PRAISE FOR *THE CAPITAL OF BASKETBALL*

"*The Capital of Basketball* provides important details
made Washington, DC, famous."
—**Mike Krzyzewski**, head men's basketball coach, Duke University

"It's a story of civil rights heroes and NBA legends. It's [336] pages of history few others could have accomplished, but John, who was born in Washington and never left the area, dedicated his life to it."
—***Washington Post***

"A must-read for anyone who wants to know about the game of basketball."
—**Morgan Wootten**, basketball coach, DeMatha Catholic High School

"John was that rare gem—an expert in DC-area sports, a generous colleague, and a caring human being. . . . Now, his expertise and insight are shared with all in *The Capital of Basketball*."
—**Liz Clarke**, sportswriter for the *Washington Post*

"John knew everything and everyone on the subject of local hoops—high school, college, and probably schoolyard. What always came through was how much he loved it."
—**John Feinstein**, columnist for the *Washington Post* and CBSsportsradio.com

"*The Capital of Basketball* highlights . . . key moments, players, games, and coaches in Washington, DC's storied high school basketball history."
—**James Brown**, host of "The NFL Today" on CBS

"When it came to basketball, John blended the knowledge of a veteran coach with the passion of a loyal fan . . . and it shows in *The Capital of Basketball*."
—**Jeff Barker**, sportswriter for the *Baltimore Sun*

"An impressive historical text that demonstrates how basketball's influence stretched beyond the simple happenings on the hardwood, helping the city contextualize the broader societal changes taking place."
—**Noah Frank**, WTOP.com

# THE CAPITAL OF BASKETBALL

# THE
# CAPITAL
## OF
# BASKETBALL

## A History of DC Area High School Hoops

## John McNamara

with Andrea Chamblee and David Elfin

Foreword by Gary Williams

Georgetown University Press / Washington, DC

The publisher is not responsible for third-party websites or their content. URL links were active at time of publication.

Library of Congress Cataloging-in-Publication Data

Names: McNamara, John, 1961–2018 author.
Title: The Capital of Basketball : A History of DC Area High School Hoops / John McNamara.
Description: Washington, DC : Georgetown University Press, 2019. | Includes bibliographical references and index.
Identifiers: LCCN 2019004745 (print) | LCCN 2019007304 (ebook) | ISBN 9781626167209 (hardcover : alk. paper) | ISBN 9781626167216 (ebook : alk. paper)
Subjects: LCSH: Basketball—Washington (D.C.)—History. | School sports—Washington (D.C.)—History.
Classification: LCC GV885.73.W18 (ebook) | LCC GV885.73.W18 M36 2019 (print) | DDC 796.32309753—dc23
LC record available at https://lccn.loc.gov/2019004745

First edition published 2019; paperback edition published 2021. ISBN 9781647121471 (paperback)

♾ This book is printed on acid-free paper meeting the requirements of the American National Standard for Permanence in Paper for Printed Library Materials.

22  21       9  8  7  6  5  4  3  2  First printing

Printed in the United States of America.

Cover designer, Tim Green, Faceout Studio.
Text designer, Faye Thaxton, Classic City Composition.
Cartographer, Chris Robinson.
Production assistant, Rachel McCarthy.

My husband, John McNamara, was a sports and news reporter for the Annapolis *Capital*. On June 28, 2018, John and four of his colleagues were murdered by a gunman who blasted his way into the newsroom where John worked.

I've spent the last year waiting, guessing, and grieving. The anguish inhabits me, colonizes me, and when I think it's heaviest, it makes its weight feel even more oppressive. But in John's den, I found the files for this book, electronic and on paper, and that gave me something more than a distraction. It gave me a sense of purpose. John wanted to be remembered as a sportswriter.

When John published his first book, *Cole Classics! Maryland Basketball's Leading Men and Moments*, about the home of University of Maryland basketball, he dedicated it to me when he wrote:

> "To Andrea: So many wonderful things happened to me during my four years at the University of Maryland. But you were the best of all."

With this, I dedicate his last book:

> To John: We promised each other we would spend the rest of our lives together. You kept your promise. You spent the rest of your life with me.
> So many wonderful things happened to me beside a basketball court, and everywhere else since I met you. But you were the best of all.

Because of a mass shooter, this is the last promise I can keep for John: By editing and publishing his book, I can make sure he will be remembered not just for how he died, but for how he lived.

Andrea Chamblee
June 2019

# Contents

# Foreword

*The Capital of Basketball* is a must read for all basketball fans. The book details how high school basketball has impacted the DC area, not just as a game but also as an instrument of change.

During my 22 years of coaching basketball at the University of Maryland, I first got to know John on a professional level, then as a friend. His love and appreciation of basketball was impressive. John's feelings and knowledge of the game jump from the pages of *The Capital of Basketball.*

John always had a special place for DC area high school basketball. I am sure he looked at high school basketball as the game in its purest form. John wanted to show that DC was and is the best high school basketball area in the country.

John writes about how high school basketball was a segregated game in the 1950s. Many great players and teams received no media coverage because of segregation during that time. John shows in this book how high school basketball was a leader in opening up opportunities for all coaches and players to be successful in basketball and as a result to have a chance to live a rewarding life. John makes it very clear that respect is gained by how well you play the game. There are no advantages when you step on the court.

For me, *The Capital of Basketball* brings back memories of great places to play basketball and the names of players and teams that made those places great. For younger fans and today's players, it shows how DC high school basketball developed into today's exciting game.

In 2010 Maryland was playing Michigan State in the NCAA tournament for the right to advance to the "Sweet 16." John McNamara was covering the game. We had just finished practice the day before the game. I was very nervous and decided to go for a walk. I ran into John, and we walked together for about two hours and talked about many subjects. His love of basketball, especially DC high school basketball, was very obvious. Along the way, John casually mentioned that he was thinking of writing a book on DC area high school basketball.

Those who knew John McNamara will miss him in their own personal way. As a coach, I will miss his ability to put down on paper his feelings as a writer of basketball. As a friend, John understood the highs and lows that are part of a coach's profession.

John McNamara's book *The Capital of Basketball: A History of DC Area High School Hoops* is a fitting and lasting memento for John's love of DC area high school basketball.

Gary Williams
Naismith Memorial Basketball Hall of Fame, 2014
NCAA Division I Men's Basketball National Champions, 2002

# Preface

I attended my first high school basketball game just after I entered high school myself at St. John's, a well-known private school that sits just off Rock Creek Park in upper northwest Washington. I was there mostly because of my father, though he was a casual sports fan at best. He thought it was important for my brother and me to get involved in some activities beyond the six-hour academic day itself, so we found ourselves one wintry night in the gymnasium at St. John's to watch the Cadets play league rival Archbishop Carroll's Lions.

I was 14 that year and already addicted to basketball. I closely followed the National Basketball Association (NBA), where the hometown Bullets went all the way to the finals in 1974–75. The University of Maryland's program was flourishing as well at the time, guided by the crafty, folksy Charles "Lefty" Driesell.

But seeing the game at the high school level was something different. If the play wasn't as polished as it was in the colleges or the pros, it was exciting nonetheless. The St. John's–Carroll game in person wasn't like watching the Terrapins on television or sitting up in the far reaches of Capital Centre at an NBA game. Seeing the action up close, getting a real sense of the skill of the players on the floor—the way you can only at a high school game—got me hooked. I could hardly wait to go back.

And why not? For a dollar or two (back then), you could watch compelling, intense, athletic basketball from just an arm's length away, played by young men not much older than I was—but whose skills were worlds beyond my own. In terms of value for your entertainment dollar, I still believe you can't beat a good high school basketball game.

And there was always a good game around. At the time, St. John's played in the Metro Conference, then as now (today it's the Washington Catholic Athletic Conference) one of the top prep basketball leagues anywhere. St. John's big rival back then was DeMatha, which annually fields one of the top programs in the country. Other league schools such as Carroll, Gonzaga, Good Counsel, and Bishop O'Connell continue to send players to big-time colleges year after year.

At the time, the public school teams in the city, not to mention the surrounding suburbs, were no less accomplished. During the 1970s, teams from the Inter-High League (then DC's public school league) finished No. 1 in the area for three straight years, with Dunbar going undefeated in 1975–76 en route to the city title. In Maryland's Montgomery County, where I grew up, high school teams won a dozen titles during the 1970s—a total county schools have failed to match in the 30-plus years since. And in Northern Virginia, West Springfield reached the state tournament three straight years (1972, 1973, and 1974), and T. C. Williams brought home the ultimate prize—a state title and an undefeated season—in 1977. In short, it was an exciting time to be discovering the game.

As I was drawn deeper into the culture of local basketball, I grew more curious about its history. Comparison and tradition—two cornerstones of any fan's worldview—require an appreciation of what has gone before, so I tried to learn as much as I could about the area's great players and teams of yesteryear.

Washington's collective basketball past seemed very close in those days. Two legendary coaches—Joe Gallagher at St. John's and Morgan Wootten at DeMatha—were still prowling the sidelines when I first came aboard. At that point, Gallagher had been at it for 30 years; Wootten was moving toward 20. The two of them—old friends and rivals—combined to win more than 2,000 games, and their firsthand knowledge of area basketball stretched back before World War II.

At that time, Bob Dwyer, the leader of the legendary Archbishop Carroll teams that won 55 straight games in the late 1950s, remained in coaching as well and taught fundamentals at tiny, exclusive St. Anselm's. Dwyer had retreated from the spotlight but was still very much in the game. One of his best players at Carroll, the towering John Thompson, was just starting to make a name for himself at Georgetown University, where he was building the Hoyas into a national basketball power.

Talk of other figures from DC's basketball past was all around me, or so it seemed. Elgin Baylor, the best player the city ever produced, had just retired from a brilliant NBA playing career to take up coaching. Dave Bing, another local legend, was winding down his professional career but took a brief turn during the mid-1970s as a member of the hometown Bullets.

After St. John's, I moved on to the University of Maryland to study journalism. There, my education—in basketball and other disciplines—continued. I attended the odd high school game for my own amusement. I also sought out local players who would someday play at Maryland and wrote about them for the student newspaper, *The Diamondback*. I kept following the game, and the game kept following me.

I still remember one brutally cold day in early 1982 when I trudged through snow piled up along Adelphi Road to Northwestern High School, about a mile from Maryland's campus. There, in the school's library, an extremely tall, exceptionally shy young man named Len Bias announced that he would play his college basketball at Maryland. A little more than four years later, after a star-studded college career that earned him All-America honors and made him the

No. 2 pick in the NBA draft, Bias was dead of heart failure, the result of a late-night cocaine binge.

His death rocked pro and college basketball, not to mention society at large. Nowhere was his loss felt more acutely than in Prince George's County, Maryland, among the people who'd nurtured him and watched him grow up. Years later, the mere mention of his name still prompts people to speak in reverent tones about how great he was and what he might have become.

After Maryland, I moved on to my first professional job at the *Morning Herald* in Hagerstown, Maryland, about 70 miles northwest of Washington. At the *Herald*, the bulk of my responsibilities involved covering high school sports. It was quite a culture shock, basketball-wise. While western Maryland has much to recommend it, the caliber of high school basketball was, in general, a good deal below what I was used to.

But I still followed DC basketball from there. One time I was assigned to cover a big tournament locally, one that featured top teams from Baltimore and Washington. I got to see St. John's, which then featured Clemson-bound point guard Grayson Marshall, go up against Cardinal Gibbons High School of Baltimore that also boasted a number of Division I–level ballplayers. St. John's won the game— 90–80, I think it was—in an action-packed display that would have impressed even the uninitiated. Afterward, someone came up to me and remarked, "I've never seen high school basketball like that!" I smiled wistfully and replied, "I used to watch it twice a week back home."

I returned to the metro area before long. After a brief flirtation with the news side of newspapers—a lapse in judgment, I grant you—I went back to sports, working for the now-defunct *Journal* newspaper in Prince George's County. There, I was once again immersed in the DC high school basketball scene, covering DeMatha along with some of the top public schools' teams in the area during the late 1980s and early 1990s.

My developing friendship with Morgan Wootten, already a legend, got me thinking once again about the area's basketball history and how there might be a book in there somewhere. It was the sort of idea one adopts for a brief time and then sets aside, putting it in that mental drawer marked "Things I'll Get to Someday." I had thought about writing such a book several times in the intervening years. But the realization that the project shouldn't be put off any longer didn't come until more than a decade later, after I'd switched newspapers again—this time to the *Capital* in Annapolis, Maryland—and had grown a bit removed from the local basketball scene.

When Dwyer, the former Carroll coach, passed away in 2007, I figured I had missed my chance. After all, you can't write about the history of local basketball without the coach of the best team the city ever produced.

That's when my wife spoke up. While I bemoaned the opportunity missed, she saw Dwyer's passing as a call to action. "Look, you've got to talk to Morgan

Wootten and Joe Gallagher and all the rest of the old-timers now!" she insisted. "It doesn't matter when you write the book; you have to get their stories written down, while they're still here." She had a point. At the time, Gallagher was in his 80s and Wootten was in his 70s.

Between the two of them, they had coached more than 90 seasons and had seen everyone and everything in area high school basketball during the previous 60 years. Gallagher, it was said, held the ladder when James Naismith first hung those peach baskets on the wall and invented the game back in 1891. Wootten, meanwhile, was simply the best there ever was in his chosen profession. Even University of California, Los Angeles, coaching icon John Wooden had said so.

The stories that Gallagher and Wootten—and others—shared with me were invaluable. Irreplaceable, really. When it comes to high school basketball, oral history is just about all we have.

The scoring wizardry of Baylor as a teenager or the grit of his one-armed contemporary, Armstrong's Gary Mays (a story in himself), exists only in the minds of those who saw them in person or in faded newspaper clippings. DeMatha's landmark victory over Lew Alcindor (now known as Kareem Abdul-Jabbar) and Power Memorial Academy of New York City in 1965 can't be found on ESPN or even ESPN Classic. The all-sports network didn't even exist back then. Nobody could put the highlights on YouTube either.

All that's left are the stories. So I set out to find these stories and the people who could tell them to chronicle the great teams and great players of my home turf.

When I started this undertaking, I thought I knew a lot about DC high school basketball. But there was much I learned, even though I'd spent almost my whole life in the area and close to the game. The journey has been a rewarding one. I am indebted to those whose voices appear herein. Their tales enriched me and this narrative immeasurably. Watching, playing, discussing, and thinking about basketball has consumed much of my life for the last 40-plus years. After all this time, I'm pleased to say that I'm still in the game.

June 2018

# CHAPTER ONE

# The Pioneers

## 1900–1950

**IT'S HARD TO IMAGINE** a summer in Washington, DC, with sunny days and muggy nights that aren't pierced with the thumps and grunts of dozens of basketballs and hundreds of players in pickup games, pounding out their frustrations and dreams on hot asphalt or in pungent gymnasiums at Turkey Thicket, Candy Cane City, Kelly Miller Junior High, or Sligo Creek.

But at the turn of the twentieth century, the sports that occupied most athletes were football and baseball. Coaches lamented the loss of physical conditioning that occurred in between the last touchdown and the first pitch. To occupy these winter months in 1891 in Springfield, Massachusetts, Dr. James Naismith developed a game with nine-man teams and two peach baskets nailed 10 feet above the floor and at opposite ends of a court. However, Naismith's new game resembled more of a hockey-rugby combination than the sport we now know as basketball.

Maurice Joyce, the founder of Joyce's Traveling Old-Time Country Circus and a sometime coach, was intrigued by the idea of the indoor winter sport. Joyce met with Naismith at the Young Men's Christian Association (YMCA) International Training School, now known as Springfield College. "Professor Joyce" brought the game with him to Washington, DC, in 1892 when he accepted a position as the physical education director at the Carroll Institute, which was affiliated with the Washington Light Infantry that served as the local militia.

Although Massachusetts had provided the baskets, after Joyce's move to Washington, the city's players revamped the game. The concept of five-man teams, fast breaks, and pugnacious defense all began and flourished in the nation's capital. Basketball may have been born in Springfield, but it was adopted and raised in Washington.

The capital was a smaller city then, inhabited by fewer than 315,000 people. The infantry was not a sporting club, but Joyce's job was to maintain the members' fitness. In doing so, the Carroll Institute often competed with athletic clubs in various contests. Joyce introduced "basket ball" to the infantry's physical training regimen.

By 1895 Joyce had decided to reduce the number of players on the court from nine players to five because, as he wrote to Naismith, with the original nine men per side, players failed to sustain the desired physical fitness. Naismith approved the change, which was adopted by the national rules committee in 1897, although some clubs continued to use more players throughout the next decade.

Joyce's five-man Carroll Institute club played numerous exhibitions and reportedly remained undefeated for three years, not that there was much newspaper coverage of basketball. Baseball, boxing, and local bowling dominated the news.

The *Evening Star* of Washington, DC, first mentioned an early high school basketball game on January 6, 1900, noting that Central High (now Cardozo) had to replay a game with the YMCA team because of the use of an "illegal" player. The paper doesn't explain the violation, and it's quite possible that the illegal player could have been black, perhaps a student from the Preparatory School for Colored Youth (now Dunbar High School). He may have been playing part-time on a professional team, thus forfeiting his amateur eligibility. Central High won the matchup 23–0 when it was replayed two days later. The *Star* praised the team's "excellent teamwork and good throwing" but was not specific on whether the throwing was passing or shooting.

Similar challenges involved paid players who tried to retain their association with the Amateur Athletic Union. On January 13, 1900, the *Star* named Harry C. Colliflower of the Eastern Athletic Club as one of the more notorious suspects (the Colliflower family name appears repeatedly in DC baseball and basketball history with players and coaches, but he played professional baseball in Cleveland, not professional basketball). In 1906 the *Washington Post* reported that "about half" the amateur players had left and "became professionals" when their status had been challenged the previous year.

After the Civil War, Washington had the highest percentage of African Americans of any city in the nation. Newcomers were attracted by the pay parity in federal employment; by Howard University, which had been founded in 1867; and, for families with children, by the Preparatory School for Colored Youth. The city's first public high school for African American students attracted college-bound students. Many of its teachers earned advanced degrees. African American residents also created hundreds of black-owned businesses. African American churches operated and supported schools as well as literary and historical societies. The churches also sponsored events promoting critical thinking and social justice as well as athletics and sportsmanship.

One of the rising stars in the African American community was Dr. Edwin Bancroft (E. B.) Henderson. In 1904 while Joyce was establishing his coaching reputation among white Washingtonians, Henderson graduated from Howard's Teachers College and headed to Harvard University's School of Physical Training, where he learned to play basketball. Henderson returned to Washington with plans to introduce the sport to African American students.

Henderson soon founded the Eastern Board of Officials and organized the Interscholastic Athletic Association before the white schools had formed anything similar. In 1906 he established the first scholastic conference, the Colored

Public School Athletic League. Henderson often played center for teams that he coached and was considered a fine player. In 1909 and 1910, his team, the YMCA 12 Streeters, claimed the designation of the unofficial "Colored Basketball World Champions."

Despite this progress, papers generally weren't covering African American athletes. The *Star* did report on games involving white players in the Washington City Basketball League, which included teams representing the YMCA, the Carroll Institute, the National Guard Ordways, the First Battalion, the Columbia Athletic Club, and the Epiphany Chapel.

B. F. Saul, whose grandfather was then founding a DC real estate, property management, and financial services empire that still thrives, was a regular for the Washington Light Infantry Armory. He would eventually manage the family business.

A *Post* article on December 16, 1906, was headlined "The Rise of Basket-Ball: Indoor Sport Has Remarkable Growth in District." The reporter said the game had "passed the stage when it was greeted with jeers and laughter." What's more, where basketball had been "simply a harum-scarum scramble, with little or no team work, each man playing the ball when and where he pleased," in the wake of the advent of professional coaches such as Joyce, it had attained "the scientific basis that it now holds."

Yet a *Post* article on February 10, 1907, declared "Basket Ball Most Harmful" of the school contests. The desirable sports, in order, were rowing, baseball, football, and track. The article declared that students should participate in only two sports, "separated by a considerable amount of time," ruling out basketball's purpose of filling the winter gap between baseball and football. It concluded by writing that basketball's "physical and moral risks are . . . serious."

A different *Post* article observed that "young ladies" were also attracted to the new game, adding that the "tumultuous entanglement of [their] arms and legs . . . would doubtless attract a full house." Local girls' teams traveled to New York City and Schenectady, New York, and Middletown, Connecticut, to compete. However, starting in 1907, DC principals ruled that no spectators would be permitted at high school games for either boys or girls. Of course, enthusiasts were still free to watch and play basketball on any available paved surface. The city's police chief advocated for more playgrounds to prevent "moral and bodily injury" on Saturdays, especially where streetcars and wagons competed with children for space in the streets.

After Georgetown University completed the Ryan Gymnasium in the fall of 1906, Joyce accepted an offer to become the university's director of physical education. Georgetown hoped that an intercollegiate team could be fielded that year, as Joyce had successfully introduced the game to students at the University of Virginia and the US Naval Academy. To that point, basketball had not been played at Georgetown, except for an obscure 1904 intramural matchup between the "Sub-Freshmen" and the "First Academics." In those early days, the coaches were students and were responsible for arranging schedules, practices, and team finances. Seasoned coaches, if available, were more like faculty advisers, teaching rules and fundamentals and providing advice when requested.

Crosstown battles between George Washington (GW) and Georgetown Universities could attract plenty of spectators. The first time that any GW team was known to have defeated Georgetown in an intercollegiate contest was in basketball in 1907. Bedlam erupted in the stands as the contest ended, with students and fans spilling into the streets. Later that week, a photo of GW's victorious squad was featured at the top of the *Post*'s sports page, under the headline "First to Lower Georgetown's Colors."

The teams met again within a week, this time at the Washington Light Infantry Armory. Before a crowd of 1,100—a then unheard-of figure in any local college sports—the players battled on and off the court. Since the sport was in its infancy, rules disputes were common. The game was delayed longer than an hour because of one such argument. As Joyce and GW coach E. Blanchard Robey debated the use of sidelines, restless spectators jeered. After the dispute was finally resolved, it was Georgetown's fans who swarmed onto the floor to celebrate the victory. A third game was delayed until mid-March. By then some players had moved on to spring sports such as baseball, and GW won, 24–10.

In all three games, homegrown star Fred Rice had led GW's Hatchetites. Rice's GW career was short lived, however. When GW failed to sponsor a team the following year, Joyce persuaded Rice to enroll instead at Georgetown's law school. Rice would be part of Georgetown's first great team, the 1908 "Champions of the South."

Joyce, who coached at Georgetown from 1907 to 1911, also coached President Theodore Roosevelt in boxing and would officiate regular exhibitions at the White House. The matches lasted until Roosevelt, who had boxed at Harvard, gave up the sport in 1908 after suffering a detached retina that blinded him in his left eye.

That same year, basketball's rules were dramatically changed in hopes of broadening the sport's appeal and reducing its injuries. Dribbling was now allowed, and a maximum of five fouls per player was instituted to limit rough play, although it was considered poor sportsmanship for opposing coaches to enforce such ejections.

Also in 1908 a gymnasium was planned for Technical High School (now McKinley Technical High). The new gym spurred a proposed league of three white high schools that had teams: Technical, Western (now Duke Ellington School of the Arts), and Business (now Theodore Roosevelt High). However, the principals couldn't agree, and the schools arranged their schedules independently. Georgetown Prep, a Catholic school then located in the District, went undefeated, which probably explained why it hadn't been invited to join the league. Prep's Hoyas traveled to locales such as New York, Philadelphia, and Baltimore for games.

By 1911 headlines revealed Washington's emerging reputation for high-quality basketball with a distinctive style featuring speed, crisp passes, and relentless defense. For instance, "Colored Boys Play Fast Basketball" featured a salute to Henderson's coaching in the *Star* on February 13, and "Fast Basket Ball: Washington Quints Show Alexandria Boys How to Play" ran in the *Star* on February 23.

The sport was rough and often violent. Teams often played surrounded by a fence to keep the ball inside and the observers off the court. Fenced in, the "cagers" soon learned to push other players against the chain links to bruise them and jar the ball loose. E. B. Henderson's new bride was worried about him getting hurt, so he promised that he would stop playing basketball after their marriage, although he did stretch the date by playing and winning in the Colored Basketball World Championship for the second year in a row *after* their 1910 wedding. Henderson then convinced Howard University to adopt the rest of the 12 Streeters as its first varsity team, one he would coach to consecutive championships.

Henderson stayed active in local sports for the rest of his working days and was a prolific writer and activist for decades. Among Henderson's many other accomplishments, in 1915 he established the Colored Citizens Protective League, which would become the National Association for the Advancement of Colored People (NAACP). He chronicled African American athletic accomplishments in *The Negro in Sports* (published in 1939 and updated in 1949). His writings, from books to letters to newspapers, are brilliant encapsulations of the struggles that blacks endured in DC and throughout the United States. Henderson retired in 1954 after 28 years as director of health and physical education for Washington's black schools. From then until his death in 1977 at age 93, he contributed to integration efforts in the city. As a tribute to all he did for the sport, Henderson was inducted into the Naismith Memorial Basketball Hall of Fame in 2013.

The DC Inter-High School Athletic Association conference had begun in 1896 with four schools: Central, Western, Eastern, and Business. Technical was added in 1902, Anacostia and Wilson in the 1930s. The District's African American schools—namely, Armstrong, Dunbar, and Cardozo—would not be part of the conference until 1958, when the formation of the DC Interscholastic Athletic Association brought all the District public high schools together as Henderson had long sought.

As for Maurice Joyce, he left Georgetown in 1911 with a 32–20 record but remained a champion of physical fitness and a notable figure in Washington athletics and social life. He served as a district court bailiff before becoming a deputy US marshal during World War I. Joyce then served in the US Department of Justice as an agent for the Bureau of Investigation, the forerunner of the Federal Bureau of Investigation. He died in 1939 at the age of 78.

As Henderson and Joyce were establishing basketball on Washington's sports scene, the *Post* published an "All-School Five" at the end of the 1911–12 season, naming two players from Army and Navy Preparatory (at 4101 Connecticut Avenue Northwest, where the Edmund Burke School is located today), two from Georgetown Prep, and one from Eastern, although players are listed only by last name. The *Post* described Army and Navy Prep's McBride and Eastern's Varela as "consistent scorers of points . . . quick as a flash to size up difficulties, and neither commits the offense of shooting at random. Once they get a chance to basket the ball at a reasonable distance and angle, it is pretty sure to drop through the netting." The article concluded that without a championship tournament, multiple claims for the top spot among the schools could not be resolved.

In November 1912 the *Post* reported the start of the season for the five-club public school circuit of Central, Western, Eastern, Business, and Technical. Schools played just one game per week until Valentine's Day (with two weeks off for Christmas). But there was talk of a contest between the public school champion and the winner of another group of teams—Gonzaga, Georgetown Prep, Sidwell Friends, and Alexandria—if they were to form a separate league. That season, numbers were added to uniforms, and new rules were instituted: players with four fouls would be ejected without an appeal to the opposing team, and the ball would be dead when it went out of bounds.

Barely a decade after basketball had begun in DC, there were now enough teams and players to make possible leagues for black and white, and private and public schools. Newspaper coverage began to include players' first names. But the game still needed improvements in its structure—for example, a better way to resolve tie games. One contest in Virginia between Manassas and Alexandria ended in an 11–11 deadlock after each team added only a single basket during a five-minute overtime. The result satisfied no one.

The first accounts of a second preparatory league in February 1915 reported that crowds estimated at 3,000 fans began to exceed capacity, packing running tracks that circled the courts. During DC's 1915–16 season, an admission fee of a nickel was charged for the first time, and game programs were available.

By the 1916–17 season, McKinley Tech joined Business, Central, Western, and Eastern in a new High School League, the first officially sanctioned conference. McKinley Tech clinched the title by beating Eastern, 25–19, in February. A year later, the *Post* declared that basketball "promises to be the most popular game in local sportdom. The floor game is having an exceptionally prosperous season in this vicinity. Hyattsville High is the only school which is not supporting the game. The war has hit the Maryland school pretty hard and it is unlikely that it will engage in varsity sports until the return of normal conditions." The Prince George's County town of about 2,000 residents ultimately lost 49 service members during World War I.

By 1919 several District schools had four teams each, divided by age or sex or both. Some schools had as many as eight teams. Only one school had no gym. Business won the title game over Eastern. Business, 12–1 against public schools, had lost twice to Gonzaga, but when Gonzaga lost to Central, Business team manager Frank H. Baxter suggested a third matchup "at any time and on any floor suitable for them." Gonzaga saw no need to respond.

J. Dallas Shirley, a guard for Eastern's 1931 Inter-High champions, had started officiating games while still in high school. After graduation, he played and officiated while attending GW on a basketball scholarship. Armed with a bachelor's degree in 1936, Shirley became a health, social studies, and physical education teacher at Alice Deal Junior High. After earning a master's degree from GW, Shirley moved on to Gordon, another junior high in Northwest DC, as a teacher, a coach, and, eventually, a principal until his retirement in 1968.

During his 33 years as a referee, Shirley officiated more than 2,000 games as well as numerous clinics. He was a member of the National Basketball Association's first officiating crew in 1946–47. Shirley officiated games for the Southern Conference, Atlantic Coast Conference, Eastern Collegiate Athletic Conference, and Mason Dixon Conference. He also officiated numerous National Invitation Tournament and National Collegiate Athletic Association (NCAA) Tournament games, as well as international contests. He was the chief official at the 1959 Pan American Games and worked the 1960 Summer Olympics.

Shirley went on to serve as the supervisor emeritus of the Southern Conference and as an observer of officials for the Atlantic 10 Conference and the Colonial Athletic Association. He was elected to the Virginia Sports and Washington Metropolitan Basketball Halls of Fame. He traveled the world with the International Association of Approved Basketball Officials and wrote numerous books and articles on officiating.

In 1980 Shirley was inducted into the Basketball Hall of Fame. Late in his career, as a member of a rules committee, Shirley helped to establish the three-point shot in college basketball. At the time of his death in 1994 at the age of 80, Shirley was commissioner of the 12-team high school Washington Catholic Athletic Conference. He had been commissioner of one of its predecessors, the Washington Metropolitan Athletic Conference, for 16 years.

In his obituary, the *Post* reported that Shirley used to tell officials at camps, "Watch the NBA game. Enjoy it. Greatest skills in the world. But don't look at the referees. Not that they're not good; it's just that their rules are so different."

In the 1930s basketball had become so popular in Washington that a group of local business leaders toyed with the idea of financing a new arena. The group included a representative from a family sports dynasty, Jim Colliflower, a former player at Central High and Georgetown who went on to coach at the Naval Academy (1915–18) and at Georgetown (1911–14 and 1921–22). Colliflower had earned three law degrees from Georgetown and had become a prominent Washington businessman and the area's first auto racing promoter. But for all his ties to basketball, Colliflower was no match for the single-minded vision of Miguel "Mike" Uline, an ice magnate. In that era before refrigerators, his product was needed for iceboxes.

Uline, who had been born in the Netherlands in 1874, immigrated to Cleveland at 16, saying that his family had lost everything they owned in one of the many floods that low-lying Netherlanders endured. Uline saved enough of his wages from various low-paying jobs to buy several ice-making plants in Ohio. After separating from his wife of 36 years in 1930, Uline moved to Washington and began making and selling ice there. But the creative Uline wasn't all about business. He helped found the still-elite Congressional Country Club in suburban Bethesda and was credited with more than 75 patents. Uline's decision to build an arena in 1940 would have a bigger impact over the next quarter century.

"I had a playground for the kids near my ice plant," Uline told a reporter, "and thought about converting it to a skating rink. But the train tracks were so close to the plant, cinders would fall and stick on the ice. So I decided I might as well put a roof on it."

Uline was 67 when he took out a $600,000 loan against his ice company to build the rink next to his business. "A lot of people have been talking about building an arena," Uline said. "I didn't do any talking. I just built one."

Uline may have had to tackle the project alone, as *Sportsweek* hinted in a 1970 article, because other possible investors "did not see things the same way Mike did." Uline was not known to compromise.

His daughter, Myrtle Uline Hill, helped publicize her father's bold move by hiring 30 striking redheaded usherettes for the arena. "Hiring day at Mrs. Hill's house" was covered by the local papers.

The 11,000-seat Uline Arena at 1132–1146 Third Street Northeast was inaugurated not by basketball or hockey but by figure skating. Sonja Henie's Hollywood Ice Revue opened the building on January 26, 1941. The arena also served as a home for Uline's hockey team, the Washington Lions of the Eastern Amateur Hockey League.

By the mid-1940s, Uline Arena was presenting hockey, basketball, boxing, and tennis games; circuses; rodeos; midget car races; and the occasional ballet or concert for white audiences. Only boxing matches were also open to African American fans. However, there was at least one notable exception: in April 1941, when the Daughters of the American Revolution canceled an appearance by Paul Robeson at Constitution Hall, Uline jumped at the chance to one-up the entertainment venue competition and booked the African American baritone and writer for the desegregated event.

E. B. Henderson, who was still striving for the inclusion of African Americans in all aspects of sports and cultural life, challenged Uline's usual segregationist policy, which was contrary to those of Washington's professional football and baseball teams—the Redskins and the Senators, respectively—that sold tickets in any section to black and white patrons alike. Henderson, along with many others, believed that Uline was particularly uncomfortable with African Americans attending ice shows where the provocative redheaded ushers worked and where "scantily dressed white women" skated.

In the wake of so many African Americans serving in World War II, the Golden

Gloves boxing tournament desegregated its bouts in 1947. Around the same time, the *Washington Post* said it would no longer support segregated boxing. The next tournament was planned for DC, and in his typical pugnacious manner, Uline wanted his arena selected to be the venue. Tournament officials indicated that wouldn't happen if Uline didn't change his segregated policy. On January 21, 1948, Uline announced that he was lifting the ban.

"Negroes will be as welcome as anyone else," Uline said. "There will be no segregation, and they will receive the same attention as other spectators. The trend of the times prompted my decision."

The arena continued to follow the trend of the times. It made its biggest splash 16 years later, or six years after Uline's death, by hosting the Beatles' first US concert on February 11, 1964.

In basketball terms, an even bigger landmark took place at Uline in 1946—the coaching debut of Arnold "Red" Auerbach. He had starred at GW and, after graduating in 1940, stayed in DC to coach high school ball at St. Albans School and then Theodore Roosevelt High School before enlisting in the US Navy.

In 1946 Auerbach was stationed at Bethesda Naval Hospital. He used the arena to stage an off-season basketball game between members of the Washington Redskins and the Philadelphia Eagles. Uline was so impressed that when Auerbach said he wanted to put together a pro basketball team, Uline agreed to finance it. Their Washington Capitols played in the Basketball Association of America (BAA), forerunner of the NBA.

Auerbach coached the fast break–oriented Capitals to a 49–11 record in his first season, including a 17-game winning streak that stood as the single-season record for 23 years. The Capitols reached the BAA finals twice in Auerbach's three seasons, but he didn't give Uline much credit. "He was the iceman," Auerbach said. "He had very little to do with the day-to-day business of running the team. He didn't know the difference between a basketball and a hockey puck."

Auerbach resigned after the 1948–49 season following a dispute with Uline about the direction of the franchise. While Auerbach went on to win a record 10 NBA championships during 16 seasons as the coach of the Boston Celtics, Uline's Capitols folded in January 1951. However, first they made history again when the team's Earl Lloyd became the NBA's first black player to actually play on October 31, 1950. Uline had managed to transform himself into the owner of an integrated basketball team. Auerbach would also select Maryland's Len Bias second in the draft in 1986. Bias would die two days later on June 19 from cardiac arrhythmia caused by a cocaine overdose.

At the same time, Uline's personal life was starting to unravel. In the summer of 1950, he got a divorce in Mexico and promptly married a former beauty parlor operator. However, the divorce wasn't legal and led to bitter marital disputes. Even worse, the ice magnate suffered a bad fall on ice in 1953 that left him disabled and partially blind. His health was failing, and his arena was facing heavy competition from the National Guard Armory. Uline had folded his original franchises, but he made another attempt to establish his own pro hockey team, the Washington Presidents. The team was skating at the arena on February 22, 1958, the night that Uline died at the age of 83.

While Uline was trying to make his arena a showplace during the early 1940s, Hyman "Hymie" Perlo and Earl Lloyd were establishing themselves as Washington's first true basketball stars. Born in Durham, North Carolina, on October 8, 1922, Perlo moved to Washington with his family in 1925. The five-foot-ten Perlo became a master of the two-handed set shot at Theodore Roosevelt High. Auerbach, who coached him at Roosevelt, called Perlo "the greatest high school player in his day." An All-Met for three years, Perlo was selected in 1940 and 1941 as the outstanding southern player in the Duke-Durham scholastic basketball tournament. Perlo was offered more than 50 college scholarships upon graduating from Roosevelt in 1941, but after briefly attending GW, he enlisted in the US Army.

Perlo, who spent 69 days in a foxhole in Anzio, Italy, received the Silver Star for swimming injured soldiers across a river to safety in the midst of enemy fire. However, Perlo's heroism ended his basketball career when he was seriously wounded in a leg. "I've never cursed my fate," he said. "I was thankful to come back alive."

Perlo graduated from GW with a degree in education and spent a decade as the director of athletics at Washington's Jewish Community Center. In the 1960s he supervised a jobs training program at the Junior-Senior High School for emotionally disturbed boys. Perlo also was the director of the Buffalo Gap summer camp in West Virginia, using his connections to bring in guests such as Auerbach and Baltimore Bullets star Wes Unseld.

In 1968 Abe Pollin, who owned the Bullets (now the Wizards), hired Perlo, his Roosevelt classmate, to perform public relations work and to handle special functions. After Pollin opened the Capital Centre in suburban Landover, Maryland, in 1973, Perlo also promoted boxing at the arena. Perlo organized visits by the Bullets and their wives to hospitalized children and to special education programs. He also distributed thousands of tickets to Capital Centre games to residents of veterans' homes, arranged for their transportation to the arena, and ensured that they were well treated while spectators.

"Those old soldiers are rotting away in their wheelchairs," Perlo told the *Post*. "They come here, and they feel like part of the community."

Perlo famously led the Bullets' summer clinics for many years. He would try to balance the youngsters' often unrealistic ambitions of basketball stardom by reminding them of the importance of academics. Perlo retired in 1992. He died in 2006 at age 83. In tribute to his high school stardom and his community service, Perlo was inducted into the Washington Metropolitan Basketball, DC Sports, and Greater Washington Jewish Sports Halls of Fame.

Six years younger than Perlo, Earl Lloyd was born in Alexandria, Virginia, on

April 3, 1928. His father, Theodore Lloyd Sr., worked in a coal yard and his mother, Daisy, cleaned houses. He was raised on Montgomery Street in "the Berg" section of Alexandria. He was a standout athlete at Lyles-Crouch Elementary because he said there was nothing else to do. He played basketball on the blacktops of Alexandria and walked across the 14th Street Bridge to play pick-up ball in the District. He didn't play organized basketball until he played for the city's segregated Parker-Gray High School and Coach Louis "Rubber Dog" Johnson. Johnson had graduated from West Virginia State University to become the school's longtime coach of basketball, football, and track.

As a high school standout, Lloyd described traveling with athletic teams to Virginia cities such as Roanoke, Charlottesville, or Petersburg in an open-bed canvas truck filled with hay. There were no hotels or eating establishments available to African Americans at the time.

"When I reflect back on Parker-Gray, I just shake my head," Lloyd said in an interview with Alexandrian Derrick Lyman of the *Connection* newspaper. "I don't know how we did it. Athletically, we had nothing—no gymnasium, no baseball diamond, no football field. Except we had a magical coach, Louis Johnson. Man, he got it done."

Lloyd was nicknamed "Moon Fixer" and then "Big Cat" because of his size. Although he was never known for high scoring, he was a formidable defender. Lloyd was named to the All-South Atlantic Conference three times and the All-State Virginia Interscholastic Conference twice.

After he graduated in 1946, he received an offer to pitch for the Brooklyn Dodgers but, with encouragement from Coach Johnson, accepted a basketball scholarship to play for the West Virginia State Yellow Jackets. Lloyd led the team to two Central Intercollegiate Athletic Association (CIAA) Conference championships in 1948 and 1949. Lloyd was named all-conference three times and an All-American twice. He received his bachelor of science degree in physical education in 1950 and prepared to go into teaching and coaching high school basketball since all the players in the four-year-old professional league were white.

Before 1950 only the Harlem Globetrotters hired black players. The owner, Abe Saperstein, was rumored to threaten other teams with refusing to play in their stadiums if they competed for black players. However, Coach Red Auerbach and owner Walter Brown drafted Chuck Cooper for the Boston Celtics in the second round as the 12th pick, and Coach Joseph Lapchick and owner Ned Irish acquired Nat "Sweetwater" Clifton from the Harlem Globetrotters for the New York Knicks. Lloyd credits their selections with motivating Mike Uline, once again refusing to be outdone, to choose him as the 100th pick for the Washington Capitols. Since Lloyd was the first to step out on the floor, he became a pioneer in his own right as the first black player to make his debut in the NBA. Cooper made his debut with the Celtics just one day after Lloyd played his first game with Washington.

Unlike other sports, the presence of the first black player in the fledging Basketball Association of America, operating in its fourth year, did not generate headlines. Earl Lloyd's milestone was barely noted in the press accounts.

After seven games with the Washington Capitols, Lloyd was drafted into the military for two years. By the time he returned to play, the Capitols had folded on January 9, 1951. He went on to play for the Syracuse Nationals (later the Philadelphia 76ers). In his best offensive year, the 1954–55 season, he averaged over 10 points and 7.7 rebounds a game for Syracuse, but he was more valuable in stopping the opponent's offensive stars, including fellow DC native Elgin Baylor. Syracuse captured the NBA title that season by defeating the Fort Wayne Pistons in seven games. Lloyd ended his nine-season career in Detroit, serving as a scout and then as an assistant coach for the Pistons. He is credited with discovering basketball talents Willis Reed, Earl Monroe, Dave Bing, Ray Scott, and Wally Jones. In 1970 he became the first full-time black head coach in the league for the 1971–72 season. He coached the Pistons for a year, but the Pistons went 20–52. Seven games into the next season, Lloyd left basketball.

"Coaching is only fun if you win," Lloyd told the NBA for his retrospective story, laughing. "I didn't win. It wasn't fun."

Lloyd went on to work for the city's board of education and the police department, and for Bing's Detroit-based steel and auto parts enterprise, the Bing Group. Lloyd was inducted into the Virginia Sports Hall of Fame in 1993, the CIAA Hall of Fame in 1998, and the Naismith Memorial Basketball Hall of Fame in 2003. In 2001 the city of Alexandria celebrated Earl Lloyd Day, and in 2007, the new basketball court at T. C. Williams High School was named after Lloyd. He died in 2015 at the age of 86.

As the 40s came to a close, Joe Gallagher began coaching the Cadets in his first basketball games at St. John's High School, as well as in baseball and football. His star player, Jack George, would appear in *Time* magazine in 1947 with illustrations of him playing each sport as well as tennis, calling him "The Boy Wonder of the Nation's Capital." After George died from cancer at age 60, Gallagher would tell the *Washington Post* that George "may have been the best all-around athlete ever in the Washington area."

Pioneers Joyce, Henderson, Shirley, Uline, Auerbach, Perlo, and Lloyd had established basketball as an essential part of Washington's sports fabric. DC high school players, coaches, and fans would see the game reach new heights in the decades ahead.

Edwin B. (EB) Henderson (center front) poses for a 1910 team portrait with the 12th Street YMCA basketball team in Washington.

The 12th Street YMCA basketball team contributed players to the new Howard University basketball team.

In 1954, when *Brown v. Board of Education* supposedly made his job obsolete, Professor Henderson celebrated his retirement from DC Schools as the Athletic Director for African American Schools with a professional photo by famed photographer Addison Scurlock.

Theodore Roosevelt High School, located at 13th Street NW, yearbook page dedicated to Coach Red Auerbach during his years of coaching (1941–43).

2. Mr. Boyd
3. Homeward bound
4. Mr. Auerbach
5. Romance
6. Billy Harward's Orchestra

Auerbach received an athletic scholarship to play basketball for Bill Reinhart at George Washington University in Washington, DC, and graduated in 1941.

Auerbach joined the US Navy in 1944 after two years of coaching high school basketball at St. Albans and Theodore Roosevelt High Schools.

Parker Gray graduating class of 1946. Earl Lloyd is in the back row, far right.

Forward Earl Lloyd (11) of the Syracuse Nationals fights for a rebound against the Fort Wayne Zollner Pistons and center Mel Hutchins (9), 4-time NBA All-Star, for the NBA title in 1955.

Earl Lloyd of the Syracuse Nationals. Lloyd was drafted into the US Army in 1951. While he was fulfilling his military duty, the Nationals picked him up on waiver.

After graduating St. John's College High School in 1949, Jack George attended LaSalle University, where he played basketball and baseball. He also excelled at tennis.

# CHAPTER TWO

# The Fifties

**DECEMBER 1949** brought a cold snap to the nation's capital. Daytime highs only reached the 20s, and nighttime lows dipped into the teens. Frigid temperatures are not uncommon for winter in Washington, but weather that cold usually came after the holidays.

And the holidays were most assuredly on everyone's minds. Stores reported record crowds and spending on the second weekend of the month and near-record levels on the last weekend before Christmas.

And why not? After years of self-imposed denial during the Depression and then government-imposed rationing to aid the war effort, the country was ready to splurge. Disposable income, according to US Department of Labor statistics, was nearly three times what it had been just a decade earlier, when the country was still in the throes of an economic crisis.

The war was over, but the economy hummed along, producing all manner of consumer conveniences and gadgets, which were gobbled up by an all-too-eager public. For $126, you could escape DC's cold with a round-trip flight to Bermuda. If you wanted to stay at home for the holidays, you could buy a 16-inch Motorola television set with a built-in antenna for $349. A five-passenger Pontiac sedan could be yours for $1,764. Even harder to believe, a house on Brandywine Street Northwest near American University (AU) could be had for $17,850.

Shoppers flocked to the downtown shopping area along F Street. Men in hats and women in dresses or skirts (never slacks) sampled the wares at once-thriving stores that have now vanished from the local landscape: Woodward & Lothrop, the Hecht Company, Garfinckel's, Lansburgh's Department Store, and W&J Sloane Furniture.

Those who weren't out shopping were probably taking in a movie. Likely they saw Bing Crosby and Fred Astaire in *Holiday Inn*, which was back at the Trans-Lux, about a block from the White House, seven years after its initial release. Or at the Playhouse at 15th and H Streets Northwest, they saw Broderick Crawford in *All the King's Men*, which went on to win the Academy Award for best picture in 1950. If your tastes ran a bit more on the racy side, you could sneak over to the

Gayety Theater at Ninth and F Streets to catch an eyeful at the burlesque "Frisky Follies" show.

Washington's sports pages were filled with football news. Sammy Baugh of the hometown Redskins had just won the sixth passing title of his 13-year career, and the National Football League announced that it would expand to include the San Francisco 49ers, Cleveland Browns, and Baltimore Colts from the All-America Football Conference.

Soon enough, space on those pages would be given over to basketball—the professional game and those of the local colleges and, of course, the high schools. "Schoolboy basketball," as the newspapers patronizingly referred to it, was about to become a very big deal. A group of eager, hustling kids from McKinley Technical High School in Northeast Washington was about to establish a new standard for excellence in their still largely ignored sport.

Even though the school itself was just two miles up North Capitol Street from the seat of our nation's government, the families of those children who went there were hardly Washington insiders. For the most part, McKinley parents were the truck drivers, the laborers, and the clerks who helped keep the gears of the city turning.

From these modest circumstances sprang an extraordinary high school basketball team, one whose body of work rivals anything produced in the decades since. The Trainers, as McKinley's teams were called, starting in 1950 won three straight Inter-High titles and three straight championships in the Metropolitan Tournament, which essentially determined the area-wide champion. The Trainers also ran off a then-record 38 straight victories.

The starters—all-around star Stan Kernan, lefty point guard "Babe" Marshall, long-range set shooter Bill Breen, center Frank Sullivan, and role player Joe Caw— were collectively known as the "Fabulous Five." The nickname still means something more than 60 years later to Washingtonians of a certain age.

"The Fabulous Five? Oh yeah! They had a helluva team," recalled feisty, funny Joe Gallagher. A local high school basketball icon himself, he coached St. John's Cadets from 1946 to 1991 and saw everyone in the interim who was any good at all.

Though its heyday was back in the early 1950s, McKinley could rightfully be called one of the city's first "modern" teams. The Trainers rejected the deliberate style of play so prevalent at the time, preferring instead to fast-break at every opportunity while daring opponents to keep up.

This approach was still unusual at the time. The rule requiring a jump ball after each basket—slowing down the game considerably—had been eliminated a dozen years before. Although the rule change regarding the center jump opened the game up, many teams and coaches were still rooted in the careful, slow-paced style of the past and opted to keep a tight rein on their players.

In contrast, the Trainers were a running team, practitioners of what sportswriters in those days called "racehorse basketball." They lacked height—the six-foot-three Frank Sullivan was the tallest man—so McKinley had to work to grab its share of rebounds on most nights. Nevertheless, the Trainers used hustle and positioning to grab the ball off the boards, and then off they'd go.

"That was the only way we knew," Kernan said. "If you didn't have [the fast break], you set it up. We more or less ran all the time. I don't remember that we ran any plays or anything. We didn't have point guards or two guards back then; you just played. We just spread out and passed and moved and shot."

If they didn't have much height and didn't run a patterned offense, why were the Trainers so good? Chalk it up to geography. McKinley's five starters during that period all grew up within a couple blocks of each other, near the intersection of North Capitol Street and Rhode Island Avenue, just a few blocks from the school itself. With little else to occupy them in those simpler times without television, laptops, or smart phones, the game became their hobby, their pastime, their passion. The only handheld device that mattered to them was a basketball. They played together every day and for as long as they could, often skipping lunch on weekend days or over the summer so as not to lose their spot in the playground pecking order.

"If we weren't home, our parents knew where to find us," Breen said. "That's all we did was play ball."

"We'd rather play basketball than eat," Marshall agreed.

If ever there was a team you could have magically transported out of Washington, DC, and dropped into the middle of some makeshift dirt court in basketball-crazy Indiana, it was the McKinley squad of the early 1950s. Nobody would have known the difference. It was a group straight out of the film *Hoosiers*.

By the time they all reached the varsity team, the group operated as if with one mind, having developed a telepathy borne of habit that enabled each player to anticipate the others' moves. The youngsters had also benefited from some useful outside tutoring sessions during the offseason. NBA coaching great Red Auerbach, who would lead the Boston Celtics to a host of titles as coach and team president, was then in the early stages of his career, coaching Washington's professional basketball team known as the Capitols. To augment the meager salary pro coaches were paid in those days, Auerbach worked in the summers managing a swimming pool near McKinley. He often gave Kernan and his buddies tips on improving their play and occasionally brought some of his own players around to shoot baskets with the local youths. "What are the chances of that happening today?" Kernan asked.

Only a couple members of the Fabulous Five were able to crack the regular rotation as sophomores during the 1949–50 season. Breen and Kernan played more and more as the season wore on, although Tony Sgro was the team's established star. Sgro scored 20 points, while Kernan added nine and Breen eight in a 57–41 win over the Eastern Ramblers for the Inter-High championship that year. Breen's modest total of 10 points led the way as McKinley edged St. John's, 35–32, for the Metropolitan Tournament crown.

The next year Breen, Kernan, Marshall, Caw, and Sullivan were back together again in the McKinley starting lineup, and "low" scores of the previous year became a thing of the past. The Trainers gave a hint of what was to come early in the 1950–51 season, routing the DeMatha Stags, 87–49, and then blasting the Bullis School Bulldogs, 75–53. Despite a loss to the American University Eagles' freshman team (high schools frequently played such games before college freshmen were eligible for varsity competition), McKinley was ranked No. 1 in the first prep poll released in the new year.

But George Washington High School (GWHS) of Alexandria stunned McKinley, 58–50, on January 17 in the area's biggest regular-season game of that year. Both teams were considered among the best in the area, but the combination of the GWHS Presidents' height—with six-foot-five Crenshaw Hardy and six-foot-four Bob Kessler—their effective zone, and their famously small bandbox gymnasium was too much for McKinley Tech to overcome.

That was the last loss for McKinley for the next season and a half. The Trainers were simply too strong for anyone else. Through mid-February they hadn't scored fewer than 65 points in a league game—an almost unthinkable figure at a time when many teams still scored in the 30s and 40s.

For McKinley's players, up-tempo basketball seemed the most natural thing in the world. Kernan, in fact, was a standout running back and sprint champion in high school. He was also a self-taught jump shooter, opting for the then revolutionary shooting style after watching "Jumping" Joe Fulks, an early NBA scoring standout. Everybody else who shot from the outside, including teammate Breen, for example, launched two-handed set shots. But Kernan ventured out in this new direction, which fit in with the more wide-open approach that was taking hold.

The McKinley coaches—head man Hiram "Dutch" Usilander and assistant Russell Lombardy—also played a role in fostering the team's unique style. Usilander borrowed heavily from his experiences as a wrestling coach to institute a rigorous preseason conditioning program. Lombardy, the more tactically savvy of the two, simply decided that the up-tempo pace the players preferred would be the best approach. As a result, Tech simply outran and overwhelmed many of its opponents. Typically, a third-quarter surge did the trick. Often, it came at a time when opponents were starting to wear down.

"They just ran too much for us," Maryland Park coach Bob Blackford explained after his team absorbed a 21-point loss to the Trainers. "My boys told me in the third quarter they were getting tired. That's the best team we've played all year."

McKinley had a couple of close calls near the end of the regular season, partly because opponents, having exhausted all other solutions, began stalling against the Trainers. A neck injury that kept Marshall out a couple of games didn't help either.

Some suggested that McKinley had grown stale, that all the success had made them complacent as the 1950–51 season wound down. But with Marshall back in the lineup, the Trainers whipped the Calvin Coolidge Colts, 73–59, for a second straight Inter-High crown. In the Metropolitan Tournament final, the Trainers thrashed Coolidge again, 62–34, in front of 4,000 people at the University of Maryland's Ritchie Coliseum.

As the *Evening Star* account noted after the Trainers' second big win over Coolidge, "The Tech unit showed a finesse not usually associated with high school basketball as Coach Dutch Usilander's players passed with precision, shot accurately, rebounded on both boards and played airtight defense—a phase of the game the Trainers had neglected before last night."

To Usilander, the difference was the return of Marshall, the player who generally set up the offense. The late-season struggles, the coach insisted, were the result of Marshall's absence. "He's our quarterback," Usilander said. "When he went out, we went down."

The next year, it was more of the same. McKinley was the center of DC's basketball universe during the 1951–52 season. Its gym had been refurbished and expanded to accommodate 3,600 fans, and all Inter-High League games were moved to McKinley, with well-attended doubleheaders played there on Friday and Saturday nights.

The Trainers opened what would be the final season for Breen, Kernan, Sullivan, Caw, and Marshall with another typically lopsided win, 90–38, over the Suitland Rams. Kernan, who had led the Inter-High in scoring as a junior with a 19.5 average, pumped in 24 points. Breen, second to Kernan in scoring the year before with a 16.5 mark, added 21. During the Trainers' reign, everyone had chances to score. That included Marshall, Caw, Sullivan, and reserve Dick DeCesare, who made some important contributions later that season.

"The main thing is, we were unselfish," Kernan said. "We didn't care who scored. We just wanted to win."

And win they did. They downed Georgetown's junior varsity, 73–60, after leading by 19 at one point. McKinley also avenged the loss at GWHS the year before with a 51–43 triumph at McKinley. McKinley's streak reached 20 straight in a 70–44 romp over the Western Red Raiders. Kernan went for 29 points.

The next landmark came at the end of January, when the Trainers overwhelmed the Bell High Vocats, 100–38. That victory also boosted the streak to 26 games, believed to be the longest in the history of DC area prep basketball to that point.

The only sour note came a few nights later in another rout, 85–34, over the Woodrow Wilson Tigers. That game marked the finale for Marshall, who was graduating a semester early and wouldn't be available the rest of the season. Marshall contributed 14 points that night and got a standing ovation when he left the game with 90 seconds left.

Even without Marshall, though, McKinley kept winning. DeCesare filled in admirably at the point, and the team won its third straight Inter-High title with a narrow 47–43 victory over Roosevelt's Rough Riders. Reserve Edgar Peyton converted a layup with 12 seconds left in the third quarter to give McKinley the lead.

The Trainers froze the ball for much of the fourth quarter—a tactic that Usilander decried when it was used against his own team. Breen scored 22 points, while Kernan was held to seven in the team's 35th straight win. Winning a third straight title was something no Inter-High team had accomplished since Eastern had in the mid-1930s.

Only the Metropolitan Tournament remained. McKinley needed three more victories to close out an undefeated campaign and a third straight season as the metro area champions. It wasn't easy. The team that had provided very little drama during its remarkable run seemed to save all the excitement for the end.

After getting a scare from the Montgomery Blair Blazers in the opening round, McKinley Tech trailed by seven with four minutes to go in the tournament final against its old nemesis from across the river, George Washington. But Tech, which hadn't been in many pressure situations, handled this one with aplomb. Reserve Don DeAtley, all of five foot seven, snuck inside for a key tap-in down the stretch. Then Kernan tied the game on a free throw with 37 seconds left. The teams remained even through the three-minute overtime before Kernan tapped in a miss that dropped through the net at the buzzer for a 58–56 victory.

The McKinley fans among the capacity crowd of nearly 4,000 people at Ritchie streamed from the stands to hoist Kernan and his mates on their shoulders. He'd scored 30 points in the tournament final—matching the earlier brilliant performance of GWHS star Bob Kessler—including the game winner at the buzzer. Kernan had been responsible for many of the 38 victories during the record streak, but he had saved what might have been his best performance for last. "That's a heck of a way to end your high school career," Kernan agreed.

If McKinley was the best basketball squad in the Washington area in the early 1950s, Kessler and George Washington weren't far behind. The six-foot-four Kessler, like the jump-shooting Kernan, was a player who would have fit in even while playing today's more highly evolved game. At that height, Kessler would have played center on almost any other team of the era. But the presence of six-foot-five Crenshaw Hardy freed Kessler from the low block and permitted him to roam the perimeter, handle the ball, and shoot from the outside—activities previously considered inappropriate for a high school player of his size.

Of course, Kessler wouldn't have been granted such latitude by his coach, Al "Rasty" Doran, had he not demonstrated the skills of a much smaller man. But Kessler, who grew up on the southern tip of Alexandria proper, honed his skills at the Alexandria Boys' Club and worked out religiously on his own as well. He remembers taking a ball with him down to the laundry room at his apartment complex and working on his ballhandling there (with his left and right hands) when he couldn't find anyone to play with. Having a big man's body with a guard's skill made Kessler a difficult man to defend.

"It was good to be six foot four and play that way," Kessler said. "I wanted to get the ball every time and control the game from there."

Kessler first made a name for himself as a 15-year-old when he helped lead George Washington to the Metropolitan Tournament finals against McKinley. The GWHS Presidents came up short in the final—as they would in Kessler's senior year—but the skinny sophomore led the tournament in scoring and made everyone take notice. "By the time that kid gets out of high school, every coach who has seen him will want him," one college scout noted after watching Kessler as a 10th grader.

As a junior, Kessler was almost solely responsible for the Presidents' upset victory over McKinley, the Trainers' lone loss to a high school squad in almost two years. And it would be the last game that Kernan and company lost as high school players.

Kessler poured in 27 points to lead the upset but didn't get another shot at McKinley in the Star Tournament that year; he came down with the mumps and was too sick to play. Still, he averaged 21 points per game as a junior and led GWHS to a 17–4 regular-season record.

Kessler's senior year, 1951–52, promised even greater things. "Kessler is even better this year," raved the *Evening Star*. "An effortless performer with all the shots and a hard-fighting rebounder despite his frail appearance."

He led George Washington to the Metropolitan Tournament finals once again, but GWHS lost in overtime to McKinley. As noted, Kernan was the hero, scoring a team-high 30 points. Kessler was just as brilliant, scoring 30 points himself as he and his rival (both were twice first-team All-Met picks in the *Washington Post*) put on a dazzling show. Afterward, though, Kessler couldn't think of himself as anything but the goat. He'd blown a breakaway layup late in the game that might have made the difference to GWHS.

When interviewed more than 50 years after the fact, Kessler brought up the subject of the missed opportunity without any prompting, still clearly upset about the gaffe. "It still bothers me," he said. "I hotdogged it instead of playing it smart. Nobody ever said anything about it, but it was a dumb thing to do."

That Kessler would point out his own mistake decades after everyone had forgotten it speaks volumes about who he was. As a high school player, he was the most admirable and admired player in suburban Virginia. Half a decade after he moved on to a 1,200-plus-point career at the University of Maryland, where he scored the first points ever in Cole Field House, the local papers still referred to him as the greatest player in Northern Virginia history.

In fact, Kessler became something of a role model for many of those players who followed. Bill Edmondson, a three-time All-Met selection from the Mount

Vernon High School Patriots, was inspired by Kessler's on-court style. The same was true for others who came along later at George Washington.

"He took [Edmondson] under his wing and helped him a lot," recalled Red Jenkins, who graduated from Mount Vernon with Edmondson in 1954. "Bob Kessler was all class."

Doug Yates, who became a first-team All-Met for George Washington in 1954 and '55, was another big fan. "Kessler was my idol when he was on the varsity," Yates said. "I've always tried to play like he did."

During Kessler's prep career, George Washington was consistently ranked among the best teams in the area. But that was nothing new. Doran had arrived at the school when it opened in 1938 and won the state Group I championship in 1945 as well as a slew of Northern Virginia titles. He retired in 1953 with more than 500 victories and ultimately earned a place in the Virginia Sports Hall of Fame—one of the few figures from Northern Virginia to be so honored.

Doran was a kindly, low-key sort. He was never one to raise his voice or make a fuss even under the most stressful of circumstances. He would often invite Kessler and Hardy over to his house on game day, making sure they were sufficiently rested for the game that night. He'd throw a couple of steaks in the oven for the two of them as well. Many thought Doran was merely taking care of his two meal tickets, but it was more than that. Kessler and Hardy weren't as well-off as most of their teammates, and Doran felt it important to spoil them when he had the opportunity.

"He was like a father to us," Kessler recalled. "He was like [Coach] John Wooden. He didn't say much. But when he talked, he got your attention. He treated me extremely well."

From a tactical standpoint, Doran liked to control the pace of the game. On defense, his teams played a lot of zone and always seemed to have enough big, long-armed players to make it work. Syracuse University coach Jim Boeheim would later operate much the same way with great success. Doran's zones were made even more effective by the cramped gymnasium his teams played in. It didn't help opponents that the gym held only about 300 people, and crowds were always standing room only. The gym wall was only about three feet from one baseline, making any drive to the basket at that end an adventure. Between the partisan crowds right on top of you and the long arms and big bodies of the Presidents' zone closing in, opposing teams found it almost impossible to win there. "It was a real bandbox," Kessler said.

As dominant as George Washington was in the early part of the decade, the Generals of Washington-Lee (W-L, now Washington-Liberty) from neighboring Arlington emerged as a worthy rival as the 1950s progressed. W-L played in the state title game in 1952 and '55; GWHS did the same in 1953 and '56. In those days, the top two Group I teams from Northern Virginia automatically were invited to the state tournament, and George Washington and Washington-Lee were always the choices. They were the elite of Northern Virginia, leaving county schools such as Mount Vernon and the Fairfax Rebels on the outside looking in. "We couldn't beat them to save our necks," Jenkins recalled. "They were at a different level."

The two schools were heated rivals as well. In 1954 Washington-Lee gained the final No. 1 ranking in the *Post*. Of course, the only regular-season loss the W-L Generals suffered came at the hands of George Washington. The GWHS Presidents also wound up winning the Metropolitan Tournament that year under first-year coach Steve Osisek, who replaced Doran.

That's how it went with the two schools: every time Washington-Lee did something, George Washington answered—and vice versa. Every game between the two, it seemed, was hard fought and hotly contested. One year the police were called to GWHS to handle crowd control for a W-L game because too many folks were trying to squeeze into the school's undersized gym. Another time, Bob Kessler appeared to hit a jumper at the buzzer to win a game over W-L, but the officials called Crenshaw Hardy for a three-second violation, which negated the shot and gave the Generals the win. Naturally, a huge free-for-all ensued. A couple of years later, there was a scuffle after a game between the two schools, and George Washington opted not to play in Washington-Lee's year-end invitational tournament, which was being held the following week, so that tempers could cool off. "Washington-Lee was our big rival," Kessler said. "It went back and forth every year."

The rivalry extended to football as well. Each year for more than three decades, the two schools met in the "Old Oaken Bucket" game on Thanksgiving Day. The contest was one of the premier athletic and social events of the fall. In the years when both teams were good, the matchup could draw crowds approaching 15,000 people.

And how seriously did the local rivals take that game? Consider this: Bob Waldorf, who would coach the W-L Generals to an undefeated season and a state football title in 1956, was hanged in effigy after his team's 1955 loss to GWHS. The next year, when W-L ended a nine-game losing streak in the series, Arlington admirers carried Waldorf off the field on their shoulders. When it came to GWHS and W-L, beating the other guys was always a big deal.

The two schools competed in other areas as well. Washington-Lee could claim—with no small amount of pride—that its school produced the best acting talent in the area. Shirley MacLaine and Warren Beatty graduated from there in the 1950s, while Sandra Bullock got her diploma from W-L a couple of decades later. George Washington, meanwhile, could boast of the noteworthy pop music stars who'd attended the school. John Phillips and Cass Elliot of the Mamas and the Papas attended GWHS, as did enigmatic Doors front man Jim Morrison, a member of the class of 1961.

Judging from the newspaper coverage of the day, sportswriters clearly believed the best basketball in the area was played in the Inter-High and the Catholic League.

George Washington and Washington-Lee were generally considered in the same class as well.

❀ ❀ ❀

For whatever reason, suburban Maryland schools were considered a notch below their neighbors. Perhaps it was because of the schools' lack of postseason success. The only metro area school to win a Maryland state basketball championship before 1950 was Greenbelt High School; long since closed, it had won a title in 1947.

But like so much else in the Washington area during that time, things were changing. The shift began in the first few months of 1951, when Blair basketball coach Tony Crème was called into military service in the Korean War.

His replacement was David Carrasco, a local youth coach with a commanding presence who never raised his voice because he never had to. At six foot four and about 220 pounds, Carrasco was a standout boxer and basketball player at Texas Western College (now the University of Texas–El Paso). He was coaching youth league and junior high school basketball in and around Silver Spring, Maryland, when he got the Blair coaching job. In those days, his teams often played at the old Silver Spring Armory, where he sometimes crossed paths with Morgan Wootten, then another up-and-coming young coach.

Given the intolerance of those times, it seems surprising in retrospect that Carrasco even got the job. He was, after all, a man who had been raised in a culture that was equal parts Mexican and American in El Paso, a west Texas border town. He had olive skin and a slight accent. The prejudices of the era extended even to celebrities of Latin descent. CBS network officials, for example, were dubious about casting Cuban Desi Arnaz opposite Lucille Ball in the *I Love Lucy* show, which was about to become one of television's first big hits. Ball, a talented, big-name comedienne at the time, had to explain to the officials that Arnaz was her husband *in real life,* so everyone should just accept him in the role. It wasn't until the husband-and-wife team went on the road with their act and drew big crowds that the network relented. This story speaks volumes about the general discomfort American society in the 1950s felt about a person of color in any kind of prominent position. The idea of a Hispanic man such as Carrasco wielding authority over basketball players, especially white ones, was an alien concept at the time.

Carrasco silenced any criticism of his background or suitability in the most definitive way possible—by winning. His Blazer teams captured state titles in 1952, 1953, and 1955, striking a real blow for Maryland suburban schools. In fact, he started a long-running tradition of excellence at Blair that lasted for three decades. From 1952 to 1979, Blair won nine state titles and reached the final two other times while competing in the state's largest classification.

Carrasco's first title winner was something of a surprise. The Blazers were just

9–7 at one point during the 1951–52 season but got everyone's attention when they nearly knocked off McKinley in the opening round of the Metropolitan Tournament. They continued to play well through the postseason, thanks largely to the ballhandling and passing by point guard Marty Sigholtz. In Blair's 42–34 victory over the Hagerstown Little Heiskells at Ritchie Coliseum, Sigholtz scored a game-high 18 points to give Blair what was then called the Class A title.

The next year, success was expected; virtually everyone but Sigholtz returned. Jack Doane—whose brother, Gene, would coach Blair to a pair of state titles in the 1970s—led the way in the 60–57 win over the Allegany Campers in the 1953 Class A final. He scored 23 points and helped give Blair a second straight state championship.

It's a testament to Carrasco's guidance and leadership that he was able to win back-to-back state titles without a single player deemed worthy of All-Met consideration. What his players recalled about him, more than any particular tactical innovation or specialty, was the respect he commanded and the leadership he showed. He was simply the kind of coach that kids loved to play for.

"He just had a way with people," said Gene Doane, who helped out Carrasco at practice and did some scouting for him as a student at Maryland while mulling a coaching career of his own. "He was low-key; he wasn't out there ranting and raving. He had a way of letting you know if what you were doing was right or wrong just by his look. I respected him so much."

Carrasco wasn't one for public displays either. Whatever mistakes his players made were discussed behind closed doors, often at halftime. He didn't want his players carrying on during games, because it might reflect badly on them. He held his own temper in check for the same reason.

"He was a fine man," said Dick Brown, who played with Blair's 1955 state champs. "When you're young, you don't quite realize some of that stuff."

The real proof of Carrasco's influence lies in the number of his players who became coaches themselves. Doane and Ed Clements later coached at Blair, Brown at the US Naval Academy, and Willie Jones—who also played for Carrasco at American University—at Robinson Secondary School in Fairfax and at the University of the District of Columbia, where he won a Division II national title.

In 1955 Carrasco had his best team ever. He inherited a number of players who had helped Blair to an undefeated football season that fall. That group helped propel the basketball team to its own 21–0 record and to Carrasco's third state championship in four seasons. In the spring, the school's baseball team—which featured Brown and pitcher Steve Barber, later the Baltimore Orioles' first 20-game winner—lost just once that season. All in all, it was quite a year for Blair's athletic teams.

During the 1954–55 campaign, the basketball team was unquestionably the class act in the area. Carrasco scheduled tough games against top teams in the Catholic, Inter-High, and Northern Virginia Leagues because he knew he was guiding a powerhouse and wanted it tested against the best competition he could find. He had six-foot-seven Herb Jacobsen in the middle, but the six-foot-three Brown, an All-Met selection that year, jumped center because he was uncommonly athletic. Supporting players such as Dick Street, Frank Corcoran, Don Shanklin, and John Stoneburner all understood the sacrifices necessary to win—lessons learned as a result of their football success.

"This is a different type of team than the [first] two championship clubs," said Carrasco, who went 61–20 in his first four seasons at Blair. "On paper, Dick Brown would appear to be the best player . . . but it has been a team effort; and not a five-, but a six-man team that has carried us along."

Brown led Blair with 21 points in the 1955 state final victory over Hagerstown, with Jacobsen adding 13. But Corcoran was the real hero. Though he finished with just 11 points, his jumper inside the final 90 seconds broke a tie at 54. He added a key free throw as the Blazers held on for a 58–55 victory that clinched an undefeated season.

"We were pretty good athletes, and we liked each other," recalled Brown, who led a balanced Blair offense with a modest 15-point average. "We just got along well. And we did everything Carrasco told us."

As good a high school basketball coach as Carrasco was, he was destined for bigger things. He parlayed his success at Blair into the coaching job at American University. There, with the aid of the administration, Carrasco recruited black players such as Willie Jones of the Dunbar Crimson Tide and Jim Howell of the Archbishop Carroll Lions, thereby integrating college basketball in the Washington area. Thanks in large part to Carrasco, AU was more than a half-dozen years ahead of the University of Maryland, George Washington, and Georgetown in this regard.

Having faced prejudice himself back in El Paso, Carrasco was determined to give his players—black and white—an education and a chance at a better life. But none of it was easy. Once word got out that AU had signed black players, many southern schools refused to play the AU Eagles. That led to lots of schedule juggling, not to mention other problems. When the Eagles went on the road, they endured taunts, opponents who tried to provoke fights, and all manner of indignities.

Jones, a fiery competitor, often fumed at the treatment he received. But it never came to anything; Carrasco wouldn't let it. One night in Roanoke, Virginia, Jones almost snapped when the fans serenaded the AU players with a mean-spirited rendition of "Bye, Bye, Blackbird." But Carrasco stepped in and made sure everyone on the team calmed down.

"I didn't bring you down here to fight," Carrasco told Jones. "You're down here to be a basketball player. You have to understand, they're doing this to you because you're good. When you score, it's like punching them in the face."

Later, school officials sent a telegram of apology, but the incident—and Carrasco's response—stuck with Jones. "He had prepared us about what our goal was—

to play basketball," Jones said. "I was ready to fight everybody, but the man took that completely away from me. I imagine that, being Mexican American, he had experienced all that stuff."

Carrasco coached six years at AU and, thanks largely to the high-scoring Jones, guided the program to three straight 20-win seasons. But after a 10–11 record in 1961–62, he was let go. He believed there was always a faction in the school administration who felt he'd pressed too hard for integration and that he'd gone too far, too fast.

He went on to become an administrator for sports programs in the Peace Corps and served as a liaison between the US Olympic team and local officials at the Mexico City Games in 1968. After that, he returned to El Paso to start a job training center aimed at bettering the lives of the at-risk youths in his hometown. The job center was rated the most successful in the country for 10 years straight, prompting *Time* magazine to run a feature story about him and his success in changing the paths of so many young people.

"Dave was the kind of guy that anyone who met him, liked him," said Morgan Wootten. "He knew basketball, he knew life, he knew people. He touched a lot of lives."

McKinley Tech, George Washington, and Blair all enjoyed dominant runs during the 1950s. But even with these successful programs, there was room on the local sports pages for the exploits of the underdog too. In 1951 tiny Herndon High School, "an upstart team from Fairfax County" in the estimation of the *Star*, put together one of the great seasons in the history of Northern Virginia prep basketball.

Herndon, an incorporated city on the northwestern edge of Fairfax County near where Dulles International Airport is now, must have seemed like a frontier outpost at the time. The city itself, now part of the bustling Northern Virginia suburbs, was home to a mere 1,461 residents, according to the 1950 US census. The high school had just 300 students, which consigned its athletic teams to Group III competition. The biggest schools in the area, such as George Washington and Washington-Lee, played in Group I.

But Herndon's modest size could not detract from its accomplishments. With first-year coach Bob Carter pushing all the right buttons, the Herndon Fighting Hornets ran off 23 victories without a loss and captured the state Group III title with a 52–47 victory over Garden High's Green Dragons of Oakwood, Virginia.

Like McKinley, Herndon outran and outhustled its competition all season. It overwhelmed the Lovettsville Lions, 99–18, and whipped the James Madison Warhawks in the regional tournament, 68–34. The Hornets won four other times that season by at least 29 points.

The big edge they had over opponents was six-foot-five center Dick Detwiler, who generally dominated the lane at both ends of the floor while averaging about 16 points per game. He had a lot to do on that team; he was the lone six-footer in the starting lineup. Ronnie Coleman, the next-tallest starter at five foot 11, provided the driving and outside scoring threat to complement Detwiler. Coleman led the team in scoring with about 21 points per game. Point guard Earl White (five foot eight), Tommy Poland (five foot eight), and Sonny Lawrence (five foot nine) filled out the starting five.

Lawrence was the one who came up big in the state finals against the Green Dragons at Virginia Military Institute in Lexington, scoring a game-high 18 points in one of the few close calls the team had that season. That contest featured a dozen lead changes in the second half, and neither team led by more than three points after intermission. But the Hornets' balance was the key to victory. Aside from Lawrence, Coleman contributed 16 points, and Detwiler netted 14 to secure the title.

Even though Herndon wasn't the year-in, year-out power that some of the bigger schools were, it did gain one major distinction that season: it became the only Northern Virginia team to capture a state basketball title—at any level—during the 1950s.

Two years later, another small school in DC rose to grab headlines from the more established teams in the area. St. Anthony's, a small coed Catholic school in the Brookland neighborhood of Northeast DC, took the measure of the best teams in the metro area in 1953 despite having a student body numbering just 250—only 106 of whom were boys. The players on the St. Anthony's team were all neighborhood kids, products of a solid middle-class upbringing where everybody knew everybody and where everybody's father, it seemed, was a fireman or a cop.

At the time, St. Anthony's didn't even have its own gymnasium. The team had to practice wherever it could—sometimes outdoors, sometimes at Gonzaga after the Eagles were done, or at any number of other spots around the city. "You name a gym, we've practiced there," quipped Coach Jack Bohne.

Bohne himself was part of that neighborhood culture. He'd grown up in Brookland and played on the St. Anthony's varsity team in 1947 and '48. He had taken the basketball coaching job fresh out of college at the age of 22.

"St. Anthony's wasn't a place that had a lot of money to pay coaches," noted Jack Sullivan, far and away the star of that St. Anthony's team. "They were always getting young guys."

But the best basketball training didn't come from Bohne or from the many gyms the team borrowed for practice. It came from games on the playground courts at Turkey Thicket, not far from the school, where the best players in the city—black and white—would gather.

"We wanted to get better, and to do that, you had to play with the best," recalled Sullivan. "If you played ball in the fifties, that's where you went."

It also helped St. Anthony's Tonies that Sullivan was on the roster. He was six foot four, strong, athletic, and just as capable of scoring from the perimeter or with a deadly running hook as he was on an offensive rebound. In 1952–53 he was a first-team All-Met in the *Washington Post* and one of the top scorers in the city with a 24-point average.

How good was Sullivan? After graduation, he became a huge star at Mount St. Mary's, back when the Mountaineers were a Division II power, and he still holds the record for career points scored at a Maryland college (2,672). Over the years, his scoring total has withstood the onslaught of even the greatest University of Maryland star players: Albert King, Adrian Branch, Len Bias, and Juan Dixon. None of them, great as they were, matched Sullivan's collegiate point production.

As high schoolers, Sullivan and his teammates were young and cocky and absolutely convinced they could compete with anybody. After all, they'd matched their talents against the best in the city on the playground during the summer. "We didn't expect to lose to anybody," Sullivan said.

The Tonies won 12 straight to open the 1952–53 season and rose to No. 6 in the rankings. But the team faded at the finish, dropping three of its last four games.

The lone victory in that stretch, over Georgetown Prep, was a critical one. It guaranteed the Tonies a third-place finish in the Catholic League. And that year, a third-place finish meant inclusion in the Metropolitan Tournament, which featured the top teams from the Inter-High and the Catholic League, among others. That year, it just so happened that the Metropolitan Tournament coincided with the Maryland state tournament. The champions of Montgomery and Prince George's Counties—Blair and the Bladensburg Mustangs, respectively—opted out of the Metro matchup, preferring to play for a state title rather than for local bragging rights.

Their decisions opened up two spots in the eight-team field that were filled on an at-large basis by the Falls Church Jaguars and St. Anthony's. Nobody gave the Tonies much of a chance; they'd participated the year before and lost in the first round. Nobody was surprised when St. Anthony's was seeded eighth, and last, in the field.

But folks were mildly surprised when the Tonies knocked off Inter-High champ Wilson in the opening round, 62–57, helped by Sullivan's 16 points and George Shugars's key steal late in the game. More eyebrows were raised after the Tonies' 53–46 upset of Washington-Lee, a Northern Virginia power with an enrollment 10 times that of St. Anthony's. Again, Sullivan led the way with 22. "They just refused to give up," Coach Bohne said afterward.

That landed the upstart Tonies in the championship game against George Washington, the other formidable Northern Virginia entry. The Presidents eventually went all the way to the state Group I final, losing on a last-second basket to the

E. C. Glass Hilltoppers of Lynchburg. They came up just short in the Metropolitan final as well, losing to the Tonies, 52–50. Sullivan was the star again, with a game-high 17 points. The de facto area championship—improbable though it might have been—was theirs.

"There wasn't any pressure on us from the start," Bohne said. "The guys could go out and played a relaxed game. If we won, it would be a surprise. If we lost, well, that would be what everyone expected."

It was a surprise, all right. The *Star*, which sponsored the event, called St. Anthony's triumph "the biggest upset in the 21-year history of tournament." The newspaper went even further than that; when it released its final high school poll, St. Anthony's was in the No. 1 spot. Nobody argued.

In terms of area high school basketball programs, DeMatha rates as the best historically, having consistently produced standout players and excellent teams under the legendary Morgan Wootten. The iconic coach won more than 1,200 games and sent more than a dozen players to the National Basketball Association.

When it comes to rating individual players, another name stands alone in the annals of DC high school basketball—Elgin Baylor. And no wonder. Baylor was a comet, a dazzling, spectacular phenomenon hurtling through space like nothing anyone had ever seen before. He was both ahead of his time and too early. Had Baylor performed his feats during the 24/7 *SportsCenter* era, his fame would be even greater than it is today. As it is, he's considered among the best ever to play the game. Some who have been around the NBA for a long time still insist he's the best forward ever. At six foot five, he scored and rebounded like few others, averaging 27.4 points and 13.5 rebounds during a career that lasted from the late 1950s until the early 1970s.

But the sheer numbers alone don't do justice to his style. In many circles, he is referred to as basketball's Wright brother—a pioneer who took the game into the air when everyone else was still earthbound. If you were to play the word association game with certain old-timers, the phrase "Elgin Baylor" inevitably would elicit the response "hang time."

Baylor, it is said, demonstrated what one could possibly do with a basketball in mid-air, setting the stage for later players like Connie Hawkins, Julius Erving, and, of course, Michael Jordan. All walked in his footsteps, even if those footsteps were a couple of feet off the ground.

"All of it started with 'Rabbit,'" said Archbishop Carroll star Tom Hoover, invoking Baylor's DC playground nickname. "He was the originator."

A bit of provincial boasting? Hardly. Here's what *The Official NBA Encyclopedia* has to say in its entry on Baylor: "From his incomparable style, grace, creativity and athleticism came the NBA that fans cheer today in all its spectacular forms."

Chapter Two

He also had the "NBA's most dreaded head fake. Add in his remarkable hang time and vast array of spectacular moves, and it's no wonder opponents were left spinning in confusion."

Those who encountered Baylor on the blacktop of Southeast DC, or at Turkey Thicket, or even during his high school days with the Phelps Tradesmen and then the Spingarn Green Wave always spoke proudly of sharing the floor with him. Locals take special delight in looking back on those days, as the game of basketball literally went skyward. They know that they were there at the start, witnesses to the game's liftoff.

"He did stuff nobody had thought of yet," said Warren Williams, a friend and rival who played at Dunbar. His recommendation kick-started Baylor's college career at the tiny College of Idaho.

"You'd swear wires were holding him up," agreed Bill McCaffrey, who played at Anacostia, then an all-white school in the days before DC school integration. "He was one of a kind."

And yet Baylor's brilliant basketball career nearly failed to launch. Most accounts say that Baylor grew up in Southeast DC, which is technically true. In reality, though, his boyhood home was closer to Capitol Hill. He grew up on Heckman Street, which doesn't exist anymore. Today it's called Duddington Place and sits in the middle of a gentrified neighborhood a couple of blocks from the Capitol South Metro station.

In those days, Baylor's neighborhood playground was segregated, as were many public facilities in the District. The only time the black kids could go there and play was at night, when nobody was watching. In the dark, it was difficult to play anything, much less a game of basketball. As a result, Baylor's interest in the game was minimal at first. Over time, things changed, albeit slowly. By his own admission, he didn't begin seriously playing the game he revolutionized until he was 14 or 15.

"Really, I wasn't interested in basketball until about then, and then they had a place called Southeast Settlement House, where kids could go," he once recalled. "So it happened that I got involved in basketball—for what reason I don't know—but it just looked like fun to do. Actually, this was the only thing we could do, because we couldn't play any other sport. We could only go on the playground when it was closed, and the only thing you could do was try to shoot baskets."

He just as easily could have moved on to some other activity, given the lack of access to the local playgrounds. It probably helped that his two older brothers played the game. They might have served as role models for young Elgin, but he never tried to emulate them. "I never tried to play like anybody," he once said.

That seemed only right. Baylor played like nobody else because nobody else played the way he did. Even his name itself is exotic and original. The story is that Baylor's father glanced down at his watch to note the exact time of his boy's birth and saw the name on the face of the watch, Elgin. Have you ever met or heard of anyone else named Elgin? Of course not. In every respect, the man is one of a kind.

Despite his late start, Baylor landed on the Phelps High School varsity team as a freshman. He even drew a mention in the team preview that ran in the old *Washington Daily News* tabloid before the 1951–52 season, which would have been only his sophomore year. Phelps—along with Dunbar, Armstrong, and Cardozo—was one of four segregated DC high schools for blacks at the time. Spingarn, where Baylor eventually wound up, wasn't built until a year later and was the final all-black segregated high school built within the city's boundaries.

According to newspaper accounts, Baylor averaged about 19 points per game as a freshman and about 27 as a sophomore. But details of his exploits are sketchy at best. The mainstream newspapers didn't give much coverage to the black schools, which were grouped together in the Inter-High's Division II.

The long-gone *Daily News* was far more progressive than its competitors were in such matters, but Baylor's talents still never got the attention they deserved. According to Baylor, it was a lack of publicity—not poor grades, as many maintain—that left him struggling to find a college at the conclusion of his prep career.

Although few actually saw Baylor play at Phelps, he was widely known throughout the city by reputation, if nothing else. Those who got to see him play for themselves—at Phelps or on the playgrounds—were quickly won over. "I thought I was a good player until I saw Elgin," said Williams, an All-Met player himself.

Baylor attracted enough attention as a sophomore to make the all-league team put together by the *Star*. However, he was listed as playing for Dunbar, not Phelps, in a clear indication that the papers weren't paying enough attention.

"People like Baylor never received the recognition they should have received in high school," said Frank Bolden, the longtime coach of the Cardozo Clerks, whose teams battled Baylor's in the early 1950s. "The big papers just didn't pay the black schools any mind."

After his standout sophomore season, Baylor's budding basketball career came to a halt. Even though he was probably the best player in the city, he dropped out of school for a time and didn't play scholastic basketball during what would have been his junior year, 1952–53. Baylor continued to play on the playgrounds and in the recreation leagues, his legend growing with every performance. At that point, his fame was widespread among those in the subculture of DC basketball, though he was virtually unknown to the public at large.

That was about to change though. After his year in exile, he resurfaced at Spingarn, then a brand-new school, in the fall of 1953. Reunited with Coach Dave Brown, who'd coached him at Phelps, Baylor's career was about to take off—again.

His average jumped to about 36 points per game that year, and only twice did he fail to score 20. Again, estimates of his scoring totals are inexact; his statistics varied from one newspaper to the next. Years later when the local papers recounted his exploits in college and the pros, they often contradicted their own earlier accounts of his high school accomplishments. But this much was clear: Baylor was unlike anyone who'd come along before in Washington and better than anybody since.

He compiled dazzling numbers despite playing only about a half in many of his team's games. Spingarn went undefeated in league play and lost only twice during the regular season. Both of those losses came on a road swing up to Baltimore during which his coach experimented with the lineup.

Word spread quickly that stopping Baylor was a nearly impossible proposition. Consequently, he faced all manner of zones and junk defenses designed to contain him, none of which met with much success.

Opponents wouldn't let him set up close to the basket, sagging inside with their zones to clog the middle. On those nights, Baylor would set up in the lane, then make a quick cut to the wing or the corner, take a pass, and score anyway. Bolden recalled one time when Baylor picked up his fourth foul against Cardozo in the early moments of the second quarter. Coach Brown sat him down at that point, leading Bolden to figure he could forget about Baylor for the rest of the game.

But Baylor sat for only a minute or two. Brown put him back in, instructing him to stay out of the lane at both ends so as not to pick up a fifth and final foul. Baylor responded by torching the Cardozo defense for 40 points, doing most of his damage from the outside. And he didn't foul out either.

That's how he played for much of his high school career. Then his college career. Then his pro career. He was indomitable. He could drive like nobody else, finding ways through the defense when his initial path appeared blocked. He also rebounded like a fiend and could score on tap-ins even when the ball didn't come his way. If the middle were closed off, he could kill you from the outside. If double-teamed, he'd find the open teammate. In fact, he was such a good passer that Red Auerbach ordered the Celtics never to double-team him. Auerbach decided his teams would take their lumps guarding Baylor one-on-one. They often did.

"I don't know if I have the words to describe him," said Marty Tapscott, who ran the point on the Baylor-led Spingarn team of 1953–54. "He was the best thing to come out of Washington before or since. He was graceful, he could jump, he could shoot from the outside, he could score inside. There was nothing on the basketball court that he couldn't do. It's a wonder we didn't all just stand around and watch him."

That otherworldly talent, combined with a real competitive streak, drove him to greatness. Whether it was playing cards, basketball, or any contest, young Elgin Baylor hungered to win. Warren Williams remembered countless tests of skill in dinky youth gyms during his high school years that involved Baylor. Those on hand were there to goof around, maybe get a little extra work in, and they would sometimes engage in shooting contests for whatever loose change they had in their pockets. Invariably, Baylor took everyone's money. "He was *very* competitive," Williams recalled with a laugh. "He wouldn't let you win at anything."

And yet for all his talent and his competitive streak, Baylor was no diva. Those who played with him and against him remembered a young man of immense talent who was all business on the court. The only thing Willie Jones could recall him saying on the court was, "I got him," when players matched up at the start of a game. Bolden described the young Baylor as "mannerly." Because he could be so quiet, some found him difficult to get to know, but everyone respected him—especially with a basketball in his hands.

"He wasn't boastful, he wasn't loud. He just went about doing his job," Tapscott said.

Over the years, Baylor's personality underwent quite a change. In later years, within the confines of the Los Angeles Lakers' locker room or inside the team's inner circle, he was known as a lovable, insufferable chatterbox, capable of holding court on any and all topics through a cross-country flight from Los Angeles to New York. In public, though, he generally maintained a low-key facade, even as he developed into one of the game's greatest stars.

Baylor's high school coach deserves much of the credit for keeping the young star's head on straight. Brown was revered by any and all who came under his guidance. Like all the best coaches, he taught his charges about much more than sports. He delivered lessons about life, about how to act, about how to get along in the world.

"You couldn't act the fool around [Brown]," said Tapscott. "He wouldn't put up with it. To be around him, you had to be respectful. [He was] a true gentleman. Not only a coach, but a philosopher and a father figure. If you didn't play by the rules, you couldn't play for him."

"I considered myself a very disciplined player," Baylor once said. "And I thank him [Brown] for instilling that quality in my game. I really respected him."

As the two were reunited at Spingarn after their time together at Phelps, together they took a step toward changing the culture of basketball and basketball coverage in the metro area. Even though newspapers devoted little space in the high school sports pages to the black schools previously, Spingarn and Baylor now were simply too good to ignore.

By late January of Baylor's senior season, Spingarn had established itself as a serious contender for the league title. The Green Wave edged Dunbar, 48–46, to assume the top spot for the first time ever in what was a typically brilliant game for Baylor. He scored a game-high 23 points, including a pair of drives that tied the game at 41 after Spingarn had trailed by nine entering the fourth quarter. In the final five seconds, Dunbar's Frank Jones stole the ball and drove in for a layup that would have tied the game. Baylor, trailing the play, blocked the shot from behind and grabbed the loose ball at the buzzer, preserving the victory.

The next time out, he went for 34 points as Armstrong Manual Training School tried to contain him with a zone defense. Against his old school, Phelps, he set an Inter-High scoring record that still stands with a 63-point outburst in a 91–48 blowout. He scored 31 in the first half and 32 in the second, despite playing with four fouls for much of the last two periods. "The only guy who can stop Baylor is the referee," marveled one observer.

If that wasn't enough to convince basketball fans of his greatness, then his next game was. It was generally unquestioned at the time that the best basketball in the city was played among the white schools in the Inter-High's Division I and in the Catholic League. Media attention focused on those schools. Baylor turned the accepted pecking order upside down by scoring 40 points in Spingarn's shocking 64–55 upset of the Archbishop Carroll Lions. The Lions weren't the power they would become at the end of the decade, but they were still a quality team. Coach Bob Dwyer deserved a great deal of credit for scheduling all-black schools such as Spingarn when none of the all-white public schools would.

The outcome and Baylor's performance did much to legitimize the level of play in the Inter-High's Division II. If Baylor and Spingarn were good enough to beat Carroll, the reasoning went, then they must play a pretty good brand of basketball in that league. And nobody played a better brand than Baylor.

"He is without a doubt the best high school player I've ever seen," said Dwyer, whose team, according to the *Star*, featured "one of the best zone defenses in the area." Dwyer gushed, "I've been coaching basketball for 18 years. And I never saw a high school player that could touch him—I mean even *touch* him."

In that game, as in many others, Baylor did whatever he wanted. Accounts of the action indicate he scored off lob passes for dunks. He also buried hooks, fadeaways, and, as the *Post* noted, "a dozen more odd-angle shots of his own invention."

Those who actually saw him play, like Dwyer, became true believers. Local papers ran letters to the editors in which fans raved about Baylor's abilities and pleaded for sportswriters to give him his due.

The groundswell of support may actually have made a difference. Spingarn finished its season 15–2 (high school teams generally played only about 20 games in those days) and wound up second only to 20–1 Washington-Lee in the *Post*'s final high school poll. Spingarn's ranking was reported to be the highest ever earned by a segregated school in the *Post* up to that point.

All of the local papers broke precedent when picking their postseason all-star teams as well. Baylor was a first-team All-Met pick in the *Star* and the *Post*, the first player of his race to be so honored. "They couldn't keep him off there," Tapscott said. The *Daily News*, which picked only all-league teams back then, went its competition one better. The scruffy tabloid named Baylor its player of the year, awarding him the Livingston Trophy as the top high school basketball player in the area.

The term "groundbreaking" doesn't begin to describe the impact he had in terms of both changing the game and changing perceptions about black schools and black players. The recognition for Baylor came late and probably wasn't as extensive as it should have been, given his abilities and accomplishments. Over time, his presence and impact locally seem to have been forgotten as well. It was so long ago, and Baylor himself hasn't returned to the area very often. He became a West Coaster after his brilliant college career at Seattle University, his Hall of Fame career with the Los Angeles Lakers, and his long tenure as the general manager of the Los Angeles Clippers.

But those who played with him or against him—and even those who just watched him play—remember. They're dwindling in number now, but they remain keepers of the flame and guardians of the legend. They remember how it was because they saw it with their own eyes, and they look askance at anyone who doesn't believe that it really happened that way—that there really could have been a kid from the streets of the nation's capital who transformed the game and did things on the court that nobody else ever did. The tales of Baylor's exploits may seem improbable, but he really was that good, they'll tell you. And if you don't believe the stories, well, then that's your problem, not theirs.

Jack Sullivan is one who knows. The former St. Anthony's star was as good a shooter and scorer as there was in the early 1950s. He was one of that crew who honed his game on the courts at Turkey Thicket and remembers Elgin Baylor when he was still largely a secret to the rest of DC, much less the world. "Any story you hear about Elgin Baylor, take it as true," Sullivan said. "He was that good."

Baylor, great as he was, made his final appearance in a Spingarn uniform in a consolation game, not a championship. He and Spingarn lost in the semifinals of the black schools' postseason tournament; it was the only game the Green Wave lost to a DC team all year. Armstrong, which had dominated the Inter-High's Division II for the previous decade, upset the Green Wave in the semifinals. Accounts of the final score differ—an indication that the local papers weren't paying attention to the black schools—but it was either 51–47 or 50–47. Baylor scored "only" 19 points; some accounts said his total was 18. At any rate, it was just the second time all season he failed to reach 20.

Armstrong coach Charles Baltimore had watched Baylor torch his team for 44 and 45 points during the regular season. So he had changed tactics. He employed a box-and-one defense against Baylor, using senior captain Gary Mays to shadow the city's best player. Mays's job was to stick close to Baylor and make it as difficult as possible for him to get free. Help would come from teammates when Baylor came into their area, but the primary responsibility rested with Mays.

"Coach said, 'I got a job for you,'" Mays recalled. "'If he [Baylor] goes into the bathroom, I want you to follow him.'"

Much has been made over the years over Mays's performance that night, although Mays himself always tried to downplay it. "I didn't stop Elgin," he'd say. "Elgin stopped himself." For the record, Mays scored 12 points himself, including the clinching free throws in the three-point victory.

"That's the only bad game he [Baylor] ever had," Tapscott said. "Elgin was just missing a lot of shots."

Ultimately, whether Mays stopped Baylor is immaterial. Mays was an incredible story in his own right, no matter what happened on the night in question. Since the age of five, when he was hit by an accidental discharge of some shotgun pellets, Mays had lived with a left arm that was just a few inches long—"my nub," he called it affectionately. In time, he became known as the "One-Armed Bandit" or just "Bandit."

But lacking a left arm hardly hindered Mays at all—not on the basketball court, where he learned to cope with his particular challenge, nor on the baseball field, where he was generally acknowledged as the best catcher in the city. "'Can't' isn't in my vocabulary," he said. "I've never had any problems doing anything."

He had a hell of a time convincing some folks, though. He was forced to practice on his own as a youth because no one would choose him for pickup games. Willie Jones, then an up-and-coming player at Dunbar, remembers seeing him on the playground one day and noticing Mays's shoelace was untied. "Here, let me get that for you," Jones said, bending over to help.

*Whap!* Mays whacked Jones on the top of the head with his damaged limb, shouting, "I can tie my own shoes! If I need your help, I'll ask for it!"

Mays didn't need anyone's help, and he didn't want their pity. He was, pure and simple, a player. A tenacious defender and a reliable scorer, he was good enough to make second-team All-League in the *Daily News* as a senior. He was too quick and too clever to be overplayed to one side, despite his handicap. He'd spin and twist while handling the ball and get where he needed to go. "I could see what they were trying to do, but I had no problems," Mays said.

"You were wasting your time overplaying him," Jones recalled. "He was that good with the ball."

At one point, Mays was even approached about signing with the Harlem Globetrotters, but the idea didn't interest him. "I didn't like the clowning part of it," he said. "If you've got only one arm, you're a freak show, anyway."

No, Mays wanted to play it straight, the same as everyone else. He always felt he could have played professional baseball, but he never got the chance. Mays was no less nimble behind the plate than he was on the basketball floor. A 1955 *Jet* magazine profile of Mays explained how he would toss the ball in the air as he got out of his catcher's crouch, flip off his glove back between his neck and shoulder, and pluck the ball from mid-air, catching the ball in the middle of his throwing motion. Then he'd whip it down to second base in a flash. After a while, base runners simply stopped trying to steal on him. "They didn't want to be embarrassed," Mays said.

Mays could hit, too, batting .675 one season, according to the *Daily News*. He homered and threw out everyone who tried to run on him during a special try-out at Washington's old Griffith Stadium. But he didn't even get a nibble from the scouts on hand, even though he was chosen as the event's outstanding player.

Mays continued to play sandlot ball and in adult leagues but never got the break he longed for. "Everyone expected me to make the majors, and I did everything in my heart to make it," he said. "But I could never get anybody to believe in me."

Had their timing been a bit better, Baylor and Mays might have achieved the kind of acclaim their talents merited. Had they graduated from high school just one year later, after DC schools were integrated, things might have gone differently for them. With greater visibility during their high school careers, maybe Baylor wouldn't have had to start his college career at the tiny, obscure College of Idaho. Maybe Mays would have gotten the professional baseball contract he so desperately sought.

Just a few months after the 1953–54 basketball season ended, the US Supreme Court handed down its landmark decision in the *Brown v. Board of Education* case, ruling that "separate but equal" educational facilities had no place in American society. In other words, the concept of segregated schools had no legal legitimacy in the eyes of the highest court in the land. Implementing the decision and changing the US educational system proved far more problematic than anyone might have guessed. In some of the more backward parts of the country, real integration remained decades away, but the decision undeniably changed education and society from that point forward.

President Dwight Eisenhower, a man who was not exactly enlightened on this issue, nevertheless mandated that public schools in Washington, DC, would integrate in the fall of 1954, presumably so they could serve as a model for the rest of the nation. The schools, as with everything else in the District, were still under the thumb of the federal government; true home rule for DC was still two decades away. So, as far as the city was concerned, Eisenhower's word was law.

High school sports such as golf, tennis, swimming, and football were all still played in supervised, carefully curated grounds. But integration had already occurred within the city's boundaries—on the playgrounds. Up until *Brown v. Board*, blacks and whites played at separate schools and in separate leagues, but they'd already come together to interact and intermingle at Turkey Thicket, Langley Junior High, or one of the other pickup basketball hotspots of the day. City recreation officials made sure the playgrounds stayed all-white during the week. But all bets were off on the weekends, when many facilities had no one on duty to enforce the rules. Consequently, blacks and whites willingly played basketball with and against each other, making young basketball players far less hung up on race than the rest of the city was.

"When I was in high school, I started going over to Turkey Thicket," McKinley star Stan Kernan said. "There would be [black and white] people sitting all over the place, waiting to watch the games. We never had a fight or an argument or anything; it was about basketball."

"We always thought we got better playing against the black players," McKinley's Babe Marshall said. "A lot of guys came over there on the weekends."

Talent was what mattered on the playground. If you won, you kept playing. If you lost, you waited for the next open game. That might take hours, because Turkey Thicket was *the* destination for the best players in the city.

Consequently, the players who frequented the blacktop proving ground at 10th Street and Michigan Avenue Northeast, not far from Catholic University, cared less about the color of your skin than the quality of your jump shot. Nobody thought much about the larger issue of segregation; they were only high school kids, after all. When asked about it later, the comment you heard over and over again from players—black and white—went along the lines of "We never really thought about it," or "That's just the way it was."

While school systems in the United States had long operated according to the fraudulent concept of "separate but equal," the ethos of the playground was exactly the opposite. There, black and white players were assuredly not separate. But—and this might have been the only place in the city where this was true—they were equal.

At Turkey Thicket, for example, everyone played hard, perspired, and grew thirsty from their exertions on the court. So what did they all do? They grabbed a swig from the water fountain. There was just one in the park, and everyone drank from it regardless of color.

Today, that might not seem like a big deal. And to the teens occupied only with pickup basketball in mid-century Washington, DC, it wasn't. But in many parts of the United States in the early 1950s, the idea of both races drinking from the same water fountain was an alien concept. This was especially true in the South, where many communities had separate drinking fountains for blacks and whites.

"We never gave that a second thought," said Edward "Monk" Malloy, the future president of Notre Dame University. He once lived three blocks away from the park and started playing there at about the time McKinley ruled DC basketball.

"You wouldn't have seen that in Mississippi or Alabama," said Dick Ridgway, another Turkey Thicket regular who played at Gonzaga in the early 1950s.

Of course, once the pickup games were over, everyone went back to a largely segregated city—the whites to their neighborhoods and the blacks to theirs. Still, for virtually everyone—even those stung by prejudice and exclusion in the world at large—the basketball memories were good ones. "Those days," said Warren Williams, a star at Dunbar and a buddy of Baylor's, "I wouldn't give 'em up for anything."

Ultimately, the Supreme Court and Eisenhower's edict merely codified what had already taken place on the outdoor basketball courts of the city. But the first instance of blacks and whites coming together within the context of an actual public school contest came on January 7, 1955, with a doubleheader at McKinley's gym, the biggest in the city at that time. For the record, Armstrong beat McKinley in overtime, 58–57, and the Anacostia Indians topped Phelps, 41–36.

No signs of trouble were reported in the newspapers. The games went off without a hitch, leading some to wonder what all the fuss had been about. "We had to be very, very careful about what went on," said Frank Bolden, the coach of previously all-black Cardozo. "But we didn't have many problems."

Black kids welcomed the chance to prove themselves head-to-head after all those years of exclusion. They also felt pressure—pressure to prove their brand of basketball was equal to that played by the more publicized white schools.

"Sure, it was a big game," Armstrong's Willie Wood told Dick Heller of the *Washington Times* for a retrospective piece more than 50 years after that groundbreaking evening. "The white schools had all the money and all the facilities, and we knew the basketball reputation of the black schools was at stake. We couldn't afford to lose."

As it turned out, Wood didn't have to worry. He went on to lead Armstrong to the Inter-High title that year and eventually became an All-Pro safety on Vince Lombardi's great Green Bay Packer teams of the 1960s. Armstrong's Inter-High titles in 1955 and '56—the first two years after integration—continued a remarkable run of success for the program under Coach Charles Baltimore. In the nine seasons prior to integration, Baltimore had guided Armstrong to six Division II titles.

There was one unfortunate casualty of the move to integrate the city's public schools—the Metropolitan Tournament. For more than two decades, it had been *the* premier event in Washington high school basketball, matching up the best teams in the Inter-High League (at least among the white schools), the Catholic League, and Northern Virginia with those of Montgomery and Prince George's Counties from Maryland.

But the tournament was scrapped for 1955 because Virginia schools were prohibited from participating in any integrated athletic contest. Several Virginia counties, mostly in the southern or rural areas, actually shut down their public schools rather than admit black students; that's how resistant many jurisdictions were to the idea of integration. (Instead of local county schools, white students were treated to "tuition grants" or vouchers for education that were not equally available to black students.)

Curiously, the Metropolitan Tournament was never revived. In time, however, officials from the Catholic and the Inter-High Leagues decided to stage a postseason contest between the champions of their respective leagues. Thus, the first City Title Game took place in 1957, with Cardozo beating Gonzaga for local bragging rights.

Naturally, the prospect of integrating DC public schools was viewed with a great deal of trepidation on all sides. However, a weeklong series of articles in the *Star* the next fall indicated the transition was remarkably smooth, with few problems reported by students of either race.

Basketball was undeniably a vehicle for bridging the gulf between blacks and whites. White kids who played pickup ball with black kids at Turkey Thicket or somewhere else were less likely to look upon blacks with suspicion—and vice versa.

That was certainly the case with two of the city's biggest stars in the mid-1950s—Wilson's Lew Luce and Dunbar's Willie Jones. Both were picked by the *Post* and the *Star* for their All-Met teams for 1956, and the two had become thick as thieves by then. Even though Luce was white and Jones was black, they shared a great deal. Both were talented, outgoing, and, as their friends would tell you, a little crazy. Every sentence spoken by them or about them seemed to cry out for an exclamation point.

Luce was a multisport star, earning All-Met honors in football as well as basketball. He was a dangerous running back and kick returner, capable of taking the ball the distance at any time. On the basketball court, he played much the same way, barreling down the lane to score, without a thought for his own well-being or for anyone who stood in his way.

"I'd drop my shoulder and just drive to the basket," Luce recalled. "They couldn't stop me. Back in those days, they didn't call charges."

Luce burst upon the DC basketball scene by scoring 32 points as a sophomore in the Inter-High championship game of 1954 and leading Wilson to the title. He was unabashedly gung ho in everything he tried. He'd dribble a basketball to and from school each day to work on his ballhandling and would go all over the city to find a pickup game. He thought nothing of diving to the pavement in pursuit of a loose ball, leading an incredulous Baylor to cry, "Man, what's wrong with you, Luce? You must be crazy!"

Jones was no less colorful or talented. Though not even six feet tall, he developed into one of the great shooters in the area by studying the game and by learning how and when he could get his shot off. He was dangerous from the outside, quick to the basket, and unafraid to let you know it. In his senior year, he averaged 29 points per game with a high of 45. "I was the best shooter you've ever seen," he would boast, well into his 70s.

When it came to talking on the court, one playground rival described Jones this way: "If there was something Willie wanted you to know, Willie was gonna tell you." During Dunbar's games, Jones thought nothing of striking up conversations with fans in the stands or of warning an opposing ball handler that he was going to steal the ball—and then doing it. "I was Muhammad Ali before Ali," Jones would say with a laugh.

Given their personalities, it wasn't surprising that Luce and Jones became fast friends. The vast difference in their backgrounds might have raised some eyebrows, but they paid no mind to such things. Luce lived in well-to-do Chevy Chase, the son of a Teamsters lawyer. Jones grew up on Lamont Street Northwest, not far from Howard University. His father worked as a railroad dining car waiter. But the two young men were more alike than different.

"What? Because he's black, he's not as good as you?" Luce said. "I was never prejudiced against anybody."

"It was very uncommon," Jones said of their bond. "It shows you the strength of athletics and respect. We were good athletes who were cocky to a point, strong in our convictions, so you couldn't say things that would intimidate us."

In fact, Luce and Jones went out of their way to demonstrate their friendship, convention be damned. Neither one minded stirring the pot a little bit. If people saw the two of them hanging out together off the court and didn't like it, well, that was their tough luck.

When Jones needed a car to take his date to the prom, he asked to borrow Luce's. Lew was only too happy to oblige. Afraid Luce might be reluctant, Jones offered to bring the car back the next day, just to put Lew's mind at ease. "Don't worry about it," Luce told him. "I'll come by and get it."

Luce, being occupied with all manner of things—as most teenage boys are—didn't make it over to Lamont Street until about a week later. Jones, delighted by the unaccustomed luxury, took full advantage. He spent the next couple of days cruising around the neighborhood just to show off.

"Man, I was a monster in that thing!" he recalled. "I drove that thing around like I was leading a parade. Not that many guys in my neighborhood had their own cars."

Years later, Luce downplayed the incident, reluctant to make too much of the gesture. But in 1956 not many white kids from Chevy Chase were loaning their cars to black kids from Lamont Street.

"I don't think many people today run across that kind of friendship," Jones said. "He never displayed any of that [prejudice] with me. He was genuinely, truly my friend."

Of course, not everyone was so color-blind. Just across the Potomac, old guard Virginia politicians dug in their heels to block school integration. The practice was so widespread in the Old Dominion that it even acquired a name—"massive resistance."

State laws, obstinate politicians, fearful white citizens, and numerous delays prevented meaningful integration from taking place in Northern Virginia until more than a decade after *Brown v. Board*. Less than two years after the ruling, in fact, the Virginia legislature passed a bill prohibiting interracial scholastic sports competition within the state's borders.

As a result, schools such as Parker-Gray—Alexandria's high school for black students—never got the chance to test themselves against white competition. That was too bad, because it might have presented some interesting matchups. Considering the long list of outstanding black players to enter the doors of Alexandria's

T. C. Williams High School in subsequent years, it seems reasonable to assume that the Parker-Gray Bulldogs boasted a similar collection of talent. It was at Parker-Gray, after all, where Jim Lewis first developed his skills in the early 1960s. When Lewis moved to Alexandria's Groveton High (now West Potomac) in 1963, he immediately was recognized as one of the top players in Northern Virginia, earning All-Met honors in the *Post* despite playing only nine games with the Tigers in his senior year.

The man who tutored him at Parker-Gray, Arnold Thurmond, had a long history of success by the time Lewis came along. Thurmond took over from Louis Johnson (the man who coached NBA pioneer Earl Lloyd) for the 1952–53 season and remained the coach at Parker-Gray for 13 years, until the school closed and its students were finally absorbed into their now-integrated neighborhood schools.

In those 13 years, Thurmond compiled a 214–87 record that included four straight state titles and regular matchups against topflight competition. The Bulldogs played against the top all-black schools as far north as Baltimore (including the local Maryland power Fairmont Heights Hornets) and as far south as Richmond, with many games against the Spingarn and Armstrong teams of the Inter-High.

Despite the meager funding that Parker-Gray received and the substandard resources at his disposal, Thurmond refused to get hung up on the inequities he encountered while trying to run his program. "It was wonderful, and I enjoyed it," Thurmond recalled. "Every bit of it."

Instead of bemoaning his circumstance, Thurmond focused on finding ways to win, coming up with innovative techniques that wouldn't be out of place in today's game. While he had great respect for Johnson, his predecessor, he was his own man too. Upon taking over at Parker-Gray, Thurmond put a greater emphasis on conditioning, running his players at practice until their tongues hung out. Every practice concluded with a couple of laps, with the two slowest players required to run again. Thurmond would occasionally grab a player's jersey while he ran to make it harder to accelerate. He also had his players practice running backward, as defensive backs do in football, to develop better footwork and coordination.

He focused on his players' eating habits, too, which was unusual for the time. Thurmond worried that they were sneaking off to a small convenience store across the street from school, so he issued printed guidelines about proper diet. He gave each player a three-by-five-inch index card at the start of each summer that described what he needed to work on and handed out more cards at the start of each season, indicating what he expected from each man on the roster. He encouraged his players to keep those cards tucked into the corner of their bathroom mirrors, where they would serve as a constant reminder of what needed to be done.

As unorthodox as some of Thurmond's methods might have seemed, they worked. Thurmond's first state title came in his third season, 1954–55, despite the fact that he had an inexperienced team. The Bulldogs played a whopping 35 games that season and finished 27–8. Five of the losses came before Christmas because the Bulldogs were so young, with just one senior on the roster. But his youthful charges responded when needed, winning two games in one day and capturing the Group II (black school) Virginia state title with a 59–52 overtime victory over the South Norfolk High Tigers.

That was just the beginning. Players such as six-foot-four Walter Griffin and Perry Lyles formed the nucleus of a squad that won two more titles before graduating. Lyles, who always seemed to come up big in the postseason, scored a game-high 14 points in a 49–38 victory over the Bruton Heights Spiders of Williamsburg in the finals the next year, and the Bulldogs (21–5) took their second straight title.

Up to this point, Thurmond's team had received only scant attention from the Washington newspapers. To its credit, the *Alexandria Gazette* devoted a great deal of ink to the Bulldogs, even though George Washington High School's athletic accomplishments were far more celebrated by the local paper. But by the time the Griffin-Lyles group became seniors, Parker-Gray had become so successful that even the DC newspapers took note.

Thurmond's Bulldogs ran off 26 straight victories in the 1956–57 season, including a third straight state title, and ran their overall winning streak to 37 games. They were one shy of the record string put together by McKinley's "Fabulous Five." Rasty Doran, the legendary George Washington High School coach, called Thurmond's 1956–57 team one of the best he'd ever seen. "They have speed and height, can shoot and run," said Doran, a man whose basketball opinions were gospel in Northern Virginia.

The six-foot-four Griffin was the key man. He operated mostly out of the corners, with too much speed and agility for those assigned to guard him. He averaged 16 points per game that season and was named first-team All-Met in the *Post*, the first (and only) Parker-Gray player to be so honored. "He was a good one-on-one player," Thurmond recalled. "He could outplay most of the big guys who were on him."

It was Lyles, though—again—who stepped forward in the playoffs. He pumped in 24 points in a 64–47 victory over Fairfax rival Luther P. Jackson Tigers in the state semifinal. Lyles added 16 points—including 14 in the first half, when the Bulldogs took control—in the 62–53 championship victory over Bruton Heights. Griffin added 14, Robert Scott contributed 12, and William Thompson had 11.

St. Elizabeth's Ironmen of Chicago eventually ended Parker-Gray's winning streak at 37 games—one short of McKinley's mark—in the National Negro High School Tournament in Nashville. That loss came after the books were closed on the metro high school basketball season, and the final rankings in the *Post* gave Parker-Gray another first—a share of the No. 1 overall ranking. The pollsters faced quite a quandary at the end of that season as Montgomery Blair (17–0), George Washington (18–0), and Parker-Gray (24–0) all were undefeated. So in the only time such a deadlock occurred, the newspaper picked all three as its No. 1 team.

The quest for a fourth straight state crown was much more difficult. The core of the three-time state champions was gone. But that didn't stop Thurmond from bringing home another title despite some adversity along the way.

In one sense, it was like starting over. Key players such as Griffin and Lyles had moved on. The Bulldogs were inexperienced and struggled at the foul line for much of the season. After eight games, the team's record stood at just 4–4, quite a drop-off from the undefeated team of the year before.

But Thurmond pulled things together, and the team earned yet another trip to the state tournament with a 46–45 victory over Princess Anne Cavaliers of Norfolk County (now the city of Virginia Beach). The Bulldogs had grown up along the way, hitting 20 of 24 from the line to pull out the victory. Leroy Butler dropped in a pair of free throws with 24 seconds left to wrap it up.

Despite the team's early season struggles, Thurmond was upbeat upon entering the state tournament. "They had to follow an unbeaten team, but it hasn't gotten them down," he noted at one point. "The hustle and spirit has been wonderful all year."

The state tournament would test the team even further. First came the news that junior Clifford Harris, the team's leading scorer and rebounder, wouldn't play because his father had suffered a fatal heart attack at work. Then on the trip to Norfolk for the tournament, the Parker-Gray traveling party encountered all kinds of car trouble, including a couple of flat tires and a wheel that came off one of the three cars transporting the team. Thurmond and the Bulldogs finally showed up in Norfolk—hours late—only to find that some of their rooms had been given away and all the restaurants were closed.

After a slow start in the semifinal, Parker-Gray roared to a 45-point second half and whipped the Albert Harris Yellow Jackets of Martinsville, 70-45. Butler led the way with 21 points, and Joseph Marshall added 20. Harris, playing with a heavy heart after rejoining his mates, added eight.

The final offered a matchup between Parker-Gray and Bruton Heights for the third straight year. It, too, was a struggle. The Bulldogs trailed by seven in the fourth quarter, but they rallied to pull out a 57–50 victory for their ninth straight win and their fourth straight title. Marshall led the way with 18 points, including the basket that put the Bulldogs up for good with about three minutes left. Harris added 14.

"This team had to fight all the way," a proud Thurmond said. "They were not loaded with the talent of my other teams. We got off to a rather poor start, and we had to finish strong [the Bulldogs wound up 21–7] to make it four straight titles."

"We had some rough times this season, but I was fortunate to have a group that takes things as they are."

And that group was just as fortunate to have Thurmond as its coach.

Even if racial attitudes in Virginia remained rooted in the past, major changes were coming all over the metropolitan area. The great migration from the city to the suburbs was under way, and local officials of the close-in counties in Maryland and Virginia could hardly build schools fast enough to keep pace with the post–World War II baby boom.

Between 1954 and 1960, the Virginia suburbs added schools such as Wakefield, Groveton, Annandale, McLean, Lee, Yorktown, Hammond, and Stuart (now Justice). Suburban Maryland's school ranks grew with the addition of High Point, Wheaton, Walter Johnson, Northwood, Peary, DuVal, and Springbrook during the same period. New school construction continued unabated for much of the next decade, further changing the prep basketball landscape. When the major metro area dailies picked their All-Met teams in the early part of the 1950s, the players were drawn from about 60 schools in all, public and private. A decade later, the number of schools the papers covered had doubled.

Changes—geographical and otherwise—were coming in the staid old Catholic League as well. St. John's College High School moved its campus from downtown Washington, near the White House, out to its current location on Military Road Northwest, in 1959. By then, the other schools in the league had begun to catch up with the Cadets.

There was a time when everyone knew how the Catholic League race would turn out: St. John's was going to finish on top. The Cadets won the league title the first half-dozen years after Joe Gallagher took over the basketball (and football) coaching duties at his alma mater in 1947. He established himself as the dean of area high school basketball coaches in the early 1950s, mentoring a succession of All-Met players such as Bobby Reese, Ralph Hawkins, and Bob Rusevlyan. After seven years on the job, Gallagher's record stood at 151–30.

"Joe was the man," said Morgan Wootten. Gallagher had plucked him from the youth league coaching ranks in 1953 to serve as his assistant for three years before Wootten took over at DeMatha in 1956.

"You hear about character-building—well, Joe stresses it," Brother Andrew (Schaefer), the athletic director at St. John's, said at the time. "And he's so well-liked around town, everywhere he goes. He's one of the school's best advertisements."

It wasn't until the 1953–54 season that anyone could unseat St. John's from atop the league. And the new champion came from an unlikely source—Gonzaga. Tommy Nolan, who had played on some of the great Eastern teams of the 1930s, had taken over the basketball program there and built a winner based on three principles: (1) play together; (2) play defense; (3) don't do anything that would reflect badly on the school.

His team that beat out St. John's for the league title had a number of fine players—Dick Ridgway, Ray Smith, Ronnie Bennett, Mike Williams—but no real star.

Nolan also had a strong bench with Tony Natoli, Frank Vita, and Hank Slevin all contributing along the way. The Gonzaga Eagles topped St. Anthony's in the league championship game when Bennett made a steal and a layup in the closing seconds. "They're the best-rounded team I've ever coached," Nolan said. "Any boy on the team can be the high scorer on any given night."

That was the start of an impressive run for Gonzaga, which won the league three out of four years. Nolan's Eagles won again in 1956, aided by the presence of first-team All-Met Tommy McCloskey. After Nolan took the Georgetown coaching job, the Eagles repeated in 1957 under Head Coach Tommy O'Keefe with an unusually tall squad that featured three starters—Tom Coleman, Tom Matan, and Dan Slattery—who were six foot three or taller. By virtue of winning the Catholic League title in 1956–57 (beating Wootten's first DeMatha team in the final), Gonzaga also earned a spot in the first-ever City Title Game against Inter-High champ Cardozo.

Since the demise of the Metropolitan Tournament, coaches and administrators had sought to come up with some kind of postseason showcase that would crown an area champion. Washington-Lee sponsored a big postseason tournament for a couple of years after the Metropolitan Tournament ended, but the W-L event never really caught on.

Carroll coach Bob Dwyer created the Washington Catholic Invitational in 1954, bringing together some of the top parochial schools up and down the East Coast and a couple of local private school teams. His event, which later became known as the Knights of Columbus Tournament, proved quite durable and became a staple of area postseason basketball for decades. But nothing seemed to capture the imagination of the basketball-crazed public like the public-private matchup of the City Title Game. Coach Frank Bolden's Cardozo teams won the first two city titles, beating O'Keefe's Gonzaga team and Dwyer's Carroll squad for the championships in 1957 and '58.

Along with Cardozo and Gonzaga, a number of other local teams enjoyed great success in the middle and late 1950s. After Carrasco moved on to coach at American University, Montgomery Blair kept right on winning with Ed Moffatt at the helm. Blair went undefeated during the 1957 and '58 regular seasons, only to lose in the state championship game both times. Injuries ruined the Blazers' chances both years. In 1957 Moffatt lost six-foot-two Barry Goss, a standout rebounder and defender, to a broken hand a week before the state tournament. The next year, it was All-Met Tom Brown who got hurt, spraining his ankle in the semifinals. He played just 12 minutes in the finals, and Blair was beaten easily.

Soon enough, all other area teams had to step aside. Over at Archbishop Carroll, Coach Bob Dwyer was putting together a team for the ages. His Carroll Lions squads of the late 1950s remain the most famous in the history of Washington area high school basketball. It's not difficult to see why. Carroll won 55 straight games and captured three straight Catholic League titles, which was no small feat considering the caliber of competition that league has traditionally featured. Carroll also won back-to-back City Title Games and captured multiple titles in the Knights of Columbus Tournament (twice in a row) and at the Eastern States Catholic Invitational (three years running).

Those teams featured some of the most recognizable names in local basketball, including future Georgetown coach John Thompson and future Notre Dame University president Monk Malloy. There were a couple of soon-to-be NBA players in Tom Hoover and John Austin, and the multitalented guard George Leftwich probably would have joined them in the pros, if not for a serious knee injury he sustained while starring at Villanova. No less a basketball authority than longtime Maryland coach Gary Williams, who grew up on Philadelphia college basketball in south Jersey, considered Leftwich to be an NBA-caliber talent in his prime.

Few teams before or since could match the Lions for star power—Carroll had three of the five players who made first-team All-Met for the *Star* and the *Post* in 1959—or for success. On-court excellence was a large part of that team's legacy, but the Carroll Lions were more than just a basketball team. In its time, that squad also provided a concrete example of what was possible when blacks and whites worked together toward a common goal. That was still very much a foreign concept in Washington as both the city and the country as a whole tried to come to grips with integration, equality, and fairness.

Much was made of the difficulties faced by the T. C. Williams football team that came along a dozen years later, a situation chronicled in the film *Remember the Titans*. Players and coaches at Carroll faced many of the same issues but in a far less tolerant time, and they did so while playing standout basketball through it all. When reminiscing about those days, several Carroll players proclaimed, in effect, "We were the Titans before the Titans!"

Truth be told, playing at Carroll in the late 1950s was far tougher than playing for T. C. Williams of Alexandria in the early 1970s. At that earlier time, blacks knew they weren't welcome in Georgetown at night; the sight of a black face anywhere west of 16th Street might arouse suspicions from local residents or even from the police. It wasn't until the early 1960s, for example, that a public facility like the amusement park at Glen Echo was open to blacks as well as whites.

Yes, district schools had been integrated since the fall of 1954; however, people's hearts were resistant to change, no matter what the law might say. There were even some inside the halls of Carroll who wondered if the racial makeup of Dwyer's teams was appropriate or in the best interests of the school at large. Such were the sensibilities of the time. "Washington, make no mistake, was in the South," noted Tom Hoover, whose defense and rebounding (along with Thompson's) helped make Carroll great.

That officials at Carroll found themselves in the middle of the ideological debate on race and education was no accident. The school was founded in the early 1950s with the idea that it would provide religious education for all manner of Washington's children, white or black. That was Archbishop Patrick O'Boyle's vision for the school. In time, he also became one of the Lions' biggest boosters.

It was left to Dwyer to navigate the sometimes treacherous waters of the school's integration policy and the public's reaction to it. His position came with tremendous headaches. But it had its advantages too. Creating schedules was difficult when some schools wouldn't play an integrated team in his early years there. Dealing with often-outspoken opponents of the team's racial makeup was a problem, to be sure. But Carroll's forward-thinking policies also made it a magnet for talented black players seeking an option outside the DC public school system.

Dwyer, an intense competitor on the basketball court or the golf course, understood that he had a built-in advantage in regard to the school's admissions policies. He was able to bring in talented black players such as Jim Howell, a first-team all-Met pick by the *Star* in 1957, plus the group that included Hoover, Leftwich, and Thompson a little later. He also understood that he was striking a blow for greater equality and opportunity. Why else, for example, would he schedule games against all-black Inter-High schools such as Armstrong and Elgin Baylor's Spingarn team?

Carroll lost both of those games, and Dwyer could just as easily have scheduled non-league games against white teams his squad could beat. Clearly, he had something more in mind than his won-loss record.

"My dad liked to win," said Bobby Dwyer Jr. "He was a competitor. But he knew what was going on socially. His interest in having black kids come to Carroll was twofold. I think he understood from an integration standpoint that he was doing groundbreaking work."

Building and guiding those Carroll teams were perhaps Dwyer's greatest accomplishments but hardly his only ones. He was already a successful coach by the time he arrived there, having previously guided the Priory (now St. Anselm's) Panthers to a 108–37 record in six seasons. He also helped establish the basketball program run by the local Catholic Youth Organization, which gave thousands of area youngsters (including the author) a chance to learn and play the game. He started the St. Anselm's Invitational tournament—now the longest-running postseason event in the metro area—and, as noted, established the Washington Catholic Invitational, which became another prestigious postseason showcase for high school basketball in the city.

The Carroll job was a start-up, and some of the early years were difficult, particularly when competing against established programs such as St. John's and Gonzaga. By 1957, though, Dwyer had the program up and running. That year, the Lions finished the regular season 22–4.

The next year, they were even better. Leftwich and Thompson joined the team as sophomores, bolstering a team that already possessed a dangerous outside shooter in Malloy and a rough-and-tumble center in Hoover, a six-foot-eight, 240-pound football player who ruled the post. Malloy was the ultimate "gym rat" and a future Catholic priest with absolutely no conscience when it came to shooting the basketball, even from what would now be considered three-point range.

"I liked to shoot from anywhere," Malloy confessed. "If they'd have had a four-point shot, I would have shot it from there. I thought I was always open. I had a gunner's mentality."

Hoover excelled in many of the less glamorous aspects of the game, such as rebounding, setting picks, and making sure nobody—but nobody—came through the lane untouched. He was one guy nobody wanted to tangle with. "Hoover could intimidate anybody," said Morgan Wootten, who was then starting his Hall of Fame career as DeMatha's coach.

"I guess I was a rough kind of guy," Hoover said. "But I didn't let anybody bother my teammates." Opponents always granted Hoover a wide berth. His teammates, though often the targets of Hoover's playful but occasionally bruising jabs in the locker room, always knew he had their backs.

"The guy had a heart of gold," Leftwich said. "He was a practical joker who didn't know his own strength. He fancied himself as the big brother of the team. That was the role he took on."

Soon enough, he had company. The six-foot-ten John Thompson, a shy and quiet young man, had loads of potential at that point but needed polish. Even though some parts of his game had a long way to go, he immediately teamed with Hoover to make the interior nearly impenetrable for Carroll's opponents.

"Nobody came through the lane scot-free," Hoover said. "I took a lot of pride in playing defense. I wanted to block your shot; I wanted to keep you down."

Leftwich recalled one time when an opposing guard got by him on a drive to the basket—quite an accomplishment considering Leftwich's quickness. The poor fellow got into the lane against Hoover and Thompson, and had his shot knocked one way and his body the other. The next time up the floor, Leftwich couldn't resist.

"Hey, that was a great move," he said with a smile. "You wanna try that again?"

"No way!" the shaken opponent replied. "I'm not going back in there!"

It was quickly apparent that with Leftwich and Thompson in the fold, Carroll was a team to be reckoned with. Carroll thrashed the Chamberlain Shipmates in its 1957–58 opener, 88–35; whipped Anacostia, 65–27; and then handled Mount Saint Joseph's Gaels of Baltimore, 83–37. Leftwich scored 24 points in that game, while Thompson added 11 points and grabbed 19 rebounds. "In Leftwich and Thompson, I believe we have the finest basketball prospects the school has ever had," Dwyer announced.

A pattern had been established. The Lions were nearly impossible to score against, and missed shots and turnovers were quickly turned into fast-break baskets. On most nights, the games involved little suspense, and the starters seldom played the fourth quarters, or sometimes even the third, because the scores were so lopsided.

Not even college freshman teams were safe. Carroll humbled the American University freshman team right after the first of the year, 71–35, and took over the top spot in the *Star*'s high school poll at 9–1.

Just as impressive was a 67–32 victory over St. John's and Joe Gallagher, then the dean of area coaches. Gallagher's Cadets absorbed the worst loss he could remember in his 11 years as coach and managed to make just two of 33 shots in the middle two periods. Entering the fourth quarter, the score stood at an unbelievable 57–17. Malloy led everybody in scoring with 25 points, bombing away from the outside.

Carroll won the Catholic League title, finished 25–3 (two of the losses were to college freshman teams) during the regular season, and met Inter-High champ Cardozo in the City Title Game at Uline Arena, located just north of Union Station. It wasn't expected to be much of a contest. Carroll was the top-ranked team in the city and had handled the Clerks by 21 points in a regular-season meeting. But Cardozo, guided by wily coach Frank Bolden, rose up and stunned Carroll, 65–62. Richard "Rip" Scott, at only five foot eight, torched Carroll's defense for 21 points, and the quartet of Gene Bullock, Marshall Johnson, Willie Jenkins, and Frank Harrison (all at least six foot four) won the battle of the boards.

The outcome made Bolden and Cardozo two for two in City Title Games, but the Lions—to a man—thought the title should have been theirs. The loss stung so badly that some Carroll players kept the newspaper clipping from the loss in their wallets to remind them of the opportunity they'd missed.

With that kind of motivation, there was no stopping Carroll the next year. The four names everyone remembers—Hoover, Malloy, Leftwich, and Thompson—were back. Walt Skinner, a six-foot-three junior, usually held down the fifth starting spot. But it didn't really matter who played. Carroll had enough weapons to win and usually by a wide margin. If someone was having an off night or got hurt, somebody else stepped up.

The Lions beat Phelps 80–35 in mid-December despite Thompson's ankle injury because Leftwich scored a game-high 29 points. Against Gonzaga in late January, when Hoover got in foul trouble early and Leftwich and Malloy couldn't find the range, Thompson (21 points) and Doug Barnes (20) took over, leading the Lions to a 66–50 victory.

The joke around town said that Carroll had the best team in the Catholic League and that the second-best team was Carroll's bench. Players such as Kenny Price and Skinner could have been stars somewhere else—John Austin, a reserve on the undefeated 1959–60 team, would later become an All-Met selection at DeMatha after transferring—but at Carroll everyone was content to play his role. Nobody wanted to rock the boat. Of course, winning made any sacrifice that much easier.

Price, a strong and quick defender, pushed Leftwich at practice each day. Skinner filled in wherever necessary. Against DeMatha he scored three key baskets in the last four minutes of a 45–39 victory, which was one of the few close encounters Carroll had in 1958–59. "Everybody—even the guys on the bench—wanted to win," Skinner said. "Call it camaraderie or cohesiveness. It was a great thing to be a part of. It was marvelous."

"Anybody on that team could have been an all-star on any other team," Price said. "Skinner fit in and complemented everybody. Nobody had to carry the load because everyone would pitch in and help."

Carroll lost to the Georgetown freshmen on January 10, 1959, the Lions' last loss until the beginning of the 1960–61 season, or a span of 55 straight wins. (By that time, Leftwich, Thompson, and all the rest had moved on.) Carroll also avenged its previous loss to Cardozo by drubbing the Clerks, 79–53, in the 1959 City Title Game. Thompson led all scorers with 24 points as the Lions built a 52–20 lead at one point. They were no less spectacular in the Knights of Columbus Tournament against a strong field of teams from New York, Pittsburgh, Philadelphia, Wisconsin, and Minnesota. Carroll gave the Washington area its first title in the six years of the event, outscoring three teams by an aggregate 207–122.

Hoover, Malloy, and Barnes graduated, but Carroll rolled on in 1959–60. Thompson, Leftwich, Price, and Skinner led the way to an undefeated season, including another City Title Game victory and another Knights of Columbus title. Leftwich was the hero of the closest call during the streak, burying a jumper from the top of the key with three seconds left to beat a team from Racine, Wisconsin, 57–55, in the Knights of Columbus finals at Georgetown's McDonough Gymnasium.

The team was so deep and so talented that Dwyer didn't need to do much from a strategic standpoint. He was more concerned about keeping the players focused, which was no small task considering how easy it would have been to grow complacent. "Dad was a great psychologist," his son said. "He would tell you himself that he wasn't the greatest Xs and Os guy. His thing was psychology."

Dwyer was also careful to shield players from some of the racial criticism directed their way, taking a lot of the heat himself. He could be blunt with the team's critics in a way that his players could not. And when he needed to, he'd bring up some of the unflattering things outsiders would say about the team in a tactic designed to motivate his players.

"He was very aware that, as an integrated team, we had our own set of challenges," Malloy said. "He kept challenging us to rise to higher levels with each progressive year. I think in his own time, he was one of the great high school coaches that ever was."

Of the players, the most important was Leftwich, even if his scoring average didn't always reflect it. A three-time All-Met, he was a player of great skill and quickness who possessed a remarkable vision on the floor and an acute understanding of what his team needed in a given situation. His ballhandling skills were critical to the team's success. He got the ball where it needed to go, and once Carroll had the lead, opponents were wasting their time trying to press. Leftwich was so quick he could foil any kind of trap or double-team all by himself. "Not to slight anybody, but George Leftwich was the MVP of that team," Morgan Wootten said.

"He was all-around good, and he had a sense of what was going on out on the floor," Skinner said. "He was a big-picture guy. He's the MVP in my book."

Malloy, Leftwich's backcourt mate for two full seasons, was just as complimentary. "He was the most important player on our team," Malloy said. "He could bring the ball up against anyone, he could shoot from the outside, and he was unselfish. In high school, he was the best player on the team, and all of us knew it."

He was also instrumental in keeping his teammates focused each day at practice, teasing, cajoling, and generally leading by example. When the best player on the team works hard, it's difficult for anyone else to slack off. His attitude was a tremendous help to Dwyer in terms of keeping the team hungry as the victories mounted. "I was always stirring things up at practice," Leftwich said. "You've got to find your niche."

"You never had to worry about George," Price said. "He never seemed to have a bad day."

Meanwhile, the huge strides that Thompson made during his high school career helped Carroll cope after the graduation of Hoover and Malloy. It is rare to find a newspaper story from those days that fails to mention Thompson's continuous improvement from one year to the next. He was simply too driven and too dedicated not to succeed; those traits would serve him well when he became a coach and revived a couple of moribund basketball programs—first at St. Anthony's and later at Georgetown. The effort and focus he devoted to the game did not go unnoticed, even by his teenage teammates. "If there was a global crisis and there was only one thing that could be done to save the planet," Leftwich said, "I'd give that job to John Thompson."

One summer, urged by Dwyer to improve his offensive skills, Thompson shot virtually every time he touched the ball in every pickup game he played. His teams invariably lost and his teammates seethed, but Thompson didn't care. He was working toward a greater goal. As a senior, he led the Catholic League in scoring with a 21-point average and drew raves from coaches all over the city for the progress he had made.

After Thompson pumped in 25 points during a win over DeMatha in his senior year, Dwyer called him "the best big man ever to play basketball in the Washington area." A couple of weeks later Dwyer gushed, "He can already do things the pros can't do. You know how they guard some of those big players. They stand around the basket, and if the big man goes outside, they forget him. If they do that with John, he'll murder 'em with that jump shot."

Some had thought that Carroll might fall back in the pack with Hoover and

Malloy gone. But the holdovers all assumed larger roles, and the 1959–60 team simply steamrolled everyone in its path. That year the Lions finished 31–0 and beat the Georgetown freshmen by 16 points, the George Washington freshmen by 18, and the Maryland freshmen by 23. In early February, they whipped Gonzaga, 81–43, to break McKinley's record of 38 straight victories.

"I didn't see how they could lose Tom Hoover and Monk Malloy without hurting," Gonzaga coach Harry Marmion said. "But they're more flexible this year, and they're playing better defense."

As the winning streak grew and the team drew more and more attention from the local media, the crowds began to swell too. It's not clear how many minds the team might have changed about integration, but in many quarters, its achievements were held up as an example of blacks and whites working together.

"The more games we won, the more championships we won, the more focus there was in the local newspapers," Malloy said. "And one of the qualities that made our team so noteworthy was that we were a successful model of integration in a city struggling against its southern heritage."

In those years, Archbishop Carroll was the biggest game on everyone's schedule. Fans packed every gymnasium to bear witness to this record-breaking team. Some were wanting to see the juggernaut for themselves; others rooted feverishly against them. Though the team drew unprecedented interest, playing on a big stage never bothered or intimidated Carroll in the slightest.

"The concept [of losing] was nonexistent," Price said. "We knew we were going to beat you; it was just a matter of how. Taunting us didn't work. We got up for all the Catholic League games, and we got up again to play the public schools. You didn't even think about [crowds] because you knew you were gonna win."

A then-record crowd of 10,500 people braved icy roads to watch the Lions down Spingarn, 68–54, in the 1960 City Title Game at Cole Field House. That Spingarn team was notable for the two future NBA stars on its roster—junior Ollie Johnson and a quick, talented sophomore named Dave Bing. Another 4,000 fans squeezed their way into Georgetown's McDonough Gymnasium to watch the Knights of Columbus Tournament while carloads of fans were turned away at the campus gate.

The hoopla surrounding the Carroll program eventually grew too intense for Dwyer. That team was so famous, so talked about, and, in some quarters, so reviled that it made the coach uncomfortable. Angry, threatening phone calls were made to his house; in one out-of-town tournament, somebody came down out of the stands and confronted him on the sidelines. As rewarding as it might have been to coach such a team, the attending mania had turned high school basketball into something it wasn't supposed to be, at least as far as Dwyer was concerned.

So he decided to leave Carroll after the 1959–60 season. All sorts of stories surfaced about his departure. Some said he left Carroll to spend more time on his insurance business; unlike most of his colleagues, he was not a classroom teacher. Others claimed he left because of a dispute with the school's administration.

But the real reason Dwyer retreated from the spotlight to coach at St. Anselm's, where he'd started, was so he could return to teaching and coaching the game without having the job feel so claustrophobic. He coached at St. Anselm's for another two decades after leaving Carroll and enjoyed himself immensely, according to those who knew him.

"He loved his time over at St. Anselm's," Dwyer's son said. "He coached the varsity, the junior varsity, the freshman team, the eighth graders. He loved it over there. He loved the kids, he loved the game of basketball. It didn't matter that those kids had different potential than the kids at Carroll."

What Dwyer and his players left behind at Archbishop Carroll was a legacy of excellence. His teams there are still talked about today, with his final squad generally recognized as the finest the Washington area has ever produced.

"I don't think anyone at the time knew how good that team could be," said Leftwich, who remains proud of all that Carroll accomplished. "The only goal was to get respect when we played. It kind of mushroomed into something nobody expected. I don't know that any of us ever guessed that it would last this long."

Stanley Kernan 1951–52 yearbook senior photo; Kernan was voted McKinley Tech's "Best Athlete."

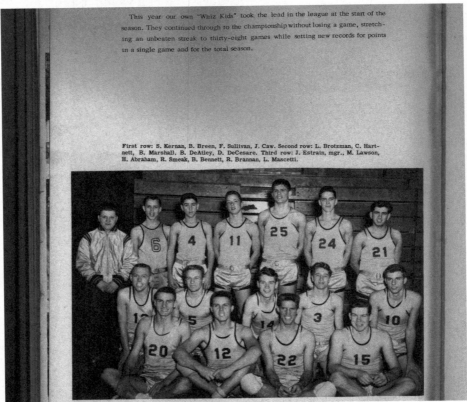

This year our own "Whiz Kids" took the lead in the league at the start of the season. They continued through to the championship without losing a game, stretching an unbeaten streak to thirty-eight games while setting new records for points in a single game and for the total season.

First row: S. Kernan, B. Breen, F. Sullivan, J. Caw. Second row: L. Brotzman, C. Hartnett, B. Marshall, B. DeAtley, D. DeCesare. Third row: J. Estrain, mgr., M. Lawson, H. Abraham, R. Smeak, B. Bennett, R. Brannan, L. Mascetti.

The Trainers, as McKinley's teams were called, starting in 1950 won three straight Inter-High titles and three straight championships in the Metropolitan Tournament, which essentially determined the area-wide champion. The Trainers also ran off a then-record 38 straight victories. The "Fabulous Five" (or the "Whiz Kids") were the four starters in the first row: Stanley Kernan, Bill Breen, Frank Sullivan, and Joe Caw; and Babe Marshall (14) in the middle row.

**PEARL EDNA ARRINGTON**

Cheer Leaders — Section Reporter

Ambition: To be a model or dress designer

*Edna Q Clark 10-2-99*

**ROSETTA FRANCES BARBOUR**

Red Cross

Ambition: Switchboard operator

**BARBARA ANTOINETTE ARTIS**

Vice-President of Section — Representative, Girls' League

Ambition: To be a teacher and a lawyer.

**BARBARA ANN BARNES**

Bank — Student Council — President of Section — Honor Society — Girl's Basketball Team

Ambition: To join the Wave

**THERESA AUDRIENNE BABER**

Red Cross

Ambition: A registered nurse

*Theresa Baber*

**MERLE ALVETA BATES**

Pres. of Girls' League — Feature Editor of Sentinel — Sec. of Student Council — Nat'l. Thespian Society — Section President

Ambition: To be a journal.

**MARY CARMELITA BAILEY**

Red Cross

Ambition: Stenographer

**CHARLES H. BATTLE**

Cadet Corps Officer — Treasurer of Section — Vice-Chairman of Constitution Committee (Boys' Union)

Ambition: To study theology

**NORMAN ALVIN BAKER**

Business Club — Vice-Chairman, Boys' Union — Program Committee — Dramatics Club — Red Cross — Section Secretary —

Ambition: To be a realtor

**ELGIN GAY BAYLOR**

Basketball Team

Ambition: To be a physic education teacher

Elgin Baylor aspired to play basketball in the only way open to him in 1953: by becoming a physical education teacher.

MRS. CYNTHIA D'A
BROWN
Mathematics

MR. DAVID J.
BROWN
Physical Ed.

MRS. VALERIE P.
BROWN
French

MR. EDGAR S.
BURKE
Office Machines

MR. LEE J.
CALLOWAY
Architecture

MR. CHARLES B.
COBBS
Social Studies

MRS. EDNA J.
COKER
Spanish

Coach David Brown in the 1953–54 Spingarn Green Wave yearbook.

**NO. 2 IN LEAGUE RACE!!**
Appearing from left to right are the members of the 54-55 Varsity basketball team who compiled a 12-5 record this year. Kneeling are James Coleman, Ralph Love, Irving Brown, Coach Dave Brown. Second row Andrew Johnson, Lloyd Murphy, Donald Wills, Tony Washington, Robert Outlaw, George Williams, Gene Johnson. Third row, John Tresvant, Carl Hunter, Dickie Wells, Francis Saunders, and Charlie Queen.

Coach David Brown and the second place Spingarn team from the 1954–55 Green Wave yearbook.

Llewellyn "Lew" Luce
1956–57 Woodrow Wilson
High yearbook photo.

The fighting Greenwave team of 1957-1958: Top—left to right: Coach Roundtree, Brian Dorsey, Leonard Frazier, James Bussey, Ernest Dunston, Charles Mayo, Michael Harkins and Wilmore Haraway. Bottom—left to right: Michael Davis, Federick Neal, Lawrence Ross, and Richard Frazier.

Spingarn's Coach (Dr.) William Roundtree and the 1957–58 team.

*Front Row: (l to r):* James Price, Tracy McCarthy, Jim Bradley mgr., Tom Berry mgr., George Leftwich, Bill Romig.
*Second row:* Coach Bob Dwyer, Walt Skinner, Monk Malloy, Bill Barnes, Doug Barnes, Mike O'Brien, Tom Moore.
*Back row:* John Thompson, Tom Hoover. Manager Dan Hogan was absent when picture was taken.

### Archbishop John Carroll High School—Varsity Basketball 1958-59
### 33-2

DC City Champions
Knights of Columbus Tournament Champions
Washington Catholic League Champions
Eastern States Catholic Invitational Tournament Champions

Bob Dwyer's team in 1958–59.

The varsity for 1959-60 *(l. to r.):* Mr. Robert Dwyer (coach), Bill Barnes, Larry Rohan, Chuck Rohan, Jim Price, John Austin, Walt Lindsay, George Leftwich, Walt Skinner, Julius Shelton, Mike O'Brien, John Thompson; *(kneeling):* John Thomas, Hank Coon (managers).

### Archbishop John Carroll High School—Varsity Basketball 1959-60
### 33-0

DC City Champions • Baltimore-Washington Catholic League Champions
Washington Catholic League Champions • Knights of Columbus Tournament Champions
Eastern States Catholic Invitational Tournament Champions

Bob Dwyer's team in 1959–60.

Bob Dwyer stands with star player Tom Hoover.

This photo of Dwyer was taken in 2001 when the Carroll teams of 1958–59 and 1959–60 were enshrined in the school's Hall of Honor.

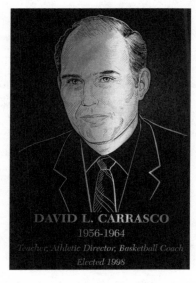

A plaque in the American University Hall of Fame.

DAVID L. CARRASCO
1956-1964
Teacher, Athletic Director, Basketball Coach
Elected 1998

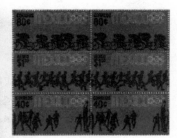

MEXICO·68

Left: Front page of the sports section of Diario de México shows Carrasco with Mexican coaches; right: U.S. postage stamp in commemoration of the 1968 Mexico Olympics.

Left: Front page of the sports section of *Diarío de México* shows Carrasco with Mexican coaches; right: US postage stamp in commemoration of the 1968 Mexico Olympics.

Presenting our gym teachers and coaches: Mr. Sylvester Hall, Mr. Marcelleous Jenkins, Mr. Joseph Drew, Mr. Frank Bolden, and Mr. Donald Porter.

15

Coaches pose for the 1957 Cardozo yearbook: Sylvester Hall, Marcelleous Jenkins, Joseph Drew, Basketball Coach Frank Bolden, and Donald Porter.

Trying to stop Buddy Frazier (11) from making two points, Petie Greene fails (22).

All Metropolitan, Ollie Johnson, displays one of his talents in driving in for a basket in the Spingarn-Eastern game at McKinley Tech. High School.

139

1959–60 Spingarn yearbook basketball page.

# CHAPTER THREE

# The Sixties

**MORGAN WOOTTEN** never figured on becoming a high school basketball coach. Today, after his DeMatha teams won 1,200 games, finished No. 1 in the Washington metro area 22 times, and sent a dozen players to the National Basketball Association, it's difficult to think of Wootten as anything but a coach.

But Wootten's career path was not preordained by any means. At Montgomery Blair High School in Silver Spring, Wootten was a good but not great basketball player on the Blazer varsity. He was a sometime starter and a sometime sixth man for Coach Tony Crème before graduating in 1950.

Though his basketball skills on the floor might have been ordinary, his oratorical skills were extraordinary. Wootten was a standout high school debater, the key member of an undefeated team. His powers of persuasion were said to be so strong that even at that age, he could win both sides of an argument and, when asked, take a position diametrically opposed to what he actually believed. No one who ever heard one of Wootten's pep talks as a coach would be shocked to learn that he could be convincing as a teenager.

Given his gift for persuasion, Wootten expected that he was headed to law school. He undoubtedly would have been as formidable in the courtroom as he was on the sidelines. While an undergraduate, first at Montgomery College, then at the University of Maryland, he coached youth sports on the side at St. Joseph's Home and School for Boys in Northeast Washington. At the time, coaching was more of a fun way to make some extra money than a career choice.

At St. Joseph's Wootten first put his legendary motivational skills to use. There was no money, no familial support—just Wootten and the kids—yet he made it work. Somehow he convinced the youngsters in his care that they could and would win even if they didn't have the best equipment or the nicest uniforms.

"If we didn't believe in ourselves, who would?" he asked. That was Wootten in a nutshell: upbeat, positive, always more eager to solve a problem than to bemoan his fate. That can-do attitude and willingness to work—and his ability to get others to work hard, too—served him well during his Hall of Fame high school coaching career, which spanned nearly five decades.

Back in those early days, Wootten was working his way through school. He also picked up some extra cash driving a cab, another job that gave him some valuable insight into human nature. After all, celebrated Marquette University basketball coach Al McGuire once suggested that six months driving a cab or tending bar was the best preparation for any job. The people skills developed in either profession would prove useful in any line of work, McGuire believed.

Wootten agreed. "I enjoyed driving a cab," he said. "It was good training, even if it sometimes showed you what kind of person not to be."

As time went on, Wootten's outlook on coaching as a career began to change. He could see he was getting through to the orphans, making a difference in their lives. More and more, the idea of working with young people appealed to him.

Joe Gallagher, then considered the dean of the city's high school basketball coaches, remembers being impressed as he watched Wootten coach youth football. Gallagher would occasionally check out such games, always on the lookout for good athletes who might want to come to St. John's. "I liked the way he handled kids," Gallagher recalled. "He had control of them but he wasn't authoritarian; he had that knack. And I could see he was a great motivator."

Before long, Gallagher added Wootten to his staff at St. John's. Wootten stayed on for three seasons. During his last two years he was a student at the University of Maryland and then spent his first year out of college teaching world history in the mornings and helping out Coach Gallagher in the afternoons. Their alliance, modest in its origins, evolved into one of the closest and longest-lasting partnerships in area basketball. Even after Wootten moved to DeMatha and the two became fierce rivals, they also somehow managed to remain the best of friends. More than 50 years after they first joined forces, one was always able to crack up the other with a new joke or an old story they'd both told a hundred times.

"Yeah, I guess his DeMatha teams cost me a lot of wins and championships over the years," Gallagher said. "But that never bothered me. I like to see people do well."

When asked about his old buddy Gallagher, Wootten was just as generous. "How lucky can a guy get to be tutored or to have as a mentor one of the greatest coaches that ever coached the sport?" he said.

Between the two of them, they won more than 2,000 games, taught the game to thousands of kids at their highly successful basketball camp, told a million stories, and never had a cross word pass between them except when their teams played each other. They knew everyone in basketball, it seemed, and everyone in basketball knew them—the by-product of having been so successful and so generous for so long. It seemed only fitting that both men taught history. In the eyes of many who followed DC basketball, they *were* history.

Wootten didn't stay Gallagher's lieutenant for long. DeMatha came calling in 1956, seeking a head coach. He'd turned the school down a year earlier because he was just out of college and immersed in his first year of teaching. Wootten wasn't sure he was ready to handle teaching a full course load for the first time while serving as a head coach too. It's stunning to think that Wootten and DeMatha—synonymous today—might never have come together after the school's initial attempt to hire him failed.

Wootten was an instant success at DeMatha. His first team, led by sharp-shooting Ernie Cage, finished 22–10. Cage, whom Wootten always called the best shooter he ever coached, made the job a lot easier. Cage scored more than 2,000 points in his high school career, virtually none of them from inside 18 feet, and held the school's scoring record until Hall of Famer Adrian Dantley came along a decade and a half later. "If they'd have had a three-point line back then, they'd still be chasing his [Cage's] scoring records," Wootten liked to say.

It took Wootten and the Stags a couple of years to win their first Catholic League title, though. His arrival at DeMatha coincided with the rise of the Archbishop Carroll juggernaut, and nobody was going to unseat the peerless Lions from 1957 to 1960. Once Carroll's run ended, Wootten and the DeMatha Stags took over as the team to beat, a perch they occupied for the next four decades. The breakup of the Carroll dynasty eased Wootten's path in one other respect: up-and-coming Carroll guard John Austin, upset that Coach Bob Dwyer was leaving Carroll, transferred to DeMatha. In so doing, the gifted young guard helped shift the balance of basketball power in the city.

Austin was ineligible for the first half of Catholic League play that season because he had transferred within the league. Even though Austin wasn't always available to them, Wootten's Stags still managed to win their first 21 games in 1960–61.

In his DeMatha debut, Austin torched Inter-High foe Chamberlain for 36 points in a 72–53 DeMatha victory. Austin was quick on the dribble and good from the outside as well; he would have been an asset to any team in the city. Johnny Jones, a six-foot-six transfer from Dunbar, took care of things inside and kept other teams from ganging up on Austin. Both later played in the NBA.

Despite the gaudy record, nobody was certain that DeMatha had the best team in the area. Sure, the Stags were No. 1 in the local high school polls, but not only had the Landon Bears (17–0), Wakefield Warriors (20–0), and Montgomery Blair Blazers (17–0) been just as impressive, they had also all remained undefeated through the month of February. Ultimately, the No. 1 ranking in the area came down to the final game of the regular season, a matchup between DeMatha and Landon, which had won 28 straight dating to the previous season.

In the years since, the exclusive Landon School became known for its athletic prowess in several sports, including lacrosse. But from the mid-1950s to the mid-1960s, the Bears were truly a basketball force as well. The team boasted such stars as Donald Dell, an All-Met selection in 1956 who became a tennis pro and later one of the first super agents of sports. Another all-league-caliber player was Maury Povich, son of legendary *Washington Post* sports columnist Shirley Povich. The younger Povich eventually became a major media figure himself, serving as Channel 5's news anchor and, still later, a national talk show host specializing in live "gotcha" programming. But Landon's biggest star of all—literally—was six-foot-eight Fred Hetzel, a rare three-time All-Met who became one of the nation's leading scorers at Davidson College under a fiery young coach named Lefty Driesell and then an NBA first-round draft choice.

Hetzel, a polished big man, served notice that Landon was to be reckoned with that season when he scored 37 points and grabbed 25 rebounds in an early season rout of Bladensburg, the defending Maryland Class A state champion. Landon's front line also boasted the six-foot-seven George Manger and the six-foot-five Bo Berger, whose father, "Boze," had been a standout player at McKinley High (1920s) and Maryland (1930s) before embarking on a career in major league baseball.

Coming in late February with both teams undefeated, the DeMatha-Landon matchup was the most anticipated high school game of the 1960–61 season. More than 6,000 people filled Maryland's Cole Field House, making it the best-attended regular-season game in Washington-area history at that time.

Wootten, in one of the great tactical maneuvers of his early career, pressured Landon's guards and choked off the passing lanes to Hetzel and Manger inside, helping DeMatha to a 57–52 victory. Austin led all scorers with 20, while Hetzel was held to 18 points and 11 rebounds. The victory gave DeMatha the No. 1 ranking for the first time ever and signaled a change in the high school basketball hierarchy that would last for decades to come.

For DeMatha, there was still the small matter of the City Title Game to be played. Spingarn, the Inter-High champion, couldn't change the final rankings. But the Green Wave could still earn local bragging rights for the summer by beating the Stags. And that's exactly what happened. The Green Wave broke open a close game in the final period and pulled away for a 63–50 victory over DeMatha not long after the Stags handled Landon.

The star of the game was the guard at Spingarn's Green Wave, Dave Bing, who must be on anyone's short list of the greatest players Washington ever produced. A smooth, elegant playmaking guard, Bing scored 22 points, including 17 in the second half, to key the victory over DeMatha. His basket early in the fourth period gave Spingarn the lead for good, and he made a pair of steals that he turned into breakaway layups, sealing the outcome.

Ollie Johnson, a talented six-foot-five forward who led the Inter-High in scoring and rebounding that year as Spingarn claimed its second straight league title, added 17 points against the Stags. Eventually, Johnson would join Bing in becoming a first-round NBA draft pick and enjoyed a long professional career. One of four future pros in the game, he had the most spectacular play of the Green Wave's triumph in that City Title win—a thunderous dunk off a rare missed free throw by Bing. Johnson was fouled on the play and dropped in the ensuing free throw for a 56–50 lead with 2:08 left.

After it was over, some wanted to call Spingarn's triumph an upset. Wootten wasn't one of them. "Not when they had Dave Bing," he said.

Despite his obvious skills, Bing wasn't as highly touted as some other players of his time. There were several reasons for this. Bing's parents were humble southern folk, and he followed their example, never really seeking the spotlight. Furthermore, Spingarn coach William Roundtree always emphasized the team rather than the individual, and that may have cost Bing a couple of points off his scoring average. Roundtree was famous for keeping a big roster—up to 15 players—and for playing everyone in uniform, especially in blowouts. Consequently, Bing never recorded the kind of statistics many high school stars do. To his credit, he never developed an inflated ego either.

"My parents never wanted you to brag or toot your own horn," Bing said. But everyone else knew how good he was. "How good was Dave Bing? He's the guy who made my hair fall out," cracked longtime Cardozo coach Frank Bolden.

Ultimately, Bing went on to become an All-American at Syracuse, an NBA scoring champion, and a perennial all-star in Detroit who was equally capable of scoring himself or setting others up for baskets. Years after his retirement, he achieved the ultimate accolade when he was voted one of the 50 greatest players in NBA history during the league's 50th anniversary season.

"On my best day, he was better than me on his worst," Carroll standout George Leftwich raved. Leftwich might have been overstating matters, but Bing's considerable basketball accomplishments were only a small part of the total man. After his playing career ended, Bing became one of the most successful black businessmen in the country and, still later, the mayor of Detroit, where he'd spent most of his NBA career.

Yet for all he achieved, Bing always downplayed his accomplishments. He never sought to set himself apart from anyone. Even as mayor, he'd cheerfully arrive at the office before anyone else and promptly brew up two pots of coffee—one regular, one decaf—for the rest of the staff before settling in to conduct the city's business.

Bing was a late arrival to the game of basketball; that perhaps explains why he never developed much of a swagger. Bing was so scrawny as a youth that he was advised to stick to baseball. He and childhood buddy Jerry Chambers (another future NBA player) would idly shoot baskets while awaiting a Saturday morning ride to their youth baseball games. Over time, Bing and Chambers came to enjoy basketball more and more. It wasn't long before they put down their baseball gloves for good.

Gradually, Bing began to ingratiate himself with the established stars at the

Watts Branch, Kelly Miller, and other playgrounds on the eastern edge of the city. He did this by willingly and frequently setting up his teammates during pickup games. Typically, that's not how a playground reputation is built. But Bing was so generous with his passes that he quickly became a welcome teammate all over the city.

Bing would get by his man, force someone else to help out, and slip the ball to an open teammate for an easy basket. It was a style that served him well throughout his career and demonstrated the extent to which he had studied the game. Chambers, who attended junior high with Bing, described his approach to the game, even as a teenager, as "cerebral."

"I always thought I could get past my man," Bing said. "I got a lot of satisfaction in setting people up, especially the big guys."

Bing and the kids in Northeast DC typically played at Watts Branch during the week and Kelly Miller on the weekends. Many of the best players in the city would gather there on Saturdays and Sundays and put on a show for hundreds of interested onlookers who'd wandered over to the playground. Bing's talent for distributing the ball was known far and wide. He'd occasionally make his way up to the Chevy Chase playground in a far more stylish part of town. There, he played with— among others—Hetzel, who marveled at Bing's talent for setting up teammates.

"He was just beautiful to watch," Hetzel said. "I can just remember seeing him at Chevy Chase [playground] and watching him distribute the basketball. It was incredible. He could score anytime he wanted to, of course. But you'd cut to the basket and all of a sudden the ball would be there and you'd just have to catch it and you'd have a layup. He was smooth as silk."

Bing, who wasn't highly recruited until a breakout performance in a postseason all-star game in his high school senior year, stayed loyal to Syracuse coach Fred Lewis for spotting him earlier than anyone else in the recruiting process. Bing also thought there might be less pressure on him to succeed in upstate New York. The school was not yet the basketball power it would become, and Bing believed that if he failed there (as if such a thing were possible!), it wouldn't be as big a deal as if he crapped out at a higher-profile place, like the University of California, Los Angeles (UCLA), or the University of Michigan.

Having played against all the top-level competition on the streets of Washington, Bing was in for a shock when he went to Syracuse. Once he arrived on campus, he quickly realized that he could take five guys from his favorite childhood playground at Kelly Miller and beat the school's freshman team and probably the varsity too. "I didn't realize my skill level until I got to college, really," he said.

In DC, there was always somebody around like Austin, Leftwich, or Bernard Levi, an earlier Spingarn guard whom Bing considered more talented than himself. At Syracuse, though, Bing finally realized that he could compete against anyone, anywhere. "I don't think any of us [in DC] realized how good we were because we only played against each other," he said.

Fortunately for DeMatha and Wootten, they didn't have to contend with Bing in his senior year; Chambers and the Eastern Ramblers knocked off Spingarn in the Inter-High championship game, a loss that left Bing in tears. With a limping Austin largely used as a decoy, the Stags defeated Eastern, 54–48, for the 1962 city title and could finally, and rightfully, claim superiority in the metro area.

At least part of the reason Wootten had to wait a couple of years to achieve that status was the quality of play in Washington and its immediate suburbs. Carroll was a powerhouse during his early years at DeMatha, and the Lions remain the most revered team in the area's rich high school basketball history. But as the emergence of players such as Hetzel, Bing, and Chambers demonstrated, outstanding basketball talent existed all over the city.

"The competition was pretty strong," Chambers said. "Every time you stepped on the court, you had to go full steam, or somebody would beat you. That was a tremendous time for basketball in DC."

Between 1961 and 1966, a half-dozen players who hailed from within the city's borders were NBA first-round picks. Phelps High's Ben Warley was chosen in 1961 and Carroll's Tom Hoover in 1963. Two years later, Hetzel and Ollie Johnson went in the first round, with Bing and Chambers taken as No. 1's in 1966. In 1966 there were still just 10 teams in the league. So any first-round selection then would be the equivalent of a lottery pick today—although not nearly as well paid, of course.

The six first-rounders don't even take into account those local players taken in the later rounds who enjoyed NBA careers of some duration: DeMatha's John Austin and Johnny Jones, Carroll's John Thompson, and Wilson High's Ronnie Watts. In fact, all five players selected to the *Star*'s All-Met first team in 1962—Austin, Bing, Chambers, Jones, and Bobby Lewis of St. John's—spent time in the NBA. Nothing like that had ever happened before locally, and it hasn't happened since either. "It's hard to compare eras, but the proof is in the pudding," Chambers said proudly.

Why were more DC players participating at the highest levels of the game? There are several reasons. Most important was integration. Once black players were able to compete on the same court as white players, they gained greater visibility. College scouts could see them play more easily, and the colleges themselves were becoming more inclusive as well. Given the greater opportunities to play at big-time colleges, black players were also being evaluated in larger numbers by NBA scouts; consequently, more black players were drafted and developed into professional players.

Second, the emergence of the incomparable Elgin Baylor as a dynamic scorer and popular star in professional basketball in the late 1950s had a marked impact on the game locally. In his day, Baylor was every bit the drawing card that Michael Jordan was in his. Even folks in rival NBA cities would make plans to come see Baylor and the Los Angeles Lakers when their traveling road show rolled into town.

Baylor's influence on those players who followed can't be overstated. Players from the same streets he'd grown up on could watch one of their own play on television virtually every week and dream one day of following in his footsteps—although, truth be told, nobody from Washington or anywhere else became the next Elgin Baylor.

"I think guys like Elgin were inspiring to the young athletes of the city," Cardozo coach Frank Bolden said. "When they see and hear about these former area high school stars playing college and pro basketball, it inspires them to try harder and do better. It gives them a target to shoot at."

Wootten and Gallagher also had their own roles in upgrading the level of local basketball. Using St. John's sprawling campus off Rock Creek Park, the pair started the Metropolitan Area Basketball School in the summer of 1961. Their enterprise was nothing less than the first-ever day camp anywhere devoted strictly to basketball. Rising players could work on their games in a fundamentals-oriented, systematic way over the summer rather than trying to improve by trial and error in neighborhood pickup games.

Friends of both men dismissed the idea when the two coaches brought it up initially, saying it would never work and that kids would never play basketball year-round. (Clearly, that discussion was a long, long time ago.) But the wily Wootten and the gregarious Gallagher had gauged local interest correctly. After a couple of lean years, the endeavor grew to become wildly successful. In fact, high school players came to view attendance at the camp as almost a requirement or else, the feeling was, you'd fall behind the kids who did. "If you didn't go there, you felt like you wouldn't play basketball that winter," noted Jack Sullivan, who coached at Gonzaga in the early 1960s.

The high quality of high school play in the area didn't go unnoticed either. Fans crowded into area gyms in record numbers to cheer on their team of choice. How else to explain the crowd of 10,500 fans who attended the Carroll-Spingarn City Title Game at Cole Field House in March 1960? At the time, it was the largest crowd ever to watch a high school basketball game in the area.

But clearly that record wasn't going to stand for long, not when a mere regular-season game between DeMatha and Landon the next year drew close to 7,000 people. Just a few weeks after that game, the 1961 DeMatha-Spingarn City Title Game had a crowd reported at 10,600 fans to Cole. In 1962 the DeMatha-Eastern City Title matchup sold out the 12,500-seat Cole, and DeMatha claimed Wootten's first city title.

Sellouts were also common for big games at places such as Montgomery Blair in Silver Spring. Some Northern Virginia high schools even experimented with showing games on closed-circuit television in the cafeteria once the gym was sold out.

And the crowds weren't limited to just the postseason or to basketball. The 1961 city football championship game was the first sellout event in the history of the District of Columbia Stadium (later renamed RFK Stadium for the late senator

Robert F. Kennedy), drawing a crowd of more than 50,000 people. Still, interest ran so high at many Inter-High regular-season basketball games that the sale of tickets was limited to students from the schools involved.

"It's the best support I've ever seen here," said former Inter-High athletics director Hardy Pearce, who'd been part of the city's prep sports scene since the 1930s. "I guess people just like a good game."

In retrospect, it's easy to see why interest in high school sports ran so high in the early 1960s. To put it bluntly, high school games were the only ones in town worth watching. The NBA and National Hockey League were still a decade or more away from finding their way to the Washington area. The two established professional teams—the Senators of Major League Baseball and the Redskins of the National Football League (NFL)—were perennial losers. The original Senators were so bad they moved to Minnesota after the 1960 season and became the Twins. Their replacements, the expansion Senators, were just as inept. The Redskins won just nine games in the four seasons from 1958 to 1961 and—even worse—didn't have a single black player on the roster because of the prejudice of owner George Preston Marshall.

The local college scene wasn't much better. The University of Maryland was mediocre in football and basketball during those years, and Georgetown was nowhere near the national force it became once local star John Thompson took over as coach in 1972. Consequently, local fans seeking athletic excellence turned to high school games with increasing frequency and passion.

They exhibited more passion than was healthy, if the truth be told. Urban areas throughout the United States had their problems with crime and violence during the 1960s, and Washington was certainly not immune to those problems. During the 1950s, city athletic contests featured a couple of minor incidents, such as some postgame scuffles and vandalism. But things turned especially ugly at the city football championship game between Eastern and St. John's College High Schools at DC Stadium on Thanksgiving Day 1962.

Passions ran high throughout the game, and a fight between two opposing players on the field only served to inflame emotions. At the conclusion of the game, a 20–7 St. John's victory, all hell broke loose.

Some fans from the Eastern side of the stadium (who were overwhelmingly black) charged the St. John's fans (who were overwhelmingly white) at the game's conclusion. Then a volatile situation veered out of control. During the ensuing clash, people threw bottles, punches, parts of dislodged seats, anything handy. The violence spilled out into the surrounding neighborhood and involved youths, adults, and bystanders not affiliated with either school. Forty people were injured, dozens of neighborhood windows and car windshields were smashed, and 150 police officers were summoned to bring the chaos under control.

Everyone weighed in on the incident: coaches, athletic officials, police, and representatives from the city's public schools and the archdiocese. Pearce, the head of Inter-High athletics, called the episode "a disgrace." *Time* magazine, which ran a story on what everyone was calling a race riot, labeled it an "explosion of hate."

From the standpoint of local high school athletics, the fallout from the incident was severe. The day after the game, officials from the Archdiocese of Washington decreed that there would be no more championship games pitting the Catholic League schools against the Inter-High schools. Emotions, they maintained, were running too high. Consequently, the brawl and its aftermath left the city without a true City Title Game—in either football or basketball—for a decade.

While DeMatha's basketball program rose to prominence in the early 1960s, Montgomery Blair High School in Silver Spring, Wooten's alma mater, returned to it. Under Coach Ed Moffatt, who had replaced David Carrasco, Blair had championship-caliber squads in 1957 and '58. The Blazers had completed unbeaten regular seasons in both years, only to lose in the state finals twice in a row because of some ill-timed injuries. Perhaps because of those disappointments, Moffatt downplayed his team's prospects as the 1960–61 season approached. "Fair with pretty good size," was his preseason assessment.

Moffatt was a poor prognosticator but a great coach. As it turned out, he didn't have much to worry about, despite his early season pessimism. His Blazers were about to win back-to-back state titles, dropping only three games over the course of those two seasons.

Blair's fortunes were fortified by the presence of two standout all-around athletes—Bob Windsor and Roland "Sonny" Jackson. Windsor played inside, while Jackson directed the offense from the backcourt. They teamed up to lead Blair to the Class AA state title in 1961. After Windsor graduated, Jackson took over and led the Blazers to the 1962 AA title.

Windsor and Jackson were the two standout athletes during a remarkable period at Blair. During the 1960s, the large, leafy, sprawling campus at the edge of Sligo Creek Park served as a sort of social incubator for some extraordinary individuals who went on to become rich, famous, or both. Windsor, a future NFL tight end, and future Watergate reporter Carl Bernstein graduated from Blair in 1961. Jackson, a longtime major league infielder, and presidential aide and actor Ben Stein were members of the class of '62. Actress Goldie Hawn graduated from Blair a year later, followed by newscaster Connie Chung in 1964 and romance novelist Nora Roberts (then known as Eleanor Robertson) in 1968.

In 1961, though, nobody was a bigger deal than Windsor. At six-foot-four and 200 pounds, Windsor was a stunning all-around athlete. He was too strong for most forwards and too quick for most big men, and basketball wasn't even his best sport. He was a one-man track team, eager to participate in as many events as the rules allowed. Even at his size, he could run a 100-yard dash in less than 10 seconds, throw the javelin and discus, high jump, long jump, and pole vault. But Windsor's real talent lay on the football field. After Blair, he played both football and basketball at the University of Kentucky before he spent five seasons with the San Francisco 49ers and four with the New England Patriots.

"He could jump like a damn deer and run like the wind," recalled Gene Doane, then the Warriors' basketball coach at Sherwood and later Blair's coach. "He was the first kid I ever saw that size who could jump and was quick."

With Windsor leading the way, Blair got off fast in 1960–61 and kept rolling. A 3–0 start included wins over the Walter Johnson Wildcats (78–46), the Northwestern Wildcats (45–28), and the defending state champion Bladensburg Mustangs (72–45).

The Blazers' 16th straight win—83–63 over the Richard Montgomery Rockets—wrapped up the league and county titles. Windsor was simply brilliant that night, scoring 38 points to go along with 17 rebounds. "He did everything you could ask of a player," Moffatt said.

Blair finished the regular season undefeated—with one hiccup. The Blazers had their toughest game of the year at High Point High and trailed the Screaming Eagles 53–51 when the final buzzer sounded. But officials determined that on a couple of occasions, the clock had continued to run when the ball went out of bounds at the far end of the court. The High Point gym was so crowded that the timekeeper couldn't see all action at the other end of the floor. So eight seconds went back on the clock, and Windsor scored with three seconds left to force a tie.

The decision outraged High Point fans, who seemed on the verge of starting a riot. Game officials and school administrators huddled to discuss the situation, which was growing more and more volatile. Both teams were sent to their locker rooms to await further instructions. Nobody wanted to incite the angry crowd any further, so the game was declared a tie. It was the *only* recorded draw in the history of metro area high school basketball. At that point, anyone associated with Blair got out of the gym as quickly as possible and sped back to Silver Spring.

Another hiccup, this one in the postseason, came in the state final, where Moffatt had already seen two other promising seasons ruined. In the championship game, Windsor and fellow starters Jim Wendt and Jim O'Neil each had collected four fouls by the end of the third quarter. Reserve Jack Townsend had already fouled out. Would misfortune strike the Blazers again? Not this time. George Davis rescued Blair by scoring 11 of his team-high 20 points in the third quarter. With Windsor, Jackson, and Gary Goubeau adding 12 points each, the Blazers prevailed, 75–63.

As an all-around athlete, Sonny Jackson was no slouch either. As a senior, he enjoyed one of the best years imaginable. In the fall, the five-foot-eight Jackson quarterbacked Blair to the county football title. In the winter, he started at point guard as the Blazers won another state basketball championship, the school's fifth in a dozen years. In the spring, he played shortstop on the Blair baseball team, which also won a county title.

Jackson was a take-charge type: quick, tough, and smart. He distributed the ball where it needed to go and could hit the jumper or drive if defenses laid off him. On defense, he harassed opponents all over the floor as the point man in Moffatt's 1-3-1 zone.

"He was a great team player," Windsor said. "He could jump, really smooth. I don't remember him being a great jump shooter, but he could drive and stop and hit that pull-up. He made a lot of great plays, a lot of steals."

And on the basketball court, he saved his best for last. Jackson scored 25 points in the victory over the Northwood Gladiators that wrapped up the county title. Then he shot 23 more points in the 87–58 state semifinal victory over South Hagerstown's Rebels. In the championship game against Bladensburg, a matchup of the previous two state champions, Jackson scored 14 of his 19 points in the first half to get the Blazers going. He also limited the Mustangs' Buddy Quinn, who'd scored 21 points in the semifinals, to just five points—all from the foul line.

After high school, Jackson very nearly made history at the University of Maryland, which did not have a black athlete on scholarship. Jackson was offered a combined baseball-basketball grant-in-aid, which, if he'd taken it, would've made him the first black basketball player in the Atlantic Coast Conference. That distinction went to the Terps' Billy Jones a couple of years later.

Instead, Jackson took a different route. Major League Baseball added another Washington franchise, which replaced the original Senators that had moved to Minnesota, and the Los Angeles Angels to the American League in 1961. The New York Mets and Houston Colt .45s (later the Astros) joined the National League a year later. More teams meant more major league opportunities, something not lost on Jackson, a talented shortstop. When the fledgling Houston organization offered Jackson a professional contract and a bonus, he jumped at the chance, bypassing the opportunity to become a trailblazer in College Park.

"I would have been the first, but doing that wouldn't have bothered me," Jackson said. "I just figured I'd have a better opportunity with an expansion team like Houston and get to the big leagues quicker."

Jackson guessed right, reaching the big leagues at the age of 19 and spending a dozen years in the majors. He made it to the big leagues to stay in 1966, contending for Rookie of the Year honors with 49 stolen bases. He later was traded to Atlanta and became the everyday shortstop for the Braves team that won the National League Western Division in 1969.

For a couple of years in the early 1960s—before it took up a more or less permanent residence at DeMatha—the center of the DC area's basketball universe was in Arlington, Virginia. Wakefield, whose campus was on the Alexandria side of the city, won the Virginia Group I-A title in 1961—the first by a Northern Virginia team since Alexandria's George Washington High School did so in 1945.

Not to be outdone, crosstown rival Washington-Lee won state titles in 1962 and again in 1963—the only school in Northern Virginia ever to repeat as state champion. W-L coach Morris Levin, who learned his fundamental, defense-oriented style while playing for Bud Milliken at Maryland, brought home another state title in 1966 and gave that little corner of Northern Virginia four state titles in six seasons. To put that run of success in perspective, consider this: over the next nearly five decades since W-L's last title in 1966, schools in the Northern Region—Fairfax County, Arlington County, and the city of Alexandria—won a *total* of four state championships.

The presence of the Hummer brothers—Ed and John, two of the best ball players ever in Northern Virginia—played a huge role in the rise of Arlington basketball. Ed starred on the first two Washington-Lee state championship teams. At six foot six, he was an outstanding all-around talent who went on to play at Princeton and helped the Tigers to a Final Four with some help from a pretty fair college player named Bill Bradley. After Bradley graduated, Hummer promptly led the Tigers to a 25-victory season and another NCAA Tournament berth. Younger brother John, even taller at six foot eight, starred on W-L's 1966 title winners. He, too, went on to star at Princeton and eventually played in the NBA.

Wakefield coach Maynard Haithcock didn't have players like the Hummers. Nobody else in Northern Virginia did either. In fact, Haithcock never had much height on his teams. He often joked that all the tall kids in Arlington (such as the Hummers) lived on the other side of town, within Washington-Lee's boundaries.

Familiarity was Haithcock's big advantage when he had taken over at Wakefield for the 1960–61 season. He had coached all of the varsity players previously during a stint as the junior varsity (JV) coach. Haithcock also inherited a good situation, taking over a team that had gone 17–2 and advanced to the state tournament.

With little height aside from the six-foot-three Gerry Spadetti, Haithcock played the hand he was dealt. Through the years, his offense was always designed to compensate for the Warriors' lack of size by emphasizing teamwork and unselfishness. Haithcock's style didn't appeal to everyone. His insistence on sharing the ball turned off some kids who probably could have played for him, but Haithcock wasn't interested in creating stars, just winning teams.

He reflected on his coaching success at a 55-year reunion with Spadetti and Rick Duques at Wakefield High's Hall of Fame inductions, captured by the Wakefield alumni through the Wakefield Education Foundation. "The main emphasis in my coaching was that you have to play together," Haithcock said when they gathered for their class reunion in 2011 over a diner breakfast.

The best players at Wakefield when I was there were not necessarily on the basketball team. The prerequisite was that you had to be willing to give up the ball. This was done with a very clear conscience. Some people had trouble loosening the ball from their hands. If I'm gonna spend two hours a day at practice from November to heaven knows when, I'm gonna pick kids I want to work with. Everybody at Wakefield knew that. If I were coaching today I'd do it the same way.

Wakefield got off to a 7–0 start in 1960–61 and held down the No. 4 spot in the *Washington Star*'s first high school poll of the season in early January. The Warriors won their biggest game to date on January 11 with a 44–35 victory over Washington-Lee. In the game they compiled a 50–26 rebounding edge despite their lack of height. And per Haithcock's instructions, the Warriors hustled, they got position, they boxed out, and they won. And kept winning.

Wakefield's team was a savvy, experienced bunch, having learned its lessons en route to the state tournament the year before. That, as much as anything else, gave the Warriors an edge over Washington-Lee, which was very good that year but not quite as strong as it would become over the next two seasons when the team had more experience.

"If we could have played them 10 times, maybe we could have won once," Levin said. In fact, Wakefield beat W-L three times that year, twice during the regular season and once in the playoffs. "They executed well," Levin said. "They were real tough at the end. They did what they had to do at the end of the game."

The Warriors finished off a 20–0 regular season and beat W-L for the third time to reach the state tournament. The Washington-Lee players were not only the Warriors' biggest rivals but also their biggest fans. "That was a very skilled team," W-L's Ed Hummer recalled. "It was not a very tall team, but everybody could do everything."

"They had a team that was a great *team*," said Ray Hodgdon, one of Hummer's teammates. The numbers bear that out. First-team All-Met Rick Duques led the team in scoring during the regular season with an 11.1 average, followed by Rolfe Russart (10.5), Jerry Francis (10.4), Spadetti (10.2), and Jim Barr (8.4).

Wakefield overcame a slow start to beat the Jefferson Magicians of Roanoke in the first round of the state tournament. Duques was the hero of the semifinal win, hitting a jumper with four seconds left to complete a rally from a nine-point deficit and deliver a 38–37 victory over the Warwick Raiders.

In the finals, 25–0 Wakefield was pitted against Lynchburg's E. C. Glass, which was 23–0. It was no contest. Spadetti and Russart scored 16 points each and helped foul out E. C. Glass center Martin Morris with 7:36 left. Wakefield outscored the Hilltoppers 26–9 in the final quarter for a 58–36 victory and the state title. Spadetti, with 41 points in the three games, was named the tournament's MVP.

In a strange way, Wakefield's state title set the stage for Washington-Lee's titles the next two years. The always gracious Haithcock sent his W-L counterpart, Morris Levin, a note after the 1961 season, saying he thought the Generals were the second-best team in the state. Those words, combined with the summer-league championship that the Generals won heading into the next season, gave W-L confidence that its chance might be coming.

Under Levin's direction, Washington-Lee had already set itself apart from virtually everyone else with its style of play. Everywhere else, it seemed, the game was speeding up. Players were growing more skilled and more athletic, and teams seemed to be playing faster and faster. Not Levin's Generals. He considered turnovers wasteful and inefficient, so his teams seldom, if ever, ran. At the other end of the floor, the Generals defended to the death. They played man-to-man defense, all the time, with no switching. Each player was responsible for stopping his man. Consequently, W-L played a lot of games in the 30s and 40s at a time when others were scoring twice as many points. Some labeled Levin a control freak, a puppeteer. But he put together a 240–112 record in 17 seasons and won three state championships.

Once Levin's Generals got a lead, they were tough to beat. They seldom made mistakes and never turned the ball over. Scoring against them was always a chore.

"When we got ahead by eight on a team," noted Ed Hummer, "the other guys felt like getting on the bus and going home. Baskets were tough to get against W-L."

"[Levin] was just very conservative, and he had the right material to be conservative," said Clay Estes, who coached at Alexandria's George Washington High in the early 1960s. "They always played good defense and always played a pretty controlled game. You can't knock success, and [we coaches] all have our own way of doing things."

Levin devised his own system of evaluating players, a kind of plus-minus system similar to the one used in hockey. If a player made a turnover or let his man drive the baseline, then he got a mark against him on Levin's ledger, with team managers tracking the transgressions and the pluses during the games. "He was a detail-oriented coach who made sure you did everything right," said Ray Hodgdon.

In the locker room before each game, Levin would write the name of each opposing starter on the blackboard along with the names of his own players. He'd go around the locker room to each of his players, saying, "You're guarding this guy. He averages 20 points a game. You're gonna have to hold him to 12." To the next man, he'd say, "Your guy averages 12. You're gonna have to hold him to eight."

And on it would go until he'd gone through the whole lineup. At the end of this exercise, he'd total up his projections and decide if his estimates were likely to produce victory. If he deemed the opponents' projected total too high, he'd moan, "That's too damn many points!" Then he'd erase the board and start over again.

In that situation, Levin was using peer pressure to his advantage, and he knew it. When he put players on the spot like that, nobody wanted to give up an easy basket or let an opponent have a big scoring night. Against W-L, few did.

"The effect of that was really profound," said Ed Hummer. "It was all about individual accountability. If your man scored a basket off you, you didn't want to look over to the bench."

Not that Hummer let anyone score very often. Even though he averaged only about 14 points per game during those championship seasons, everyone recognized his value as a rebounder and defender. "He was just like a cat; he would spring any minute," Levin recalled. "A great helper on defense. Guards could play tight, knowing there were big guys back there."

Levin's emphasis on defense came in handy during the first championship season. W-L played shorthanded for much of the year as Bob Sutton was slowed by ankle injuries and Hodgdon was out for a long stretch with a broken wrist.

A late January loss to the Hammond Admirals (the final was a typical 44–41) didn't draw much attention at the time. As it turned out, it was the Generals' only loss in the next season and a half.

The Generals (20–1) won the Northern Region tournament and headed to the state playoffs, avenging their lone loss with a 42–28 victory over Hammond in the tournament final. The six-foot-four Hodgdon, who'd been squeezing tennis balls like crazy to rehabilitate his injured wrist, led the way with 18. Ed Hummer added 17. Even better news was that the six-foot-five Sutton had sufficiently healed as well, leaving W-L at full strength going into the state tournament.

The Generals beat the Marion High School Hurricanes in the first round, 53–32; the Andrew Lewis High Wolverines, 61–49, in the semifinals; and the Maury High Commodores in the finals, 49–38. Marion shot 29 percent from the floor, as did Andrew Lewis, while Maury managed just 26 percent accuracy.

The next year went much smoother as Ed Hummer led a group of seven seniors to a second straight state title. Mark Mengering hit the winning jump shot from the corner at the buzzer to beat Wakefield, 32–30, during the regular season. Lynn Moore, the football team's star quarterback, scored with six seconds left to beat GWHS, 43–41, in the region semifinals.

One of the few other close calls came in the state finals against the Douglas Freeman High Rebels. Hummer (17 points, 13 in the second half) hit a pair of free throws with 57 seconds left to give W-L the lead for good. Mengering added two more in the closing seconds to wrap up a 44–41 victory, a second straight state title, and the Generals' 39th straight victory.

Three years later, W-L struck again but this time with John Hummer, Ed's younger brother, leading the way. The pursuit of a state title had become a mission for John, who didn't want to end his high school career without a championship after his big brother had brought home a pair of them. "Two times, Ed won the state title," John told their father. "I've got to do it once."

John was more skilled at a younger age than Ed was, according to Levin. Then again, he'd been able to watch and learn from his older brother. John averaged almost 17 points per game as a senior; that was an almost unheard-of figure for one of Levin's players. But W-L was much more reliant on him for inside scoring than it had been on Ed, simply because the older Hummer had a stronger supporting cast.

One thing hadn't changed as John replaced Ed as the Generals' cornerstone—Levin's insistence on an airtight defense. When the playoffs began in February 1966, Washington-Lee ranked 18th of the 20 Northern Virginia teams in scoring (52.8 points per game), but the Generals were first in defense, allowing 41.2 points per game.

"We really worked on it, and it became a thing of pride for us," John Hummer said. "We picked guys up at half-court. We didn't let people breathe. They didn't know what hit them."

With Hummer closing off the middle and Tyrone Epperson locking down opposing scorers, the Generals, who entered the state tournament at 18–2, moved toward another title. In their first-round victory, they allowed the Hampton Crabbers just 41 points. In the quarterfinals, W-L upset the second-seeded Edison High School Eagles of Alexandria (featuring future NFL defensive lineman Pat Toomay) while allowing just 32 points. Then the Princess Anne High School Cavaliers (Virginia Beach) scored just 36 against the Generals in the semifinals.

In the state final, the story was much the same. The Generals downed the top-seeded Patrick Henry High Patriots of (Roanoke) for the championship, 54–39. Hummer scored a season-high 28 points and grabbed 14 rebounds.

W-L's defense also made a statement, limiting its foe to 2-for-17 shooting in the first half and 19 percent (10 for 52) for the game. That performance must have come as a shock to Patrick Henry coach Len Mosser, who'd claimed before the tournament that his team was the best defensive squad in the state.

"This team [W-L] probably isn't as good—particularly on offense—as the '62 and '63 teams," Levin said. "It had to work a lot harder to win this championship."

The Hummer brothers were the most successful players in Northern Virginia during the 1960s. But several other individuals distinguished themselves during the decade as well.

Mount Vernon's Marty Lentz was as prolific a scorer as the metro area has ever seen, even if his name might draw some blank looks today. Lentz was a six-foot-six wonder, blessed with quickness, jumping ability, and an uncanny knack for putting the ball in the basket. Those who saw him play estimate that he hit close to two-thirds of his shots from the field. Right-handed, left-handed, in close, or out on the perimeter, it didn't matter. Lentz could (and did) score from anywhere. "He could shoot with either hand. He could jump. He made it look easy," said his coach, Mike Skinner.

"He was silky smooth with a great touch," noted longtime W. T. Woodson

Cavaliers coach Red Jenkins, who was still working his way up to a head coaching job during Lentz's senior season in 1960–61. "Every shot looked good."

Most of them were. Lentz lacked the supporting cast that might have enabled the Majors to overtake Wakefield and Washington-Lee for supremacy in Northern Virginia. But he put on quite a show anyway.

Though he might have looked like a natural, Lentz was anything but. He couldn't even make his eighth-grade team, and he managed just 104 points during his sophomore season. However, Lentz took off in his junior year. He pumped in 45 points in the third game of the season, an 87–55 wipeout of McLean's Highlanders. By the end of February, he'd broken the state's regular-season scoring record with 567 points in 20 games en route to a 28.7 points per game average. Mount Vernon's season ended with an upset loss to the Annandale Atoms in the playoffs, even though Lentz pumped in 37 points.

"When I saw him his junior season, I just handed him the ball and said, 'Shoot, Marty!'" recalled Skinner. "He was a complete player who was very tough inside and out. He did things nobody was doing in those days."

Nobody figured out how to stop Lentz in his senior year either. He was so good, in fact, that he forced W-L's Levin to abandon his beloved man-to-man defense in favor of a zone designed to keep the Mount Vernon star from even catching the ball. W-L held Lentz to 17 points in the final game of his career—a playoff loss. But there was plenty of sizzle before the fizzle.

Lentz riddled opposing defenses in that final season for a 36.6 average, earning Virginia's state Player of the Year award—the first player from Northern Virginia so honored. He also became Northern Virginia's top career scorer (surpassing George Washington's Walt Densmore), and his single-season scoring average still ranks among the top 10 in state history.

And on February 25, 1961, Lentz went where no local player had gone before or has gone since. On that night, Lentz pumped in an area-record 74 points in the Patriots' 107–63 blowout of J.E.B. Stuart's Raiders. Lentz had games of 52 and 44 points in the weeks leading up to his record outburst, but no one was quite prepared for such a performance. On the night he scored 74 points, Lentz scored 19 in the first quarter, a mere 12 in the second, a ridiculous 27 in the third, and 16 in the fourth. He hit 27 of 51 shots from the floor and 20 of 25 from the line, and went to the bench to a huge ovation for a well-deserved rest with 3:10 left. Stuart coach Herb Duvall raved afterward, "He could have kicked the ball up there, and it would have gone in."

Ed Hummer, the best defensive player of that era in Northern Virginia, was awestruck by the performance, which he witnessed in person. "He could do anything with the ball," Hummer recalled. "I was mesmerized. Most guys couldn't score 74 points if you included their baskets in warm-ups!"

Lentz wound up playing college ball at West Virginia University, where he had an undistinguished career. But while many have forgotten or have never even heard of him, remember this: nobody in local basketball—not Elgin Baylor, Adrian Dantley, Austin Carr, or Grant Hill—has ever enjoyed a game quite like the one that Lentz produced on that magical February night nearly sixty years ago.

"He could score from anywhere," Levin said. "He played the post, he played the wing. He could bring the ball up. He could pass. He could do it all."

Area fans might recall Jim Lewis as the first coach of the Women's National Basketball Association's Washington Mystics. More astute observers would remember Lewis as the coach who took the women's basketball program of the George Mason University Patriots into Division I. But Lewis's greatest impact on the local basketball scene came much earlier. When Lewis stepped onto the court for Groveton High School (Alexandria) in a game against Mount Vernon in December 1963, three weeks after John F. Kennedy's assassination, he became the first black basketball player at a previously all-white Fairfax County school.

If Lewis was nervous, he didn't show it. He pumped in 25 points in Groveton's victory, including a perfect 10-for-10 performance from the field.

Lewis's big night wasn't that much of a surprise. He was well known around Alexandria as an outstanding player, having played for Arnold Thurmond at Parker-Gray. But the summer before his senior year, Lewis's family moved out of Alexandria proper and into Groveton's school district, a move that put him in a position to make history.

Because of his December birthday, Lewis was eligible for only the first semester of his senior year, according to the rules in effect at the time. But he had quite an impact, averaging 18 points and 22 rebounds for the Tigers, who won nine of the 10 games in which he played. He could handle the ball, slash to the basket, and go get it off the boards, too. "Jim Lewis was the real deal," recalled Coach Jenkins, who saw everybody in Northern Virginia during his coaching career, which spanned nearly 40 years.

At six foot three and 190 pounds, Lewis already had the physique of a full-grown man. He was tough, strong, and athletic, and not many could keep up with him. He'd also been tested against the area's best players across the Potomac River in DC.

"You tried to find competition, so you played everywhere. I was very advanced physically," said Lewis, who could touch the backboard a good foot and half above the rim in those days. "I had a reputation, if you will. I had somewhat of a name before I went to Groveton."

According to Groveton coach Verne Canfield, Lewis's talent was so apparent that his presence didn't cause any fuss. Black students were still quite a rarity in

Fairfax County schools at that point; a *Post* story about the opening of school in the fall of 1963 counted 420 African Americans in a school system that served 78,000 students. But Lewis was so good that he was accepted without complaint.

"I'm sure there was some [grumbling] behind the scenes, but nobody said anything to my face," Canfield said. "I think the parents probably felt like 'This guy's gonna help us.' The players knew what kind of player he was, ability-wise, which made some of our other kids even better. He was very, very coachable. [I] never had a minute of trouble with him."

Lewis recalled few problems—a sign that times were indeed changing, albeit slowly. He heard the occasional comment from the stands, but generally he was left alone to play basketball, just like anyone else. One of the few unpleasant incidents he encountered left him with a smile on his face and a warm spot in his heart for his teammates: one night, the entire Groveton team visited the Dixie Pig, a local barbecue joint, for a meal. The proprietors refused to serve Lewis, so the entire team walked out.

"It didn't bother me," Lewis said. "I'd been discriminated against in other places. But any situations like that were overridden by the guys I played with and the coaches I played for."

Lewis might have been snubbed at the Dixie Pig, but plenty of others took notice. The *Post* made him a first-team All-Met pick even though he'd played fewer than a dozen games as a senior. He made the all-district and all-state teams in Virginia as well.

As it turned out, Lewis's career as a pioneer was just beginning. After leaving Groveton, he became part of the first integrated recruiting class to play at West Virginia University. As a coach, he became the first black assistant in Duke University's Blue Devils basketball program in the early 1970s before blazing trails at George Mason and with the Mystics as well.

The biggest white star in Alexandria during the mid-1960s, not to mention its most colorful character, was Harley "Skeeter" Swift. He came from a broken home, a place of abuse and alcoholism, and seemed to find solace only when on his own, playing basketball. Swift became an expert ball handler by dribbling along the city's cobblestone streets; he became a deadly shooter by launching thousands of shots in the snow and the wind and the rain.

A child of the streets, reluctant to return to an unhappy home, Swift was basically a combination of Huck Finn, Babe Ruth, and Larry Bird. He moved easily in the black community, too, often staying with black friends in the city at a time when such things just weren't done. Unlike the white folks in Alexandria, the city's blacks never judged him; they never looked down their noses at him because his mother ran a saloon and basically allowed him to run wild in the streets as a youth.

And make no mistake, he did run wild. You name any kind of trouble a kid could get into—truancy, shoplifting, underage drinking, petty theft, foul language—and Skeeter not only did it but also reveled in the doing.

The thing was, Swift didn't need to do anything to draw attention to himself; his appearance alone was sufficient. At George Washington High School, the six-foot-three Swift played at a Charles Barkley–like 230 pounds. His ears stuck out like the open doors of a taxi cab. Those ears, his mother once remarked, looked like a mosquito's wings, and the nickname "Skeeter" stuck.

His appearance and reputation naturally made him a target for other teams' fans. But that never bothered Swift. In fact, he loved the attention he got for playing basketball (and football and baseball). He loved the spotlight and loved to make the big play.

"I was cocky, I was abrasive, [and] I was someone driven to be successful," Swift said. "I was like an arrogant type of player. It's the confidence, the will, the desire."

He helped win a football game against Annandale High in 1963 when he drop-kicked a field goal through the uprights after a bad snap—on Friday the 13th, no less. Three months later—on another Friday the 13th—he tossed in a full-court shot at the first-half buzzer against Washington-Lee, then the preeminent team in Northern Virginia. In a subsequent game against W-L, Swift tried another full-court shot to beat the halftime buzzer—and hit John Hummer in the back of the head with it. Hummer was certain that Swift had been aiming for him, but it was almost impossible to stay mad at Skeeter. He just had that way about him.

One time he bicycled over the bridge from Virginia and tried to get into a game at DC's most competitive playground, Kelly Miller. The regulars took one look at the funny-looking white kid and refused to pick him for their teams. So Swift pedaled back to Alexandria and rounded up some buddies. They piled into a car, drove back to Kelly Miller, got on the court, and won five or six straight games.

Then Swift and his mates hopped back in the car, satisfied that they'd proven their point. Except Skeeter wasn't done yet. Before making their getaway, the driver circled around the parking lot one more time, and Swift mooned everybody on the playground, sticking his bare butt out the car window. "That's a true story," Swift said.

Even before Swift arrived at George Washington High, basketball coach Clay Estes had heard all about him—what a character he was, how difficult he would be to handle. But Estes, who was also a guidance counselor, saw something endearing in the high-strung youngster. "I never had any real problems with him," Estes said. "Usually, you'd just tell him how far he could go, and that was it."

Estes recognized that Swift was a braggart because he was so self-conscious about his appearance, about not having nice clothes like the other kids, about his upbringing. For example, when Swift would get a ride home from practice, he'd never let friends drop him off in front of his house. He'd get out at the nearest corner because he didn't want his friends to see where he lived.

Knowing all this, Estes made sure never to show up Swift in front of the other players. He'd pull Swift aside when the huddle broke up and explain quietly what needed to be done. "I never did get on him too much in front of the other kids," Estes said.

The extra care Estes took was worth it. Swift was a huge asset on the court. He could handle the ball, rebound, and score. Estes's offense wasn't built around Swift as it might have been at other places, but opponents concentrated so much on stopping him that his teammates were often left all alone.

The Presidents' basketball program had fallen on hard times in the late 1950s and early 1960s as Wakefield and then Washington-Lee dominated in Northern Virginia. But with Swift—twice an All-Met—running the show, George Washington made the state tournament in both his junior and senior seasons.

In his junior year, Swift (17 points per game) led the Presidents to the Group I-A regular-season championship, the school's first in seven seasons. In the game that wrapped up the title and a 17–1 regular-season record, he racked up 34 points in a 75–54 win over Groveton.

The next year, Wakefield won the league title, but GWHS earned another trip downstate by beating the Warriors in the Northern Virginia Group I-A tournament. GWHS's 67–66 victory in double overtime was fueled by 21 points from Swift, including a free throw that made the difference.

GWHS never had much luck in the state tournament, though. The Presidents went out quickly in both 1964 and 1965, with Swift struggling to duplicate his regular-season success. He wanted to succeed so badly, but he just couldn't make it happen. "He didn't have good games down there," Estes recalled. "He tried so hard. Guys like him, they feel like they've got to do so many things."

Despite his lack of postseason success, his outsize personality, and his antics, Swift was always recalled warmly by those who crossed his path back in those days. "Skeeter was unique," said Wakefield's Haithcock. "He was something of a clown, but he could have played for me anytime."

Swift went on to star at East Tennessee State University before playing five years in the old American Basketball Association (ABA).

While Lentz could claim to be the best player in Northern Virginia at the start of the 1960s, Jim O'Brien of J.E.B. Stuart High in Falls Church held that honor when the decade drew to a close. "I'm not sure he's *not* the best player ever in the [Northern] region," said Chris Knoche, who watched his brother go head-to-head with O'Brien in the late 1960s. Chris himself played at W. T. Woodson in the 1970s and later recruited in the area as American University's head coach. "He was a kind of once-in-a-generation type of player."

O'Brien shook things up, all right. First of all, there was his scoring. He led Virginia's Group I-A in scoring twice—in 1967–68 and 1968–69. He averaged 26.6 points for his high school career at Stuart and wound up with more than 1,600 points, which was the highest total in Northern Virginia history to that time.

But O'Brien was more than just a scorer. Other players have put up dazzling numbers, but O'Brien was something else. He was a complete player, the kind nobody in Northern Virginia had ever seen before. At six foot seven, he could and often did bring the ball up the floor. He possessed remarkable vision and thus an ability to slip passes through openings that nobody else saw.

Though skinny and gangly—his weight in those years was listed at 170, which might have been a stretch—O'Brien was as smooth as they come with a basketball in his hands. He could handle the ball and fire away from the outside like a guard. Underneath the basket, he might have looked frail, but he always seemed to be where the ball came off the rim. He led Stuart in scoring, rebounding, and assists in all three of his varsity seasons, and he averaged 30 points and 18 rebounds per game over his last two years, making first-team All-Met in the *Post* and the *Star* as a junior and a senior.

O'Brien brought a certain flair for the game as well. He delighted some who watched him and infuriated others who believed basketball should be played in a more traditional manner.

"He did stuff nobody else did," said John Knoche, who played for Woodson against O'Brien in the late 1960s. "He was really tough to cover that way. He could score with either hand. He could make passes that were just scary. He was like [flashy Hall of Famer Pete] Maravich."

The redheaded O'Brien would throw passes behind his back and dribble between his legs. He was doing things that nobody else was doing in Northern Virginia at the time and certainly nobody who stood six foot seven. "A lot of people weren't used to seeing big guys do those types of things," said O'Brien, who went on to star at Maryland and play in the ABA.

O'Brien learned those skills as a youth in Uniontown, Pennsylvania, watching the local high school team win a pair of state titles in the early 1960s. O'Brien also frequented the same playgrounds as the other locals and thus was exposed to black players and a more freewheeling style than was played in Fairfax County at the time. "That was how everyone played in Uniontown," he said.

Despite his unorthodox style, O'Brien could count any number of fans among the Northern Virginia coaches, even those who would never dream of letting their own players throw no-look passes or dribble between their legs. Nobody was more old school in this regard than Washington-Lee coach Morris Levin, who always kept a tight rein on his own players, largely because he abhorred turnovers. What was Levin's take on the flashy Stuart star?

"Oh my god," Levin exclaimed when O'Brien's name came up. "What a ballplayer!"

By the end of the 1962–63 season, DeMatha coach Morgan Wootten was looking for new worlds to conquer. The Stags had won three straight Catholic League titles, three straight Knights of Columbus tournament titles, and a pair of Eastern States Catholic Invitational Tournament titles. DeMatha's three-year record was an astonishing 92–8.

Wootten had become the area's preeminent high school basketball coach, but he wanted more. He wanted DeMatha to be recognized nationally, not just locally, so he went after the biggest prize of all—a game against the Power Memorial Academy Panthers of New York City and seven-foot Lew Alcindor, probably the most hyped prep basketball player ever. "To be the best, you have to beat the best," Wootten insisted. Alcindor, who later changed his name to Kareem Abdul-Jabbar and became the leading scorer in NBA history, had already been profiled in *Time* magazine and was being sought by every college in the country. (He would wind up at UCLA, where he led the Bruins to three straight NCAA titles.)

Prior to the 1963–64 season, Wootten contacted Jack Donahue, Power's coach, and proposed a game. The two teams would meet at the University of Maryland's Cole Field House, with Washington's best going against New York's best in a marquee matchup that seemed sure to draw a huge crowd. Power had won 46 straight games; the Stags' streak stood at 23.

As the game drew closer, Wootten decided on a simple strategic approach against Alcindor, who was averaging 28 points per game—play him more or less straight up while trying to limit the rest of Power's lineup. "We will use a man-on-man defense and [six-foot-eight] Bob Whitmore will guard Alcindor," Wootten announced. "But we plan to give him some help."

The enormity of DeMatha's task became all too clear at a special dinner the evening before the game that brought both teams together. When it came time for the invocation, everyone in the room stood up, including Alcindor. As the New York giant rose from his chair, DeMatha forward Sid Catlett elbowed his buddy Whitmore in the ribs to get his attention and nodded toward Alcindor.

"He just kept going up and up—like a rocket ship," Whitmore recalled. "And my heart started going down, down, down. I'm realizing I have to contend with this guy at six foot seven or six foot eight."

Whitmore's worst fears were realized: Alcindor was every bit as good as advertised. He dominated inside, scoring 35 points on 16-for-24 shooting. He also grabbed 17 rebounds and was clearly the difference in Power's 65–62 victory. "We figured he wasn't good enough to beat us all by himself," Wootten recalled. "But he was."

DeMatha led for much of the game but got a tough break when Whitmore fouled out in the closing minutes. A five-foot-nine guard named Charlie Farrugia hit a couple of key baskets late for the visitors, and the Power Panthers escaped.

But clearly DeMatha proved, if anyone still needed convincing, that it could play with anyone.

Wootten couldn't have asked for anything more from his team or the game—except, perhaps, a victory. The game was a sellout, with 12,500 fans squeezed inside Cole Field House and thousands more turned away at the door.

Having come so close, Wootten was determined to get another crack at Power and Alcindor. Coach Donahue readily accepted the challenge. He was pleased with the size of the crowd and the big-game atmosphere. Power's continued excellence was old hat back home. With so many other social and athletic opportunities available, New Yorkers didn't consider high school basketball that big a deal. "We never get these kinds of crowds in New York," Donahue said.

With a rematch on the horizon, DeMatha became Power's biggest booster. Wootten wanted the New Yorkers unbeaten when they came back to Cole in January 1965, and he made sure that his own team didn't slip up in the interim either. He got his wish. Power's winning streak stood at 71 when it arrived in Washington for the rematch, and DeMatha boasted another 23-game winning streak of its own. The last game the Stags had lost was to Power.

If anything, the rematch was an even bigger deal. Alcindor was a senior by then, and his legend had grown with each successive game. Cole Field House was sold out a week in advance, and on the night of the game, scalpers were getting $25 for a ticket—or almost $200 in 2019 dollars. For perspective, Beatles tickets would go on sale in the next two years for the first US tour for less than $6.

In preparing for that second matchup, Wootten decided a change in strategy was in order. He opted to double-team Alcindor every chance he could, using the six-foot-eight Catlett and six-foot-three Bernie Williams to come over and help Whitmore from the weak side. Wootten wanted Whitmore in front of Alcindor, denying him the ball and the position he wanted. Another forward would position himself behind Alcindor, between the Power star and the basket. "A hero sandwich," Wootten called it.

The tactic might not have worked for everyone. But DeMatha possessed considerable size with those three, and they made it difficult for Alcindor to catch the ball on his preferred spots on the floor. Wootten also instructed his backcourt to pressure the Power guards, making it difficult to get the ball inside.

Over the years, much has been said about DeMatha's unique practice regimen leading up to the Power Memorial showdown. In preparation for Alcindor, Wootten had Catlett wielding a tennis racquet on defense in practice. The ploy was designed to get the Stags to put more arc on their shots so that Alcindor's reach might not seem too intimidating under game conditions. But the key to DeMatha's 46–43 upset victory in the rematch—the biggest high school basketball game in Washington area history—wasn't DeMatha's shooting. It was DeMatha's defense.

The magnitude and pregame hype of the rematch seemed to affect both teams; neither shot well. The winning Stags were just 17 for 55 from the floor. But their defense on Alcindor was strong enough to enable Wootten to pull off an upset for the ages.

Alcindor finished with just 16 points—14 below his average—and 14 rebounds. He was able to attempt just 11 shots, thanks to Whitmore's ability to deny him the ball and the guards' ability to cut off the passing lanes. "It was definitely a team victory," Whitmore said. "The rest of the team made my job easier."

"It was not a single-person effort by any means," agreed Catlett. "It was a collaborative effort. Depending on where [Alcindor] was, there were always two people on him. We'd beat him to a spot, take him out of his comfort zone and away from the particular places on the floor he liked, move him further out. It worked."

Catlett was the offensive star in the low-scoring, defensive struggle. He scored seven of his team-high 13 points in the last four minutes, including a tip-in for a 43–38 lead in the final minute that essentially clinched the game.

Alcindor was impressive, even in defeat. As DeMatha whooped it up in the locker room after the monumental victory, Alcindor led his vanquished teammates over from their own locker room to congratulate the victors. It wasn't the only loss of Alcindor's high school career, as has been written so many times; Power had dropped a couple of games during his freshman year with the varsity. But still, it had to hurt to make that walk, something everyone in that DeMatha locker room appreciated.

"I always had the utmost respect for Lew and the way he carried himself," Whitmore said. "For him to come into the locker room and congratulate us—that was classy, as classy as it gets."

If DeMatha was the best high school basketball program in the East (or even in the country) at that time, its league rival Mackin Trojans couldn't have been far behind. The tiny private school at 14th and V Streets in northwest DC never had more than a couple hundred students, but it produced a parade of outstanding players and teams before it closed in 1989.

Mackin's basketball tradition really began in the early 1960s with the arrival of Paul Furlong as head coach. Furlong was blunt, fundamentally oriented, and determined to build a certain toughness in his teams. He felt they'd need that quality because the school's cramped gym forced the Trojans to play all their games on the road. His teams were always athletic and high scoring, and they played with more than a hint of edginess.

Much of that edge came from Coach Furlong. One season he picked up seven technical fouls. He drew a suspension for the remainder of another season when he supposedly bumped an official while arguing a call. But the highly competitive New Jersey native was respected by his peers for his ability to develop great players and put together outstanding teams.

"He was a solid coach and really cared about his kids," Wootten said. "He was very fiery, and he drove his players because he wanted them to be the best they could be."

For much of the 1960s, Mackin couldn't be the best; DeMatha saw to that. But the Trojans were usually only a half step behind. Mackin wound up ranked No. 2 behind the Stags in the local newspapers' polls in 1964 and 1965. DeMatha's regular-season record during that span was 47–3; Mackin's was 49–8.

During that time, Mackin also lost twice to Power Memorial—once by eight points on a neutral court and once by three points while playing in Madison Square Garden. Even more agonizingly, Mackin lost five straight times to DeMatha in the mid-1960s by a combined total of only 12 points.

"They always had great ball clubs, and we always knew we were gonna have a real battle with them," DeMatha's Bob Whitmore said. "Somehow, we were always able to get the job done."

Many DeMatha opponents bemoaned this same phenomenon over the years. Most of the time, DeMatha had superior talent. Even on the odd occasions when it didn't, though, the Stags almost always found a way to prevail.

Some blamed the officials. Opposing fans and coaches swore that DeMatha always got favorable calls in key situations. It's a charge that's been levied at all great teams at all levels of the game since basketball began. More objective observers credited Wootten for maintaining his team's poise in a tight game. He himself always remained calm on the sidelines, and his players seemed to draw strength from his unruffled demeanor. "He looked like royalty over there on the bench," a rival coach once said.

Wootten, the master psychologist, convinced his teams that adversity wasn't to be feared; it was to be welcomed. It was only under duress, he explained, that real growth could take place. "If I was gonna get discombobulated, that would rattle my team," Wootten said. "Adversity is your asset; emotion is your enemy."

But whatever edge DeMatha had over Mackin, it was a slim one. For a half-dozen years during the 1960s, Mackin made things as tough on DeMatha as any team did. That was quite an accomplishment for a school with no previous basketball tradition.

Furlong and the "Three Bs"—Art Baylor (Elgin's nephew), Butch Braxton (a super leaper), and Bill Butler (a quiet, smooth player who would become a three-time All-Met)—initially brought Mackin to prominence in 1961–62. That year the Trojans went 23–10 in the regular season with victories over public school powers such as Montgomery Blair, the Bethesda–Chevy Chase Barons, and Fairmont Heights. They also knocked off St. John's twice. After losing badly twice to DeMatha during the regular season, Mackin nearly upset the Stags in the Knights of Columbus Tournament final before losing, 46–44, on a pair of Gary Ward free throws with 1:25 left.

The next year, Mackin finally did beat DeMatha, but the victory came in a holiday tournament, not in league play. The Stags came out on top in the two regular-season meetings: 50–48 in double overtime and 66–63 in a game that was not decided until the closing seconds. That's how it always seemed to go.

In 1963–64 Furlong unveiled more stars in Tom Little and Austin Carr. Little was the owner of a deadly accurate flat jump shot. As a player he was so good he'd show up at the famed Turkey Thicket playground on summer evenings after working construction during the day and still dominate while playing in jeans and work boots.

Little torched DeMatha for 31 points in a 56–55 loss to the Stags in early 1965 that Wootten recalled more than four decades later as among the best performances ever against one of his teams. "You want to talk about a night? He had a night," Wootten gushed. "Tom Little could fill it up from anywhere."

Almost anyone from Mackin could hurt you. Five of Furlong's players were named All-Met at least once between 1962 and 1967, 10 selections in all. Furlong drilled his players relentlessly at practice but then turned them loose once the game began. He wanted everyone to be able to handle the ball and shoot; he thought it made his teams more dangerous. "I would like to have a team where nobody was afraid to shoot," he said.

Of all the great players Furlong had, one stood above the rest. That would be high-scoring guard Austin Carr, another who would be on anyone's short list of the best players the city ever produced. In college at Notre Dame University, Carr was one of the great scorers in NCAA history and would be the first player taken in the NBA draft. His record of 61 points in an NCAA Tournament game seems likely to stand forever.

But Carr was a different kind of cat in high school. With all the talent on hand, he had to learn how to blend in before he became a star. "I was kind of a flow-in guy," Carr said. "I was better without the ball. I eventually learned how to play with the ball."

Even when he didn't have the ball in his hands, Carr was always moving, trying to shake defenders so he could receive a pass and score. "He was always open, somehow," Furlong recalled. "He never stopped making cuts. If a guy turned his head for a second, Austin was gone."

Carr's ability to move without the ball was far from the only thing that set him apart. He was quick, he could jump, and he could shoot. Plus, he never coasted. "He always went hard," Furlong said. "I can't remember in four years that he wasn't at practice and didn't go hard the whole time. He was never anything but what you'd hope a kid would be."

Carr worked so hard that Furlong worried about his strength and stamina. At school Carr almost never ate lunch with the other students. Instead, he'd grab a ball and head to the gym to get up a few shots while everyone else ate.

As a sophomore, he averaged 18.5 points per game, improving his figure to 21.3 as a junior. As his senior year began, he was ready to take over as the star, and everyone knew it. The Three Bs were gone and so was Little. All attention was focused on Carr.

But he didn't have to go it alone. Furlong had a valuable guard in Richie Ford and a couple of Inter-High transfers—point guard Sterling Savoy (a great basketball name) and six-foot-eight, 235-pound Garland Williams. The latter took care of the rebounding and inside scoring while also setting plenty of picks to get Carr free. When Carr came open, Savoy usually didn't miss him. A confident, aggressive player, Savoy was a great distributor as well. "He was pretty damn good," Carr recalled. "The ball was always there when I needed it."

Mackin was pretty damn good too. Carr hit a free throw with time expired to edge Cardozo, 61–60, right before Christmas, although the Clerks eventually went on to become the Inter-High champs that year. Coaches from the universities of Virginia, Duke, Wake Forest, Syracuse, and West Virginia were on hand to scout Carr.

A couple of days after the calendar flipped to 1967, Carr pumped in 22 points. Williams had 13 to go with 14 rebounds as the Trojans blasted one of Maryland's top teams, Fairmont Heights, 85–52. "It's the worst beating I've taken in 17 years here," said Fairmont Heights coach Ken Freeman.

But none of those big wins meant much unless the Trojans could finally knock off DeMatha. That's exactly what happened in late January. In front of a raucous crowd of 2,800 people in Arlington, Mackin ended DeMatha's 24-game winning streak and its own years of frustration with a 56–51 victory. Naturally, Carr led the way with a game-high 19 points, including a three-point play with 2:10 left. He also led all rebounders with 10. Savoy added 15 points as he and Ford helped force 17 DeMatha turnovers.

To put the victory in perspective, consider this: The Stags had gone 67–1 in Catholic League play since the start of the 1960–61 season. Their only loss in that six-year span came at the hands of St. John's and their standout jumping-jack forward Bobby Lewis in 1963.

To no one's surprise, Mackin took over the top spot in the local high school polls that came out the next day. It was the Trojans' first-ever view from the top.

"Trying to reach the level that Morgan has established at DeMatha has helped us," Furlong said. "DeMatha has pride; they've had it for a long time. And now we have it. Morgan built up that pride, and the kids who play for him each year live up to it. I hope we can continue it, just like DeMatha has."

Nobody at Mackin wanted to stop there though. Carr and his teammates wanted the big prize—the Catholic League title. DeMatha had won it six years in a row; they'd win it another nine years in a row beginning in 1967–68. But this year belonged to Mackin and Carr.

The Trojans made sure of that, five weeks after knocking off DeMatha the first time. They met the Stags again in the first week of March to wrap up the league title in front of 8,500 people at Cole Field House, but the change in venue made little difference. Mackin prevailed, 54–48, with Carr scoring 21 points, including six straight free throws down the stretch to keep DeMatha at bay.

"We just kept knocking at the door so many times," said Carr, who'd surpassed 2,000 career points in the first quarter of that game. "Eventually we were able to get through. It was getting frustrating being No. 2 for so many years."

Mackin never finished No. 1 again, but not for lack of trying. The Trojans handed DeMatha its only loss in 1967–68 and remained a perennial contender for area honors through much of the 1970s and 1980s before the school, always on the brink of financial collapse, finally closed in 1989.

Coach Furlong lost his job after the 1970–71 season following a clash with the administration. He felt that the clergymen who ran the school were out of touch with the times, and he said so. The reward for that kind of honesty was a pink slip. Still, he'd established a tradition of excellence, going 215–67 in 10 years at Mackin.

Even after Furlong was gone, that winning tradition continued with Coaches Harry Rest and Steve Hocker, and outstanding players such as Donald "Duck" Williams (who went on to Notre Dame), Anthony "Jo Jo" Hunter (Maryland), and Johnny Dawkins (Duke). Furlong and his players had unquestionably established a winning tradition.

"I was very happy to be No. 2," Furlong said. "Mackin wasn't anywhere near No. 2 when I got there. You're facing the best coach in the country with the best players. We had some very, very tough games with them."

In the Inter-High League, Cardozo climbed back on top once again during the middle of the 1960s, winning three league titles in four years. Those three championships, combined with the three straight league titles they had won in 1957–59, made Cardozo the most successful Inter-High basketball program during the first dozen years after integration. In some years, the Clerks were better than in others. But they were always good, and the program's sustained success could be attributed to two factors—its faculty and topography.

Frank Bolden, who became the basketball coach in the early 1950s, was responsible for much of the program's success. Bolden directed Cardozo to a 188–55 record in a dozen years at the helm, winning five Inter-High titles. During a four-year stretch that included the three straight titles, Bolden's teams won 46 of 48 league games. Cardozo also won the first two City Title Games in 1957 and 1958, stunning heavily favored Carroll in the latter contest.

The bald Bolden was a distinguished, gentlemanly presence as coach, always preaching discipline and fundamentals. Eventually, he became an assistant principal at Cardozo and later the head of physical education instruction for all DC schools.

How good a coach was he? When John Thompson became the first African

American coach to win an NCAA title at Georgetown in 1984, he cited Bolden and Spingarn's Dave Brown as two coaches who could have done the same thing, had they been given the opportunity.

Thompson was hardly alone in his high opinion of Bolden. "To me, he was the best of all those [Inter-High] coaches," said DeMatha's Morgan Wootten.

But it was Bolden's fate, as it was Brown's, to coach in the days right before and right after integration, when the world was not yet ready for the idea of a black man coaching white kids at any level beyond high school. That hardly diminished the accomplishments of either man. Both won and won big before high school sports in the District were integrated, as well as afterward. Both men—and they were hardly alone among Inter-High coaches in this regard—were the best kind of coaches, as they taught life lessons as well.

"Coach Bolden impressed upon us the importance of discipline and how that would help you later in life," noted Vaughn Kimbrough, who played point guard at Cardozo for Bolden and his successor, Harold Deane, in the mid-1960s. After Kimbrough finished college, Bolden helped him get a job with the DC public school system, in which he eventually became an elementary school principal. "I think I led some people down the right path," Bolden said modestly.

In terms of basketball, Bolden was a fanatic about conditioning. He made sure his players were ready for the rigors of the season by making them run the steep hills of 13th Street Northwest right next to the school. Over time, dozens of Cardozo players came to know every dip and divot of those hills. When it was raining or snowing or too cold to run outside, Bolden had his players run the halls to maintain their stamina. Bolden had begun his teaching and coaching career with the track team at Dunbar in the 1940s. The joke around Cardozo was that Bolden never really stopped coaching track; he just did it during basketball season.

All the players grumbled about Bolden's methods, huffing and puffing as they slogged up and down those hills. But the old track coach knew what he was doing. His teams were known for their refusal to wilt in the fourth quarter and their penchant for coming on strong late in the season. He always believed conditioning was the reason.

"He was a task master, but he got us in shape," recalled Kimbrough, who played on Bolden's last two teams that won Inter-High titles in 1964 and 1965. "Running the hill was a rite of passage. Even though it was trying, it was something we enjoyed doing. It was part of the territory, and it prepared us for the last three or four minutes of the fourth quarter."

Kimbrough was intimately familiar with the other cornerstone of Bolden's philosophy—the importance of point guard play. If Bolden was a stickler for conditioning, he was just as fixated on the play of his guards, especially his playmakers.

"We had some of the toughest little point guards," Bolden said. "We had some excellent, excellent ball handlers. I used to tell them, 'Until we get somebody out there who can handle that "pill," we're not going anywhere.' Those little guys can move the ball to the basket, and that always helps to even things up when you lack size."

In the 1950s Bolden had a succession of small guards, including Richard "Rip" Scott, Hillary Brown, and Everett Lucas, who ran things the way he wanted. If they didn't, there was always a spot on the bench waiting for them. None of the three was taller than six feet, but all could play. Brown poured in 29 points in the 1957 City Title Game victory over Gonzaga; Scott lit up Carroll for 21 in the 1958 game. When Cardozo won its third straight Inter-High title in 1959, Lucas scored a team-high 15 in the championship game victory over Spingarn. He also directed an offense that turned the ball over just eight times, while Spingarn turned it over 23 times in a 68–58 defeat.

In the 1960s it was no different. Spingarn (1960–61) and Eastern (1962–63) won back-to-back Inter-High titles, but Cardozo was back on top the next two seasons, Bolden's last two as coach, and then won another in 1966–67, the second year after Harold Deane took over the program.

Right to the end, Bolden was focused on point guard play. Two-time All-Met Billy Gaskins, the star of the coach's last two Cardozo teams, was an accomplished shooter whose long-range, high-arching jumpers were widely imitated throughout the city. Coming into the program, Kimbrough had assumed he would also become another scorer, like Gaskins. Bolden had other ideas. On the first day of practice, he handed Kimbrough the instruction manual "The Role of the Point Guard," and Kimbrough's responsibilities were set thereafter.

"I was a shooter on the playgrounds," Kimbrough said. "My idea of being a guard was being a shooter. But that book kind of paved the way to show me what my role really was. I wasn't supposed to be shooting all the time. I was supposed to be facilitating."

So he facilitated. Kimbrough had big shoes to fill. He had to replace Phil "Bo" Scott at the point, a player so in sync with Bolden that it was said that the coach never had to correct him.

For the 1964 Inter-High championship, center Aaron Webster scored 21 points, including the game-winning, last-second corner jumper, and Scott added 19 to lead the Clerks over Jim McBride (26 points) and Dunbar, 64–62. The next year, Gaskins fired away from the outside, Kimbrough handled the ball, and up-and-coming Ed Epps contributed inside and out to help Cardozo to a second straight title. The Clerks topped the McKinley Trainers, 76–67, for Bolden's last title, with Kimbrough scoring a game-high 23 points.

"All of the guys had confidence in their own abilities," Kimbrough said. "Billy was the marquee player, but the rest of us thought we were just as good. We were a good crew. The nucleus was pretty levelheaded."

Epps, who kept improving throughout his high school career, starred on Deane's Inter-High title winners in 1967 as the lone senior on a very young Clerks team.

That was a role for which Epps was ideally suited. Years later, he became a beloved coach and mentor to hundreds of District kids.

It should be added that Cardozo achieved all this success without a home court. Cardozo had moved into what was previously Central High School—the alma mater of actress Helen Hayes and ex-FBI chief J. Edgar Hoover—in the early 1950s, only to find that the building lacked a regulation-size gym. So from then on, the Clerks played their home games at McKinley, Theodore Roosevelt, DeMatha, or wherever they could.

Inadequate facilities began to become a big problem for the Inter-High in the 1960s as schools became overcrowded and fell into disrepair. For much of the decade, only about half of the league's teams played in gyms that league officials considered suitable for interscholastic games. Consequently, many league games were played on neutral courts. At a time when the school system was becoming increasingly diverse, its dearth of adequate athletic facilities was another reminder that complete equality remained an elusive goal.

Ken Freeman, the longtime basketball coach at Fairmont Heights in Prince George's County, Maryland, knew something about inequity. He began his coaching career in virtual obscurity in 1950 because Fairmont Heights was a segregated school serving the county's African American community. The Hornets didn't get much mention in the local papers at first. Prince George's County was far slower than neighboring Montgomery County to integrate, but gradually things began to change. Fairmont Heights' Wilbur "Ducie" Smith earned All-Met honors in the *Post* and the *Star* in 1956 and 1957, the first player from a segregated Maryland school to achieve such recognition.

Smith was just one in a long line of big-time scorers who played for Freeman's Hornets from the early 1950s to the early 1970s. In 1957 Smith scored 39 points in the state Negro basketball championship game as Fairmont whipped the Bates High Giants of Annapolis, 97–48. The description of Smith in the *Star*'s All-Met profile noted that he was a fine outside shooter who could also dunk, despite being just six foot three. As a senior, he led the entire metropolitan area in scoring with a 31-point average.

It was Freeman's good fortune that he always seemed to have talented players such as Smith at his disposal. He was doubtless helped by the school's location, which was just over the line from the eastern edge of Washington, DC, where some of the best pickup basketball in the city was being played at places like the Watts Branch and Kelly Miller playgrounds. "Those were just tremendously talented teams, from top to bottom," recalled Earl Hawkins, a big star at rival Gwynn Park in the late 1960s.

"I always had good players who were easy to coach," Freeman told the *Post*. "I was tough on them, but I felt I was fair. Some I had to make do the right thing, but I enjoyed every team I coached."

And Freeman, to his credit, never tried to overcoach the talent on hand. If a player made a mistake with a turnover or a bad shot, Freeman pulled him aside, told him to make up for it on defense, and sent him back into the fray. Because Freeman's approach was low key—gentle, even—his players remained fiercely loyal. It wasn't uncommon for his former players to come back and scrimmage against the current varsity to help them improve. Freeman's players wanted to play for him.

"He knew your potential, and he knew how to get into your mind and get you where you needed to be," said Julius "Pete" Johnson, a two-time All-Met who starred on the state championship team in 1964. "He was just excellent at that. It was a wonderful atmosphere to play in. You just really wanted to get out there and please him on the court."

Because Freeman was an unassuming man who coached with a light touch, the talent his players possessed was able to express itself. Freeman's teams played up-tempo, running and pressing opponents into submission.

"He had such dominant personnel," recalled Larry Gandee, who coached the Gwynn Park Yellow Jackets, one of Fairmont Heights' top rivals. "He wanted kids who could shoot from the perimeter, and his big guys were [supposed] to rebound. He didn't run anything super-organized, but everybody knew their roles."

According to Ken Ledbetter, who played on some of Freeman's standout teams in the 1960s, "All his teams were fast-breaking. Get the ball off the backboard and get it out quick to the wings. Practice was all run, run, run."

On the bench, Freeman was always calm, and his players adopted the same approach. Even in a tight game, the Hornets could almost always be counted on to make the right play, and that helps explain Freeman's seven state titles, the most by any coach in Maryland public school history.

"He always sat there like nothing was ever wrong," Johnson said. "That's the way coach Freeman was. We became exactly like him. If we made mistakes, we didn't worry about it."

Though known for a laissez-faire approach, Freeman wasn't the kind of coach who just rolled out the basketballs at the start of practice. He cared about the youth in his community and was known to open up the gym on weekends so the kids would have some place where they wouldn't get into trouble.

Freeman took great pride in his program, to the point where he made sure players' uniforms, shoes, and socks were properly cared for. If you arrived early enough before a game, you'd see Freeman, in his practice togs, sweeping out the gym himself before he changed into a suit. When it came to appearances, everything with Freeman had to be just so. If nobody could sweep out the gym in a way that met his standards, well, then he'd do it himself. "Kenny was just a first-class person," said Gandee. "He was a real gentleman."

Because of Freeman's understated personality, players new to the program might have thought they could take advantage of his pleasant nature. They were quickly disabused of that notion. Freeman's players from the mid-1960s still talk about the time one of their teammates fell behind in his classwork, and the coach found out about it. He simply pulled a desk out of a classroom, carried it to the gym, and made the offender complete his assignments while the rest of the players practiced.

"He could let you know where his foot was going if you didn't get it right," said Ledbetter. "He'd get somebody else out there to take your place."

After a decade at Fairmont Heights, Freeman's skill and expertise began to find a much wider audience. In 1962 Maryland officials finally saw the light and opened up the state basketball tournament to all comers, including the all-black schools such as Fairmont Heights. That was also the first year that Freeman's team was able to compete in the county league. Despite being lumped in with much bigger schools such as High Point and Bladensburg (a Class AA state finalist in 1962), Fairmont Heights captured the county title (though it lost in the playoffs). They repeated, winning the county title in 1963–64.

That 1964 team, led by All-Met Pete Johnson, went even further, winning the Class A state title with a 72–55 victory over the Beall Mountaineers. Johnson scored a game-high 25 points, including eight straight in the fourth quarter despite his injuring an ankle earlier.

"That state title was a highlight because Fairmont Heights was never a part of anything like that before," said Johnson, who joined the Towson Generals' Billy Jones at Maryland to break the color line in Atlantic Coast Conference basketball. "It gave the school some credibility. The school was excited, the community was excited. Now we belonged, because we had won."

Memorable though it was, that was just the beginning. Freeman's team wasn't able to compete for the state title in 1965 because of an eligibility problem with a player who had transferred from the District. But Fairmont won state titles—four in Class A, one in Class B—in five of the next six seasons, including four straight from 1968 to 1971. During that run, Freeman guided such All-Met players as John Hampton, Eugene Oliver, and Jerome McDaniel, who was twice picked to the *Post's* first team.

McDaniel and the Hornets dominated in the state tournament, trashing the Southern Bulldogs of Anne Arundel County, 87–57, in the 1971 state semifinals. In the finals it was even more lopsided, as Freeman's fast-breaking Hornets trampled the Atholton Raiders of Howard County, 120–69. McDaniel, with 49 points in the two games, was voted state tournament MVP. The Hornets' total of 120 points in the final and 207 points in two state tournament games are records that still stand more than 40 years later.

Eventually, Freeman decided to move into school administration, and the rules at the time prevented administrators from coaching varsity sports. "I just had to help kids from another angle," he said. Though he was leaving the sidelines, Freeman could take comfort in the knowledge that he was leaving quite a legacy. Since the state began separating schools into four divisions in 1961, only his Fairmont Heights teams won four straight Maryland state championships.

Fairmont Heights might have enjoyed even greater success had it been able to hang on to Mark Christian and Harold Fox. Those two developed into a powerful inside-outside combination as the Northwestern Wildcats won back-to-back Class AA state titles in 1967 and 1968. Both players had started out at Fairmont Heights. But when Prince George's County changed its policies (left over from the days of segregation), black students were able to attend their neighborhood high schools rather than getting shipped all over the county. That's how Christian and Fox wound up at their neighborhood school of Northwestern High in Hyattsville, where they should have been all along.

The six-foot-three Christian was an energetic inside player and a good enough all-around athlete to win state track titles at 100 and 220 yards. He was also a team leader, a player who always was able to keep his teammates in line. Fox, however, was Northwestern's star, a rare three-time All-Met who could score, pass, and rebound. Fox was smooth too. He never looked as though he was working hard, but he was. He never looked that quick, either—until he went by you.

"He could handle it well, get to the rim and shoot," recalled Billy Gordon, whose Richard Montgomery team lost to Northwestern in the 1967 state final. "If you tried to muscle him, he'd go around you. If you laid off him, he'd shoot the jumper."

Gordon teamed with Willie Allen, an athletic six-foot-six rebounder with telephone pole arms, to win the Class AA state title in 1966. Allen, like Fox, was also a three-time All-Met. He and the hot-shooting Gordon returned for the 1966–1967 season, making the Rockets a heavy favorite to repeat as state champs, something no school had done in Class AA since Blair had in 1961–62.

Throughout that 1966–67 season, Northwestern and Richard Montgomery eyed each other from a distance, hoping for the chance to meet for the title. Allen, Gordon, Fox, and Christian had become buddies during the summer on the playgrounds, adding another intriguing element to their rivalry.

"We think we have the best team in the area, as well as the state," Christian had said at the time. "I wish we could play Mackin or DeMatha, but beating Richard Montgomery would be satisfying enough. I'd enjoy playing against Willie too. He's great, so it would be a real challenge."

In general, Northwestern's players didn't feel they got the respect and attention Richard Montgomery did, so the desire to face the Rockets in the state tournament grew with each successive week. By the end of February 1967, the teams clearly were headed for a showdown. Northwestern was 18–1 and had won 16 in a row.

Richard Montgomery was 18–0 and had won 24 straight, dating to the end of its 1966 championship season. Allen (25.2 points per game) and Gordon (21.2) were one of the area's most prolific duos, as were Fox (22.7) and Christian (21.1).

In the state semifinals, Northwestern rocked South Hagerstown, 77–41, and Richard Montgomery dispatched Towson, 82–66, as Gordon poured in 36 points. The showdown so many had anticipated would finally come to pass.

The big matchup turned out to be no contest at all. Northwestern dominated from the outside in a 72–41 victory, an outcome that stunned everyone. The Wild-cats led 38–11 at the half as Richard Montgomery missed 24 of 28 shots in front of a sellout crowd of 12,500 fans at Cole Field House. "I didn't believe it myself," Fox said later.

Rockets coach Earl Walthall, worried that Northwestern might try something unorthodox to stop his two big scorers, had made some last-minute changes to the Richard Montgomery offense. All it did was throw his players out of synch though. Gordon finished with five points and Allen managed just four. "We should have just stayed with what we were doing," Gordon recalled. "It was an absolute disaster. We were just terrible."

Christian was the tournament MVP, having scored 37 points and grabbed 45 rebounds in the Wildcats' two victories. Fox added 36 points and 31 rebounds.

Christian was gone the next year, and Fox was the lone returning starter for the Wildcats, leading many to conclude that Northwestern had no chance to repeat. But Fox and his rapidly improving teammates proved everyone wrong again. Fox started with a bang and never let up in 1967–68. He scored 84 points in his first three games, including a 27-point, 20-rebound performance in a 62–58 victory over Bladensburg.

With Christian gone from the middle, Fox was driving to the basket more, putting himself in better position to rebound. He averaged 14 rebounds per game, carrying the load until complementary players such as Mel Francisco and Doug Walls adjusted to new roles.

"[Harold's] the best player in the area," said Northwestern coach Bill Longs-worth. "I believe in him. He's an instinctive player. He knows what he has to do and he does it."

Fox said that pride was driving him and his teammates. "It means something to all of us to be state champions," he explained. "We don't want to give up the title."

When Northwestern found itself in dire straits, Fox always seemed to have an answer. Most of the time, he *was* the answer. Northwestern took over first place in the Prince George's Class AA standings and stayed there for all of January. But a loss to Bladensburg High in early February created a tie between the two schools.

The next time out against the Oxon Hill High School Clippers, Fox took mat-ters into his own hands. He poured in 64 points in a 107–83 rout, getting 28 in the final quarter, for 41 in the second half. His total was the second highest in metro area history at the time, behind only the 74 points scored by Mount Vernon's Marty

Lentz six years before. Fox topped Elgin Baylor's total of 63 on a layup with 20 seconds left and walked off the floor to a standing ovation. He might have diversified his game in his final high school season to accommodate the rest of the team, but there was no doubt that Fox could score—anywhere, anytime. He finished the year with a 31-point average.

Northwestern made it back to the state finals, thanks in part to Fox's 41-point outburst in a 74–63 semifinal victory over the Dundalk Owls. He shot 15 for 28 from the floor, grabbed nine rebounds, and handed out six assists, including a couple on flashy behind-the-back passes.

That set up another marquee matchup in the final against Bethesda's Walt Whitman High Vikings and its own prolific scorer, Gary Browne, who was averaging 32.6 points per game. With another sellout crowd at Cole Field House, Fox once again demonstrated a flair for the dramatic. He took a nasty fall late in the first half and went to the locker room while the game continued. Fox wasn't with his teammates when they came out to warm up for the second half, but he trotted onto the floor to wild cheers just before the second-half tip.

With Northwestern clinging to a 56–55 lead with about five minutes left, Fox scored eight points during the decisive 15–4 Wildcat run, sewing up a 71–63 victory and a second straight title. Walls had stepped up nicely, scoring 20 points in the final, while Francisco added 11 points and 17 rebounds. But the day belonged to Fox, who finished with 21 points, 21 rebounds, and seven assists to cap his brilliant high school career.

"He was probably the best we ever went against," Gwynn Park coach Larry Gandee said. "He just played with people. He could do anything he wanted to on the basketball court. He's at the top of the list for me."

In Washington, as in many metropolitan areas, there was always a healthy debate over who had better basketball—the public schools or the private schools. Since the demise of the City Title Game in 1962, one could settle that debate only theoretically. The Catholic League schools and the Inter-High schools met only occasionally during the regular season during the 1960s, but there was never much at stake except for another win or loss for the teams involved.

All that changed in 1967. Officials from the two leagues were still wary of getting together for any type of championship game, and perhaps rightly so. No one wanted a repeat of the violence and chaos that had erupted after the city championship football game five years before. So it took outside organizers, with an eye on the profit motive, to bring together the best teams in the two leagues.

It started with the M Club, the fund-raising arm of the University of Maryland Athletic Department. Officials in College Park had seen the kind of interest that a Power Memorial–DeMatha matchup could generate, and they began the practice of hosting a pair of doubleheaders at Cole Field House between two New York teams and two Catholic League teams two years before. The gate was much smaller than anticipated, so the M Club decided that in 1967–68 the mid-season tournament would feature the first- and second-place teams in the Catholic League (DeMatha and whoever else) playing the first- and second-place teams in the Inter-High.

The organizers of the Knights of Columbus Tournament at the end of the season followed suit. Previously, their event had been for private schools only, but the rules were relaxed for the 1968 event so that an Inter-High team could participate. Neither event carried quite the cachet of an actual City Title Game, but the M Club doubleheader and the Knights of Columbus Tournament at least offered chances for the best teams in the two leagues to go head-to-head.

The timing couldn't have been better. The two events—one in the middle of the season, one at the end—created a great deal of excitement and speculation as they brought together two of the top teams and some of the decade's top players.

DeMatha entered the 1968 M Club Tournament as strong as ever. The Stags were top ranked at 18–0 and had beaten all but two of their opponents by at least 20 points. McKinley, meanwhile, was 9–2 and beginning a remarkable two-year run of 34 straight victories over their Inter-High opponents. Their matchup on the first night of the two-day event was all anyone could have asked. DeMatha edged McKinley, 60–59, on a late corner jumper by guard Aubrey Nash, who would be named All-Met after averaging 19 points per game. Nash had also quarterbacked the Stags' football team to a league title, earning All-Met honors in that sport too.

The game drew a crowd of 7,356 fans on that early February night, even though a bad snowstorm had hit the DC area. The crowd was equal to the two-day totals for the Cole doubleheaders of the previous two years. The next night, DeMatha (20–0) blasted Cardozo (14–1), and McKinley handled Mackin with 11,246 people on hand.

As fate would have it, the Stags and Trainers met again for the Knights of Columbus Tournament title at the end of the season and staged another classic. DeMatha came into the final 26–1. Led by All-Met Ernest Lewis, McKinley was 18–3 and had won 17 of its last 18, with the lone loss coming from DeMatha.

McKinley, buoyed by an effective zone defense, held an 11-point lead early in the fourth quarter before DeMatha roared back. The Stags rallied to take the lead before McKinley's Michael Bossard forced overtime by hitting a short hook with four seconds left. In the extra session, Nash (21 points) took over with a basket and a couple of free throws as DeMatha pulled out a 63–58 victory for its sixth straight Knights of Columbus title.

Those two clashes set the stage for the 1968–69 season, when the DeMatha-McKinley rivalry reached its zenith. By that time, James Brown—who would shine at Harvard and then become the host of the NFL halftime show on CBS—was DeMatha's star. Brown, who actually grew up in the same Northeast DC neighborhood as McKinley's players, was greatly admired in the subculture of DC playground basketball for his exceptional leaping ability. Even when he was just a young reserve on the DeMatha roster, people would come to games in the hope of seeing him go up for a rebound or to block a shot. Even the coolest of the cool dug the earnest young DeMatha star for what he could do on the court.

But Brown had a much wider appeal as well. The smiling, genial gentleman you see on television is just the same off-camera as on, and he always has been. For all his athletic talent, Brown also has a gift for charming anyone he encounters. He seemingly remembers the name and life story of every cafeteria worker or custodian at DeMatha and, in later years, every production aide at CBS and every doorman in New York. By Morgan Wootten's estimation, Brown was the most popular student at DeMatha. "And it wasn't even close," the coach said.

Brown's personality was so engaging that his teammates got used to having their parents and brothers and sisters bypass them right after the games so they could rush over and get a hug or a kind word from Brown. "Everybody loved James," recalled Ray Hite, who became the outside shooting complement to Brown's powerful inside game that season.

McKinley didn't lack for star power, either. Coach McKinley Armstrong (who won three Inter-High titles in his first four years as coach) taught basketball and life skills, even if some of his lessons seemed a bit harsh to the teenagers in his charge. He yelled at and drove them because he cared. He even used his spare time to paint banners on the gymnasium wall to commemorate his team's tournament wins and championships.

"He cares about a lot more than whether we win or lose," center Michael Bossard said at the time. "He cares what kind of men we are, whether we can get into college—things like that. If you can't play for him, you can't play for anybody."

The Trainers could certainly play. Four of their five starters—Bossard, Tim Bassett, Ronnie Hogue, and Randolph "Apple" Milam—gained some kind of All-Met recognition after the 1968–69 season. The one starter who didn't, speedy little point guard Kevin Tatum, was the one who made the Trainers' fast break go.

They all had their roles. The six-foot-six Bossard was the go-to guy inside when McKinley needed a basket. The similarly sized Bassett was less polished and responsible primarily for hitting the boards. Professionally, he went the furthest of any one of them, playing alongside Julius "Doctor J" Erving in the ABA and, after the ABA-NBA merger, for several more years in the NBA with the New Jersey Nets.

Hogue was the outside shooter. He and Bassett later broke the basketball color line at the University of Georgia. Milam was the swingman, the wild card, and the kind of player who was good, who knew it, and who had no problem taking over in a tight situation.

"He dressed sharp, he looked good, the girls loved him," Bassett recalled. "He was not intimidated by anyone. That's the kind of guy you need on your team when the Xs and Os don't work for you. You gotta have a guy on your team who can get it done."

Those starting five, plus reserves Tyrone Bradshaw and Robert Brown, were known collectively as the "Magnificent Seven." They formed one of the best, and best-remembered, teams ever in the Inter-High.

Naturally, the Trainers wanted another crack at DeMatha, believing that with another year of seasoning, they'd take the Stags. Their matchup in the M Club Tournament in February 1969 was widely anticipated throughout the city. The buildup for the game was considerable. McKinley was 13–0 and top ranked in the area going into the two-day event. The Trainers had just flexed their muscles with an astonishing 136–58 victory over the Chamberlain Shipmates as Milam scored 28; Bossard, 25; and Hogue, 22. Bassett grabbed 27 rebounds.

But the Trainers were so focused on beating DeMatha (15–2) that they looked past Mackin and were beaten on the opening night of the M Club Tournament, 68–65. Before a crowd of 9,674 folks at Cole Field House the next night, determined to redeem themselves, the Trainers handled DeMatha for the victory they had so long sought, 68–55. Hogue, hitting from the wings, led McKinley with 20 points. James Brown was even better, finishing with a game-high 26 points, but not even he could save the Stags.

As good as McKinley was, the margin was still a surprise. DeMatha didn't lose often, especially to local teams. When it did, the margin was usually a basket or two. Nobody could remember the Stags' last loss by double figures to a local team.

As fate would have it, the two teams weren't finished with each other. Both were invited to join the field for the Knights of Columbus Tournament in mid-March. By that time, McKinley's record stood at 24–1; DeMatha was 22–3.

There was no guarantee, given the overall strength of the tournament field, that the two teams would reach the final. Nevertheless, that's what everyone hoped for, including the participants. "Oh, man, do we want another shot at McKinley!" Brown said before the tournament.

It was an unusual position for DeMatha—being the hunter and not the hunted. McKinley had already been voted No. 1 in the *Star*'s final poll, thus denying DeMatha the honor that was one of its goals every season.

The Stags' chances of capturing the Knights of Columbus title seemed all but gone when Brown collapsed during DeMatha's semifinal victory over the St. Agnes Cathedral High Stags of Long Island. The pressures of the recruiting process— somehow his home telephone number got out, and James had been besieged by college coaches—had taken their toll. A victim of his own graciousness and generosity, Brown was hospitalized because of "physical and emotional exhaustion," according to doctors. Had it been easier for James to tell people no, he might not have suffered from so much stress.

With Brown under orders to rest at home for the championship game against McKinley, a rout seemed likely. Wootten, trying to fire up his undermanned team, draped Brown's warm-up jacket over a seat on the bench. No one was permitted to sit there, but his teammates still had to find a way to make up for the absence of his scoring, rebounding, and leadership.

That's just what they did. With Ray Hite scoring 31 points and a specially devised blitz-trap defense that confused McKinley, DeMatha rolled to a stunning 95–69 victory and another Knights of Columbus Tournament title. After the final buzzer, Brown, who couldn't stay away, came out of the stands to be with his teammates as they accepted their trophy. He'd left his sick bed, slipped out of his house, and found his way to Cole Field House to witness one of the landmark games in Washington area high school basketball history.

The loss stung McKinley, but the Trainers already had wrapped up the No. 1 ranking in the area regardless of their loss to DeMatha. Or had they?

McKinley was No. 1 in the *Star*, no question about it. The *Post* was another matter. Typically, both newspapers released their final rankings on the first Monday in March, unwilling to wait until the various postseason tournaments had wrapped up. In 1969 the *Star* continued to observe this policy. The *Post* did not, which was the source of quite a controversy that March.

The Knights of Columbus Tournament was typically held the last week in March, but since it was held earlier than usual that year, the *Post* decided it wouldn't release its final high school basketball poll until after the championship game. The problem was, the newspaper didn't tell anybody. Coach Armstrong had accepted the bid to the Knights of Columbus Tournament with the understanding that it wouldn't affect the final rankings, which, he assumed, had already been compiled. He argued—with some merit—that the local rankings shouldn't be affected by how a team like McKinley (or DeMatha) might do against out-of-town competition. But on the morning on March 17, the *Post* sports section featured the final top 20 ranking with DeMatha (25–3) at No. 1 and McKinley (26–2) in the runner-up spot.

The voting set off howls of protest from McKinley supporters. About 1,600 of the school's 1,900 students signed a petition protesting the ranking, charging the *Post* with "obvious bias against the public school teams." McKinley principal William H. Rumsey weighed in as well, claiming the ranking—though not racial in nature, he emphasized—involved "a CYO [Catholic Youth Organization], suburbia, closed-shop type of bias."

The next day, some 200 McKinley students protested outside the *Post*'s offices, and officials from the newspaper listened to their grievances. Trying to resolve the dispute amicably, the newspaper tried to drum up support for a third game, winner take all, but nothing ever came of it. Seeing no way out, the paper reversed itself and reinstalled McKinley as the area's No. 1 team. "The *Washington Post* considers it fair at this point to cancel its final ranking and revert to the previous listings as its final ranking for the season, moving McKinley Tech back into the No. 1 position," officials from the newspaper explained.

That was fine by McKinley. Even DeMatha players such as Brown and Hite conceded that the Trainers probably had the best team that year. But the decision irked Wootten, perhaps even more so because officials from the *Post* pleaded with him to let them flip-flop on their final decision.

"You can't ask me to do the rankings," Wootten recalled telling editors from the *Post*. "If I said that was all right, I couldn't look my kids in the eye ever again."

Forty years after the fact, the episode still bothered Wootten. "It was a fiasco," he said, rendering his final judgment.

Presentation of Interhigh Championship Basketball Trophy

From left: Spingarn's co-captains Leonard Frazier and Ollie Johnson, who teamed up with Dave Bing to win the DC Inter-High Titles in 1960 and 1961, and the City Championship vs. DeMatha in 1961, stand behind DC Supervising Director of Athletics Hardy Pearce to present the 1961 Inter-High Championship Trophy to Coach (Dr.) William Roundtree.

Coach (Dr.) William Roundtree poses with his 1960 Inter-High championship team. Dave Bing is in the front row, third from the right. Roundtree's practice of giving everyone playing time likely resulted in lower numbers for Bing than he would have had otherwise.

BASKETBALL

1959–60 Green Wave Triple Champions Prevail!

1959–60 Spingarn Green Wave yearbook captures Dave Bing (22) dribbling past Eastern High.

ALL
OF
THEM
RIGHT
IN
THE
BASKETS

Inter-High champion Spingarn team's yearbook page dedicated to the 1959-60 basketball season.

# VARSITY BASKETBALL, 1961-62

### GREEN WAVE'S SUCCESS
By Tyrone Thompson

In a three year period the Spingarn Varsity has won 60 games while losing only 6 games.

The 1961-62 "Green Wave" Basketball Team, *Defending City Champions*, had another successful season, winning 19 games while losing only 3 games. The team was successful in winning the East-Division title for the fourth straight year. Also for the fourth straight year the team was selected as *one* of the East-Division representatives in the Inter-High Play-Offs between the East and West Divisions.

Spingarn was runner-up in the Inter-High Championship Competition. For three consecutive years the Green Wave has had the honor of playing at Maryland University's Cole Field House in the championship games. During this period a total of 35,000 spectators witnessed the games. This year the team won the Consolation Trophy by beating Mackin, the Catholic League runner-up team for the city championship, by a score of 65-58 in overtime.

| | SCHEDULE | | |
|---|---|---|---|
| Springarn | 72 | Hoffman-Boston | 39 |
| Springarn | 84 | Parker-Gray | 53 |
| Springarn | 62 | Western | 51 |
| Springarn | 58 | Mackin | 44 |
| Springarn | 108 | Douglass | 38 |
| Springarn | 58 | "Alumni" | 59 |
| Springarn | 52 | Eastern | 47 |
| Springarn | 80 | Ballou | 49 |
| Springarn | 53 | McKinley | 54 |
| Springarn | 69 | Chamberlain | 52 |
| Springarn | 68 | Anacostia | 37 |
| Springarn | 83 | Phelps | 58 |
| Springarn | 73 | Eastern (overtime) | 68 |
| Springarn | 65 | Ballou | 32 |
| Springarn | 82 | American Univ. Frosh | 69 |
| Springarn | 55 | McKinley | 57 |
| Springarn | 77 | Chamberlain | 58 |
| Springarn | 62 | Anacostia | 46 |
| Springarn | 78 | Phelps | 51 |
| | **PLAY-OFFS** | | |
| Springarn | 74 | McKinley | 68 |
| Springarn | 78 | Coolidge | 61 |
| Springarn | 54 | Eastern | 59 |
| Springarn | 65 | Mackin (overtime) | 58 |

VARSITY TEAM MEMBERS —*Front Row*: Dawson, Kirkey, Hicks, Bing, Logan, Davis, Queen. *Second Row*: Hopkins, Campbell, Harrison, R. Hill, Phillips, Swilling. *Third Row*: Clayton, C. Hill, Jones, Robinson, Franklin. *Fourth Row*: Thompson, Assistant Coach George, Coach Rountree, Smith, McQueen.

TEAM MEMBERS Donald Hicks, Clarence Dawson, David Bing, Byron Kirkley, and Garland Logan present to Coach Rountree the Consolation Trophy they won for being the runner-up team in the Catholic-Public School Championship Competition for 1961-62.

93

Spingarn 1961–62 Green Wave yearbook page, including Dave Bing, summing up its season.

◄ DAWSON GOES HIGH FOR REBOUND against Eastern's Willie Johnson.

◄ GARLAND LOGAN OUTJUMPS Eastern for a tip.

At left: DONALD HICKS PASSES OFF to LOGAN for an easy basket.

## ACTION SHOTS

BYRON KIRKLEY GOES AROUND EASTERN PLAYER for a lay-up.

94

BING GOES LEFT!

## EASTERN Vs. SPINGARN

1961–62 yearbook page dedicated to the Spingarn-Eastern game.

TEAM MEMBERS Donald Hicks, Clarence Dawson, David Bing, Byron Kirkley, and Garland Logan present to Coach Rountree the Consolation Trophy they won for being the runner-up team in the Catholic-Public School Championship Competition for 1961-62.

Spingarn players Donald Hicks, Clarence Dawson, David Bing, Byron Kirkley, and Garland Logan present Coach (Dr.) William Roundtree with the Consolation Trophy as the runner-up team in the 1961–62 Catholic–Public School Championship Competition.

# VARSITY "S" CLUB HOLDS...

THE VARSITY "S" CLUB OF SPINGARN HIGH SCHOOL is composed of athletes who have earned letters for outstanding performance in varsity sports.

The club renders service to the school by furnishing ushers for assembly programs, guides for school visitors, and assistants for intra-mural and varsity basketball games.

OLD MEMBERS OF THE VARSITY "S" CLUB—*Front Row*: Byron Kirkley, Thomas Simmons, Maurice Hunt, James Davis, William Lindsay, David Bing. *Second Row*: Walter Harris, Thomas Queen, Garland Logan, Phillip Faxio, Wyzeal Scott, Wendell Anderson. *Third Row*: Melvin Moore, James Ware, Elmore Hunter, Johnnie Smith, Harold Williams, Louis Mack. *Fourth Row*: Paul Simmons, Raymond Scarborough, Albert Byrd, Earl Mayo, George Pace, Elmer Winters. *Fifth Row*: Mr. James J. Smith; sponsor of Spingarn Varsity "S" Club.

Dave Bing (front right) is among those honored for athletics and service in Spingarn's "S" Club in 1961–1962.

## THE SENIOR COUNCIL
### By Betty J. Daniels, Pres.

The Senior Council, 1962, was an organized group composed of three officers, eleven regular members, and eleven alternate members. The officers were Betty Daniels, president; Cheryl Roach, vice president; and Hazel Barksdale, secretary.

The purpose of the Council was to represent the entire senior class in executive meetings with the class officers. The Council presented to the officers suggestions and ideas that were the general opinion of the whole senior class, and in turn reported to the class section groups all decisions of the executive body.

One of the Council's first tasks was to select candidates, to hold an election, and to install senior class officers. Other tasks were the preparations for the senior class dance, the banquet, and the commencement exercises. All these tasks were supervised by the class sponsor, Miss Mary Price, and a faculty committee.

SUPERVISE the casting of ballots for the officers of Senior Class, 1962.

SENIOR COUNCIL—Vice-President, Cheryl Roach, and President, Betty Daniel confer with Senior Class President, William Lindsay.

BETTY DANIELS, PRESIDENT, INSTALLS SENIOR William Lindsay, *pres.*; Olivia Lucas, *vice pres.*; Jean Gibson, *sec'y.*; David Bing, *treas.*; Patricia Wood, parliamentarian; Byron Kirkley, Historian; Phillip Faxio, sergeant-at-arms; Wilson Breaker, chaplain.

131

**Dave Bing (5th from the left) is sworn in as Spingarn class treasurer 1961–62.**

# HI-Y CLUB

...erguson, William Smith. *Fourth Row:* Rountree (sponsor), David Mason.

Dr. William Rountree sponsors the Spingarn Hi-Y Club, a high school organization affiliated with the YMCA. The club attempts to create, maintain, and extend throughout the home, school, and community high standards of Christian character. It is composed of a group of Spingarn boys, banded together in fellowship and loyalty to their highest ideals, seeking to make living better for themselves, for their community, for their country, and for their world. Their personal ideals of the club are: clean speech, worthy scholarship, true sportsmanship, and Christian living. The club is pictured below.

**Dave Bing (center front) poses for the Spingarn yearbook with the members of the HI-Y club, associated with the YMCA in 1962.**

Coach (Dr.) William Roundtree exits his TWA flight to Spain on a 1962 summer break in a Spingarn yearbook photograph.

DR. ROUNTREE ARRIVES in Spain for his summer vacation via TWA Airlines.

Dave Bing, class of 1962, in the Spingarn yearbook.

Coach Morgan Wootten calls a huddle at the January 30, 1965, game with Power Memorial, a rematch of a rivalry that introduced the country to DC Metro basketball.

Roland Thomas "Sonny" Jackson ('62) attended Montgomery Blair High School with future journalist Carl Bernstein ('61), future Nixon speech writer and TV actor Ben Stein ('62), and actor Goldie Hawn ('63), who is in the second row from the top, far left.

Coach Morgan Wootten's DeMatha Stags starting 5 basketball team, taken before the 1967–68 season. Bottom row, left to right: Mark Edwards ('69), Ray Hite ('69), and Phil Whatley ('68). Top row, left to right: Bruce Mitchell ('68), James Brown ('69).

James Brown (41) of DeMatha takes a jump shot in heavy traffic against McKinley High.

Harold Fox (24) of Northwestern High School of Prince George's County gets some air to score on a layup against High Point in 1968. Other players are Billy Jett (45) of High Point and Charley Smith (30) of Northwestern. Northwestern would win the state championship in 1967 and 1968.

Senior James Brown of the DeMatha Stags during the 1968–69 season.

Senior James Brown of the DeMatha Stags during the 1968–69 season.

Senior James Brown (41) takes a jump shot against McKinley in 1969. McKinley defeated the Stags 68–55. In the rematch tournament semifinal, Brown sneaked out of his hospital bed to watch the Stags rout McKinley, 96–69.

On December 26, 1968, Michael Bossard (45) of McKinley prepares to go back up for a layup after grabbing a rebound against Ballou. Ken Clark (15) watches Bossard's move. The unbeaten McKinley Trainers won, 69–51.

# Number-One Rating

lfred West adds insult to Cardozo's injury in title runaway.

Another Trainer All-Met, Randolph Milam, scores two points on a fast break.

Coach Armstrong (right) directs his concern towards a referee's de
ision.

145

McKinley Trainers 1969 yearbook basketball page. Rudolph Milner (1) made All-Met that year.

An 18-year-old Harley "Skeeter" Swift (left) playing in a GW High School basketball game in 1965.

Skeeter Swift (left), John Wheatley (Wakefield '64) and John Hummer (Washington and Lee state champion '66 team) at a 2011 athletic reunion at George Washington Middle School. The reunion was organized by Swift just months after his diagnosis of lymphoma.

Alexandria basketball standout Skeeter Swift, shown during his college days at East Tennessee State University.

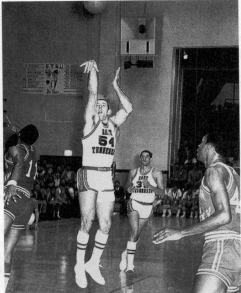

Skeeter Swift during his college days at East Tennessee State University (1966–1969).

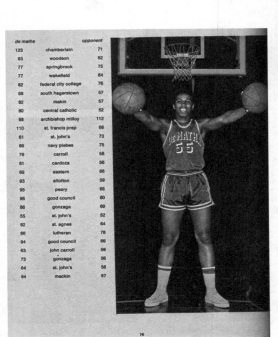

| de matha | | opponent |
|---|---|---|
| 123 | chamberlain | 71 |
| 83 | woodson | 62 |
| 77 | springbrook | 75 |
| 77 | wakefield | 64 |
| 82 | federal city college | 76 |
| 68 | south hagerstown | 57 |
| 82 | makin | 57 |
| 80 | central catholic | 52 |
| 88 | archbishop milloy | 112 |
| 110 | st. francis prep | 68 |
| 61 | st. john's | 73 |
| 89 | navy plebes | 75 |
| 79 | carroll | 58 |
| 61 | cardoza | 56 |
| 69 | eastern | 66 |
| 93 | altolton | 59 |
| 95 | peary | 65 |
| 98 | good council | 80 |
| 86 | gonzaga | 69 |
| 55 | st. john's | 52 |
| 82 | st. agnes | 64 |
| 86 | lutheran | 78 |
| 94 | good council | 66 |
| 63 | john carroll | 56 |
| 73 | gonzaga | 56 |
| 64 | st. john's | 58 |
| 84 | mackin | 67 |

76

DeMatha knew Adrian Dantley was special in his freshman year (1969) when the team went 25–2.

# CHAPTER FOUR

# The Seventies

**AS THE 1960S** drew to a close, an unlikely power emerged to challenge DeMatha, McKinley, and the rest for local supremacy. Tiny St. Anthony's, not far from Catholic University in northeast Washington, featured graduating classes of about 60 students and a gymnasium that held perhaps three times that many fans.

The Tonies hadn't been any kind of factor in local basketball since the great Jack Sullivan led them to a stunning upset in the *Washington Star*'s year-end tournament in 1953. In fact, after St. Anthony's went winless in the old Catholic League in 1960, the school dropped out of the conference. But by the end of the decade, the Tonies were back. In the interim, the school's basketball program had acquired one indisputable asset, Coach John Thompson.

After graduating from Archbishop Carroll in 1960, Thompson starred at Providence College and was drafted by the NBA's Boston Celtics. After two seasons with the Celtics, he was left exposed in the league's expansion draft. At that point, he decided he'd had enough of the travel and the lack of security of an NBA career, even though he had won a pair of championship rings. Thompson also sought some way to make a more meaningful contribution to the world, and professional basketball didn't offer that kind of reward.

So Thompson took a job with the United Planning Organization, part of President Lyndon Johnson's War on Poverty program. He also worked at the National 4-H Council. His old high school coach, Bob Dwyer, helped land him the coaching job at St. Anthony's. Thompson would work all day and trade his tie for a whistle after 5:00 p.m.

"We've been there before, and there's no reason we can't get there again," he said upon taking over at St. Anthony's. "We're going to start up the ladder."

It didn't take long. Thompson's Tonies went 12–12, 17–9, and 20–3 in his first three seasons. He had all five starters back for the 1969–70 season and figured to challenge for the top spot in the local high school polls. "The team made a goal for itself at the beginning of the season to try to become the area's No. 1–ranked team," Thompson said as that season started. "Unfortunately, we don't play DeMatha, so it might require a little luck to achieve that No. 1 ranking."

Thompson had put together a local juggernaut, using his contacts throughout the city to find players who could turn the program around. The Tonies and Stags, however, never did get together on the court in an actual game; that became a huge topic of discussion among local basketball fans and a source of friction between Thompson and DeMatha coach Morgan Wootten.

But St. Anthony's played everybody else that season. The Tonies blew out Bethesda–Chevy Chase in the opener, 83–47, beating a Barons team that eventually reached Maryland's state semifinals. They beat the DuVal Tigers, Maryland's eventual Class AA state champion; the always-tough Fairmont Heights; and the previously unbeaten Archbishop Carroll to start off 12–0. St. Anthony's also beat Eastern, the eventual Inter-High champ, on a basket by reserve guard Jonathan Smith with five seconds left. In that same game, forward Merlin Wilson (another backup) grabbed 18 rebounds and blocked four shots.

All-Met six-foot-nine center Donald Washington was the Tonies' star, a player sought by just about every major college program. Washington was a true Thompson find—an awkward but eager young man whom the coach discovered on the playgrounds playing in overalls ("like he'd been pitching hay," Thompson said). Thompson urged Washington to apply to St. Anthony's but soon went even further. Washington's mother had died and his father was hospitalized and seriously ill, so Thompson became Washington's legal guardian. Over the years, Thompson became known for his ability to tutor big men such as Georgetown University stars Patrick Ewing, Dikembe Mutombo, and Alonzo Mourning, but Washington was his first such project.

There was much about the program at St. Anthony's that would look familiar to those who admired Thompson's Georgetown University teams of later years. He had quality big men, aggressive guards, and a hard-nosed, physical defense. "You got playing time if you played good defense," said Dwight Datcher, who played for Thompson and later became St. Anthony's coach. "He didn't change that when he got to college."

Thompson himself displayed many of the traits he later became known for at Georgetown. He was fiercely protective of his players, blunt, and unconcerned about what anyone outside the school thought. Once during a game in Connecticut, he pulled his team off the floor and took a forfeit because he didn't think his team was getting fair treatment from the officials. He also sat out Don Washington for disciplinary reasons from a key game during the 1969–70 season, saying, "It was tough for me to do, but some things are more important than being No. 1."

He also lashed out when his team's invitation to a holiday tournament at Bishop O'Connell was withdrawn. The O'Connell Knights wanted DeMatha in its event and wanted St. Anthony's too. Wootten knew the game would be a huge draw and didn't want to play such a game only to have a third party profit handsomely from it. So he offered to withdraw. But O'Connell officials opted to keep the Stags and snub the Tonies.

"I guess it all depends on who you know, how good you are at politics," Thompson said. "If you know the ropes, you get invited. Having a good team isn't enough."

Thompson had reason to be upset. All of a sudden, many teams were finding reasons not to schedule St. Anthony's. The Tonies were a tough opponent for anyone. Consequently, teams that once eagerly accepted games with St. Anthony's were backing out or not returning Thompson's calls. "Nobody minded playing St. Anthony's when it was losing every game by 20 points," he noted sourly.

The Tonies missed a chance to meet the Stags in the postseason Knights of Columbus Tournament, the area's crowning event of the season. The Metro Conference (which included DeMatha) voted to send its best two teams to the Alhambra Catholic Invitational Tournament in Cumberland, Maryland, three hours away. All kinds of reasons were offered from all quarters for that decision. Conference officials said they thought the opportunity to travel made the Alhambra a more appealing option. Some wondered if lingering concerns over the Eastern–St. John's riot eight years before played a role or if the league chose to go the Alhambra route to avoid another unpleasant dispute over the polls, as had happened the year before with DeMatha and McKinley.

Whatever the reason, the bottom line was this: St. Anthony's would not meet DeMatha, which had won the event seven straight times, in the 1970 Knights of Columbus Tournament.

Thompson got more bad news the week play began when Washington tore ligaments at practice and couldn't play. Washington, a junior, had averaged 18 points and 16 rebounds through 30 games. Without him, the Tonies' 26–4 campaign looked destined for a disappointing end. But playing without Washington, the Tonies pulled together, proving once and for all that they belonged among the area's best.

They beat the Georgetown Prep Hoyas and the Thomas More Chancellors of Connecticut, both of whom had beaten the Tonies in the regular season, to reach the tournament finals. There, St. Anthony's pulled out a 54–52 victory over Our Saviour Lutheran Falcons of New York for the tournament title. Ironically, the event was played at Georgetown University's McDonough Arena, which would be Thompson's home court soon enough.

Everyone contributed in Washington's absence. Usual reserve John Butler scored 16 points in the first round. Jonathan Smith scored 21 points, and Tom Walters hit six key free throws down the stretch in the semifinals against Thomas More. In the final against New York's Our Saviour Lutheran, Smith led the way with 17 points and intercepted a desperation pass at the end to preserve the victory. Paul Wagner added 15 points and 13 rebounds. Wilson, subbing for Washington, contributed 11 rebounds, and Al Baker was named the tournament MVP.

"This is what we've been working for," a delighted Thompson said. "I don't care if we ever finish No. 1 or play DeMatha. We can't top this."

"Forget DeMatha," Baker crowed. "We're the best. We proved it."

The Stags and Tonies never did actually play—save for one memorable summer-league game in 1970. Literally thousands of fans flocked to the outdoor courts at the Jelleff Boys Club on Wisconsin Avenue near the edge of Georgetown, but what they saw was a fiasco instead.

Thompson, who didn't attend, used the game as a forum to bring attention to the lack of a regular-season meeting between the two schools. He sent a team of non-varsity players out on the court against the Stags, and they were overwhelmed, 108–26.

Thus, the cries for a game between the two local powers intensified. The two schools actually sat down a couple of times to discuss dates, times, and potential sites, but nothing ever came of it. Wootten preferred to play the game at Cole Field House (which was in DeMatha's backyard), although he offered Georgetown as an alternative. Thompson pushed for a weekend night game at Howard, feeling that would give his team more of a home court advantage.

The downtown riots in the spring of 1968 were still fresh in everyone's minds, and DC suburbanites largely kept their distance from many parts of the city, crossing the district line only for work or to visit museums, monuments, or RFK Stadium. It wasn't exactly politically correct, but it was the truth: that's how many people felt in those days.

"The city was hard-core," said Alonzo "Cheese" Holloway, the quick, heady point guard on a couple of those St. Anthony's teams. "There was a lot going on in Washington back then."

The game never came off, and relations between Thompson and Wootten were frosty for years after that, although each was complimentary of the other in their public pronouncements. Years later, when Wootten went on Thompson's radio show as a guest, the two said stories of any enmity between the two had been overblown.

But those who remember that brief period when Thompson's teams were the equal of Wootten's will swear that the feud was real. "At that time, the both of these teams were great," said Holloway, who was tight with DeMatha's biggest star at that time, Adrian Dantley. "Morgan Wootten and John Thompson weren't on the same page. That's the best way I can put it."

"I never ducked anyone in my life," Wootten said, insisting he really wanted to see such a game come off. In truth, Wootten was never shy about scheduling the best out-of-town competition or taking on the Inter-High's best in a regular-season game, even when he knew his team might get beat. Consequently, he objected when people claimed he tried to dodge St. Anthony's.

"We wanted to play DeMatha, of course," said Dane Edley, who also played for Thompson at St. Anthony's. "But as a player, there were so many things that were beyond our control. We were 24–1 my senior year [1972], won the Knights of Columbus Tournament [again]. We didn't have anything to prove. It would have been good for the city [to play the Stags]; it probably would have sold out Cole Field House. Our thinking was, if it happens, it happens. If it doesn't, we'll just move on."

Edley couldn't resist adding: "We would have won, though."

In 1971–72 Donald Washington had moved on to play at the University of North Carolina. But Holloway, Edley, Wilson, and Smith returned, and the Tonies were just as powerful as ever. St. Anthony's beat Eastern, which would win the Inter-High title, during the regular season and Prince George's County powerhouse Fairmont Heights as well. In fact, the team's only loss came at the hands of yet another strong McKinley squad.

St. Anthony's remained near the top of the polls all season, but the team had to deal with a major distraction as the all-important Knights of Columbus Tournament approached: Thompson, owner of a 122–28 record, had been hired by Georgetown University. The move was a stunner, although Thompson had earned the promotion. The surprise was that his new employer was Georgetown. The school had integrated its basketball program only a few years before. It also had developed a reputation locally as a kind of Catholic ivory tower, staying above the fray when it came to racial issues and the local turmoil that affected so much of Washington during the 1960s. Now, Georgetown had made Thompson one of only about a half-dozen black head coaches of predominantly white Division I basketball programs.

As it turned out, Thompson's final hour at St. Anthony's was one of his finest. The Tonies sent their coach out on top, winning the Knights of Columbus Tournament against a formidable field. "We wanted to win for Coach Thompson, we wanted to win for ourselves, and we wanted to win for our school," Edley recalled.

In the semifinals, St. Anthony's edged the Mount Vernon (New York) Knights, which were state champions and included future pros in guards Earl Tatum and Ray Williams as well as power forward Rudy Hackett. Holloway scored a game-high 18, including the free throws that clinched the 75–73 victory. Wilson was strong on the boards, as always, with 12 rebounds.

In the final against the unbeaten Eagles of St. Peter's Boys High of Staten Island, the New York City champs, it wasn't even close. The Tonies raced to a 38–25 lead and won going away, 73–52. Edley and Smith led the way with 22 points each.

"I wanted the guys to win so much I was ready to play," Thompson said afterward. "I've been emotionally split all week, trying to end this program successfully and starting the new one."

And for all the wins and the acclaim that Thompson brought to St. Anthony's, which fielded some excellent teams in subsequent years as well, it was the life lessons that stuck with his players from that time, especially the understanding that basketball was a means to an end and not just an end in itself.

"Why were we playing basketball? In order to get a college scholarship," said Edley, who went on to play at Loyola University of Chicago, joining so many of Thompson's St. Anthony's players at the next level. "He kind of put things in focus.

We knew that if we could go to college, we could change our lives and maybe our families' lives. He gave us lessons that would help you later in life—things that carried over, like work habits. I didn't understand it then, but I understand it now. He was trying to instill some values in you."

As the Northern Virginia high school sports season moved from football to basketball in December 1971, the school uppermost in everyone's minds was T. C. Williams. The Titans (of *Remember the Titans* movie fame) had just steamrolled to a 13–0 record that included nine shutouts and the state championship.

School consolidation aimed at promoting a greater degree of integration in Alexandria had combined three schools into one, leaving T. C. Williams the largest school in the state, with a pool of more than 4,500 students to draw on from ninth through 12th grade. The athletic programs at the school were going to be so superior, in all sports, that officials in Northern Virginia devised a plan that would shift the school among three districts over the next few years, so that nobody would have to compete directly against the Titans two years in a row.

For much of the 1971–72 season, it seemed as if the Titans' basketball program would duplicate the success of the football program. Under Coach Tom Wriston, T. C. Williams won its first 21 games but was upset by Groveton in the Northern Region tournament. The Titans were only a couple of games short of the state tournament berth everyone had assumed would be theirs.

Instead, the Northern Region title went to Gunston District champion Spartans of West Springfield, a school not even a decade old that hadn't enjoyed much athletic success to that point. "We came out of the woodwork," said West Springfield coach Don McCool.

It was easy to overlook the Spartans, especially given the more established programs such as T. C. Williams, Groveton, and W. T. Woodson in Northern Virginia at the time. Then, too, West Springfield was not a team that struck fear in opponents' hearts during pregame warm-ups. The team's two big men, Bob Ferris and Ed Tiernan, both missed significant time with injuries that season, leaving the six-foot-two Dale Watnee as the team's tallest regular.

"[Other teams] look at the lineup and sometimes they'll laugh at us," McCool said. "But they find out what we're all about when they throw the ball up, and we start running on them."

Senior guard Jeff Jeremiah agreed that their lack of size didn't faze the Spartans. "We run and press like the devil," Jeremiah said. "We've got eight different presses, we're shooting 50 percent as a team, and we're in better shape than anybody we play. Everything we do is run, run, run, press, press, press."

That wasn't exactly true. Yes, McCool loved to press; he did it at every stop in his coaching career. In fact, he was so intent on making sure the Spartans were ready for his style of play that each player had to complete a preseason two-mile run in 12 minutes. But West Springfield had a half-court weapon as well in the person of six-foot-one deadeye shooter Dave Koesters, who averaged a shade less than 20 points as a sophomore in 1971–72 largely because opponents figured they should concentrate on the Spartans' more experienced players. In time, though, Koesters would become the focus of every opposing team's defense, although few had much success.

Koesters, a first-team All-Met as a junior and a senior, was so dedicated to his craft that he even watched films of himself in action to detect any flaws in his shooting stroke. But if there were any, they weren't apparent to anyone else. "Shooting comes natural to me," said Koesters, who had more than a dozen scholarship offers for baseball and a dozen times that many for basketball by the time his prep career was through. "I guess I have a God-given talent for it."

"He's a natural," agreed McCool. "I never even thought about fooling with his shot."

As a sophomore, Koesters showed folks what was in store for the next two-plus seasons when he hit nine of 14 shots and scored a game-high 22 points in a 64–57 win over Groveton in the Northern Region championship game. The victory earned heretofore unknown West Springfield a trip to the state semifinals downstate, and, suddenly, everyone began to take note. West Springfield fans descended on Charlottesville with a vengeance, giddy at the prospect of their hometown heroes in the state tournament. The spirited Spartans supporters required 21 chartered buses to transport them to the tournament.

The roughly 2,000 fans who had made the trip south got what they wanted in the semifinals. Koesters pumped in 33 points, including the first 12 of the fourth quarter, as the Spartans downed the George Washington Eagles of Danville, 75–59. West Springfield also got a big boost from six-foot-four center Tiernan, making a rare start amid a career plagued by knee problems. Tiernan scored 14 points and pulled down a game-high 19 rebounds to earn his team a spot in the final.

There, the Spartans' luck ran out. They couldn't contend with the Hopewell Blue Devils' Willie McCray and lost, 63–55. McCray, at six foot five and 240 pounds, controlled play inside with 18 points and 27 rebounds. Koesters put up another 20 points to keep his team close, but Hopewell pulled away late.

Ultimately, Koesters and West Springfield went on to win three straight Northern Region titles and made three straight trips to the state tournament—a run equal to almost anyone's in the history of Northern Virginia basketball. While the Spartans had a lot going for them in those years, they were also cursed with a bad sense of timing.

In each of the next two seasons, they navigated their way through a talented group of teams in Northern Virginia, particularly T. C. Williams, only to run into the one player they couldn't handle—Petersburg's star six-foot-eleven center Moses Malone. With a rare combination of quickness, strength, and desire in someone so tall, Malone became the first player to jump from high school to the pros and established himself as one of the great players in the history of professional basketball. Moses and the Petersburg Crimson Wave dispensed with West Springfield, 52–41, in the 1973 state semifinals, although the Spartans acquitted themselves well considering Koesters had broken his arm earlier in the postseason and wasn't available.

The bigger story for West Springfield and Northern Virginia basketball during the 1972–73 season was how the Spartans reached the semifinals. That year T. C. Williams moved into the Gunston District, which put the Titans in direct competition with West Springfield. The two teams, among the best in the area at the time, were slated to go head-to-head twice in the regular season. Two more playoff matchups were possible, too, because the teams could meet in the district and regional playoffs as well.

The first regular-season matchup between the two, in Alexandria on January 9, went to the Spartans, 79–73. The second game, scheduled a month later, never happened. School officials at West Springfield, the site of the game, didn't put the tickets for the game up for sale until 5:30 p.m. the evening of the game. All the tickets were gone by 6:50 p.m., some 70 minutes before the scheduled tip-off.

T. C. Williams fans didn't arrive at West Springfield until a short time later, but the doors were closed. Angry at being denied entry, some T. C. Williams supporters forcibly entered the gym and elbowed their way into the few open spaces in the stands. It didn't help matters that West Springfield was almost all white, while the T. C. Williams team and its fan base were considerably more diverse. The police were summoned to restore order. They quickly concluded that the atmosphere inside the gym was too volatile, and the game was called off.

"The tension was unreal," one West Springfield teacher told the *Washington Star*. "I was petrified."

There was plenty of finger-pointing on both sides, with committees created and reports issued. Although the Titans' players had nothing to do with the whole affair, T. C. Williams was placed on probation and warned about creating any future disturbances.

West Springfield closed out its regular season 19–0, while T. C. Williams entered the district playoffs on a 10-game winning streak. This time, though, it was West Springfield's turn to see its unbeaten season ruined—in more ways than one. The 91–71 pasting at the hands of the Titans hurt, as did the 30-point effort by Darryl Turner that made it happen. But the most damaging blow of all came when Koesters fell and broke his arm in the second quarter and was lost for the season.

To their enduring credit, the Spartans turned around and beat T. C. Williams the next night in the rematch. The game determined which of the two teams—one, the Gunston regular-season champ; the other, the tournament champ—would earn the higher seed for the regionals. But that game featured a bit of upheaval as well. In the closing minutes of the 70–65 loss, Turner threw a punch at a West Springfield player and was ejected.

Given all that had already happened, the Virginia High School League, the governing body for prep sports, ruled that T. C. Williams was barred from the regional tournament and lost its chance of competing for a state championship. Initially, the ban also extended to any and all sports for the rest of the school year, although the league eventually relented and instituted the penalties for the basketball program alone.

West Springfield went on to repeat as region champs, getting a pair of Bob Ferris free throws with 19 seconds left to beat the Lee Lancers, 51–49, to earn a second straight trip downstate. But the Spartans didn't stand much of a chance against Moses Malone with Koesters on the sidelines in a cast.

It probably helped head off any further problems between the local school rivals that as part of the agreement made after the 1971 football season, T. C. Williams changed districts again the next year. Several interested parties, including community-oriented Redskins wide receiver Roy Jefferson, organized a sit-down luncheon for the two schools before they met during the 1973–74 season. It also helped that the game was moved to a much larger venue, the 5,000-capacity gymnasium at Robinson Secondary School, with three days of advance ticket sales.

The game drew an overflow crowd of nearly 6,000 people, and with good reason. Both teams were 16–0 coming in and ranked in the area newspapers' top five. West Springfield prevailed, 74–66, getting 20 points and 13 rebounds from six-foot-three Bob Wetesnik, who had taken over as McCool's nominative big man. Best of all, the game came off without incident.

"It was a fine game and a fine crowd," said West Springfield principal L. Ray Volrath. "They were a credit to both schools."

It was inevitable that the two teams would meet again in the regionals, and that is exactly what happened. There was, if anything, even more hype for their second meeting. West Springfield was 22–0; T. C. Williams, 22–1. The game also featured two of the area's top players in the Spartans' Koesters (21.8 points per game) and the Titans' wonder Carl Jackson, who thrived inside despite being six-foot-three and only about 150 pounds.

"He was like balsa wood," recalled Woodson coach Red Jenkins. "He got major-league air under his feet." That year, Jackson averaged 26.9 points per game, which was the best mark in the area and second only to Malone's stratospheric 37.6 average in the state.

In a playoff game a few days before the West Springfield matchup, Jackson racked up 49 points and 26 rebounds in one of the great high school performances by anyone, anywhere. But the region final and the berth in the state tournament, the third straight, belonged to West Springfield as Koesters poured in a game-high 34 points in a 74–69 triumph. Fourteen of those points came in the fourth quarter when it looked as if the Spartans' perfect season might be coming to an end.

"I didn't think we could win unless I got back into the offense and started looking for my shot," Koesters said. "I did, and it paid off."

Against Norfolk's Maury Commodores in the state semifinals, Koesters scored 23 before Steve Lanier hit a pair of free throws with nine seconds left to wrap up a 64–60 victory and set up a rematch with Malone and Petersburg. Both teams were 24–0, with the defending champs working on a 49-game winning streak. Malone, meanwhile, had become the state's first 2,000-point scorer.

"In all my years, he was the best high school center I ever played against," said McCool, whose teams subsequently went up against the likes of Ralph Sampson and Alonzo Mourning. "Moses was skinny back then, but he could get it done. He was the greatest player I've ever seen."

Though outmatched, West Springfield conceded nothing. As he had the year before, McCool had his players shooting over assistant coaches wielding badminton racquets to get them used to shooting with a higher arc against Malone. McCool also had the Spartans work on a more deliberate offensive strategy in hopes that it might help limit Malone, at least a little bit.

Those strategies almost paid off. Playing before another 20 busloads of West Springfield faithful, Petersburg won, but just barely. West Springfield had the ball in Koesters's hand in the closing seconds, but his attempted lob pass to a wide-open teammate underneath the basket was tipped and then controlled by Malone, who held the ball aloft—where no one else could get it—as the final seconds ran out in the 51–49 escape.

Malone finished with 26 points and 19 rebounds. Koesters was brilliant again with 29, closing out his prep career with another outstanding performance.

"We've been together since the eighth grade working for this," said Spartans point guard Steve Bacon. "We outhustled them. We outplayed them. I really think we gave all we could. But in the end, winning is the only thing."

Perhaps. But Bacon, Koesters, and the rest of the Spartans could take some solace in their three straight region titles, three straight trips to the state tournament, and a glittering 72–6 record during their memorable varsity run.

With only one starter, Joe Wilson, back in 1974–75, McCool was still able to steer the Spartans back into the Northern Region final. This time, however, T. C. Williams took the prize and earned the long-sought trip downstate. The Titans lost in the semifinals, but the young players on that team formed the nucleus of the T. C. Williams squad that finally broke through and won the Virginia state title in 1977.

Though not quite as successful as McCool was, Wil Jones, the Rams' coach at newly opened Robinson in Fairfax County, was infinitely more entertaining. Jones, in fact, might have been the most entertaining coach in the history of Northern Virginia or of the whole area, for that matter.

"Oh, he was a character," McCool recalled. "A fun guy who could tell great stories. He always made everybody laugh and was always the center of every conversation. He kept you in stitches."

And he generally had folks laughing so hard, they didn't notice he was a trailblazer. The pressures and problems of Herman Boone, the black coach who took over the T. C. Williams football program in 1971, were well-documented in *Remember the Titans*. Jones faced the same sort of obstacles at roughly the same time (his first season as coach was 1972–73), albeit with a great deal less fanfare. He was Northern Virginia's first African American head boys' basketball coach and took over what had been an all-white team.

Jones had worked as a physical education specialist with younger children in Northern Virginia and was one of several candidates for the Robinson coaching position before the school opened in the early 1970s. To the surprise of many, he got the job. Some believed he might have been a compromise candidate, because the others in the running were all established county coaches, and the selection of one would have alienated the others. There was also some feeling among county school officials that the time had come for somebody to hire a black coach, something the individual schools themselves might have been reluctant to do.

Jones thinks he was given the job to fail, just so people could say, "Well, we tried hiring a black coach, and it didn't work out." Well, Jones worked out, all right. He went 73–25 in four seasons at Robinson, qualifying for the regional tournament every year. It was quite an achievement for a start-up program.

But it wasn't the wins so much as it was Jones's antics, his demeanor, and his wardrobe that left an impression. For if those who chose him for the job expected him to step lightly in what some might have viewed as a delicate situation, then they had picked the wrong guy.

"That was not Wil's style—to be walking on eggshells," said longtime W. T. Woodson coach Red Jenkins. "They caught a doozie," Jones said. "I did not change."

"Willie" had been one of the great shooters and great trash-talkers in the city while playing for Dunbar during the mid-1950s and brought the same irrepressible outrageousness to the sidelines at Robinson. Nobody was more stylish: berets, *Saturday Night Fever*-style open-collared shirts, gabardine suits with platform shoes. No one showed such passion, such enthusiasm during the action on the floor. The games at Robinson became happenings, and Jones came to love the grand theater of it all.

"He had charisma, he had fashion, he was cool," said Craig Brewer, one of the stars of those Robinson teams. "He was a rock star."

Jones once—famously—wore a purple tuxedo on the sidelines one night and thought nothing of strolling over to the opposing team's layup line to chat up the rival players. Woodson's Chris Knoche recalled one episode in which Jones dropped a $5 bill on the floor some 20 feet from the basket and told Knoche: "It's yours if you can hit one from there."

Coaches weren't restricted by coaching boxes back in those days, but nothing could have restrained Jones anyway as he urged his team on. It wasn't uncommon to see him running from one end of the court to the other along the sidelines, shouting instructions to his players.

One time, Jones even walked out on the court to question a call while the game was going on, waving his arms like a stranded motorist trying to flag down a passing car. The game was stopped, and once the ruling was explained to his satisfaction, the action resumed. The opposing coach eyed the referees and asked if they would call a technical foul. "Aww, no, Coach," one of them replied. "You know how Wil is."

Jones left Robinson after the 1975–76 season to join Lefty Driesell's staff at Maryland. Later, Wil guided the University of the District of Columbia to the 1982 NCAA Division II national title.

But those who came of age in Northern Virginia during the early 1970s remember those crazy days of Jones's early coaching career. He had the misfortune to coach at a time when West Springfield and T. C. Williams were so strong, it was almost impossible for anyone else to take a Northern Virginia team to Charlottesville for the state tournament. Jones came close a couple of times, but his team never was able to break through.

If he had, he might be remembered for more than his sideline shenanigans and his sartorial splendor. With a little luck, he might have become another Herman Boone. As Brewer astutely pointed out, with a couple more wins in the right places, Hollywood might have made a movie about Jones rather than Boone. Denzel Washington played the part of the no-nonsense T. C. Williams football coach. But for the part of Wil Jones, you'd have to go a different route. Maybe Eddie Murphy.

During the 1960s, Morgan Wootten and the players he had at DeMatha set the standard for high school basketball excellence in the Washington area. When Adrian Dantley came along, he raised the bar even higher. By the time Dantley graduated and moved on to Notre Dame, he had led the Stags to a sparkling 111–8 record, four straight league titles, and four straight years of No. 1 rankings in the local newspapers. Forgotten were the years that Mackin beat out DeMatha for the league title and the area's No. 1 ranking in 1967, or the protest and controversy that ended with McKinley beating out Wootten's bunch for the *Post*'s No. 1 spot in 1969.

The timing of Dantley's arrival at DeMatha is an important part of his story. He'd grown up in Northeast Washington, the same part of the city as James Brown, and idolized the popular, talented DeMatha star. That, as much as anything else, prompted him to attend school there. Also, Dantley already was well known in high school basketball circles before he entered DeMatha in the fall of 1969. Mackin and Carroll both had sought him to play on their teams, but Dantley, having attended summer school at DeMatha, was convinced that was the place for him.

Wootten had seen Dantley play, though almost by accident. The legendary coach had watched a Backus Junior High School game prior to Dantley's arrival at DeMatha, but he had gone to see one of Dantley's teammates play. In fact, Wootten was shocked when Mackin coach Paul Furlong told him at one point during the summer of 1969, "You've just gotten the best player you're ever going to coach."

Wootten wasn't sure what exactly to do with Dantley at first. At about six foot three and 240 pounds, the promising freshman was, using the word of everyone who remembered him in those days, "pudgy." Wootten wasn't sure how much he could count on Dantley as a freshman player, though he sensed the ninth grader could probably contribute at the varsity level. But in order to impress upon Dantley what level of effort would be needed, Wootten had him practice with the JV team for a couple of days while the coach went out of town. When Wootten returned, he asked his assistants, "Has Adrian learned his lesson?"

Frank Fuqua, one of his assistants, replied: "I've learned my lesson. He doesn't belong on the JV!"

So Dantley became just the third player in Wootten's tenure at DeMatha to make the varsity as a freshman. The Stags' star was guard Ray Hite, who had played so brilliantly against McKinley in the Knights of Columbus victory the previous March. Dantley's assignment was to gather rebounds at either end of the floor. When he grabbed a teammate's miss and found himself close to the basket, he might score. Thus, Dantley averaged about 11 points and 10 rebounds per game that season, in which DeMatha finished with a 27–3 record.

But even in those modest beginnings, there were signs of what was to come. DeMatha routed Chamberlain (which was on the wrong end of many lopsided scores in those days) in the opener, 123–61. The starters didn't even play the whole first quarter, so quickly did things get out of hand. But the rout created a situation where Dantley could shine, and he scored 18 points off the bench in his varsity debut.

By the first of the year, Dantley had joined the starting lineup and began making his presence felt on a more regular basis. In the M Club Tournament in mid-January, his layup with 12 seconds left beat Cardozo, 61–60. The next night, against a 13–0 Eastern team, Dantley scored nine fourth-quarter points—including a pair of free throws with 24 seconds left—enabling the Stags to prevail, 69–66. When DeMatha faced St. John's in early March for the Metro Conference title, Dantley's 24 rebounds helped enable the Stags to overcome some foul trouble and pick up a hard-earned 64–58 victory.

Dantley could be surprising off the court as well. He was a student in Wootten's freshman world history class and needed a good grade on a particular test to ensure the same for the semester. Wootten, meanwhile, designed the test to be as hard as he could make it and figured he'd grade the results on a curve if he had to. As it turned out, everyone in the class needed the curve except Dantley. Understanding the importance of the test, Dantley had thrown himself into the task of reviewing the material and scored a 98 on the test. Nobody else in the class managed better than an 80.

Wootten, not sure what to make of the results, quizzed Dantley relentlessly in front of the class after the tests were handed back. Dantley answered every question correctly. "You thought I cheated, didn't you?" Dantley said to his coach and teacher, his jaw set.

For one of the few times in his life, Wootten didn't have a snappy reply. But he'd learned something from that test as well: never underestimate Adrian Dantley.

The young man was talented, to be sure, but he worked like no one else to develop his talent. That determination and drive enabled Dantley to become a three-time All-Met, an All-American at Notre Dame, an NBA scoring champ, and, ultimately, a Hall of Famer.

He never seemed to take a day off, to rest on his laurels, to be satisfied with all he'd accomplished. One day Dantley knocked on Wootten's door, asking for the keys to the school gym so he could squeeze in a workout. It was Christmas Day.

Dantley always stood a little bit apart from the crowd, because no one else would go over to the University of Maryland campus and run the steps of Byrd (now Maryland) Stadium in the sweltering summer heat. When Dantley would get invited to a party, he'd go late or not at all, preferring to work on his game at the Turkey Thicket playground or even in an alley near his house where someone had put up a backboard and rim on a telephone pole. There'd be plenty of time for parties when he reached the pros, Dantley told himself.

Dantley was so devoted to improving that he tried to persuade Wootten to let him try some weight lifting, believing it would help him get stronger and quicker. He'd seen what it had done for Kermit Washington, who'd turned himself from a scrub at Coolidge High into a star at American University and a first-round NBA draft pick.

Wootten was dubious. Back then it was believed that weight lifting was bad for basketball players. Many thought it made them too muscle bound and that it would adversely affect the soft touch necessary to shoot the ball effectively.

To his credit, Wootten took Dantley to Maryland and discussed the potential benefits of weight training with the Terps' outstanding track coach, Frank Costello. Later Wootten was so impressed with the results of Dantley's weight training program that he adopted a similar regimen for his teams from that point forward, years before anyone else was doing so.

Strength was just one of the attributes that set Dantley apart. In his entire career, including the pros, he probably got 90 percent of his baskets from 17 feet in. Even if you were bigger than he was, if he got you behind him, then you were a goner.

Dantley's abilities set him apart in one other respect. Unlike anyone who has lived in the DC area since the region's postwar boom, he loved traffic—on the court. In the lane, Dantley had an uncanny knack for finding or creating openings invisible to the normal eye. Ball fakes, head fakes, shoulder fakes—he had an entire array of moves designed to gain him a sliver of daylight heading to the basket or to draw a foul. For his entire career—high school, college, or the pros—the man lived at the foul line, leading the NBA in free-throw attempts three times.

When Ray Hite went to North Carolina for the 1970–71 season, the Stags became Dantley's team, a state of affairs that lasted for the next three seasons. He was the main man for the Stags but hardly their only weapon. Billy Langloh, a poised and heady guard, joined the varsity that season from the JV, where he had averaged 25 points per game. Dantley and Langloh were quite a pair all by themselves, but they got plenty of help from the likes of Kenny Roy (a future standout defensive back at Maryland) and the tough, aggressive Carroll Holmes. Holmes's nickname around school was "the Chairman of the Boards," because he generally grabbed any rebound that Dantley didn't.

That quartet, plus such players as Ronnie Satterthwaite and Buzzy O'Connell, propelled DeMatha to a 27–3 record in Dantley's sophomore year. The Stags won another league title after putting down another severe challenge from Wootten's friend and mentor Joe Gallagher and his St. John's team. For his part, Dantley averaged 22 points and 15 rebounds per game that season.

In his junior year, Dantley and DeMatha kicked it up another notch. The Stags finished 28–1, their best record ever. Their only loss was to the Lions of Archbishop Molloy, a New York area power, on a night when Dantley was saddled with foul trouble.

There were no other sour notes for DeMatha or for Dantley, who upped his averages to 26 points and 16 rebounds per game. He went for 28 points and 16 rebounds in an early showdown against the Springbrook Blue Devils. He scored 33 points and grabbed 14 rebounds in just a half (!) against Chamberlain. He poured in a school-record 43 points (plus 16 rebounds) in a victory over the previously unbeaten All Hallows Gaels of New York, right before the Molloy loss. A 93–70 victory over Good Counsel's Falcons, in which Dantley scored 38 points and grabbed 28 rebounds, gave DeMatha a fifth straight Catholic League title.

All but one starter, along with the top five reserves, was back for Dantley's senior year of 1972–73. The Stags picked up where they left off the year before, running their winning streak to 43 games before Skip Wise and his Baltimore Dunbar Poets team, which had won 37 straight themselves, finally downed the Stags at the Baltimore Civic Center in front of a crowd of 8,000 people.

The loss didn't slow down DeMatha for long. The next time out, Dantley went for 29 points and 25 rebounds in a 75–60 victory over Archbishop Carroll (a team that included future Washington Wizards coach Eddie Jordan). The next day, DeMatha was voted the No. 1 team in the area by the *Star* and the *Post*.

There was more to come. By winning the Metro Conference title, the Stags took part in one of the seminal moments in the history of area high school basketball—the resumption of the City Title Game. The private-public series had been discontinued after the riot following the St. John's–Eastern football game in 1962, but officials felt tensions had eased to the point where such a postseason matchup could be held again. St. John's and Coolidge had played in the first football City Title Game in November, and DeMatha was slated to meet the Western Red Raiders (featuring super-quick guard Larry Wright, who would be a key backup on the Washington Bullets' 1978 NBA championship team). For Wootten and the Stags (who had won the last city basketball title in 1962), it was a landmark moment. Certainly, Wootten wanted his team to win, but it was perhaps even more important that the game go off without any untoward incidents.

"That was special," Wootten recalled. "We wanted to show that things were back on course and that the game could be played and should be played. It was more than a basketball statement, and it came off beautifully. The sportsmanship on both sides was great. It was very important that it come off well. It was maybe the most important game that we played that year."

The game at Cole Field House was almost worth the decade-long wait. Western went on a 12–0 run to pull within 59–55 after three periods. But thanks in part to Dantley (20 points and 10 rebounds despite constant double-teams), the Stags pulled away late for an 89–77 victory in front of 10,763 people, including droves of college coaches wanting to get Dantley's signature on a letter of intent. DeMatha's Kenny Roy did a great job of making Wright work for his 28 points. Billy Langloh was no slouch, either, scoring 27 points himself.

"People think we rely only on Dantley," Wootten had said earlier that season. "But we really have a well-balanced club. If you concentrate on one man, somebody else has to be open."

Langloh continued his strong late-season play at the Alhambra Catholic Invitational Tournament in Cumberland as the Stags sought their third straight title in the event. He had 44 points and 16 assists in the first two games of the tournament, but Dantley had one big moment left in his high school career. He'd been bothered by a sore knee during the tournament and was something less than his usual dynamic self.

Wootten, afraid that his star might be brooding a bit, took him aside before the final, which would be played against St. Leo, the Chicago Catholic League champion. "It's your last high school game," Wootten told Dantley. "Why don't you go out there and show everyone the All-American that you are."

Responding nobly, Dantley discarded his knee wrap and scored 38 points and grabbed 17 rebounds during a 116–67 rout in the championship game. The result made DeMatha 29–1, thus eclipsing the previous year's record as the best ever in school history. Once again, Dantley had risen to a challenge. It was a fitting end to one of the great high school careers in DC area history.

Almost four decades later, when the 1972–73 team was inducted en masse into the DeMatha Hall of Fame, Wootten's assessment of that group was both succinct and on target. "There was none better," he said.

Even though Adrian Dantley was only six foot four, he cast quite a shadow over Washington area high school basketball. He was so good—already the subject of newspaper articles while still in eighth grade—that his successes tended to obscure most anything else going on in the city. In that sense, he was what the music industry would call a "crossover" star, as he was known not just within the circles of high school basketball but also by the public at large.

Dantley's legend only grew once he left Hyattsville. He played at Notre Dame, where he was on television virtually every weekend in those pre-ESPN days of college basketball coverage. Before his career at Notre Dame was completed, Dantley joined fellow ex-DeMatha Stag Kenny Carr and led the US team to recover the Olympic gold medal in 1976 that it had lost to the Soviet Union in 1972.

DeMatha's pervasive success tended to overshadow that of other teams in the city. Just ask the other schools in the Catholic League/Metro Conference of that era that produced such standouts as Eddie Jordan, Arthur Daniels, and Chris Redding (Carroll); Collis Jones (St. John's); and Donald "Duck" Williams and the Herron brothers, Larry and Keith (Mackin). None of these players probably got the notoriety they deserved, because DeMatha was always on top of the area high school basketball scene.

The great players and teams in the Inter-High also were overshadowed by DeMatha's excellence in the early 1970s. The city's public schools enjoyed more than their share of high points such as McKinley's 1971 Knights of Columbus Tournament victory over a Mount Vernon (New York) team that included three future NBA players (Hackett, Tatum, and Williams) or Western's triumph in the same tournament in 1973. However, DeMatha wasn't entered in that tournament either season, opting instead to travel to the Alhambra Catholic Invitational Tournament.

Part of the perception problem for the Inter-High was that the public school teams didn't often get a chance to play against DeMatha because the City Title Game had been suspended following the 1962 riot at the football championship game. All that changed when the private-public basketball series was revived in 1973. And even though DeMatha took care of Inter-High champ Eastern in the matchup, at least going forward the city's public schools would have a chance to test themselves against whoever won the private school league title—and that was almost always DeMatha.

In the 1973–74 season, the second after the resumption of the City Title Game, the tide began to turn. DeMatha, which had finished No. 1 in the final polls in both the *Star* and the *Post* 11 times, took a back seat to Inter-High teams Eastern (No. 1 in 1974 and 1975) and Dunbar (undefeated and No. 1 in 1976).

"They were the dominant team in the city," said Gerald Gaskins, a sixth man on Eastern's city champs in 1974 and the starting point guard for the Ramblers in

1975. "All you heard was DeMatha, DeMatha. In '74 and '75, we put it on them. We wanted to beat DeMatha to show that the Inter-High had some ballplayers also."

The intensity of those games was felt on both ends. "It definitely felt like they [Inter-High teams] were coming after us," said Pete Strickland, who played the point at DeMatha in 1974 and 1975. "You definitely felt like it was you against the world. It really was a great rivalry."

Eastern had generally fielded strong teams over the previous dozen years, going back to the teams coached by John Moffatt and led by such All-Mets as Jerry Chambers, Reggie Greene, Ronald "Biggie" Cunningham, and Louie West in the 1960s. Chambers and the Ramblers dethroned Hall of Famer Dave Bing and Spingarn to win the Inter-High title in 1962. Eastern won the league the next year as well.

After Cardozo and McKinley had their turns at the top of the Inter-High in the late 1960s, Eastern, under young head coach A. B. Williamson, became a power again. The Ramblers won the Inter-High's regular-season title in 1973 with an unblemished record, but they were upset by Bell in the playoffs to finish 24–4.

The next year, with a deep, talented veteran crew led by six-foot-six Mike Oliver, six-foot-five Slim Joiner, and five-foot-nine dynamo Tyrone Jones, the Ramblers became unquestionably the best team in the city, including DeMatha. "This season, Eastern has a lot of discipline," noted Western coach Bob Piper. "They have more confidence and less cockiness. They've played before big crowds, and they've been together for three years."

The Ramblers proved it with a 70–65 overtime win over the Stags in early January, handing Wootten his first-ever overtime loss at DeMatha and the first defeat by one of his teams to an Inter-High squad in six years. Jones led the Ramblers with 20 points, atoning for a key missed free throw the year before in a 66–61 loss to DeMatha.

After beating DeMatha, the Ramblers rolled on. Williamson had loads of talent at his disposal and did a good job keeping everyone in line. He had so much talent, in fact, that he could afford to bench anyone who displeased him.

In the Inter-High tournament final, the Ramblers shut down Wilson. They held the Tigers to just six points in the first quarter and only two in the second, as Eastern cruised to a 58–35 win.

That hard-nosed defense was on display again in the City Title Game when the Ramblers dispensed with DeMatha as well in a resounding 74–58 victory in front of 11,000 fans at Maryland's Cole Field House. Jones again led the way with 20 points, scoring on a combination of twisting drives and long jumpers. He scored 10 of his points in the fourth quarter to break open a close game, while Oliver did the dirty work inside, keeping DeMatha off the boards.

"When you feel in your mind you can win, the physical part usually takes care of itself, Williamson said afterward. "And we knew we could win."

That was quite a statement, considering how dominant DeMatha had been in previous years. Even Wootten, to his everlasting credit, made no excuses and gave Eastern its due. "They were so good defensively that we couldn't run a thing offensively," he said. "They were super. Eastern has excellent team speed. They rebound well, play tough defense, and have a great floor leader in Jones. He's the best guard we've faced this season."

To the players and coaches who had felt as if they'd always played second fiddle to DeMatha, those comments must have been music to their ears. And after Eastern beat DeMatha twice in 1973–74, the pollsters had no choice but to vote the Ramblers No. 1 at the end of the season.

"That [1974] team was a mature team, a team of destiny," Williamson recalled. "We felt like we were the best team. Winning [over DeMatha] really did a lot for me and for Inter-High basketball."

But Inter-High basketball's reawakening was just beginning. In 1974–75 Williamson had another athletic, talented team, with James "Turkey" Tillman and Gerald Gaskins assuming larger roles outside since Joiner and Jones had graduated. Inside, the six-foot-seven Mike Morton, who had transferred from DeMatha, took over for Oliver.

That team established itself right after Christmas with a 59–58 victory over Wootten's Stags, thus becoming the first team since Carroll's tremendous squads of the late 1950s to beat DeMatha three times in a row. Eastern rallied from a 55–48 deficit with 2:44 left. Gaskins hit a critical jumper with 25 seconds left, and Tillman (20 points) clinched it with a couple of free throws 20 seconds later. "They hung in there and won with their hearts and their guts," Williamson said. "They fought back."

But DeMatha wasn't Eastern's only obstacle in its quest to repeat as No. 1. Dunbar, under second-year coach Joe Dean Davidson, had emerged as a serious Inter-High threat after going 13–10 the previous season.

In 1974–75 the Crimson Tide was boosted by the transfer of the dazzling Stacy Robinson, the player Notre Dame coach Digger Phelps once called "the best guard in the country." A flap over Robinson's participation in a postseason all-star game rendered him ineligible to play in Prince George's County, where he lived. That's how he landed at Dunbar, joining a talented lineup that already featured John and Lonnie Duren, Craig Shelton, and Joe Thweatt. Robinson, Shelton, and Thweatt all earned All-Met recognition.

Any doubts about Dunbar's abilities were erased when the Crimson Tide knocked off Eastern, 77–73, just two weeks after the Ramblers had beaten DeMatha. Robinson buried a pair of crucial corner jumpers in the late stages against Eastern, helping to rally Dunbar from 15 points down in front of an overflow crowd of 1,500 fans at Spingarn. It was the first league loss for Williamson and Eastern in more than two years. As it turned out, the outcome decided the Inter-High regular-season champion since neither team lost the rest of the season. Thanks to Robinson's heroics, Dunbar would represent the Inter-High in the City Title Game against—who else?—DeMatha.

But first there was the matter of the Dunbar-Eastern rematch in the Inter-High tournament final, which took on the air of a heavyweight championship fight back when boxing was still on sports fans' radar. Dunbar came in with a 21–2 record, having won 16 straight. Eastern had run off 12 straight victories of its own. The showdown at Georgetown's McDonough Arena was the biggest game of the year to that point. And for once, that distinction didn't apply to a game that involved DeMatha.

A crowd of about 4,000 fans shoehorned its way into the gym, and the roads running through that part of campus closed an hour before the opening tip. What the crowd saw was brilliant basketball—and much more. For the record, Eastern (sort of) settled its score with Dunbar as Tillman scored 12 straight points down the stretch to lift the Ramblers to a 75–70 victory. The game was every bit as taut and tightly contested as the first. The aggregate score of the two encounters was Eastern, 148–147.

"Eastern and Dunbar's basketball teams proved very little about which is the best high school team in Washington," wrote Thomas Boswell, then a young high school reporter for the *Post*. "But it's hard to believe after that performance that one of them is not."

The fans got a taste of what they were in for early, when Gaskins threw a 40-foot lob pass to Tillman, who grabbed the ball a foot above the rim and was about to bring it down through the hoop. Then, out of nowhere, Shelton swooped in and pinned the ball on the backboard, drawing a goaltending call. Everyone oohed and aahed and then laughed at the ridiculously spectacular act they'd just seen— and that was just in the first couple of minutes. The rest of the game was just as good.

"This is the greatest rivalry the city has ever seen," Williamson crowed. "The public schools have never had the No. 1 and No. 2 teams before, and there's never been a crowd-pleasing match like this one."

Davidson agreed: "The players this year aren't necessarily better than in other years, but the brand of ball definitely is."

To everyone's delight (and relief), there were no incidents in the stands. In years past, big games had often devolved into some kind of postgame disturbance, involving injuries, police, suspensions, or some combination thereof. Shots had even been fired after a big matchup between Spingarn and McKinley a few years before. For a period, the starting times of certain Inter-High games weren't permitted to be published in the newspapers and the tickets were sold only to the students at the participating schools in an attempt to keep out potential troublemakers who had no connection to either school.

But the atmosphere was nothing like that this time, even with the passionate, jammed-in crowd and the evenly matched teams. The tone was set by Shelton and Tillman, the game's two biggest stars, who'd been neighborhood pals as youngsters. The two blood rivals had spent two hours on the phone together the night before, chatting about everything and anything but the game just ahead. Before the opening tip, each made a point of going around the midcourt circle and shaking hands with everyone on the opposing team.

"Five years ago, you couldn't have had a game like this with controversial calls and the packed gym, and not have 15 fights," Williamson noted. "The chances for that were there today, but everything seems to have changed."

Added Inter-High official Otto Jordan, "Hell, you couldn't even hold an assembly five years ago. We're all proud of the players and coaches, but we're even prouder of the students."

As memorable as the Eastern-Dunbar game was, a couple of more twists and turns were left in the season. In the City Title Game, DeMatha slipped past Dunbar, 67–62, despite a 26-point, 18-rebound effort by Shelton. DeMatha's Charles "Hawkeye" Whitney was nearly as good, taking home MVP honors after his 18-point, 14-rebound performance.

A few weeks later, the same two schools met in the Knights of Columbus Tournament, which was played at George Mason University in Fairfax because no venue could be secured closer to town. Dunbar won in a rout, its full-court press taking a severe toll on the Stags, minus Strickland, who sat out with a sprained ankle.

When the dust finally settled, both papers agreed: Eastern was No. 1 again. The Ramblers had beaten both Dunbar and DeMatha at full strength, and that seemed to tilt the scales in the minds of the voters. In truth, it was almost impossible to separate Eastern (25–2) from Dunbar (25–3) and DeMatha (25–6). Dunbar was second and DeMatha third in the *Star*'s final poll, which was released before the Knights of Columbus Tournament. The *Post*'s ranking, which came out afterward, had DeMatha and Dunbar reversed.

There was no such room for debate the next season. Dunbar, particularly Shelton and John Duren, saw to that. In 1975–76 the Crimson Tide put together one of the greatest seasons in metro area history. *Sport* magazine voted Dunbar its 1975–76 "Dream Team." And with good reason. The Crimson Tide finished 26–0, including victories over the eventual Virginia state AAA champ, Maggie L. Walker's Green Dragons of Richmond; Baltimore's best, the Lake Clifton Lakers; St. John's; and, in the City Title Game, DeMatha.

Davidson's squad probably wasn't as talented as the 1974–75 team. But with the tone set by the hustling Shelton and the hardworking Duren, Dunbar had no peer. "They're a disciplined, well-organized, well-coached basketball team," North Carolina State University coach Norm Sloan said on one of his many recruiting trips to the DC area. "I think they're the finest high school team I've seen this year."

Shelton, a relentless rebounder, led the Inter-High in scoring that season with a

23.3 average while averaging 19 rebounds per game. Duren, who made the offense go, averaged 18.1 points, plus 11 assists per game. Both were first-team All-Met in both papers. Shelton was also named the *Post*'s Player of the Year. The two of them would also be instrumental in Georgetown's rise, leading the Hoyas to within a whisker of the Final Four (upsetting a Maryland team led by Albert King and Buck Williams along the way) as seniors in 1980.

"He was probably the best player I ever played with as far as being a guy who was competitive and worked hard," Duren said of Shelton. "I don't think I ever met a guy that worked harder than Craig and had the confidence in himself that he did. You see the top guy working hard, and the other guys fall into line."

Duren's rise that season caught many off guard. Davidson had put him at forward in his junior season as someone had to move to make room for Robinson. But the coach entrusted Duren with the offense in his senior year, and he responded brilliantly. He carried the team for a time early on while Shelton recovered from a knee injury, and Duren never really stopped.

"Somebody had to sacrifice some things and give up some things," Duren said. "I did that my junior year. Senior year, coach came to me and said he thought I could handle the point. I knew I could handle it."

Shelton rebounded and started the break with his outlet passes, while Duren would finish with either a shot or an assist of his own. It was a potent combination. It had to be for Dunbar to stay undefeated and No. 1. The Crimson Tide faced a strong challenge by Eastern, which had lost Coach A. B. Williamson to Howard University but still remained dangerous. Dunbar beat Eastern twice that season by a total of four points, and those two losses were the only ones the Ramblers suffered that year. The final in the Inter-High championship game was 59–58 in front of 3,500 people at the DC Armory. The regular-season matchup between the two at the same venue drew more than 5,000 fans.

But the biggest game of the year was the Dunbar-DeMatha rematch in the City Title Game. It was also the biggest game of John Duren's high school career. Entrusted with the responsibility of running the team, Duren responded brilliantly but never more so than against DeMatha in the matchup for bragging rights in the city. Duren scored 24 points, grabbed seven rebounds, handed out six assists, and made a pair of steals as Dunbar closed out its unbeaten season with a 70–66 victory. With the game tied at 63 with 2:16 left, Duren canned a pair of free throws to put his team ahead for good.

"The great thing about him is he's cool under pressure," marveled Williamson. "He's got nerve. He doesn't fold." Or as Duren's future college coach, John Thompson, put it, "The man can play the game. That's all there is to it."

Shelton provided his share of heroics too. Down by just a basket, DeMatha missed a shot in the closing seconds, as well as two tip-in tries. Before the Stags could try one last time for the equalizer, Shelton soared to grab the loose ball and shut the door by hitting a pair of free throws with three seconds to go.

"I knew I had to get one more rebound so the game would go our way," he said. And so it did.

⚆　　⚆　　⚆

DeMatha might have finished behind Inter-High powers Eastern and Dunbar for a couple of years during the mid-1970s, but the Stags remained unquestioned kings of the Metro Conference. Even with Dantley gone, they extended their run of titles to 15 in 16 years from 1961 to 1976. The only interruption in that span had come in 1967, when the Austin Carr–led Mackin Trojans beat out the Stags for the Catholic League title.

Clearly, it was going to take an exceptional team to beat out the Stags, who always had a wealth of talent, poise, and, of course, coaching. In 1977 Joe Gallagher's Cadets were just such a team.

St. John's won 27 games and the Metro Conference title in 1976–77, beating the Stags three times along the way—a rare accomplishment, to be sure. It would be another seven years before someone other than the Stags would wear the league crown, making St. John's the only team to interrupt DeMatha's string of league titles in a 17-year span.

Gallagher's team drew comparisons to the best squads that he had ever coached, going all the way back to his first team, which featured future NBA All-Star Jack George in 1947–48. In the intervening years, Gallagher gained the admiration and respect of his coaching colleagues for his ability to devise some sort of tactic or gimmick to compensate for whatever his team lacked: speed, height, depth. In 1977, though, the beloved and venerable coach needed no such trickery; the Cadets were good enough for him to play it straight.

Gallagher's team that year had everything, a rare occurrence for all but a few select coaches. For a man who had labored so long, it seemed only right and fair, somehow, that he finally got to coach a team that good.

The Cadets had an elite star in senior Mark Pitchford, a talented all-around player who seemed driven to be successful at anything he tried. In addition to being the Cadets' leading scorer, Pitchford was a topflight student, the second-ranking officer in the Cadet corps, and the sports editor of the newspaper. He went to Stanford University on a basketball scholarship and seemed destined for greatness there before a back injury effectively ended his career. He went on to become a highly successful lawyer in California.

"He was so good at everything," recalled teammate Billy Barnes, who was a first-team All-Met himself in 1978. "At times, it drove us crazy."

Pitchford made first-team All-Met in the *Post* and second team in the *Star*. The other obvious standout on that team, six-foot-ten center Justin Ellis, earned first-team honors in the *Star* and second team in the *Post*. Ellis, as much as anyone, set that particular St. John's team apart. Gallagher had had good big men on his teams before, including future pro Collis Jones ten years earlier. But as few other coaches had, he'd never had a player who was quite so big and so capable of shutting off the inside.

Ellis, like most kids that size and that age, was raw at first. But he learned quickly and soon established himself as the area's best big man. He scored, he rebounded, and he made up for any defensive missteps by his teammates by blocking shots. He was, literally, the last line of defense for St. John's.

"You probably had a typical St. John's team and you throw Justin Ellis in there and that made it special," Barnes said. "If you got beat defensively, he was there to fix it, blocking a shot or intimidating."

There was also a host of eager, hustling, skilled supporting players, the kind of kids a military school such as St. John's always seemed to have in droves. Dennis Dempsey was a standout point guard and long-range shooter, Bobby Boyd was the defensive stopper in the backcourt, and Barnes and Mike Hoyle were the complementary pieces in the starting lineup, splitting time at one of the frontcourt spots.

The other quality that distinguished that team from many of Gallagher's others was the depth of its talent. Aside from Pitchford, Ellis got a scholarship to Wake Forest and finished his college career at Colorado, while Boyd and Barnes played at the College of William & Mary. Dempsey started out at Catholic and transferred to Mount St. Mary's. Even reserves such as Mark Townsend and Bill Freitag played college basketball at Loyola University Maryland and the Naval Academy, respectively. The roster also included a couple of Division I football players in Tom Fitzpatrick (Villanova) and Kevin Jez (Boston College). "There were guys on our bench who were pretty good players when they got the chance to play," Dempsey noted.

Experience was another big advantage. Pitchford, Dempsey, Boyd, Ellis, and Hoyle—all were seniors coming off a 21–6 season and knew what to anticipate from one another on the court. "We knew each other's moves before we even made them," Pitchford said.

The season opened with great promise. The Cadets won their opener, 70–63, over the Cardinal Gibbons Crusaders of Baltimore, a team that featured future NBA player Quintin Dailey. In a nonleague game played at Catholic University, the Cadets defeated DeMatha, 64–58, in a mutual fund-raiser for both teams' athletic departments. DeMatha rallied from 12 points down to cut its deficit to 55–52 with 2:43 left. But Boyd scored on a drive and then hit a couple of free throws to keep the Cadets out of danger. Gallagher was pleased but restrained in his praise: "We held our poise like a senior team should."

Perhaps it was a letdown, but the next game provided the only real clunker of the season, a 38–27 loss to the Loyola Dons of Baltimore that left Gallagher fuming about the hometown officials. The Cadets were disgusted with their performance, which included a 19-for-60 effort from the field. In a team meeting after the game, the players vowed they wouldn't lose again.

They kept their word for more than two months, running off 17 straight wins to establish themselves as one of the area's best teams and one of the best in school history. Along the way, the Cadets set a school scoring record with a 108–60 demolition of the Annapolis Panthers. In late January at St. John's, they beat the Stags—who had won 14 straight—74–56, and again the game counted in the league standings. As usual, Pitchford led the way with 24, while Ellis went for 20 points, 11 rebounds, and five blocks. Dempsey scored 12 points and handed out 10 assists.

That string also included Gallagher's 600th victory, a 68–49 wipeout of Carroll. The streak finally came to an end against Mackin, which edged the Cadets, 86–83. That left both DeMatha and St. John's at 9–1 in the league, with the teams set to meet just three days hence to decide the league title and to earn the spot in the City Title Game.

At that point, any edge that St. John's might have developed seemed to be gone. Gallagher's team would have to win at DeMatha, a venue where no local team had triumphed in more than a decade and a half. But this wasn't like other years. The Cadets made an emphatic statement, scoring 99 points in a 12-point victory.

Ellis controlled play at both ends with 25 points and 18 rebounds, while Pitchford added 22 points. St. John's also got a huge boost from Hoyle, who pumped in 21 points and grabbed nine rebounds in a performance that seemed to come out of nowhere. Hoyle hadn't scored in the first game between the two rivals and hadn't even played in the second game. To have him produce such a performance in such a big game—well, it was just that kind of year for St. John's.

After it was over, Wootten, to his credit, didn't mince words about what had happened. "They beat us three times, so I guess that's a good indication of who has the best team," he said. "I guess I can learn to live without one championship after 10 years."

Next up for St. John's was Inter-High champion McKinley in the City Title Game. The Trainers put on quite a show during warm-ups, with their dunking and acrobatics drawing oohs and aahhs from the Cole Field House crowd of 8,000 fans. But Gallagher brought his players back to the locker room, calmed them down, and urged them to play just as they had all year long.

That's just what they did. Executing almost flawlessly, they shot 65 percent in the first half, hitting 24 of 37 shots, and raced to a 50–34 lead at the half. The final was 83–73, but it wasn't really that close. St. John's led by 20 at several points during the game.

"I thought it was one of our better games at both ends of the court," Gallagher said. "It's always a good win when it's over an Inter-High team and especially in the city championship game."

But a 27-win season, a league championship, and the city titles failed to net him and the Cadets the area's No. 1 ranking at the season's end. Instead, that honor went to T. C. Williams of Alexandria, the first Northern Virginia team to finish No. 1 since Washington-Lee did so a decade and a half before. St. John's players claimed they were the better team because they handled T. C. Williams in a preseason scrimmage. But it was tough to argue against the Titans' résumé—a 28–0 record and the first state title for the Northern Region since the last of Washington-Lee's champs in 1966.

@ @ @

School consolidation in Alexandria (three schools joined to form one) left T. C. Williams the biggest school in Virginia and with huge athletic expectations. "Once you lost two games, people thought you were a failure in Alexandria," said long-time W. T. Woodson coach Red Jenkins.

In that regard, the coaching job at T. C. Williams was at once the best of situations and the worst. You always had talent to work with as the city's youth programs were strong, and interest in high school sports there ran high. So Titans coach Mike Hynson could always count on a large talent pool to draw from and big crowds at the games.

But Hynson was always trying to establish some kind of reasonable balance in terms of the team's style of play—less discipline than he would have perhaps liked but more than the players wanted. It was a quandary many coaches face when dealing with a young, skilled group of players. And T. C. Williams was a place where anything short of a trip to states was a disappointment, and the most demanding fans, who often sat right behind the team bench, weren't bashful about voicing their opinions about his coaching moves.

Unfortunately, in the early 1970s Hynson ran into the same problem as everyone else in Northern Virginia—West Springfield. The Spartans made three consecutive trips (1972–74) downstate for the state tournament. T. C. Williams finally broke through and won the region title in 1975 but was quickly eliminated at the state tournament. So hopes were high at T. C. heading into the 1977 season. The team had a solid core of veterans from a team that had gone 17–8, with the losses coming by a total of just 30 points.

"We'd been playing with each other or against each other all our lives," said Craig Harris, the Titans' shooting guard. "One of our main goals growing up was winning the state championship. We'd always talked about it. We really admired guys like [previous T. C. Williams stars] Myron Contee and Carl Jackson, and we wanted to be talked about in the same conversation. So we really set goals. I learned a lot about what being a teammate is that year. It's not really about talent; it's about who's willing to sacrifice."

The five-foot-nine Harris (named first-team All-Met after averaging 19 points) was the Titans' nominal star, although anyone in the starting lineup was capable of a big game. Harris teamed with five-foot-five Willie Jackson to form perhaps the smallest backcourt in the area, but it was probably the most explosive.

At six foot five, Anthony Young was the eraser on the back line. Though prone to foul trouble, Young keyed the defense with his shot blocking and keyed the fast break with his rebounding. George Richardson, Frank Holloway, and Reggie Davidson, who was injured late in the season, helped up front. Holloway, who became the school's all-time leading scorer that season, told Harris early on that he should focus on scoring. Holloway was a big-time football recruit dealing with shoulder and back injuries on and off, so he vowed to concentrate on the less glamorous parts of the game. "Don't worry about passing [me] the ball," he told Harris. "I'll just go get the rebounds."

Harris remembered, "The guy had so much heart. He just motivated you with his toughness. He'd play with one arm if he had to."

With speed on the outside and athletic big men on the inside, it was no secret how Hynson's team was going to play—all out at both ends. "We are going to run and run and run and run some more and shoot while we are doing it," Hynson said during the preseason.

And with few exceptions, that's what the Titans did. Jackson's leadership and ballhandling gave T. C. the ability to slow it down on the rare occasions a half-court set was called for, but mostly the Titans played racehorse basketball, pressing and fast breaking their way to an average of 84 points.

"Basically, we tried to wear everybody down," Harris said. They made no secret of their goals, either, counting off the victories as they went. Everyone focused on reaching 28, which would mean the long-sought-after state title.

The Titans rolled through December, winning the Armstrong-Walker Christmas Tournament and knocking off defending state champion Maggie Walker en route to the title. When the calendar turned to 1977, T. C. Williams found itself atop the local high school polls, the first Northern Virginia school to hold the top spot at any point since Washington-Lee was voted No. 1 in the Star's final 1963 poll. St. John's took over the top spot for a time, but T. C. Williams simply wouldn't lose and wound up atop both polls at the end of the season.

A week after being ranked No. 1, the Titans blitzed W. T. Woodson, 86–60. Richardson, normally one to score his points on follow-ups, exploded for 29 points. Harris added 24, plus eight assists, and Young blocked eight shots.

Davidson went down with a broken ankle in early February, but T. C. never missed a beat. Mike Daniels moved into the starting lineup and contributed 15 points and eight rebounds in a 61–54 victory over Robinson, one of the few close calls the Titans had.

The return match at Robinson in mid-February was a different story. The Titans closed out a perfect 21–0 regular-season mark with an 80–52 wipeout. Although some might have been impressed by the margin and the performance, Hynson wasn't. After all, the Titans had much bigger goals in mind. "We did what we were supposed to do," he said.

They beat Woodson again, 89–74, to win the Northern District tournament title, with Young taking center stage. He'd struggled with foul trouble in several games, but nothing slowed him down that day: 19 points, 20 rebounds, and five blocked shots. Young's thunderous slam off a missed free throw broke open what had been a close game. Richardson led the scoring with 22 points, Jackson added 16, and Holloway had 10 with 11 rebounds.

When the same two teams met for the Northern Region title, Woodson coach Red Jenkins figured he'd try something different. His team had lost three times to the Titans already, all by double digits. So he figured he'd slow things down. Way down. And it almost worked.

T. C. Williams managed to survive the slowdown and punched its ticket to the state tournament with a 21–18 victory. Only two field goals were scored in the entire second half, with Young's last-second dunk clinching the victory. Woodson had come close, but the Titans had prevailed, even if it had been more nerve wracking than anyone had anticipated.

When Hynson went to greet Jenkins afterward, the Woodson coach couldn't help but notice that Hynson's hands were shaking badly. Even though Woodson had nearly pulled off the upset with an inspired bit of trickery, Jenkins couldn't help but admire the grit and talent of the Titans, now 26–0. "It would have been a damn shame if we had won that game," he said.

So off to Charlottesville the Titans went, carrying the hopes and dreams of the Alexandria basketball community with them. The local fans had seen the 1971–72 squad go unbeaten in the regular season only to lose to Groveton in the region playoffs. In 1975 the Titans had finally knocked off West Springfield to earn a trip downstate—while Harris, Holloway, and Young were sophomores—only to lose in the semifinals.

"They [previous T. C. Williams teams] just went down there for the ride," Harris said. "We're going down there to win it."

Harris's bravado seemed a bit misplaced, considering how the semifinal game against the deliberate Henrico Warriors began. The Titans were tense and, even worse, cold. They hit just four of their first 16 shots. However, Young took over until his teammates came around. He scored only 12 points but grabbed 23 rebounds and blocked six shots in a tense 68–64 victory. The game wasn't sewn up until Richardson hit a pair of free throws, and Harris added another inside the final two minutes.

"I was real tight in the first half, as tight as I remember being for a game," Harris said. "We are all feeling some pressure, but we're just going to have to play as best we can."

The truth was the Titans hadn't shot the ball well through most of the postseason. Maybe they were feeling some pressure and maybe their opponents were finding ways to combat their high-powered attack.

In the state final against the William Fleming Colonels of Roanoke, the Titans took a collective deep breath, relaxed, and proceeded to play their kind of basketball. They romped 95–73, setting a state tournament record for points in one game

(95) and in two games (163). Jackson led the charge with 26 points and six steals. Holloway added 20 points and 13 rebounds. There was no doubt about this one as the Titans sped to a 40–26 halftime lead.

"We haven't been shooting well the last couple of weeks, and with our style of basketball, it can really make a big difference," Hynson said. "We haven't talked about it much because we didn't want the kids to start pressing. We knew it was just a matter of time, and tonight, they cut loose. That's the way we've been playing all year."

After the remarkable St. John's team of 1977 had knocked DeMatha into second place in its own league for the first time since Austin Carr and Mackin did it a decade before, some people were starting to wonder about DeMatha. After the brilliant four-year run with Adrian Dantley ended in 1973, DeMatha had failed to regain the No. 1 spot in either the *Post*'s or the *Star*'s final poll in any of the next four years. That's how high the standards were at DeMatha, which had won more than 100 games during that stretch, including 29 in 1977, matching the highest single-season victory total in school history.

If anything, Coach Morgan Wootten and the Stags were victims of their own success. Because they were always so good, everyone expected them to win everything in sight. Then, too, because DeMatha set the standard for excellence, it was inevitable that occasionally another team was going to rise to that level and be dead set on knocking off the kings of local hoops. It would not be an exaggeration to say that DeMatha raised the level of play throughout the area. And during the mid-1970s, the Stags were beaten by the kinds of teams their success, in some way, helped create.

As usual, Wootten had the ultimate response to those who suggested DeMatha might have slipped a bit: his 1978 squad took on all comers and became the first in school history to finish undefeated at 28–0.

Wootten had produced several one-loss seasons during his tenure, including the last two years of Dantley's career. At that time, Wootten speculated that it would be difficult to go through an entire season undefeated simply because DeMatha was always the biggest game on everyone's schedule, and Wootten insisted on playing the topflight competition in addition to the rigorous Metro Conference schedule. The Stags had gained valuable experience the year before, and an August trip to Brazil to play a dozen games helped build camaraderie and cohesion.

The 1978 Stags gave an indication of what kind of season it would be on opening night. They blasted a quality W. T. Woodson team, 105–66, with Tommy Branch (whose younger brother Adrian would become DeMatha's main man two years later) leading the way with 25 points.

That was just the beginning. Eight times that season, DeMatha topped 100 points. The DeMatha team was unique not only because of its record but because of its makeup as well. Over the years, Wootten's teams had boasted stars such as Ernie Cage, who was followed by John Austin, who was followed by Bob Whitmore, and on down through James Brown, Adrian Dantley, Kenny Carr, and Hawkeye Whitney.

This particular team didn't have anyone similar to those players. Branch was the top scorer on the team, averaging about 15 points. He also was the lone All-Met. But what the Stags might have lacked in star power, they made up for with depth. This team came at you in waves. When curious college coaches would drop by and ask Wootten who his best player was, he would innocently reply, "I have no idea."

Said senior point guard Dutch Morley, "We probably had 10 guys that were interchangeable. If someone had a bad night, there was no reason he couldn't be taken care of by the other guys. There wasn't that much of a letup. We pretty much had two [starter-level] teams."

And because Wootten could use 10 players with no drop-off, the Stags pressed relentlessly every game, usually wearing down their opponents. According to Morley, having all that talent made the competition for playing time "pretty intense"; it kept anyone from letting up as the victories mounted.

Wootten's biggest challenge then was keeping everyone happy. Sidney Lowe and Dereck Whittenburg would lead North Carolina State to an improbable NCAA title in 1983, but at DeMatha neither could crack the starting lineup as juniors. "We had to keep 10 guys happy," Wootten recalled. "The big thing was to make sure everyone felt wanted, felt loved."

Wootten was the main reason nobody broke ranks. He was tough but fair, a coach whom everyone respected. "You were told when you did things wrong, and you were praised when you did things right," Morley said. "He was in charge. Nobody rocked the boat. If you did, you fell off."

Winning helped head off any bruised egos too. DeMatha went to 11–0 with a 78–56 blowout of Eastern while causing 35 turnovers. After the Stags crushed Gonzaga, 90–53, *Basketball Weekly* rated them the No. 1 high school team in the country—a designation some felt didn't go far enough. "They're the best high school team I've ever seen," said awestruck Gonzaga coach Dick Myers.

Once again, DeMatha was the team everyone was talking about, and Wootten took great delight in responding to folks who congratulated him on DeMatha's being "back," whatever that meant. "We never left," he would tell them. "We've always been right here. Those were just great teams that beat us out."

As the winning streak grew, DeMatha's players never really felt any pressure to stay undefeated, according to Morley. All too often, the games would be decided before halftime, and the Stags didn't waver in the rare close games they had because they'd all been stung previously by the program's first home losses in almost 20 years against St. John's and the Bishop Eustace Crusaders of Philadelphia.

"There was certainly some business to take care of senior year," Morley said. "We did a pretty good job of it, I do believe."

In late February, DeMatha got its league title back, wrapping it up with an 85–59 victory over Good Counsel, for the Stags' 16th conference title in 18 years. That victory ran their season record to 22–0 and set up another matchup against Joe Dean Davidson and Dunbar in the City Title Game, the third time in four years that the Stags and Crimson Tide would play in the ultimate contest. They had split the first two meetings, with DeMatha winning 67–62 in 1975, while Dunbar took the title the next year with a 70–66 triumph to cap its unbeaten season.

The Crimson Tide came into the 1978 title game with a 25–2 record and a 19-game winning streak and was every bit DeMatha's equal for three quarters, pulling to 42–41 early in the fourth. That's when DeMatha went on an 11–0 run, from which Dunbar couldn't recover. The final was 63–55, with Paul DeVito and Branch sharing scoring honors with 15 points each. "We came back like a No. 1 team should," Wootten said.

Davidson, to his credit, was gracious in defeat. He said, "We are a proud team and we gave it our best shot and that's that. It's gonna take a helluva team to beat DeMatha."

All that was left was the season-ending Alhambra Catholic Invitational Tournament, where DeMatha would need to handle a strong Mackin team for the third time that season. Mackin star Mark Nickens was limited by some foul trouble, and DeMatha trailed by one at the half. But Branch, who finished with 28 points, helped DeMatha get going again, and the Stags coasted home with a 74–64 victory and their perfect season at 27–0.

"You could see this team coming," Wootten said with a gleam in his eye after the season was over. "We utilized some different things [like pressure defense] to take advantage of the depth. And most importantly, we didn't try to create a superstar where there wasn't one. At the beginning of the season, we told the players that a lot of them could be all-stars somewhere else, but that we weren't going to worry about that."

The concept of "all-stars" loomed large over the DC high school basketball landscape at the end of 1978. For the fifth year in a row, a team of local all-stars was slated to play a team of national all-stars in the Capital Classic. The game, which was played at the Capital Centre, gave local fans a chance to see future college and professional stars such as Moses Malone, Albert King, and Gene Banks.

The problem was that the national stars were so good, the Capital Classic was anything but classic. In the first four years the game was played, the locals never came closer than 18 points of their guests, with one of the games being an embarrassing 31-point runaway.

More of the same was expected in 1978. The local team, which included Morley, the Churchill Bulldogs' Eric Smith, and Spingarn's Bryant Johnson, wasn't considered particularly strong by DC standards. Nobody expected the Capital squad, coached by Churchill's Les Lombardi, to put up much of a fight.

The *Star*'s article previewing the game proclaimed, "There's a good possibility that the record 31-point margin of victory . . . may be in jeopardy." The *Post* was no less harsh in its assessment: "Probably the only thing that could save the Metro All-Stars from embarrassment in tonight's Capital Classic against the U.S. All-Stars at Capital Centre would be a last-minute change in the rules. As has been the case the last couple of years . . . the U.S. Stars are loaded and the Metro Stars are out of their league."

Lombardi and his players, understanding they were at a disadvantage talent-wise, figured they'd have a chance if they stuck together and played as a team instead of like a collection of all-stars. "I know the team concept is the only way," said DeMatha's Branch, who learned that lesson well during the course of the Stags' record-setting season. "I played on an undefeated team this season, and that's why we won. It's our only chance."

So the locals played it straight, opting to play the game as if it were a real basketball game instead of a showcase event. They stayed disciplined on offense, shared the ball, and got a couple of outstanding performances in a stunning 87–73 victory.

Smith, who had been awful during the practices leading up to the game, came off the bench and hit his first five shots, staking his team to a 25–14 lead. He finished with 16 points to lead the Capital team.

Johnson, the tallest of the locals at six foot seven but still at a height disadvantage against the nationals, grabbed a share of the MVP honors with 15 points and 20 rebounds. Because of him, the US team's rebounding edge in the game was a mere 52–49.

The other half of the MVP tandem was Morley. He scored only seven points but handed out five assists and so clearly controlled the tempo of the game that his stardom was obvious even to the neophytes among the crowd of 14,923 fans. Morley also made the game's key defensive play, drawing a charge to stop a three-on-one break during a key stretch late in the game. "We knew we couldn't run with them, so we just spread them out and kept control of the game," Morley said.

It was the first victory in the series for the locals, and it was a bit untraditional perhaps but, oh, so sweet.

"People thought we were gonna get beat by 50," Morley recalled. "But those kids believed they could win. That was all you needed. That was great for local basketball. It just showed that talent level that we had in the DC area. It wasn't your traditional all-star game, but it was a W."

Throughout the offseason, coaches and fans would come up to Lombardi and congratulate him on the victory, on striking a blow for area basketball. His greeting at Churchill High School the next day wasn't quite as big an ego boost. He'd arrived at school the next morning, pleased to have the opportunity to bask in the glow of the victory and receive the compliments and praise of his colleagues. Instead, he found himself assigned to cafeteria duty, and the question he found himself asked more than any other was, "What are you doing here?" Lombardi could only roll his eyes and laugh. Anyone who has ever taught and/or coached for a living at the high school level knows exactly how he felt.

When it comes to boys' high school basketball, players and fans tend to be provincial. The era that any one person played in, or the players he played against, or the ones he watched are always deemed superior to any other.

But it's not that simple. Comparing players across the years is difficult at best, folly at worst, given the changes in the game, training methods, coaching, or any number of factors. That said, it would be difficult to argue that the 1970s represented anything but the zenith of public school basketball in Montgomery County.

The numbers are beyond dispute. In the 23 years between the end of World War II and 1970 (there were no state tournaments from 1940 to 1946), Montgomery County teams won a total of 11 state basketball championships. From 1980 to 2010, county schools captured a dozen state titles, including an impressive five straight in Class 4A from 2006 to 2010. That span also included a nine-year dry spell (1989–97) during which county teams failed to win a single title.

In between those two eras, Montgomery County teams enjoyed a remarkable run of success. In the nine years from 1971 to 1979, county teams brought home 12 state championship trophies, a total that took the next 30 years to match. And unlike what happened in neighboring Prince George's County in the 1960s and 1970s, that period wasn't dominated by any particular team, at least not to the extent that Fairmont Heights and Gwynn Park reigned in their particular classifications.

To borrow a phrase used regularly in well-to-do Montgomery County, it was "everybody into the pool." Montgomery Blair was the big winner among county teams of that era, winning state championships in 1975, 1977, and 1979. But the Rockville Rams (1971, 1973) and the Wootton Patriots (1978, 1979) each won twice, with single titles going to Springbrook (1972), the Woodward Wildcats (1977), the Paint Branch Panthers (1977), Churchill (1978), and the Sherwood Warriors (1979). That roster doesn't even take into account the success during that era of a program such as that of Bethesda–Chevy Chase, which went to the state finals four times from 1970 to 1976 and lost each time.

Coaching, by almost universal agreement, was the reason for that run of success. For men such as Springbrook's John Barrett, Blair's Gene Doane, Paint Branch's Hank Galotta, Sherwood's Mel Laughner, Rockville's Jim Conner, and Woodward's Tom George, coaching wasn't a job; it was their *life*. And they didn't just field a succession of teams; they built *programs*.

"When you use the term 'program,' it can be used very casually," said Barrett, who guided Springbrook's basketball fortunes for more than two decades, won more than 500 games, and had the court at the school named after him. "A program to me is when you do it over a long period of time. I went to lots of clinics, I studied the game from all different angles. There's not as much of that now. I'm not sure a lot of high school coaches want to do that now. They come and go."

Barrett and the men he coached against during that period weren't dabbling in coaching; they were in it for the long haul. Laughner coached at Sherwood for 29 years; Galotta for 25 at Paint Branch. George was the only basketball coach in the now-closed Woodward's 21-year history, while Conner was Rockville's lone coach for that school's first decade and a half. The court there is named for him. Galotta won more than 400 games, and Laughner and George (if you include his years in Pennsylvania) won more than 300. Conner went 274–104, a .724 winning percentage. Doane spent a quarter century in the school system, spreading his time between Sherwood, Blair, and the Seneca Valley Screaming Eagles and winning a pair of state titles.

"The coaches you had then—they worked at the game," Doane said. "They worked at the game, so you had to be good to beat them." That's one thing that virtually every coach from that period mentioned—the need to have yourself and your players ready every night because of who you were going up against.

"There were very few nights off," recalled Laughner, who became an institution at Sherwood, coaching from the mid-1970s until the turn of the century. "It made everybody better, and it made everyone work harder. It made everyone totally prepared. It was a real challenge to coach against those guys, and it was really fun."

Well, it wasn't always fun. These schools were all battling for county championships and a few select spots in the state tournament. Every game was big, every game mattered, and every loss hurt, even the ones in the regular season, because it meant that somebody had gotten the jump on you.

Consequently, there were some hard feelings between certain coaches on many nights. Whoever was mad at somebody else usually depended on who'd won the last game between their two teams.

"We were all a little crazy back then," said Les Lombardi, who coached Churchill to the Montgomery Class AA title in 1977 (only to lose to Blair in the playoffs) before winning the state Class AA championship the next season. "But we all had talent, and that's why the championships came."

Barrett agreed: "When you're coaching, you don't love every coach you're playing against. But that fades away after a while. Of course, I never told my players that."

Everyone wanted to win so badly that sometimes it was difficult, right before the game or right after, to observe the requisite proprieties. One time Barrett expressed his amazement that Laughner could go up to an opposing coach just before the game and exchange a bit of light-hearted banter. It was an act of fellowship the Springbrook coach couldn't fathom. "I don't dislike you," he once told Laughner. "But I do on game night."

But it wasn't always so contentious, for there was bonding too. Dale Miller, who coached at Bethesda–Chevy Chase and Wootton, recalled going on early morning fishing excursions with Conner, a man whom George respected so much he let his own son play for him at Rockville. And when Lombardi coached the Capital All-Stars to their first-ever win over the US team in the Capital Classic in 1978, the most heartfelt congratulations he received came from Barrett, a man whom he'd competed so fiercely against during the season.

Galotta, who took over at Paint Branch in 1973–74, was surprised at some of the hard feelings he encountered among his colleagues. He was used to a more gentlemanly approach in the Catholic League / Metro Conference, where he had served as Morgan Wootten's assistant at DeMatha during the James Brown–Adrian Dantley era. Wootten and Joe Gallagher, two longtime friends and business partners, set the tone in that league, so the hard feelings never became too severe.

Of course, Galotta didn't endear himself to anyone by upsetting the pecking order in the county. He came in and had the audacity to go 17–5 in his first season, with kids who previously would have gone to Springbrook or Sherwood before Paint Branch opened. As a young coach, he could sense the initial resentment from some of his more established brethren. In time, though, he became a Montgomery County fixture himself, adding a title of his own to the county's collection in 1977 and guiding Paint Branch's basketball fortunes for more than two decades.

At the center of all this intense competition was the rivalry between two of the county's primary Class AA powers—Springbrook and Blair. Any game between the two schools was a battle for bragging rights in and around Silver Spring, as players from both schools congregated on the courts in Sligo Creek Park near Blair or at Hillandale near Springbrook.

Brian Magid, Blair's deadly All-Met shooter from the mid-1970s, grew up near New Hampshire Avenue and Adelphi Road, so he lived right on the border of the two schools. When enrollment levels changed later on, his Oakview neighborhood became part of Springbrook territory.

The "Blond Bomber" recalled spending more time with Springbrook's players than with his own teammates during the summers, at least in part because Springbrook's gym was open more often once school was out and offered a chance to play indoors rather than on the unforgiving blacktop. That's the way it was for a lot of kids who played at those schools. Young men who had been teammates in youth league basketball in Silver Spring found themselves blood rivals during the season because of where they happened to live and where the school boundaries were drawn.

"I remember the great atmosphere of those games," said Willis Wilson, who played on the Blazers' 1977 state title team. "We played ball with Springbrook guys all summer. There was a familiarity there. But the loyalty and allegiance to your school was much greater back then."

Cedric Boatman was an imposing six-foot-six rebounder and outlet passer who triggered the fast break for Doane's 1975 state champs, a team many consider the gold standard in Montgomery County. "You respected them so much, but you wanted to beat them," Boatman said of the Blue Devils. "You'd talk a little smack on the playground. That kind of rivalry isn't there anymore. It's different. A Blair-Springbrook game was packed all the time. It was incredible. People would be scalping tickets."

By the time Springbrook opened in 1960, Blair had already won three state championships under Dave Carrasco and had been to two other state championship games under Ed Moffatt. Springbrook, meanwhile, became a successful program almost immediately, advancing to the state tournament in 1962 and '63. But the basketball rivalry between the two schools really began to heat up when Barrett and Doane took over at their respective schools within a year of each other in the early 1970s.

Both coaches were fiery, demanding, and, most of all, successful. To outsiders, they might have appeared grouchy, insensitive, and single-minded. But both were more complicated than that.

"He wasn't a touchy-feely guy," said Craig Esherick, a reserve on Barrett's 1972 state champion Springbrook team and an All-Met as a senior in 1974. Yet nearly four decades after graduating, Esherick still couldn't bring himself to call his old coach anything but Mr. Barrett.

"My name's John, you know," the old coach chided him one time.

"I know," Esherick replied, "But I just can't make my mouth say the word."

Esherick wasn't alone. Barrett was held in the highest esteem in the Springbrook community, even if he might not always say hello when you passed him in the hall. When the court at the school was named in Barrett's honor, a good 20 years after he'd retired from the sidelines, hundreds turned out for the ceremony.

And why not? With no disrespect to the men who preceded him and followed him, John Barrett *was* Springbrook basketball. His team won the state title in 1972, buoyed by the presence of Buzzy Braman, who was one in a long line of standout shooters: Ed Peterson (who tutored Magid, among others), Chuck Driesell (son of the longtime Maryland coach), Kevin McLinton, and Chris McGuthrie.

Barrett had Springbrook back in the state tournament again in 1973 and '74, putting together a three-year run that ranked with anyone's. Barrett's record after his first four seasons was a fabulous 72–16. And yet the year that Springbrook won its first state title (1972), the Blue Devils got into the state tournament on a fluke. The Blue Devils actually lost in the county playoffs to Peary that year, but because the Huskies had played one more than the permitted 20 games during the season,

Springbrook took Peary's place in the state tournament. There was nothing tainted about Springbrook's play once it reached Cole Field House though.

All-Met Braman pumped in 28 points in a 75–61 victory over Annapolis in the semifinal, including a perfect 12-for-12 performance from the foul line. Braman scored 24 in the 72–59 state championship conquest of Bladensburg, hitting 10 for 16 from the floor. No wonder that he went on to become a nationally renowned shooting instructor, tutoring a number of NBA players on proper form and technique.

"They shot too well for us outside," said Bladensburg coach Roy Henderson, offering a lament heard from numerous Springbrook opponents over the years. "They had a great shooting game. They deserved to win."

That Springbrook, which would otherwise have been the second-best team in the county, could step in and rather easily win the state title in place of the on-court champion was perhaps the best indication of the caliber of play in Montgomery County during that period.

Doane, who was every bit as intense as Barrett, took over as the king of the hill after Springbrook's three consecutive runs to the state tournament ended in 1974. He led Blair to state titles in 1975 and '77 and had the 1979 team poised to win another. It eventually did, but by that time Doane had taken on the challenge of building the program at newly opened Seneca Valley. Like Barrett, Doane had his detractors. But, again, just as Barrett's players did, Doane's players always spoke well of him.

"Coach Doane could be loud and abrasive, but he was very close to his players," Magid said. "And it was not something you noticed if you weren't on the team. He really cared, and not just for us as basketball players either."

During a Blair-Springbrook game, there was no better show than watching Doane or Barrett make strategic moves and then try to counteract the other. That game within a game was a treat for anyone interested in basketball at the tactical level. To keep Magid under control, Barrett liked to have a different player guard him every couple of minutes and give him a different look. Doane would run Magid through an obstacle course of screens and picks to get him open, or he would try to isolate Boatman inside where no other Springbrook players could offer help.

"You want to talk about a hell of a coach? He was a hell of a coach," Doane said of Barrett. "The rivalry was intense because we overlapped those two areas. My kids knew his kids and vice versa. They'd hang together. When we laced up the sneakers, that upped the ante because they were all close friends. You were gonna defend your turf. He would do something in a game that I'd have to react to and I'd have to counter. And I'd do things he'd have to react to."

Said Boatman, "I knew deep down inside [that] Doane and Barrett had a lot of respect for each other, even though a lot of people thought they were like oil and water. There was this image of [Doane] being so hard-nosed and not caring. But he wasn't really like that. You had to get to know him. He had a good heart. During a game, though, he was crazy."

Doane was crazy enough to gather his players the first day of practice in the fall of 1974 and congratulate them on the state championship they were going to win. The Blazers had lost in the county semifinals in 1974, denying everyone what might have been an epic championship game between Blair and Springbrook for the right to go to Cole Field House.

"That playoff loss [to Peary] totally informed the next year," Magid said. It hurt so bad that nobody connected with Blair basketball was going to let it happen again. That's why Boatman led his teammates on summer runs through Sligo Creek Park and kept everyone in shape. That's why practice began, on an informal basis, as soon as school started in the fall.

Of course, Blair's run to the 1975 state title would not have been possible without talent, which Doane had in abundance. First of all, Magid was perhaps the area's best pure shooter. Up front were the formidable big men Boatman and Van Buren Vaughn.

"We were big and strong and talented," Magid said. "There weren't too many teams that could contend with us inside. As far as I was concerned, the planets were aligned. You couldn't play us man, so you'd have to play us zone."

Laughner, who was just starting his coaching career at Sherwood back then, called the Blazers "unreal." And even though the Blazers won their first six games and nipped Loyola, Baltimore's top-rated team, in December, they couldn't protect their home court against Springbrook, which hung a 58–57 loss on them in late January. But aside from an upset loss to Whitman a couple of weeks later, the Blazers didn't trip again. They won the return match with Springbrook and beat the Blue Devils again in the county playoffs to earn a trip to states. At 21–2, they were ranked fourth in the *Star*'s final poll. After the two state tournament victories, they occupied the same spot in the *Post*'s final balloting.

Magid, who'd become Blair's all-time leading scorer during the season, managed just 12 points in a 73–55 semifinal blowout of the Parkville Knights, preferring to find open teammates, a testament to his unselfishness and his overlooked passing abilities. In the state final against DuVal, the cold-blooded, fair-haired boy next door turned assassin again, scoring half of his team's total in a 66–61 victory. Magid had heard some whispers from those who'd thought he was overrated after the semifinal performance, so he set out to prove them wrong. He hit 10 of his first 12 shots—most from far beyond what would be three-point range today—and 16 of 22 overall. With 2:16 left, he drove right-handed, found his path blocked, and switched the ball to his left hand for the layup that essentially sealed the deal. "I'm glad I could show people the real me," he said happily.

The superb performances by Braman and Magid were hardly singular among county ballplayers in that era in the state tournament. Every year, it seemed, something magical would happen when a county team finally got to Cole Field House.

In 1977 Blair, Woodward, and Paint Branch all won state titles. Back in those days, most folks didn't even know where Paint Branch was. Indiana coach Bobby Knight supposedly got lost trying to find the school on a scouting trip, and opposing fans used to taunt Panthers players with the cry, "What's a Paint Branch?" But Galotta and Tracy Jackson, the player who attracted Knight's foray to Burtonsville, put the program on the map.

Jackson, who went on to become a big star at Notre Dame before playing for the pre–Michael Jordan Chicago Bulls, was the best player ever produced by the Montgomery County school system. No less an expert than Barrett, a man not given to idle praise, called Jackson the best he'd ever gone up against in Montgomery County. "We had a hard time doing anything with him," Barrett said.

At six foot five and 205 pounds, Jackson could, and did, do it all. He played center, he played power forward, he could shoot from the outside, and he could handle the ball. Against DeMatha, St. John's, and Mackin—the three best teams in the area that were also on the Paint Branch schedule—Jackson scored 105 points and grabbed 44 rebounds. Those totals were the unimpeachable response to those people who claimed Montgomery County's best couldn't compete with the top players from other jurisdictions. In fact, those three-game totals mirrored Jackson's senior-season averages almost perfectly: he led the area in scoring with 30 points per game, averaged 16 rebounds, and shot 60 percent from the floor.

"What could he do?" asked Galotta, who had tutored the likes of James Brown and Dantley as a DeMatha assistant. "Whatever it takes to win the game. He was as good a high school player as I've ever seen."

And he was no prima donna either. Galotta compared Jackson to Brown for his generosity of spirit and his sweet disposition. Jackson always had a smile on his face, had a kind word for everyone, and never got into trouble. "The only time you'd see him out on Friday night was at the McDonald's on New Hampshire Avenue," noted Blair's Wilson, who played youth basketball with Jackson.

"Even his opponents really, really liked him," Galotta said. "You can't say that about a lot of high school stars."

As the state tournament approached, Jackson had nothing left to prove. The *Post* named him its Player of the Year, the first from Montgomery County to be so honored. Though his future and his legacy were assured, Jackson was determined to close his prep career with a flourish. He scored 29 points and grabbed 16 rebounds in an 86–61 wipeout of the Francis Scott Key Eagles in the state semifinals. In the championship game against the Edgewood Rams, Jackson scored 34 points on 16-for-20 shooting in a 76–52 rout.

Without a doubt, Jackson had one of the great senior seasons in county history. But the next year, Churchill's Eric Smith went him one better—sort of. During the

1977–78 school year, Smith turned in one of the great performances in the history of Maryland public school athletics.

In the fall, he quarterbacked the Fred Shepherd–coached Bulldogs to a state championship, the program's second in succession. Smith ran Churchill's option attack to perfection. In the state final against Woodlawn's Warriors, Smith ran 23 yards for the game's first score and passed for another in a 21–16 victory.

He was slow to adjust once basketball season began, a common experience among football players making the transition indoors. Consequently, Churchill got off to a sluggish start. But led by Smith, the team jelled near mid-season and wound up tied for the best record in the county's AA league at 10–2. "We kind of got on Eric's shoulders," remembered Lombardi. "He was just the kind of guy who could make things happen."

In the playoffs, Springbrook beat Blair in Doane's finale before Churchill topped the Blue Devils to earn a trip to Cole Field House despite a good-but-not-great 17–8 overall record. But the record was deceiving; behind Smith, Churchill had caught fire. He dominated in the 85–78 semifinal victory over Annapolis, scoring a school-record 35 points, including eight in the last 2:50 after the score was tied at 76.

Churchill was one of four Montgomery teams to reach the state finals, with one in every classification for the first time ever. The Bulldogs faced a Bladensburg team that featured six-foot-eleven future NBA star Thurl Bailey, but it was Smith's show again. He and the rest of the Bulldogs simply shot down the Mustangs, hitting 17 of 28 shots in the first half en route to a 77–63 win. All Smith did was score 29 points on 9-for-11 shooting from the floor and 11 for 13 from the line.

"It was just unbelievable how everything worked out in the state final," Smith said, sounding as if he still didn't quite believe what happened himself. "I got hot when we needed it. I can't explain it."

Montgomery County won three more titles in 1979, with Blair, Wootton, and Sherwood taking home the ultimate prize. But as the decade wound to a close, so did that era of unprecedented success for county teams.

The first blow came when Wootton's Dale Miller retired from coaching after the 1979–80 season. The rough-hewn western Pennsylvania native sometimes seemed out of place in genteel Montgomery County, but he had built a solid record (190–74) with back-to-back state titles in 1978 and 1979 and four other trips to the state final in 11 seasons at Bethesda–Chevy Chase and Wootton.

"I never liked to see a great one sit down," Doane said. "He comes at you like a tiger. You had to be well-prepared when you played him. I enjoyed going against him because he was the best. Dale's team played any style. They ran, they pressed,

Chapter Four

they were deliberate. They played zone, and they played man. He did what was best for his personnel—that's what I call a coach."

Miller's departure was the start of the exodus. Conner stepped down after the 1981–82 season; Doane retired after the 1985–86 campaign. George was done when Woodward closed shortly thereafter, merging with Walter Johnson High. Barrett, Galotta, and Laughner did last into the 1990s, with Barrett winning another state title in 1988. But the depth of quality coaches, with the night-in, night-out battle of wills and wits, was over.

Then, too, private school programs were becoming a more attractive option, especially with the county growing more affluent with every passing year. Even without any kind of aid, many families could afford the tuition at a Metro Conference school or somewhere else. After all, private schools had more relaxed rules about how many games they could play, or how far they could travel to play at an in-season tournament. The varsity coach could coach his guys in summer-league basketball, but that wasn't permitted for public school coaches. More and more, the private schools seemed to offer a better alternative for high school basketball players.

All those factors detracted from the quality of play in the county. Someone like Johnny Dawkins—who grew up playing at Sligo Creek Park with the kids who would attend Blair, Northwood, Kennedy, and Springbrook—wound up at Mackin. There he enjoyed an outstanding career, which led him to Duke and eventually the NBA.

"Part of it was the opening up of the recruiting rules," said Galotta, who went to St. John's and coached at DeMatha. "I think we lost a lot of players that normally would have stayed home and played. We lost some pretty good players, and we couldn't compete with that."

Lamented Barrett, "Private schools were always telling kids they could go there and play before bigger crowds and play in more games. To me, that's BS. But now, when you're a public school coach, you have to really convince people that you have a good program."

Most Washington-area high schools with a history of success in basketball are close to the city. That only makes sense. Those areas are more populous than the outlying suburbs, and players at places such as Fairmont Heights, Blair, and T. C. Williams could always cross the boundary into the District and find any number of hot spots for pickup basketball against the best players in the city.

Gwynn Park, winner of 10 state basketball championships, had a geographic advantage: the school was far from the hustle and bustle of the city yet was still the centerpiece of its southern Prince George's County community. Located in rural Brandywine, Gwynn Park was considered quite remote during its basketball heyday in the 1960s and 1970s. For many years, a large sign welcoming "the future farmers of America" proudly stood by the entrance of the school near the intersection of Routes 5 and 301. "It was Mayberry," said Larry Gandee, who coached the Yellow Jackets to a half-dozen state titles from 1969 to 1980.

It was the kind of time and place that Webb's Grocery, the former center of what little activity there was in Brandywine then, would close down for the Yellow Jackets' big games in the state tournament, reasoning that nobody was going to be doing any shopping that day anyway. Plus the proprietors might have been eager to catch Gywnn Park in action themselves. The oft-told joke around those parts was that the ideal time to commit a crime would be during a Gwynn Park basketball game, because everybody in town would be there.

The run of championships actually started in 1967–68, when Gandee's friend Tim Carney coached the team. Gandee was an assistant coach then and took over the next season from his fellow Glenville (West Virginia) State College alum. Gwynn Park hadn't enjoyed any basketball success to speak of until integration came in the mid-1960s. Basketball success helped ease that major transition. There wasn't much else going on in Brandywine in those days, so the games themselves became a big deal and a sort of rallying point for the entire school community, which extended to the Charles County line and then remote Waldorf. As the games became even a bigger and bigger deal in the community, sustaining the program's success became easier. Youngsters in grade school and junior high got hooked on the excitement and passion of the games played by their older brothers and friends, and they in turn worked hard to develop their own skills so that they, too, could play for the Yellow Jackets when their time came.

It also helped that youngsters in the rural community were familiar with the concept of hard work. Gandee knew a lot of students who helped on their family farms, cutting tobacco or doing whatever other chores needed to be done. That work ethic seemed to carry over to the basketball court; Gwynn Park players were known to be hardworking and generally got better over time because they diligently developed their skills. Then, too, they didn't have the distractions of more urban areas such as shopping malls and fast-food joints to divert their attention from sports.

"Every one of my players lived at the end of a dirt road," recalled former Carroll great George Leftwich, who coached Gwynn Park to a pair of state titles in the 1980s. "That's what I loved about those kids."

Gwynn Park was far and away the smallest school in the county. Enrollment in the early years of Gandee's tenure was fewer than 400 students, making it the area's smallest public school. In one of the Yellow Jackets' state championship seasons, only 145 boys were in the entire school. As the county's lone Class C school, Gwynn Park was forced to consistently face good teams from bigger schools such as the Douglass Eagles, Central Falcons, and Fairmont Heights Hornets. The

Yellow Jackets had a big advantage once they reached the state tournament since they had been so tested during the season compared to other Class C schools from the Eastern Shore or western Maryland. The Yellow Jackets seldom lost once they got to Cole Field House, the site of the state tournament.

A strong youth program in the area also helped sustain Gwynn Park's success. Most of the credit for that goes to a man named Howard Mathews, beloved in the community although virtually anonymous outside of it. Many a Gwynn Park basketball player over the years came under Mathews's tutelage, and he made sure they learned the game the right way. His son Steve became Gwynn Park's coach in the 1990s. But the influence of the senior Mathews on those he coached went far beyond his own children and beyond sports. "He was a father to the little ones, a big brother to those who didn't have big brothers, and a friend to those who went on to college," one of his former charges recalled.

While the Gwynn Park community's rural nature was a major part of the school's athletic success, it also created some rather unique problems. The young man most responsible for the school's first two state titles was six-foot-six center Walter "Shorty" Simmons, who patrolled and controlled the lane. Simmons was hardworking: he was a custodian at a local elementary school during his high school summers and would sneak out on his breaks to shoot baskets. He was selfless too. He was willing to score when needed but was perfectly happy to let others make the baskets while he rebounded, just so long as Gwynn Park won.

"Shorty was a heck of a player," Gandee recalled. "As long as we won, he didn't care who scored."

Simmons lived in the small community of Baden, near the Charles County line. This often required him to walk or hitchhike home after basketball practice since the school activity buses had long since been locked up for the night. Simmons claimed not to mind the walk; somebody usually picked him up before he made it all the way home. "I don't mind it," Simmons once said. "Besides, the fresh air is healthful."

The concern was that Simmons's home was so remote that any difficulty he might have in getting to school or games could jeopardize the team's success. Gandee recalled driving Simmons home one evening and having the rocks and dirt on those remote country roads do all kinds of damage to the underside of his car.

When Gwynn Park made the state tournament for the first time in 1968, Gandee, then still the assistant coach, knew Simmons would be there for the semifinals. The game was played on Thursday, so all Simmons had to do was catch the bus from school with the rest of the team. Saturday's championship game posed another problem. Not wanting to risk having Simmons miss the game because he couldn't find a ride, Gandee let the star center stay at his place on Friday night before the title game. It was a brilliant coaching decision. Simmons scored 34 points and grabbed 23 rebounds in leading the Yellow Jackets, who finished 21–4, to their first state title.

The experience taught Coach Gandee the first commandment of any basketball coach's cannon: always make sure your big man has a ride to the game. "I may not be that smart, but I was smart enough to figure that out," Gandee said with a laugh.

Gandee took over from Carney the next year, but little changed. Simmons led a 22–2 season, while Ronald Jones and Dale Adams provided the kind of balance that prevented teams from double-teaming Simmons inside. Those people who dismissed Gwynn Park because it was a mere Class C school didn't have much to say when the Yellow Jackets beat powerhouse Fairmont Heights twice in a week, the only two losses the Hornets suffered that season en route to the state Class B title. The Yellow Jackets later gave top-rated Mackin all it could handle in a 76–74 loss. For the most part, Gwynn Park's games were more like its 115–46 rout of the Laurel Spartans that set a school record for points. Gwynn Park defended its state title by trouncing Somerset Dragons of Princess Anne County, 85–59, in the final.

In 1969–70, Gwynn Park and Gandee made it three in a row. Along the way, they hung a 111–47 loss on Douglass, scored 48 unanswered points in a 95–28 wipeout of Thomas Stone's Cougars, and blasted Laurel again, 108–72. In the 60–50 victory over the Mount Savage Indians in the state title game, Earl Hawkins, having replaced the graduated Simmons at center, scored 20 points and grabbed a tournament-record 31 rebounds.

Gandee's team lost in the state final in 1971 and again in 1975, but the Yellow Jackets won it all in 1972, 1974, and 1976. Just for good measure, the coach's final triumph came in the 1980 finals.

Much of the Yellow Jackets' success in the mid-1970s was due to five-foot-eight dynamo Sonny Proctor, who thought he could hit from anywhere in the court and was right more often than not. As a sophomore, Proctor averaged 19 points per game and scored 22 points in the state championship victory over Pocomoke's Warriors. Cornell Banks, also a sophomore, added 19. Banks wound up starting in a state title game three years in a row; that's quite an accomplishment.

That state title in 1976 might have been the most impressive of all of them. Proctor was a senior but went down early in the season with a knee injury and eventually had to have surgery. Banks stepped up, as did Mark Clark and six-foot-four, 225-pound point guard Ed Jackson. Gwynn Park didn't have its best player and had been bumped up to Class B due to school expansion, but it didn't matter. Playing a more team-oriented game with Proctor out, Gwynn Park lost only three games and by just seven points combined. A five-point loss to Mackin, a powerful team that boasted the area's leading scorer in Maryland-bound Jo Jo Hunter, convinced the players that they were good enough to win another title even without Proctor.

In the state final, now in Class B, it was no contest. Gwynn Park ripped the Southern Garrett High School Rams of Garrett County, 79–59. "This one means more to me than the others," said Gandee, whose record stood at 145–46.

After the 1976 final, someone asked Gandee if he'd ever consider moving up the coaching ladder. "The kids are great," he replied. "They're fun to watch. Why would I want to go to a bigger program?"

Gandee's last championship title in 1980 came with a different kind of team, one that was spotty, though balanced, on offense but suffocating on defense. Ultimately, the Yellow Jackets squeezed out a 75–74 overtime victory over Rockville for the Class A title. Jeff Adams, a six-foot-one center, led the way with 21 points and 10 rebounds, while Robbie Spencer and Andy Smith added 14 each. Shawn Clark contributed a pair of key blocked shots in the first overtime as well.

"We play team ball, and if you play team ball, you can go a long way," Adams said after the semifinal victory. "Everyone on the team knows each other, and we just play together real well."

Tim Raune (14) of Georgetown Prep is called for an offensive foul as he crashes into St. Anthony's Charles Barrett (42) while trying to score in the January 27, 1970, game. Don Washington (54) is trying to block the shot.

Jerome McDaniel (11) of Fairmont Heights cuts down the nets after a record 120–69 victory over Atholton for the Maryland Class A Championship on March 20, 1971.

Adrian Dantley goes up against St. John's in 1973. While at DeMatha, Dantley was a three-time All-Met selection and helped lead the Stags to four straight No. 1 rankings in the Washington area.

Adrian Dantley gets the rebound against Spingarn in 1973.

Earnest Johnson
Head Football Coach

A. B. Williamson
Head Basketball Coach

The 1973 Eastern High School yearbook page includes basketball coach A. B. Williamson, who would move to Howard University in 1975.

Gene Doane was one of the winningest basketball coaches in Montgomery County history. He coached at Sherwood, Blair, and Seneca Valley with a combined record of 447–113.

Dunbar's John Duren started out with a shot in mind, but when he moved under the basket, he found a Crossland defender in his way, so he tried to pass instead. It went astray in the game on December 7, 1975.

WE ARE NUMBER ONE!! say Ba-Ba, Jeff and Steve.

# DUNBAR DEFEATS DEMATHA

All-Metropolitan and All-Interhigh selection . . . Craig "Big Sky" Shelton

The Mighty Crimson Tide floated th
with a record of 26-0 as the Interhigh a
The Tide has defeated such comp
idge, Bell and Eastern twice, Woodso
for the city title.

The Dunbar Crimson Tide yearbook page celebrating the 26–0 championship season in 1975–76 includes photos of John "Ba Ba" Duren (30) and Craig "Big Sky" Shelton (33).

Montgomery Blair's Brian Magid passes around Springbrook's Rick Dagen after being trapped in the corner in a playoff game February 17, 1975.

Solid defense was one of the major reasons T. C. Williams defeated West Springfield, 63–57, to win the 1975 Virginia AA Northern Region Basketball Championship at Hayfield. Williams got equally solid instruction from Coach Mike Hynson.

The Mighty Crimson Tide floated through the season undefeated and finished with a record of 26-0 as the Interhigh and City Champions.

The Tide has defeated such competitors as: Maggie Walker, Spingam, Coolidge, Bell and Eastern twice, Woodson, Cardoza, McKinley Tech and DeMatha for the city title.

He's called the ball handler . . . John "Ba-Ba" Duren.

Matha's Hawkeye up against the "Big

The man behind the number one team Coach Joe Dean Davidson.

125

Dunbar Crimson Tide yearbook page celebrating the 26–0 championship season 1975–76. Features John "Ba Ba" Duren (30), Craig "Big Sky" Shelton (33) facing DeMatha's Charles "Hawkeye" Whitney (42), and Coach Joe Dean Davidson.

Junior dynamo Sonny Proctor drives for a Gwynn Park basket, February 22, 1975. Gwynn Park would win the state championship that year and the next, although Proctor would be out for most of his senior year for knee surgery.

Mackin's Jo Jo Hunter (35) drives in for a layup and charges DeMatha's Clarence DesBordes (34) in the 2nd quarter of the game on February 25, 1976.

DeMatha's 1978 team included Dereck Whittenburg ('79), future men's head coach at Fordham University; Sidney Lowe ('79), future NBA player and coach, and men's head coach at North Carolina State University; Ron Everhart ('80), future head coach at Northeastern and Duquesne Universities; and Adrian Branch ('81), future NBA player. The teams met at the state boys' championship at Cole Field House in 1978. Dunbar's Crimson Tide came into the 1978 title game with a 25–2 record and a 19-game winning streak. The game was close until DeMatha's late 11–0 run. The final score was 63–55, with Paul DeVito and Branch sharing scoring honors with 15 points each.

DeMatha's 1978 team included Dereck Whittenburg ('79), future men's head basketball coach at Fordham University. Dutch Morley (21) is in the background.

Social media collage of Brian Magid at Montgomery Blair.

# CHAPTER FIVE

# The Eighties

**EARLY MARCH 1980** was an uneasy time for followers of DeMatha basketball. It was bad enough that Spingarn, led by seven-foot transfer Earl Jones, had handled the Stags in the City Title Game, 77–69. The victory ended the Stags' string of two straight wins in the annual Inter-High–Metro Conference matchup.

Now an even bigger loss loomed. Word got out that North Carolina (NC) State was making a serious run at Morgan Wootten to replace departing coach Norm Sloan. It was the Florida-bound Sloan himself who had recommended Wootten to North Carolina State athletic director Willis Casey. And why not? Sloan had recruited a host of DeMatha players over the years, and Kenny Carr, Sidney Lowe, and Dereck Whittenburg had all flourished for the Wolfpack.

Not only was Wootten the leading candidate for the job but, according to those at NC State, he was also *the only* candidate. To secure the coach's services, Casey went all out, dangling a five-year, $700,000 package that guaranteed the sale of Wootten's home, as well as college educations for his five children. That helped get the coach's attention.

"NC State is a great school, although I'm extremely happy here," Wootten said. "But maybe I've been too close-minded in the past. I'm trying to be as open-minded as possible this time. It comes down to what's best for my family. They're the jury."

Wootten had ignored such overtures in the past, but the possibility of moving up to the college ranks intrigued him. For one thing, he was approaching his 50th birthday and realized that if he didn't take this opportunity, such an offer might not come again.

Another factor was in NC State's favor: Lowe and Whittenburg were already there, and they had helped Wootten to his first undefeated season at DeMatha just two years earlier. "If you come down here, we could win a national championship," the players told him.

Then, too, there was the money. Wootten was not a greedy man. But having worked his way through college, he knew the value of a dollar. The possibility that his children's education would be taken care of made NC State's offer very attractive indeed.

Wootten's kids, meanwhile, had some other perks in mind. One asked if the new job offer meant that he could quit his paper route. Another wanted to know if the Woottens could get a swimming pool if Daddy got this high-paying new job.

James Brown, Wootten's big star a decade before, urged him to make the jump. "It would be great to see him be successful at that level," Brown said at the time. "And he would be successful."

Wootten was convinced of that as well. The issue, in his mind, was not if he could win as a college coach. The question was, Would he be happy? Friends and colleagues who were involved in the college game advised him that his family life would suffer; he'd simply be home a lot less. Recruiting was a never-ending rat race, they said, a necessary evil of the job that offered the promise of success as well as the possibility of long stretches on the road.

Friends assured him that he had nothing to prove from a coaching standpoint. His record at DeMatha was an incredible 649–92. He was recognized and respected from coast to coast and in tremendous demand as a speaker and clinician. Was chasing success at the college level really a mountain he wanted to climb?

These questions and others kept running through his mind as the DeMatha community held its collective breath and as local reporters sniffed around for hints about which way he was leaning. Wootten agonized over the decision for two full weeks, and his dilemma grew into one of the biggest stories in Washington that spring. Everyone offered opinions on what Wootten might do and what he should do. Casey was calling constantly in an effort to land the big prize. In the middle of all the speculation and hubbub, Wootten wasn't sure where he stood.

"If you've ever seen a guy sitting on dead center, you're looking at him," he confessed at one point. "You can build a favorable case for both sides. I have to decide."

In the end, he decided to stay. Score another victory—a big one—for DeMatha. Wootten's explanation was heartfelt and eloquent. "As for climbing mountains, they are where you find them," he said at a news conference held to announce his choice. "Any time I help a student in one of my classes, get a better start in his formative years, or touch the life of one of my basketball players, I feel I have climbed another mountain. That's the kind I prefer climbing."

At DeMatha, everyone exhaled. The student body gave him a 10-minute standing ovation at a special school assembly after the announcement. They were grateful, they were appreciative, they were relieved.

"I don't know what we would have done without him," said school secretary Nancy Westover. "These kids need him more than those college kids do."

The story had a happy ending for NC State as well. After Wootten turned down the school's offer, Casey hired a hilariously funny, up-and-coming young coach named Jim Valvano. Just three years later, Valvano led the Wolfpack, featuring Lowe, Whittenburg, and Bladensburg's Thurl Bailey, to the national championship by slowing the pace in a stunning upset of Houston's "Phi Slama Jama" crew in the NCAA final.

The victory made Valvano a star; he was recognized all over the country. With a never-ending supply of one-liners, he was in huge demand on the banquet circuit. On one occasion, though, Valvano was in the audience as Wootten stepped to the podium to speak. The DeMatha coach caught Valvano's eye and leaned toward the microphone. Wootten deadpanned, "How's that NC State job? Pretty good?"

In DeMatha's first season after Wootten's near departure, 1980–81, the Stags showed that, on the one hand, they could get along just fine without their longtime coach—albeit for a short time. On the other hand, what happened at the end of the season might just have proved that Wootten's powers were even greater than previously thought.

The Stags, led by All-Met Adrian Branch ("a very charming guy with a lot of style," Wootten recalled) and Bobby Ferry, the son of the Washington Bullets general manager, finished first in their league for the fourth straight season and the 19th time in 21 years. At the end of the regular season, the Stags were 23–3 and directly in the path of 24–0 Dunbar. The schools would meet in the City Title Game for the fifth time since the resumption of the private-public year-end series in 1973.

DeMatha had won three of the four previous meetings but was the underdog this time. Joe Dean Davidson's Crimson Tide boasted a couple of big stars in forwards Anthony Jones and Sylvester Charles. Some were calling this Dunbar's best team since the undefeated squad of 1976.

"We were supposed to get beat, no question," Wootten recalled. That seemed even more sure when Wootten was laid low by a severe sinus infection the week of the game.

With Wootten dizzy and unable to coach, his assistant Joe Mihalich would direct the Stags. Wootten would stay apprised through a telephone hookup on the DeMatha bench. Mihalich and Wootten went over strategy the day before the game and chatted at length during halftime. But Wootten was loath to provide too much input because he knew he wouldn't have the same feel for the game as someone who was actually there.

Even though their legendary coach wasn't there, the Stags played as though he were; that's how well drilled they were after months of practice. Dunbar raced to a 10-point halftime lead, with Charles dominating inside with 14 points. DeMatha focused on shutting down the inside after intermission and rallied. By the end of the third quarter, the deficit was 50–45, and DeMatha kept coming. Branch (22 points, 10 rebounds) hit a pair of free throws with 42 seconds left to put the Stags in front for the first time. Ferry (19 points) added two more with 13 seconds remaining, and Branch closed out with another pair from the line for the 67–62 upset.

"I did some coaching over the phone, but Joe did a great job taking care of things," Wootten said. Mihalich respectfully disagreed. He didn't think he deserved any credit—and didn't want any. "People can say I coached that game all they want," he said. "Morgan Wootten coached that game. By the end of the year, [the players] know what they're supposed to be doing."

The next season figured to be a transitional one for DeMatha. The Stags were very young. Promising six-foot-nine freshman Danny Ferry would become one of the great players in DeMatha history, but success figured to be a way off for him and the rest of his largely untested 1981–82 teammates.

The Trojans of Mackin, coming off a 24–5 season, were the chic preseason pick for the top spot in the Metro Conference and the area. DeMatha was picked sixth overall in the preseason poll, its lowest such ranking in years.

Those placements were hard to dispute. Mackin featured high-scoring guard Johnny Dawkins, to whom the *Washington Post* referred—with good reason—as "a jump shot artist." Trojans coach Paul DeStefano also had a tough inside player in Dominic Pressley and a talented point guard in Darnell Swinton. And all three were seniors. Mackin hadn't beaten DeMatha in a half-dozen years, but Dawkins voiced what everyone secretly believed when he said, "We definitely believe this is our year."

Except that it wasn't. DeMatha blasted Mackin, 90–67, in mid-February for its 15th straight win over the Trojans. Wootten's team didn't have much in the way of experience, but he did have a long bench, which he used to great effect. DeMatha's reserves accounted for 53 points in the victory, offsetting Dawkins's sparkling 29-point performance. A week later, DeMatha clinched the Metro title by beating Carroll, while Mackin was upset by St. John's.

The Stags' 53–52 victory over Spingarn for the city title was eerily similar to the win over Dunbar the year before. The Inter-High champions' big man, Michael Graham, enjoyed a big game (20 points, 12 rebounds) but scored only six points in the second half as DeMatha shut off the inside after halftime. Drew Komlo's free throws with 46 seconds left put the Stags back on top, and a last-second shot by the Green Wave rimmed out.

DeMatha had done it again and showed no signs of stopping. Ferry, Komlo, Carlton Valentine, and their teammates now were seasoned, which offered the promise of even better things to come.

"We had very little experience, and I said if they [Mackin] didn't get us this year, it will be very hard to beat us the next two," Wootten said. As usual, he was right.

With a well-seasoned club at his disposal, Wootten and DeMatha won an unprecedented third straight City Title Game in 1983. Nobody—not even the great Archbishop Carroll teams more than two decades earlier—had done that.

DeMatha sealed its league crown and recorded its 27th straight 20-victory season with a 69–63 victory over St. John's on February 20. Bennie Bolton led the way with 19 points.

Awaiting the Stags (23–4) in the City Title Game was—who else?—Dunbar (20–4). "They always seem to show up, darn it!" Wootten cracked.

As usual, Dunbar was formidable. Davidson's front line included six-foot-seven

Bernard Campbell, who averaged 20 points and 12 rebounds; six-foot-six Tyrone Jones, who averaged 16 points and 12 rebounds; and six-foot-nine Sean Alvarado. Davidson would leave for Delaware State University after the season, and his last Crimson Tide team was one of the few capable of matching up with DeMatha. And that is just what happened.

The Stags needed a couple of Bolton free throws with 13 seconds left to tie the score at 55, and the game went to overtime when Dunbar's last-second shot was off the mark. DeMatha's Leroy Allen, a senior guard who had lost his starting job, delivered the decisive play in overtime: he snuck inside to tap in a teammate's miss, drawing a foul and converting for a three-point lead to spark a 7–0 run.

That was the maddening thing about playing DeMatha: The Stags were usually better. And even when they weren't, they always seemed to come up with the key play to turn the game their way.

In Wootten's mind, winning begat winning, which was one of the reasons for the Stags' success. Because DeMatha had always won, its players expected to win and somehow always (or almost always) managed to make it happen. It was true in league play, in nonleague play, and in the City Title Game, where the Stags pulled out so many narrow victories.

"We were there every year," Wootten recalled years later. "We were always more used to being out there than the other guys."

Wootten didn't need any magic formulas to succeed in 1983–84. He had talent and plenty of it. The core group included Quinton Jackson at the point, Juan Neal at the off guard, Komlo at one forward, Ferry at the other, and Valentine in the middle. All but Ferry were seniors, and they understood what Wootten wanted and what any given situation required. Together, they embarked on one of the great seasons in school history.

"The group complemented each other very well," Ferry remembered. "We'd been together for a while. We knew the system."

Yes, the Stags were good, and they knew it. To them, it was no surprise when they opened the season by ending Baltimore Dunbar's 59-game winning streak or when they knocked off the Mater Dei Monarchs of Santa Ana, California—the nation's preseason No. 1—66–51, right before Christmas.

DeMatha opened league play with a 74–42 blitz of Good Counsel. The Stags were 10–1 and ranked No. 1 in the area. "We were simply overmatched," Good Counsel coach Rich Seel admitted. "I look at them and see four or five Division I players. They're so fast and so big and take up so much room on the court."

That was especially true of Danny Ferry, who was one of the most famous high school players in the country. Despite the hype, Ferry was just one of the guys. Like his dad, he was a first-class agitator and always ready with a good-natured jibe for one of his teammates. "Off the court, he was a jokester," Valentine said. "Danny was cool."

On the court, Ferry was like nothing his teammates—or anyone else—had seen. Even at that age, he had a great feel for the game and a remarkable knack for making the perfect pass. Had he been even the slightest bit selfish, there might have been some resentment, considering all the publicity he got, but there was none.

"He was an amazing passer," Valentine recalled. "It was just amazing to play with a guy like that, a very unselfish guy. He could have scored more, but he was all about winning."

Despite being six-foot-nine, Ferry played forward—an indication of how tough and talented Valentine was inside at six foot six and 225 pounds. "I did a lot of the dirty work, a lot of the stuff around the basket," Valentine said. "I was tough and rugged. I always played with an edge."

His talents were perhaps most appreciated by Ferry, because Valentine's style enabled him to play more freely away from the basket. "His hands were so soft, and his touch was so good," Ferry said. "We complemented each other extremely well. I was a skill guy with some toughness; he was a tough guy with a lot of skill. We fit together."

Actually, they all fit together, including reserves such as Steve Trax, who made some big plays at key times, and Steve Hood, who would become an All-Met as a senior. When the Stags traveled, it wasn't uncommon to see players scurrying up and down the hallways into one another's hotel room to relax, hang out, talk trash. On bus rides to the games, somebody—usually either Jackson or Valentine—would start singing in the back, everyone would join in laughing, and Valentine would keep time by banging on the wall of the bus. Wootten, knowing what a talented squad he had, didn't keep as tight a rein on this group as he did with some others.

"It was the loosest team ever," recalled Mike Brey, then a DeMatha assistant. "They never felt the weight of the world on their shoulders. They were comfortable in their skin. They'd get on each other. Just a pleasure to be around. You looked forward to going to practice every day with that group."

The one time the Stags might have been a little too loose was against league rival Archbishop Carroll. Trailing 48–30 midway through the third period, the Lions got hot, rallied, and stunned DeMatha in overtime, 88–81. The star of the comeback was Carroll center Derrick Lewis, who scored 14 points, grabbed 14 rebounds, and blocked 10 shots.

But that was just a hiccup. The Stags closed their season with 18 straight victories to win the Metro Conference, finished atop the local polls, and were ranked No. 1 in the nation, according to *USA Today*.

Their 18th straight victory was an 88–69 blowout of Carroll in front of an overflow crowd at Montgomery Blair, avenging one of their two regular-season losses. The Stags were ruthlessly efficient, shooting 63 percent from the field. Valentine (25 points, 12 rebounds) led the way. In the late stages, he punctuated the victory with a thundering reverse dunk and drew a lecture from Wootten about showing off. But Valentine couldn't help himself; he was too excited about the victory. "That was the icing on the cake for me," Valentine said.

In the game that had mattered most, DeMatha had justified the hype and achieved what was always one of the program's goals—winning the competitive Metro Conference—but there was more to do. The top-ranked Stags claimed the City Title as well, winning over second-ranked Dunbar in a similar fashion. Most years, the public-private matchup was close, but not this year. The Stags won, 61–50, clearly establishing their local superiority. Valentine was front and center again, with 24 points and 10 rebounds.

At the season-ending Alhambra Catholic Invitational Tournament, the story was much the same. The Stags downed St. John Neumann's Pirates and Monsignor Bonner's Friars of Philadelphia to reach the final against the Cathedral Memorial Gaels (31–2) from Ontario, Canada, in a game that was billed as the high school basketball championship of North America.

It was no contest. DeMatha jumped out to a 25–6 lead after one quarter against Canada's best team and cruised to a 70–53 victory. Valentine was brilliant again, with 28 points and 15 rebounds.

After it was over the jubilant players tossed the straitlaced Wootten into the shower. They nearly got Brey, too, but he dashed out of the locker room, fled the arena, and didn't stop running until he reached the team hotel. He was one of the few guys who ended the day completely dry.

"We were throwing everybody in there," Valentine recalled. "It was one hell of a year. You didn't want it to end."

After that season for the ages, DeMatha went through an atypical three-year City Title drought. Spingarn, led by future Syracuse star Sherman Douglas, took the 1985 crown by going undefeated. Gonzaga knocked DeMatha from the top spot in the Metro Conference in 1986, and Dunbar finally toppled the Stags in the 1987 title game despite 35 points from John Gwynn, a championship game record.

However, DeMatha topped the *Post*'s preseason poll in 1987–88 thanks to six-foot-ten senior Jerrod Mustaf, a player with uncommon shooting range for a big man that was similar to Ferry's. Mustaf had been bothered by an Achilles' heel injury for much of his junior season, but he still had scored 23 points and grabbed nine rebounds against Coach Roy Westmore's Crimson Tide, whose scoring depth was too much to overcome.

The 1987–88 Stags knocked off Archbishop Molloy of New York—the top-ranked team in the country—68–66, at Takoma Academy in mid-December. Superstar guard Kenny Anderson scored a game-high 26 for the New Yorkers, but Mustaf countered with 19 points, 12 rebounds, and a steal that ruined Molloy's last chance to tie. A month later, DeMatha needed all of Mustaf's 25 points (on 11-for-15 shooting), 16 rebounds, and four blocked shots to edge Metro foe Bishop McNamara's Mustangs in a 54–53 victory. But no one in the league would beat the Stags, who went 14–0 against their biggest rivals.

Winning the league title meant a 14th City Title Game appearance in 16 years for the Stags. Mustaf figured to meet his match in Inter-High champ Coolidge's six-foot-ten star, Donald Hodge, a fellow *Parade* magazine All-American. Mustaf was averaging 21 points and 14 rebounds for the 26–3 Stags; Hodge was averaging 22 points and 14 rebounds for the 27–2 Colts.

The game turned out to be almost dead even too. Mustaf scored 27 points, grabbed 11 rebounds, and blocked four shots. Hodge only was slightly less brilliant with 17 points, 11 rebounds, and four blocks.

In the end, though, the game was decided by someone a foot shorter than either of those two—a player with a surname well known to all, obscure though he might have been to most of the 7,895 fans watching at Cole Field House. Brendan Wooten, the son of DeMatha's legendary coach, dropped in a pair of free throws with 24 seconds left to make it a four-point game as the Stags prevailed, 57–54. "He earned his keep for another week," the proud papa quipped.

It took the DC basketball world almost a whole season to catch up to Gar-Field High in 1979–80. Teams in the state of Virginia never did.

In terms of Northern Virginia basketball, the big focus in the preseason was on Don McCool and defending state champion Mount Vernon. In the *Post*'s high school basketball preview, Mount Vernon merited four paragraphs, while Gar-Field—in Woodbridge, Virginia, the outer reaches of the suburbs—merited only two. At that time, a lot of people outside of Northern Virginia didn't even know where Woodbridge was.

The Indians were expected to be good, coming off a Commonwealth (VA) District championship. But the level of play in the district was considered a good deal lower than that being played in what most people thought of as Northern Virginia: Fairfax County, Alexandria, and Arlington. After all, no Commonwealth District team had ever made the state tournament, and no Northwest Region team (Gar-Field was in the Northwest Region, not the more familiar Northern Region) had won a state title in Virginia in a decade.

"Back then, the only teams considered good basketball teams were in Washington or Maryland, or maybe close-in Virginia, like Alexandria," remembered Othell Wilson, whose addition to the Gar-Field roster that season helped carry the Indians to an undefeated (25–0) season and a state Class AAA title. "Nobody paid any attention to us and didn't really give us a look until we got down close to playoff time."

An early season matchup against DeMatha fell through because of an administrative foul-up. A victory in that game might have clued people in that Gar-Field was a squad to be taken seriously. But a loss in such a game would have ruined the team's undefeated season.

The Indians were good, no doubt about it, but how good wouldn't be decided until the postseason. The team got a huge lift when Wilson transferred in from the crosstown rival Woodbridge Vikings because of a change in school boundaries. The muscular Wilson—he looked like a safety or a running back—could score inside and out, run the break, and distribute the ball. He was also an absolute nuisance on defense. In a district playoff game, he stole the ball on five straight possessions, a feat that might never have been duplicated.

Wilson played with his new teammates over the summer in the Jelleff League, where the Indians proved themselves against the area's best. Those games also gave him a chance to bond with the Gar-Field holdovers and learn how they played.

"They had good players already," Wilson said "We had a lot of talent. When we played together in the summer league, we were killing people. We started feeling like we could be pretty good."

The other key man was the six-foot-five Steve Perry, perhaps the best shot blocker in the state that season. Perry was thoughtful, bright (he would be nominated for an ultra-prestigious Rhodes Scholarship), and low key. His acceptance of Wilson made the newcomer okay in everyone else's eyes too.

Along with the two big stars, guard Steve Smith and forwards Kevin Smith (no relation) and George Suggs gave Gar-Field an all-senior lineup. They rolled undefeated through the regular season, winning 19 straight games, and they won over at least one area basketball veteran in the process. The Indians' two closest games of the regular season were victories by 14 and 15 points over Lake Braddock. Bruins coach Carl Hensley knew what a winner looked like, having taken a couple of his former Edison High teams to the state tournament in the 1960s. Hensley was impressed with the Indians, to say the least.

"I wouldn't be the least bit surprised to see them in the state finals," Hensley said after a late February loss to the Indians. "I know nobody in Northern Virginia can run with them. I think if a team can beat them, it will be with tempo."

Gar-Field finished the regular season 19–0, then tacked on another four postseason victories to reach 23–0 and earn a berth in the state semifinals. The Indians were the first-ever team from its district to do so.

Five busloads of true believers made the trip down to Charlottesville for the state tournament, and they got to see quite a show. Gar-Field beat the Marshall Walker Cavaliers of Richmond, 80–73, in the semifinals. The Indians endured their only real scare in the championship game against Booker T. Washington of Norfolk before pulling out a 67–65 victory. Wilson made the two biggest plays: he hit a driving bank shot with 23 seconds left to give Gar-Field a 66–65 lead; then he drew a charge on Bookers star Billy Walker with five seconds left.

Though everyone contributed, the stars—Wilson and Perry—made the difference. Wilson scored 44 points combined in the semis and the finals, adding 16 assists and eight steals. Perry matched Wilson's 44-point output to go along with his 19 rebounds and nine blocked shots.

Gar-Field had its state championship, a No. 2 ranking in the *Post* and the *Star,* and some well-deserved name recognition. To top it all off, when it came to assemble the local team for the Capital Classic All-Star game against the national squad, Wilson and Perry were selected; they were also the first Commonwealth District players ever chosen.

"Oh my gosh, I was really fortunate to have that team," said Frederick (Rick) French Jr. "They were so enjoyable to coach. They were like a machine. I probably didn't realize myself how good we were until the 10th or 11th game. Those kids never had a bad night."

Coach French had his own distinguished history. After a preseason injury ended his pro career before it began for the Baltimore Bullets, he switched to semi-pro baseball during the summers, while he taught physical education and coached basketball at Lee High School in Springfield (1968–71) and then Gar-field (1971–80). He became the head coach in 1976. He designed and implemented a multiple defense system, achieving winning seasons from 1977 to 1980. The *Post* ranked his team No. 1 in the metropolitan area throughout 1979–80, and the team won the Maryland AAA state championship with a 25–0 record.

If many thought Gar-Field's state championship came out of nowhere, the state title that the Robert E. Lee High School Lancers of Springfield won in 1981 was just as improbable. Coach Charlie Thompson always felt that the regular season didn't matter much; what mattered was having your team ready for the playoffs. The Lancers' postseason run in 1981 served only to reinforce that notion in Thompson's mind.

As Lee was coming off a 20–3 season, expectations were high, but the team struggled through most of the season, dropping three straight at one point to fall to 11–6. Thompson felt his players needed to relax, so he gave them some time off heading into the Gunston District tournament. With nothing to lose, the Lancers began playing as a loose, confident bunch and got red hot from the field. "We went on an unbelievable roll," Thompson recalled. "The pressure seemed to be relieved. We really came together."

And then crazy things started happening. After beating Groveton in the district semifinals—a win that guaranteed the Lancers a berth in the region tournament—they beat top-seeded Mount Vernon (who'd beaten them twice during the season) in the playoff game to win the Gunston District title.

In the Northern Region tournament, they survived an overtime scare from crosstown rival West Springfield in the opening round. Point guard Rod Wood scooped up a loose ball and sank a shot with just a second left to force overtime. Rick Hancock then supplied the winning free throws in a 69–68 escape.

Next, the now-dangerous Lancers ended the South Lakes Seahawks' 17-game winning streak with a 70–52 victory. That set up a fifth meeting with Mount Vernon for the Northern Region title to gain a berth in the state tournament. Lee worked its magic once again, although nearly blowing a six-point lead with a minute left before holding on for a 56–51 win.

The triumph was Lee's eighth in a row and its third straight in that postseason over the Mount Vernon Majors, who were the 1979 state champs and had been ranked No. 1 in Virginia for most of the season. Once things started clicking for the Lancers during that postseason run, "we were never afraid of losing," Wood recalled.

Thompson, who almost always kept his bench short throughout his three decades as a high school coach, got key contributions from all of his senior regulars: Tom Estepp, Tony Farris, Hancock, and Wood. The five-foot-nine Wood was the key man, though. He averaged 18 points per game that season while serving as the team's inspirational leader.

"The lynchpin was Rod," Thompson said. "He called all our defenses, he called all our offenses. We were un-pressable with him at point guard. Plus, he was such a fierce competitor and such a great leader. He just did it all."

Naturally, the Lancers were considered something of a fluke going into the state tournament. After all, they had more losses (six) than the other three participants did combined. But Lee knocked off a pair of perennial powers—Patrick Henry of Roanoke and Booker T. Washington of Norfolk—to win Fairfax County's first championship in the state's largest classification.

In the semifinals against Patrick Henry, Lee trailed by 10 points midway through the third quarter, but the Lancers stormed back to take a seven-point lead with 2:44 left. The Patriots answered with a 10-4 run of their own to close within 59–58 with 17 seconds left. But Lee came away with a critical jump ball, and Wood drained a pair of free throws to wrap up the 61–60 victory. Lee had hit 10 of 12 free throws in the last 3:38.

Against Booker T. Washington—which featured future NFL Hall of Famer Bruce Smith—the Lancers came out on top, 50–46. Hancock made one of the biggest plays of the game when he grabbed a teammate's missed free throw, enabling the Lancers to keep possession inside the final minute. The Bookers were forced to foul, and Wood—of course—canned a pair of free throws to ice the championship, 50–44, with 12 seconds left.

Having proven conclusively that the regular season didn't mean much, Thompson saw no reason to adjust his philosophy in the years that followed. He didn't sweat his team's losses in December, January, or February, believing that those three months were just a prelude to the most important part of the season—the playoffs.

"I put the pressure on the elimination games, not the regular-season losses," Thompson said. "We never really varied from that philosophy. . . . I never said, 'We lost that game so we're dead in the water.' If you do that, then what do you have to play for? Mentally they would be fried if every game was a crisis. That's why I could never coach football—one loss and you're done."

Everything his teams did was geared toward the postseason. Thompson wanted his teams to focus on execution and playing physical ball, because he believed that the pace of play slowed down in the postseason and that referees tended to permit more contact as well. "Pretty much everything we did was for the postseason," said Wood, who eventually served as Thompson's assistant and became a college coach himself.

That unique approach served Thompson well, no matter where he went. He had a 10-loss team that went all the way to the state finals in 1985, and the Lancers were back there again in 1988. He changed schools a couple of times after that, coaching the Robinson Rams, the Oakton Cougars, and the Hayfield Hawks, and he rarely stopped winning en route to a career record of 417–207. But what stands out is Thompson's versatility. He took every school he coached to the state tournament at least once.

In the fall of 1975, few people had heard of Flint Hill, a tiny private school in Northern Virginia. And nobody had heard of the Huskies basketball coach, an eager young man from Manassas, Virginia, named Stu Vetter.

Flint Hill had been around since the mid-1950s, but the school hadn't built much of an athletic reputation. At the time Vetter took over the program, Flint Hill's enrollment was fewer than 100 students. Vetter's ambitions for the program were quite modest initially. He hoped to raise the quality of play in the program so that it could better compete in the Interstate Athletic Conference with the likes of the Episcopal Maroon, the Landon Bears, the St. Albans Bulldogs, and the Georgetown Prep Hoyas.

Flint Hill's gym was actually more like an elementary school's all-purpose room. It had a tile floor and doubled as the school's auditorium and cafeteria. The uniforms for the eight varsity basketball players didn't even match, with some of the jerseys featuring the school's name across the front and with others just blank. All in all, it was a laughably primitive starting point for what would become one of the most successful and recognized high school basketball programs in the country.

Vetter turned out to be a very good coach, a fact that was overlooked in subsequent years because so much of the talk about his methods focused on player procurement. Flint Hill was 92–20 in his first four seasons, with the program's schedule being upgraded significantly in the process. Vetter's best player during the early years was a scrappy, hustling point guard named Mike Pepper, who didn't make All-Met but was good enough to bring Flint Hill some attention. The Falcons went 21–4 in Pepper's senior year and won the Tri-State Conference title for the second straight season. Playing in a league that included the likes of the Quantico Warriors, the Colonial Beach Drifters, and the Heights School Cavaliers, Flint

Hill's scoring surpassed 100 points five times in Pepper's senior year. And folks were beginning to take notice. "Little Flint Hill Is No Laughing Matter" read a February 1977 headline in the *Star*.

Neither was Pepper. Vetter was getting calls from lots of big-time schools about Pepper. It was an eye-opening experience for the coach and for many in the area's basketball community. Pepper's recruitment proved that college recruiters would find you even at an obscure place like Flint Hill, and it was a huge deal when lordly coach Dean Smith of the University of North Carolina (UNC) made a personal visit to the school.

The bond that grew between Smith and Vetter proved mutually beneficial. Smith got a steady stream of players from Vetter's teams, and Vetter gained entrée into the world of big-time college basketball. Pepper went on to captain the 1980–81 Tar Heels, who went all the way to the national championship game.

Vetter, meanwhile, joined the inner circle at North Carolina. He became a frequent visitor to Chapel Hill, where he'd sit in when the UNC coaching staff broke down game film—a practice that helped accelerate his development at a coach.

Pepper's presence at UNC—the Tar Heels were always on television in the Washington area—lent legitimacy to Vetter and his program. In time, his ability to send his players to the most prestigious college teams became a major selling point for Vetter at Flint Hill and then with the Colonels of Harker Prep (now St. Andrew's), the Vikings of St. John's at Prospect Hall (now St. John's Catholic Prep), and the Mustangs of Montrose Christian.

Thanks to Pepper and the success Flint Hill enjoyed during his time there, Vetter began setting his sights a little higher. By 1979–80 the school had dropped out of the Tri-State Conference to become an independent. That switch gave Vetter more flexibility in scheduling and enabled him to set many of his own rules.

That year the Flint Hill Falcons also picked up Carlos Yates, a six-foot-five transfer from Oakton who became the first of Vetter's players to garner All-Met recognition. Powerful inside despite his relative lack of size, Yates was a third-team selection in leading the Falcons to a 23–4 record.

In 1980–81 Yates was a first-team All-Met after averaging 24.5 points as Flint Hill finished 23–6. The Falcons also earned their first end-of-the-year ranking in the *Post* at No. 12. Flint Hill had reached a level nobody—including Vetter—could have imagined just a couple of years earlier.

Vetter was an entrepreneur who dabbled in real estate and restaurant ownership when he wasn't coaching, and he saw the potential for more. Flint Hill dipped slightly (18–8) the year after Yates graduated, but in 1982–83, it finished at No. 6 in the final *Post* poll while posting a 24–6 record.

The troubling thing to local coaches, especially those in Northern Virginia, was the number of transfers making their way to Flint Hill. The 1982–83 Falcons included Kevin Sutton (initially at Falls Church), Darrick Simms (Edison), and Gerald Jackson (Washington-Lee). Jackson actually switched schools in the middle of his senior year and was a real talent, averaging 18.3 points and 7.3 rebounds per game while making first-team All-Met. Opposing coaches didn't like losing their best players to anybody, much less a local private school that regularly showed up in the *Post*'s rankings, not to mention the national poll that ran in the fledgling *USA Today*.

It also rankled some that players who transferred to Flint Hill often were required to repeat a grade upon their arrival, giving them another year to grow physically and develop their skills. Many coaches saw having the opportunity to use fifth-year seniors against 15- and 16-year-olds as an unfair competitive advantage. But that requirement wasn't Vetter's; it was the school's. Flint Hill's rigorous academic program had specific requirements, and if an incoming student failed to meet them, he or she was asked to repeat a grade. Still, the setup at Flint Hill enabled Vetter to compete on a playing field that wasn't level. The more Flint Hill won and the more notoriety it got—in *USA Today* and elsewhere—the more attractive it became to good players and the more local coaches complained. In time Northern Virginia public schools stopped playing the Falcons, and many of the top private schools—including those in the Metro Conference—did as well because of the fifth-year exception and charges that Vetter recruited players.

As time went on, Vetter paid less and less attention to his critics. Because of the recognition his program received, Vetter's teams were in huge demand at tournaments all over the country: Las Vegas, New York City, the Virgin Islands, and Hawaii. That made the school an even more desirable destination for starry-eyed young players. Vetter's teams were able to play in more of these tournaments than most teams were because the Huskies were from an independent school and not bound by the rules of any particular league.

Vetter and his program enjoyed a much greater reputation nationally than locally, and that was fine with him. By that point, Vetter was well on his way to changing a lot of the accepted ideas about how a high school basketball program should operate. And like any maverick with his own ideas of how things should operate in the world of sports, he encountered some resistance.

"There was some bitterness," Robinson coach Bob McKeag told the *Post* in 1986. "There are several schools in this area that have lost good players to Flint Hill. And they didn't lose them when they were seventh- or eighth-graders; they lost them when they were established players."

While some viewed Vetter as a renegade, the values he preached and the habits he tried to develop in his players were old school all the way. If you played at Flint Hill, you wore a coat and tie on the road. You shook hands firmly and looked a visitor in the eye. And you didn't do anything crazy in the pregame layup lines, because an assistant coach was always lurking about to report on any shenanigans back to Vetter.

"Coach Vetter went into such detail, from how we stood for the national anthem, to training us to deal with opponents and adults with respect," said Bruce

Butler, one of Vetter's early players who went on to become the principal at South Lakes High School in Reston. "I never knew I could work so hard at anything as I worked at basketball. That experience of working hard and committing to something bigger than me, committing to the team, and committing to something for all the right reasons has impacted me. I didn't quite get it at the time, but as I moved on through life I understood what it all meant."

Even with all the glamorous travel and tournaments, Vetter also always kept his team's schedule to about 25 games, so the players didn't miss too much classwork. His players have gone on to graduate from Duke, UNC, Virginia, and Wake Forest, among others, so he certainly didn't neglect that part of his players' development.

"The [academic] prep and everything you do is the same. . . . It's just exactly the way college teams run it," said Randolph Childress, a Flint Hill star in the late 1980s who later starred at Wake Forest. "That's why he's so successful with his players in college. The culture is the same."

Amid all the things said about Flint Hill—good and bad—the Falcons kept winning. When Vetter added Loudoun County Raiders transfer Dennis Scott for the 1983–84 season, Flint Hill went to another level. That squad finished 23–3 and No. 2 in the final *Post* poll, behind only one of the best DeMatha teams ever.

Scott was the complete package. At six foot seven and about 220 pounds, he looked more like a football player than a basketball player. Despite his bulk, Scott possessed good ballhandling skills and an uncanny long-range shooting ability. During his senior year at Flint Hill, the *Post* gushed that Scott had "enough skills to play all five positions."

In college Scott's three-point shooting ability helped carry Georgia Tech to the Final Four. That same skill then propelled Scott to a 10-year career in the NBA.

Scott was everything you envision in a young basketball prince. He played for a famous program at Flint Hill that garnered national attention, traveled to exotic locales, and stayed in the finest hotels. In large part because of Scott's national reputation, Flint Hill was the featured team in the first high school game ever televised live on ESPN.

Scott was only too happy to take advantage of the perks and the exposure, as most anyone his age would be. He sometimes enraged opponents (and Flint Hill critics) because he always seemed a little too sure of himself, a little too cocky. For those critical of Flint Hill already, Scott's demeanor only reaffirmed their suspicions.

"I'm not arrogant or cocky," Scott said. "I love to play, and I enjoy what I'm doing out there. I smile a lot, and people misunderstand that. I play hard all the time."

Vetter echoed that assessment. "Dennis had a great personality," the coach said. "He was outgoing, personable, and obviously had a certain flair for the game. He enjoyed playing to the crowd. But when it came time to play, Dennis was one of the most focused players I've ever coached. He loved the competition. He loved the challenge."

Led by Scott, Flint Hill finally climbed to the top in 1985–86, finishing with a 23–0 record, and was ranked No. 1 in the DC area for the first time. Scott, then a junior, averaged 22.5 points, 8.8 rebounds, and 5.1 assists en route to making first-team All-Met.

He repeated that honor as a senior while leading Flint Hill to a second straight 23–0 season and another ranking atop the *Post's* final poll. The Falcons were also voted the top team in the country by *USA Today*. Scott upped his averages to 24 points, 11.4 rebounds, 6.0 assists, and 3.5 steals and was named the national high school Player of the Year.

Scott was the last of Vetter's fifth-year players, though. *USA Today* decided it would cease ranking schools that granted an extra year of eligibility. Vetter, mindful of how much those rankings helped raise the profile of his program, finally got the school to change its rules about repeating a grade. The move also placated some—but not all—of the coach's critics.

Even with Scott's having moved on to Georgia Tech, Flint Hill was able to sustain its success in 1987–88. After consecutive unbeaten seasons, Vetter's team was on the brink of eclipsing the ultimate local high school basketball record—Carroll's 55-game winning streak. Adding a bit of intrigue to the approaching milestone was that Ronny Thompson—the son of Georgetown coach John Thompson, who had been a huge part of that Carroll dynasty—now played for Flint Hill.

The Falcons achieved that historic 56th straight victory with ease, routing Theodore Roosevelt, 73–44, at George Mason on December 12. The younger Thompson contributed 12 points and five steals.

"Ronny has been running his mouth all week, and I can't talk trash anymore about our record," John Thompson said. "I told him we would play teams like his in the morning and go out and play another team at night."

Responded Ronny, "I'm glad to see it go from Thompson to Thompson. He told me his team would have beaten us by 50. I said, 'No way, you were too slow.'"

Regardless of whether Flint Hill could have beaten the Lions of John Thompson's era, Vetter clearly had built one of the area's strongest programs. The Falcons were 22–2, buoyed by out-of-state transfer Arron Bain, who made first-team All-Met. Then Bain and George Lynch, a transfer from Roanoke, Virginia, both made first-team All-Met as the Falcons went 23–3 in 1988–89. Flint Hill kept it going in 1989–90 with a 23–3 mark, and Bain and Lynch became the first high school teammates to be named McDonald's All-Americans, putting another feather in Vetter's cap.

Vetter's record was a staggering 377–53 in 14 years at Flint Hill, and he built his reputation to the point where players from all over flocked to his program. But changes were coming at Flint Hill. A new administration had taken over and was perfectly happy to have the basketball program compete at a less advanced level. Thus ended the days of Flint Hill as a national power.

But it was just the beginning for Vetter. He moved on for two seasons to Harker

Prep in Potomac. There he fashioned strong teams populated exclusively with transfers who wanted nothing more than to play for Vetter, to develop their skills, and to gain national exposure. After Harker closed in 1992, with the Colonels atop the *Post* rankings, Vetter moved on to St. John's at Prospect Hall in Frederick, Maryland, and won another national "championship" in 1997–98. After a difference of opinion with Prospect Hall's administration, Vetter took over at Montrose Christian in 1999. Montrose quickly became the fourth tiny private school that he developed into a national powerhouse. Kevin Durant, an eventual NBA MVP, and Greivis Vásquez, a Venezuelan who became Maryland's last star under Hall of Fame coach Gary Williams, both came to Rockville to play for Vetter.

Over time, Vetter's critics calmed down. After all, Vetter wasn't going to change, and he was always going to play by a different set of rules than others. So why fight it? Also, after a coach sends enough players on to successful careers on the Tobacco Road of college basketball, criticizing him looks foolish.

Vetter's website (how many high school coaches have their own website?) featured raves from college coaches such as University of Texas's Rick Barnes and Duke's Mike Krzyzewski. "In Vetter's program, kids are prepared for college as well as any other program in the country," reads the Krzyzewski blurb on Vetter's website. "They learn responsibility, discipline; and they identify with team goals. And the discipline is not just on the court but off it as well. His kids are not just good players, but gentlemen."

As time went on, other private school coaches began to imitate Vetter rather than criticize him. They began to recruit local, national, and international players more openly; began playing more games each season and traveling more; and began to tout their schools' programs as gateways to a college scholarship rather than just as a mere extracurricular activity.

"We were criticized early, but we became the model for what people wanted to do," Vetter said. "Coaches call me up and say, 'We want to do what you did.' Some of the people who were critical of me would like nothing more than to have some of the teams that I have had. High school basketball has really changed. . . . I get most of the credit for that and most of the blame."

By the fall of 1979, the Spingarn basketball program was ready to break out. Not much had been heard from the Green Wave since the days of Ollie Johnson and Dave Bing nearly two decades earlier. But when former Spingarn track star John Wood took over its basketball program in 1972, all that began to change.

Even though Wood wasn't a basketball guy per se, he'd learned a lot about the game watching Hall of Famer John McLendon run practice at Tennessee State University. He'd been highly successful as Spingarn's baseball coach and had no doubts about his ability to succeed in basketball as well.

"I've been competitive all my life," Wood said. "Any challenge I was confronted with, I worked hard to get it done. I grew up in [nearby housing project] Barry Farms, so people knew me and knew what I was about. I felt like whatever I put my hands to, I could get done."

Wood was certainly right about his ability to coach basketball. In 1976, 1977, and 1978, he had the Green Wave at Cole Field House, albeit as the Inter-High runner-up playing the Metro Conference's second-place squad in the warm-up to the City Title Game. As the 1979–80 season began, Wood's program seemed destined for even bigger things. Spingarn had defeated DeMatha for the Jelleff League summer title, so that seemed to bode well. And then six-foot-ten transfer Earl Jones landed in Woods's lap at the beginning of the school year.

Jones was considered one of the top players in the country, but he was miserable in his hometown of Mount Hope, West Virginia, a down-on-its-luck mining community of about 2,000. Jones had missed 63 days of school during his junior year to stay home and care for his ailing mother while also trying to avoid the oppressive scrutiny of teachers and classmates. He'd fled West Virginia over the summer to play Amateur Athletic Union basketball in Washington, where a couple of his sisters lived. Ultimately, Jones decided that environment was much more hospitable than the one back home, so he moved in with relatives and showed up at Spingarn.

There was a hitch, though. Because he'd missed so much class as a junior, Jones was able to play just one game for the Green Wave before being ruled ineligible. He could return for the second semester as long as he kept his grades in order. His absence didn't seem to matter much. As Eastern coach Herman Cannon pointed out, "Even without Jones, Spingarn is the team to beat."

By early February, Wood's team was 18–1 overall and 8–0 in the Inter-High, and the *Star* ranked it No. 1. The Green Wave had savvy guard Jeffrey Hughes, who got the ball where it needed to go, and rugged Clifton Cottom and John Jones up front.

Jones finally joined the team on February 6 and contributed 10 points, 14 rebounds, five blocks, and six assists in a 60–51 victory over Coolidge in front of a standing-room-only crowd, which had come out to see what all the fuss was about. With Jones or without, Spingarn simply had too many weapons for most of its opponents.

"They were double- and triple-teaming him all day," Cottom noted. "But that's where they made their mistake. They concentrated on stopping [Earl] too much. They forgot that we were 8–0 in the league without him."

Dunbar used a sagging 2-1-2 zone to limit Jones in a 57–53 victory over Spingarn in front of 3,500 fans at the DC Armory in mid-February. But that was the last game the Green Wave lost that season. Wood's squad finished 25–2, going 12–1 without Jones and 13–1 with him. Spingarn finally earned a spot in the City Title Game with a 77–50 rout of Eastern that wrapped up the Inter-High crown. Jones led all scorers with 27 points, and Cottom added 17.

Finally, Spingarn had broken through, and the ultimate opponent awaited—DeMatha. At that point, the Stags (22–3) had won two straight city titles and five of the seven titles contested since the end-of-year showdown had resumed in 1973. And yet DeMatha seemed more wary of Spingarn than the other way around.

"Earl Jones is good enough right now to step into the NBA, according to a few of the general managers I talked to," DeMatha coach Morgan Wootten said. "But they're not just a one-man team. I wish they were. Spingarn is solid all the way down the line."

Wootten's assessment was correct. Jones saved his best game at Spingarn for his last, scoring 28 points and grabbing 13 rebounds to lead the Green Wave to a 77–69 victory over DeMatha in the City Title Game at Cole Field House.

"He was a man among boys out there," Wootten said afterward, saving plenty of praise for Jones's Spingarn teammates. "They're a great team without him. With him, they're . . . whew! Their front line was just too big and strong for us. They just wore us down."

Wood, meanwhile, couldn't have been any more pleased. He'd not only knocked off Dunbar for the league title but he'd taken down DeMatha too. And he'd done it his own way—by insisting that his players follow the rules and comport themselves to his standards, no exceptions. This went for Jones, too, despite his obvious talent and his past problems. "He just fell right in," Wood said years later, recalling Jones's assimilation. "He saw we had some good guys and he just blended in."

Jones was headed for bigger things. He moved on to the University of the District of Columbia Firebirds, where he teamed with Michael Britt and Coach Wil Jones to win the Division II national title in 1982. The Firebirds fell in the 1983 championship game before Earl Jones headed for the NBA.

That 1980 championship also awakened a wider audience to Wood's abilities. By the end of that season, his eight-year record at Spingarn stood at 140–60. But the best was yet to come. He guided the Green Wave to another Inter-High title in 1982 and yet another in 1985, as well as a second City Title Game victory over DeMatha.

Discipline was always at the foundation of Wood's system. Players had to check in with him every day before homeroom so he could be sure they were in school. He'd grown up in the same neighborhoods as his players, faced many of the same problems (Wood's father died when he was very young), and understood the hurdles they had to overcome. Wood always had a strong rapport with his players. His door was always open, and anyone could call him at home, while still exerting his authority. "I don't put winning ahead of discipline," he once said. "I'd bench my momma."

Years later, one of Wood's players said, "What I got from Mr. Wood was beyond basketball. You have to stay around the right crowd. If you're around the wrong people, you'll get into the wrong stuff."

Despite his old-school values, Wood remained flexible enough to adopt his on-court tactics as necessary. "I played according to my personnel," he said. "I didn't have one style."

Wood's 1982 Inter-High champs were led by the rugged junior and big man Michael Graham. The Green Wave finished 20–6 after hanging with DeMatha in the City Title Game before the Stags' Drew Komlo hit two late free throws for the 53–52 victory.

In 1985 Spingarn surpassed all others again. The Sherman Douglas–led Green Wave went undefeated (31–0), set an Inter-High record for victories in a season, and could rightly take its place among the greatest teams in league history, along with the McKinley Tech squads of the early 1950s and late 1960s, the Bing-Johnson Spingarn teams of the early 1960s, and the Shelton-Duren undefeated Dunbar squad of 1976. Everyone recognized that Spingarn would be good in 1984–85. Wood's team was coming off a 22–6 season in 1983–84 and was No. 2 in the *Post's* preseason rankings behind DeMatha and Danny Ferry, its senior star.

While Wood knew his team would be good, he worried about its size. He had two six-foot-five players up front in Emmanuel Johnson and Anthony Duckett but no true center. Ernie Hall, a transfer from Coolidge, provided size off the bench. Thinking outside the box, Wood opted for a three-guard lineup, with Melvin Middleton, Robert Smith, and Douglas in the backcourt.

Douglas served notice immediately that he and Spingarn were to be reckoned with, pumping in 48 points in the opener against DuVal and another 36 against Oxon Hill in the next game. By New Year's Spingarn was 10–0 and averaging 90 points—an unheard-of scoring rate for a team playing a 32-minute game. In late January, Douglas and company whipped Dunbar, 87–61, handing the Crimson Tide its worst loss in a dozen years.

By then it was obvious that Spingarn was something special. And there was no better show in the Inter-High than the high-octane, fast-paced, dunk-happy Green Wave squad.

"No Spingarn team of the past could have matched this year's squad for sheer entertainment value and—perhaps—success," wrote Donald Huff of the *Post* as the season wound down.

"Rebound, fast break, dunk. We're pretty exciting to watch," Hall said.

In the middle of it all was Douglas, awarded the area's Player of the Year, which was no small achievement in Ferry's senior season. A lithe six-foot-one, Douglas dominated games from the backcourt with his scoring (26 points per game), passing (seven assists per game), and defense (three steals per game). He even rebounded when Wood needed him to do so. It would have been easy (and tempting) for Douglas to focus solely on scoring—his most obvious talent—but he did what was asked of him and whatever Spingarn needed because what he really cared about was winning.

"I thought Sherman was one of the best players in the city," said Dunbar's Darryl Prue, who could've made the same claim about himself. "He was smart, tough as nails, and would do anything to win. He didn't need a lot of attention. He was never a guy who was greedy. In my era, he was the best guard to come through DC."

Thanks to Douglas and a strong supporting cast, Spingarn rolled through the rest of its schedule. The Green Wave won the regular-season Inter-High title and the league tournament as well, raising its record to 30–0 heading into the City Title Game. DeMatha was formidable again at 29–1, and at Cole Field House a crowd of 12,116 fans awaited what the *Post* called "as good a matchup as the area has had in years."

Spingarn completed its undefeated storybook season with a 54–46 victory over the Stags, making Wood one of the few coaches who could say he beat Wootten twice with everything on the line. Douglas led Spingarn with 14 points and seven assists, but the unheralded Green Wave front line and a sagging zone defense that limited Ferry to 10 points (half his average) on 3-for-11 shooting keyed the triumph. Jones, Hall, and the others also enabled Spingarn to claim a 42–27 rebounding edge.

When it was over, even Wootten had to admit the Stags had met their match. "Spingarn was the better team," he said. "No question."

The Green Wave drew praise from an even higher authority than Wootten—if such a thing were possible—when the team was invited to the White House after the season and honored by President Ronald Reagan. "You have brought honor to this city," he told them during a Rose Garden ceremony that March.

An undefeated record, a city title, a trip to the White House—in every way imaginable, it was the ultimate season. Wood was even named *USA Today's* national Coach of the Year. So Wood decided to step down with a superb 263–85 record. He had dealt with the long hours and the bumpy bus rides for 13 years. He'd been very successful as Spingarn's baseball coach as well.

"That was a good one to go out on," Wood said, reflecting on that magical 1984–85 season. "I mean, what more could I do?"

The departure of Wood and Douglas from Spingarn cleared the path for Coolidge to ascend to the top of the Inter-High ranks. Truth be told, Coolidge had one of the best teams in the area in 1985, but nobody noticed because Spingarn produced one of the all-time great squads in Inter-High history. Although overshadowed, the Colts, under the fatherly guidance of Coach Frank Williams, set a school record with 25 victories. With a host of players coming back in 1985–86, Coolidge was all set to take its turn at the top of the pecking order among the city's public school basketball programs.

That's just what the Colts did, but it wasn't easy. The team was severely shaken when reserve guard Andre Jackson was shot and killed on his way to school one fall morning before preseason practice began. Jackson, who was expected to see a lot of time off the bench, pushed the starters in practice and made sure they were sharp every day. Coolidge's fortunes took another hit before the season when six-foot-nine center David Butler was ruled academically ineligible.

However, with coolheaded point guard Carl Weldon leading the way, they caught fire after a slow start. It didn't even matter that the Colts lacked an adequate gym on school grounds in which to play home games.

Coach Williams deserved much of the credit for keeping the team on track. He had been a standout himself two decades before at Coolidge and had a special appreciation for the issues his players had to face. "He embraced you," recalled Milt Newton, who graduated from Coolidge in 1984 and went on to start on the University of Kansas's 1988 NCAA championship team. "There were a lot of kids who came from broken homes, and [he was] not only the coach but . . . that parent away from home—with greater influence than a parent."

Newton recalled many a time when Williams would press a dollar bill or two into a kid's hand so he wouldn't go hungry at lunch. "He did things like that on a consistent basis," Newton said. "Guys would think, 'This person cares about me so much, he's willing to give me his last dollar.' Even with the hardest kid, that softens them up a little bit."

The 11th-ranked Colts established themselves as contenders in late January when they knocked off fourth-ranked and previously unbeaten Dunbar, 81–67. Coolidge went 18–2 in the league. In the Inter-High Tournament, the Colts rallied to beat Dunbar in the final, 61–50. Derrick Davis finished with 23 points, nine of them during a late 12–0 run that clinched the victory that put the Colts in the City Title Game for the first time.

Their opponent was a surprise. Gonzaga had beaten out DeMatha for the Metro crown. It was the first time since 1977 that the Stags had failed to win the league. Against Gonzaga in front of 9,800 people at Cole Field House, the Colts found themselves down three inside the final minute. But Weldon got a layup off a steal, and after a missed Gonzaga free throw, Davis canned an 18 footer with five seconds left. The Colts were city champs, 62–61.

"Even though we might have been behind," Weldon said. "We knew not to panic." Clearly, Williams had taught them well.

By all rights, the beloved coach should have been on top of the world at this point. After a decade and a half at the school, he had brought the program to the point where it could compete with anybody. Plus he could count on the completion of a new field house on campus during the 1986–87 season.

But fate intervened, and he was unable to enjoy the fruits of his labors. Williams suffered a series of seizures before preseason started, and later he had a bad reaction to medication to treat them. He was in and out of the hospital for six weeks as trusted lieutenants Len Farello and Jerrell Robinson ran the team. The Colts started 12–2, going 8–0 in league play, but faltered as everyone came to realize just how sick their coach was. They finished 18–11, going 13–7 in the league. The sad end for Williams came on Memorial Day 1987, six days after his 43rd birthday, when he succumbed to brain cancer.

He had compiled a 255–131 record at Coolidge, but the numbers didn't come anywhere near to telling the real story. The true measure of the man wasn't how many times he won or lost but how many times he *cared*. "It was easy to get along with him and see that everything he had to say was the truth," Weldon recalled nearly three decades after Williams's death. "Even though he was quiet, he got his point across. All of his players respected him."

Though Spingarn and Coolidge took their turns atop the Inter-High, the league's premier program—and in fact the area's premier public school program—remained Dunbar. The Crimson Tide won Inter-High titles in 1981, 1983, 1984, 1987, 1989, and 1990, with three city championships to its credit during that decade. It didn't matter if the team was coached by Joe Dean Davidson (240–40), Roy Westmore (88–20), or Mike McLeese (180–40). The stewardship of those three coaches produced a two-decade run—from the early 1970s to the early 1990s—that resulted in a 508–100 record and an .835 winning percentage.

The Dunbar program during that era had a certain glamour. Thanks largely to Davidson, the school had become a magnet for top talent from all over the city. Players wanted to be part of Dunbar's winning tradition.

Consequently, Dunbar coaches always had top-level talent at their disposal—a collection of gifted, athletic, disciplined players who enjoyed nothing more than making steals, blocking shots, getting out on the fast break. "Nobody's dunking on us and we're dunking," one Dunbar player recalled Davidson saying at one point.

At schools such as Spingarn and Coolidge, a Dunbar game meant a showdown, a matchup of two top teams. At the less successful schools, the arrival of Dunbar made for a great show. There were sure to be some memorable shots and plays whenever and wherever the Crimson Tide played, so the team became a huge drawing card, even on the road.

"The crowds at our games were incredible," recalled Dunbar forward Darryl Prue, a first-team All-Met in 1984 and 1985. "I loved the attention, and I loved the aura that we had."

The man most responsible for creating that aura was Davidson, who turned the basketball program into one of the area's best in the 1970s and kept right on winning until he moved on to take the Delaware State coaching job in 1983. Player development was Davidson's specialty. In his decade at Dunbar, the coach molded a parade of players into first-team All-Mets and some *Parade* All-Americans as well. There were Stacy Robinson, Joe Thweatt, Craig Shelton, John Duren, Kenny Matthews, and Joe Holston in the 1970s. In the 1980s, Anthony Jones, Sylvester

Charles, Bernard Campbell, and Prue all achieved first-team All-Met status in either the *Post* or the *Star* or both.

Davidson was rightfully—sometimes defiantly—proud of what he had wrought at Dunbar. "I'm running a program here, know what I mean?" he said at one point. "There's a difference between having a team and having a program."

Over and over again, his former players cited Davidson's ability to instill discipline, build confidence, and develop talent as what they remembered most about him. He'd even take an interest in players from other schools and try to help them along, both as basketball players and as young men trying to find themselves.

"He would talk me through stuff; he would tell me how good I was gonna be," Prue recalled. "He gave me confidence."

Even the mercurial Robinson came to understand that Davidson wanted only the best for him. The coach refused to cater to Robinson, one of the city's top players, after he transferred to Dunbar. Davidson even brought him off the bench, not starting Robinson in an effort to make the dazzling guard get more serious about his studies.

It never quite worked out for Robinson, but he appreciated Davidson's efforts and understood years later that the coach really was on his side. "I had a big head," Robinson recalled. "All he was doing was trying to help me. He'd tell me to get to class, do the right thing. Now that I'm older, I can see that all he wanted for us to do was achieve."

The names changed over the years, but the success continued. Davidson had one of his best teams in 1980–81, featuring area Player of the Year Jones and Charles. That frontcourt duo kept Dunbar unbeaten and at the top of the local rankings almost all season.

The only hitch all year came at the end when DeMatha, even with Coach Morgan Wootten at home with a bad sinus infection, upset Dunbar in the City Title Game. That loss left the Crimson Tide 24–1 and so incensed Davidson that he refused to speak to reporters afterward. He declared his players off-limits to the media as well. "No interviews!" he snapped. "You saw the game, write what you saw!"

Michael Graham–led Spingarn nosed out Dunbar for the Inter-High title in 1981–82, but Davidson went out with a flourish the next season—his final one at Dunbar, as it turned out. At the end of the year, the fourth-ranked Crimson Tide (20–4) faced top-ranked DeMatha (23–4) in the City Title Game. The Stags prevailed 64–61 in overtime, as Davidson's squad had a last-second 15 footer in regulation that simply wouldn't go down. DeMatha had finished on top—again. Davidson, however, had brought Dunbar to the point where it was practically DeMatha's equal. As everyone who competed against Wootten's squads over four-plus decades understood, that was a feat in itself.

Following Davidson was easy in some ways, difficult in others. He'd had his backers and his enemies in Dunbar's administration, so some wanted Westmore to be exactly the same while others wanted him to be the complete opposite. Dunbar had not only plenty of talent but also high expectations. Westmore kept the winning tradition going. He earned Coach of the Year acclaim from the *Post* after his first season, 1983–84, when Dunbar went 24–4, won the Inter-High (again), and lost in the City Title Game (again).

Westmore might have done an even better job in his last year, 1986–87. Dunbar trailed in the Inter-High standings by two games with five left to play, but the Crimson Tide came on strong to win the league. In the City Title Game, Dunbar overcame a record 35 points by DeMatha's John Gwynn to beat the Stags, 91–85. Balance was the key to offsetting Gwynn as Tyrone Gibson, Anthony Beagle, Kevin Sams, and Dion Lewis all scored at least 19 points.

Westmore, who always wanted to have everyone involved offensively, left on the perfect note. It was Dunbar's seventh appearance in the City Title Game since the game had resumed in 1973—DeMatha was the opponent each time—but only its second victory.

McLeese took over as coach the next season, fully aware of what he was getting into but eager to accept the challenge. He'd paid his dues by coaching at Lincoln Junior High and serving as the Dunbar girls' basketball coach, succeeding in both capacities. "I thought it was the best job in the city," he said. "Even though you had Spingarn and Coolidge who were good, I thought Dunbar was a great opportunity."

But there were high expectations as well. Chuck Taylor, who'd played for Westmore, had summed up the prevailing attitude about Dunbar's program. "We know people around the school expect us to win," he said. "So do we."

So McLeese's 11–14 record in that first year wasn't exactly well received. In fact, McLeese heard a Dunbar assistant principal speculate over who might replace him when the team struggled. But McLeese survived and picked up some valuable tips while helping John Thompson as the latter coached the 1988 US Olympic team.

"I had an opportunity to observe how he formulated practice plans, the drills he used," McLeese said. "I was like a sponge, soaking it all up. I was at every practice, every meeting. I saw how it was supposed to be run."

Armed with Thompson's methods, McLeese immediately returned the Dunbar Tide to glory. "The next year, we got it going," McLeese said.

Not only did McLeese's teams win three straight Inter-High titles in 1989, 1990, and 1991 but they also won back-to-back city crowns. That matched the total won by Davidson and Westmore combined, and in repeating as the City Title Game champions, Dunbar became the first Inter-High school to do so since Frank Bolden's Cardozo teams won the first two games way back in 1957 and 1958.

"Coach Mac was one of the best," recalled Michael Smith, the linchpin of those back-to-back city champs and an eventual NBA player. "We had good players and a good coach—a general who led us. His teams had talent, but he knew what to do with it. Kids would come from all over just to play for Coach 'Mac.'"

McLeese's tutelage helped make Smith the most effective inside player in the city. He averaged 23 points and 16 rebounds as a junior, teaming with Donald Ford to carry the team to the Inter-High title. After sitting out much of the season with academic woes, Ford was the hero in the City Title Game, hitting a desperation 35 footer that beat Lawrence Moten and Archbishop Carroll, 81–79.

Smith was the star, though. He scored 26 points and grabbed 10 rebounds in the victory that enabled Dunbar to finish 27–5. "He rebounds the ball, hustles, and is just as quick as any other player on the floor," Moten said.

The next year, it was more of the same. Dunbar, its profile as high as ever, was invited to play holiday tournaments in Las Vegas and Florida, and the Crimson Tide rolled to a school record 34 victories. Dunbar hounded teams with its defense, forced turnovers, grabbed the ball off the boards, and scored in bunches. In the half-court, McLeese could turn inside to Smith (who averaged 24 points and 12 rebounds in another first-team All-Met season) or to second-team All-Met Deon Murray outside.

McLeese also had another emerging star in future Maryland standout Johnny Rhodes. Dunbar had so much talent, in fact, that a couple of players transferred out in search of more playing time and wound up playing prominent roles at other Inter-High schools.

"Junior year we were good, but senior year, we were better," Smith said. "Everybody knew what everybody could do. You didn't have to teach everything all over again. It made us better because everyone knew what they needed to do."

At the end of the year, DeMatha stood between Dunbar and the city title. As with so many of their previous matchups, the 1990 game was a classic. The Crimson Tide held on to win, 71–69, surviving the Stags' six shot attempts to tie the game in the last 15 seconds. Just as they had all season, Smith and Murray came up big in the finale. Smith took care of the inside with 22 points and nine rebounds, while Murray led all scorers with 24 points and handed out five assists.

While the basketball programs at Spingarn, Dunbar, and Coolidge established themselves among the area's best in the 1980s, the fortunes of teams from Montgomery County faded a bit. Many of the coaches who had brought such success to the Maryland county were still prowling the sidelines, and some of them were still getting excellent results. But collectively they weren't able to bring home the state titles that they had in the previous decade.

Then, too, some of the men who'd brought such attention and acclaim to county basketball were stepping down from their posts. Dale Miller left Wootton in 1980 to become an administrator and, later, a football coach. Jim Conner, the only coach Rockville High School had known since opening in 1968, retired in 1982. Conner, who won a pair of state titles in the 1970s, certainly went out in style, leading the Rams to the state finals in 1980 and 1981 and to the semifinals in 1982. Unlike many coaches who attempt to fit players to a system, Conner succeeded by adapting his game plans to his players' strengths. He won with big teams, small teams, fast squads, and slow ones. "Creative" was one word a former player used to describe him.

"The best thing about him is that he doesn't have a set way of doing things," said his son, Jimbo Conner, the point guard on his father's final squad. "He coaches to the ability of his players. He comes into each season with an open mind, looks at the talent he has, and coaches according to what he has."

Gene Doane, who won a pair of state titles at Blair in the 1970s, was up to his old tricks as well. Doane had left a state title contender to succeed Marty Dickerson for the 1978–79 season (the Blazers did win the Class AA crown) to take the program at up-county Seneca Valley. The Germantown school, which opened in 1974, had already won two state football championships, but many considered Doane's 11–11 debut as something of a miracle. He was just getting started though.

"[Initially] I really felt like we could be a winning team," Doane said. "Maybe 15 or 16 wins. That wasn't great, but it was on the plus side. Once I got into it and got the support, I figured if we can win this thing in football, we can win it in basketball. I went there with the idea of being successful and building a program that could be competitive with anybody."

Doane was spot-on. By 1982 the High Point Screaming Eagles were good enough to knock off Inter-High power Dunbar and ascend to the top of the *Post*'s rankings for a good portion of the season. Seneca Valley was unbeaten until a playoff loss to the eventual Class AA state champion High Point. But that was the high point for Doane, who retired in 1986, having guided winners at Sherwood, Blair, and Seneca Valley during almost three decades in Montgomery County.

Tom George—the only basketball coach in the 21 years that Woodward High School was open—ended his career the next year when the school was absorbed into nearby Walter Johnson. Those departures left only John Barrett (Springbrook), Hank Galotta (Paint Branch), and Mel Laughner (Sherwood) from the extraordinary group of coaches who had made Montgomery County basketball so special in the 1970s. At one point in that decade, *eight* county schools had coaches who had won at least one state championship.

Galotta reached the state finals in 1985 and the semifinals in 1988, and he kept the Panthers as winners through much of the 1990s. As for Laughner, after winning the state title in 1979, he had the Warriors back in the finals in 1987 and again in 1999.

But Barrett was the veteran coach who enjoyed the most success in the 1980s. He had the Blue Devils in the state semifinals in 1981 (with Chuck Driesell, son of Maryland coach Lefty Driesell, on the team) and again in 1987. Springbrook won the Class AA state title in 1988, beating a top-ranked Crossland Cavaliers team led by Walt Williams—soon to be Maryland's star—and a vaunted full-court press that was thought to be unbeatable. "If they put out betting lines on high school games, we probably would have been 20-point underdogs, but we knew what we thought we could do to take away their strengths," Barrett said of the Cavaliers, who were in their third straight state final.

While the lineup of Darrel Asson, Shawn Clifton (a transfer from Blair), Anthony Jennings, Mario Manderson, and the future Terps guard Kevin McLinton lacked Crossland's marquee value, Springbrook was no slouch at 24–1. "It was just a tremendous bunch of players to coach," Barrett said. "We played good defense; we shot the ball good from the outside. We got the ball inside well against teams. We had balanced scoring. I think that really was a key."

In the championship game, the Springbrook Blue Devils repeatedly foiled Crossland's press with deft passing and heads-up play. Once the pressure was beaten, the Blue Devils often had 2-on-1 or even 3-on-1 advantages, helping them hit 17 of its 29 baskets from close range. The result was a 77–73 upset.

"One must give credit where credit is due," Crossland coach Earl Hawkins said. "And that is to a fine Springbrook coach and team."

Asson led the way with 22 points. McLinton added 18, and Clifton contributed 17 points and 10 rebounds. Springbrook held off a late charge by hitting all 12 of its free throws in the final three and a half minutes.

The game bore Barrett's trademark. For two decades, his Blue Devils might vary in size or talent from one year to the next, but they were always tough defensively and well drilled offensively. They seldom beat themselves.

"One of the things I was pretty proud of was that we were always in contention and usually ranked," Barrett recalled. "That's pretty good when you consider I took whoever came through the door."

Barrett's methods certainly proved enduring. He won two state titles, 16 years apart. He was one of just a handful of coaches (Doane, Galotta, and Laughner were among the others) who made trips to the state tournament in three different decades. When Barrett finally left Springbrook in 1992, he was replaced by assistant Bob Cilento. Using the same methods and system, with a couple of adjustments, Cilento took Springbrook to the state semifinals in 1993 and the championship game in 1994 and 1995.

"We were always prepared," noted Chris McGuthrie, who played on Barrett's final team. "We had like 10 different defenses, and everyone knew exactly what their job was. He was just so clever. I didn't lose many games playing for that man."

With some of its most successful coaches gone, the heights that Montgomery County schools reached during the 1970s became a distant memory. After Springbrook's title in 1988, 10 years passed before another county school—in any classification—went to the state tournament at Cole Field House and brought home the ultimate prize.

In the 1980s neighboring Prince George's County became the dominant force in Maryland high school hoops. That success continued unabated into the middle 1990s, until Baltimore City's schools joined the Maryland Public Secondary Schools Athletic Association.

From top to bottom, the level of competition in Prince George's County may never have been better than it was during the 1980s. From 1980 to 1989, 15 county public school teams won state championships with 10 different schools winning at least one state title. (County teams managed 10 titles from 1970 to 1979 and a dozen from 1990 to 1999.)

Individual talent was everywhere, it seemed. Nine players who grew up in the county and graduated from high school between 1981 and 1990 eventually played in the NBA. The group included private school products Adrian Branch, Danny Ferry, and Jerrod Mustaf of DeMatha along with Randolph Childress of Flint Hill. Childress actually played for a time at Gwynn Park before transferring. The De-Matha trio all grew up within the county's borders, even though they opted for private school. Walt Williams (Crossland), Monty Williams (the Potomac Wolverines), Mike Morrison (Northwestern), John Turner (Eleanor Roosevelt Raiders), and Dickey Simpkins (Friendly Patriots)—all went from a Prince George's public school to the NBA.

There's even more supporting evidence that attests to the county's superior basketball programs during the decade. Between 1983 and 1989, four players from the county were named high school Player of the Year by the *Washington Post*: Rodney Rice (St. John's, 1983), Derrick Lewis (Carroll, 1984), Mustaf (1988), and Michael Tate (Oxon Hill, 1989). In 1987 four county players were named to the 10-player All-Met first team. In 1988 a whopping six from the county were selected, and Crossland's Earl Hawkins was Coach of the Year. In 1989 three county players were first-team All-Met, while High Point became the first-ever Prince George's team to finish the season ranked No. 1 in the *Post*.

Of course, on that aforementioned list of pros, Northwestern grad Len Bias ('82) would have been the 10th to go pro. His Northwestern team went to the Class AA state title game, losing to High Point 54-52 on a Hail Mary shot at the buzzer. Bias, a sculpted six-foot-eight force of nature, could dunk over you, drive by you, or shoot his feathery jumper over you. Also in 1982, Bias, with 18 points and 11 rebounds, won co-MVP honors with Johnny Dawkins as the Capital All-Stars beat the All-American All-Stars 82-79 at the Capital Classic. And he stayed home to become a two-time Atlantic Coast Conference Player of the Year at Maryland.

"When I think of Len, I don't think of how great he was in games," his high school coach, Bob Wagner, told the Washington, DC, *City Paper* 10 years after Bias's death. "It's about watching him practice, because it was in practice that you could see how hard he worked to get to the level that he did and how much he loved the game. That enthusiasm—that incredible spirit—is what set him apart.

Everybody around him, not just me, could see that Len was special. It sounds silly, but you could see it in his eyes. That's what I choose to remember."

After his All-American career at Maryland, the Boston Celtics made Bias the second pick of the 1986 NBA Draft. But Bias never lived to wear the No. 30 Celtics jersey he'd been given. He never got to add to the Celtics' string of championships. On June 19, 1986, less than 40 hours after being taken by the Celtics, he was dead of a heart attack, the result of a celebratory late-night cocaine binge in his Washington Hall dorm room.

Bias's death stunned the nation. How could this have happened to someone so young, so strong, with so much ahead of him? The tragedy had huge repercussions in the academic world, the athletic world, and the legal world. His death wasn't a pebble tossed into a pond that set off ripples; it was a boulder. It affected how the public and the government viewed the scourge of crack cocaine and prompted tougher sentencing guidelines. At the University of Maryland–College Park, Bias's death resulted in seismic changes. Academic requirements were raised, and Chancellor John Slaughter, Athletic Director Dick Dull, and legendary basketball coach Lefty Driesell all lost their jobs.

Nowhere was the shock and hurt felt more acutely than in Prince George's County, especially among those who had nurtured Bias and watched him grow up. Even as he became a huge star, Bias always embraced his roots. He returned again and again to Northwestern High School and the Columbia Park Recreation Center, where he had learned to play basketball. Bias sought refuge in those places where he could relax and be himself, free from those who were part of the outside world who always seemed to want something from him.

The weight of what happened fell hardest on Bias's younger brother, Jay. A talented player in his own right, Jay was a rising star on Northwestern's varsity—just as his late brother had been just a few years earlier. The 1986–87 season promised to be a difficult one for Jay and everyone else at Northwestern. The tragic death of the school's biggest hero seemed to cast a pall over the whole building when classes began that Fall.

The situation only grew worse when Coach Wagner stepped down right before the start of the season, leaving the team in the hands of assistant Cornell Jones. The Wildcats, though talented, looked to be in for a difficult season.

Northwestern dropped three of its first four games as Jones tried to get the hang of his new responsibilities. A one-point loss to DeMatha offered some hope, but that was offset by Jay Bias's troubles. He was ejected from the opener for throwing an elbow and was suspended for a game. It was the first of several incidents involving Bias, whom some saw as a sympathetic figure and others as a target.

During a particularly ugly incident at Eleanor Roosevelt, all hell broke loose when an opposing player slugged Bias, knocking him down. Players—some wanting to settle the score, some wanting to make peace—got involved. Some fans even came out of the bleachers to join the melee during which Jones was actually pushed out the door of the gym. Bias was treated for a bruise at Doctors Community Hospital in nearby Lanham. Northwestern was awarded the victory because it had been ahead when the brawl broke out.

As troublesome as that episode was, it came about the time that the Wildcats were pulling together. Jones was getting the hang of his new responsibilities, and the veteran team—led by point guard Clinton Venable—was talented enough that Bias didn't have to do everything himself. Venable was the key as he was quick, smart, and able to score. He was the kind of player and leader that his teammates respected and even opposing coaches admired. He averaged 22 points, nine assists, and six steals, making first-team All-Met.

"He was the catalyst," Jones said. "He kept everybody in line, and he wasn't gonna let anything stand in the way of a state title."

Venable's 15 footer with two seconds left beat High Point, 66–65, and earned Northwestern a trip to the state semifinals. The triumph was the team's 14th in 17 games after a 3–4 start; it was quite a turnaround, considering all the adversity. "It makes us play harder," said the Wildcats' Joe Freeman at the time.

Northwestern was the fourth seed out of four teams in the Class 4A tournament. But the Wildcats were rolling. The players and coaches had buried the problems of the past and evolved into a dangerous, confident bunch. Northwestern knocked off top-seeded Annapolis in the semifinals, 69–56, with Bias scoring 24 points and grabbing 14 rebounds in a performance that would have made his brother proud.

The venue—Cole Field House, where his brother had played so brilliantly for Maryland—made the performance that much more special for Jay. "I started having flashbacks of coming to see my brother play," he said. "This was always his spot."

In the state final, it was more of the same. Northwestern trailed by nine at the half and by eight after three quarters against Crossland, which had won the regular-season matchup. But Venable (17 points, with 15 coming in the second half) tied the score with 2:49 left on a steal and a layup. That keyed a decisive 9–0 run that turned the game Northwestern's way. The final was 73–63.

Bias was the star again, finishing with a game-high 25 points and 11 rebounds. To pay tribute to his brother, he'd written "Len" on the back of his left shoe and "Bias" on the back of the right one. With the clock ticking down and the game secure, Bias, still out on the court, pointed to his shoes and then up to the sky.

"I felt a lot of pressure after Len died," Jay admitted. "I think people expected me to do what he did when he wasn't here. It bothered me a lot, and I didn't have the patience to deal with it. I'm better now."

Jones agreed: "He's come a long way. All he wants is his own identity. He wants to sink or swim as Jay Bias."

The championship gave Jay a claim to fame that his brother never achieved. For all Len accomplished in basketball, he never led Northwestern to a state title. The closest he came was as a senior in 1982, when the Wildcats fell in the state final after that miracle last-second shot by High Point's Vernon Butler, who would star at the Naval Academy.

Jay added to his own legacy in 1987–88. Northwestern wasn't as good, but Jay established himself as one of the area's best players. He averaged 26.5 points and 10.3 rebounds and made first-team All-Met. He and two of his buddies—Oxon Hill's Michael Tate (now known as Michael Venson) and Parkdale Panthers' Henry Hall—also staged perhaps the greatest can-you-top-this scoring battle in area basketball history.

Hall, a bombardier of the first rank, emerged victorious in the three-man challenge. He averaged a stunning 37.1 points per game, benefiting tremendously when the high school game adopted the three-point line that season. Hall's range was, conservatively, anywhere inside half-court. Hall had pumped in 40 points in a game against Crossland the year before, a total that Cavaliers coach Earl Hawkins estimated might have been 60 with a three-point line.

The six-foot-seven Tate, a year younger than Bias and Hall, also could score with anybody. With his great leaping ability and deft shooting touch, he finished at 30.7 points per game, producing eight games of at least 40 points.

The trio had become close prior to that season, having played on a youth all-star team together. Their scoring battle was great fun for all involved, especially those basketball fans in Prince George's County.

Bias still had his dark moments. Jones had to suspend him for a time as a disciplinary measure, and he grew sullen at times, especially when the Celtics came to town to play the Bullets. Jay knew that he should have been at the Capital Centre, cheering for his brother.

But even for Bias, his senior season was mostly a time of fun, excitement, and laughter. The members of the high-scoring trio were constantly on the phone with one another, teasing about what somebody had or hadn't done in the most recent game, not to mention what one guy might do to the other the next time they met on the court.

"We were friends all the way," Venson recalled. "We were tight, we would trash talk. People used to call us 'The Three Amigos.' One of us would do something big, and you'd say, 'I'm gonna outdo that.' It became competitive. Somebody would say, 'You're not gonna catch me,' and you'd come back and say, 'We'll see about that.' You'd come out of the locker rooms for those games, and you'd see rows and rows of people—that was the ultimate. Seeing that added a couple of inches to your vertical."

No matter which of the three you would go see, one or both of the other players would do something spectacular in another game the same night. The only way to keep up was by reading about it the next day in the *Prince George's Journal*. "When any of us play, you are going to get a show," Bias said at one point.

On January 19, Hall erupted for 51 points in a 106–92 win over Oxon Hill, while Tate countered with 39. Tate poured in 51 a couple of nights later in his

Chapter Five

team's loss to the Bowie Bulldogs. A little more than a week later, Hall got 40 points in a 90–75 win over Northwestern, with Bias scoring 35. On and on it went.

All three made first-team All-Met, and promising futures awaited. Hall went to the University of Texas–El Paso and enjoyed a fine career there. Tate was the *Post*'s Player of the Year before moving on to Georgetown and then James Madison University.

A different fate awaited Jay. He played some at powerful Allegany Community College (now Allegany College of Maryland) in western Maryland, but unlike his brother, Jay never made it to Division I. In December 1990, when he would have been starting his junior season, he was shot and killed as he sat in a truck outside Prince George's Plaza. The shooter said that Bias had been flirting with his wife. Jay Bias was only 20 years old.

Amid all the individual talent in Prince George's County, one team stood apart. Crossland went all the way to the Class 4A state finals three years running, winning the title in 1986 but falling in the championship game the next two seasons. That three-year run under Coach Earl Hawkins produced a 71–8 record, part of a 10-year-long stretch under his stewardship that produced a 164–79 mark.

Hawkins had been a key man on Larry Gandee's championship-caliber Gwynn Park squads of the late 1960s and early 1970s, and he adopted much of what he had learned from Gandee. Hawkins's Crossland teams were up-tempo but disciplined, prone to press, and always capable of turning defense to offense by making steals or forcing turnovers.

Hawkins was never one to take anything for granted, always pushing his teams to keep up the intensity. Hawkins, after all, had once grabbed 31 rebounds in a state playoff game. How could he be any other way?

"He demanded control, and he was in control of everything," said Walt Williams, Crossland's biggest star of that era and later a standout at Maryland and in the NBA. "He had the respect of everyone. We always went out and tried to execute to the best of our ability."

High Point coach Ernie Welch called Hawkins "a good coach, a good guy. He was great with his kids. Those kids did what he led them to do, and he didn't let them do bad stuff."

Hawkins was also fortunate to have a pair of point guards—Mike White and Anthony Higginbotham—who understood their roles and ran things the way Hawkins wanted during that three-year run. White, who ran the Cavaliers to the 1986 state title, always thought to pass first rather than shoot. Big man Clarence Alford swept the boards clean and scored on a lot of putbacks.

That team had a certain toughness; the Cavaliers always seemed to be rallying to pull out a game that looked to be a loss. Alford scored nine points in the fourth quarter in a late-season victory over Eleanor Roosevelt and NBA-bound John Turner. White scored five points in the last 59 seconds, including a pair of free throws with nine seconds left, as Crossland nipped High Point, 64–62, to reach the state final.

"It's not necessarily the skill level of the players you have, but how tough they are," noted Williams, who was just a sophomore bit player on that team but marveled at its resolve. Crossland didn't need any late-game heroics in the state final against Bethesda's Whitman High. The Cavaliers hit nine of their first 11 shots and played keep-away at the end of their 64–58 triumph over the Vikings for the Class 4A title.

The personnel on and off the court were a lot different the next two years in Temple Hills, but the success continued. Alford was the only senior returnee, but Williams's game continued to evolve as Hawkins uncovered another unselfish point man in Higginbotham. "Anthony was just like Mike," Hawkins recalled. "A tremendously heady point guard who understood how to play the position."

Because of those two players, things just seemed to flow better offensively for Crossland than for its foes. Everyone was on board with Hawkins's program—he wouldn't tolerate anything else—and even his opponents were impressed with the Cavaliers' cohesiveness.

"Coach Hawkins had a good crop of kids," recalled Oxon Hill star Michael (Tate) Venson. "Everyone complemented each other."

It helped, too, that Williams—the best player on the team and one of the best in the area—was eminently coachable. He was a dazzling talent who was capable of bringing the ball up court and shooting the lights out from the outside, even at six foot eight. He was a matchup nightmare for almost every team Crossland faced but remained as level-headed in stardom as he was in obscurity.

"He was a tremendous, tremendous person—with no ego," Hawkins said. "He was everything you could ask for as a player and as a person, even to this day. Because of him, the other players were easier to coach."

Williams and the Cavaliers weren't able to duplicate that 1986 state title, but they went all the way to the final before losing to Northwestern and Springbrook, respectively. They spent most of the 1987–88 season ranked No. 1 by the *Post*, winning 25 straight before the Blue Devils foiled their press in the finale. But Williams and the rest had made their mark.

"I do believe we've finally reached the stage where our program has been accepted with the DeMathas, Dunbars, and Flint Hills," Hawkins said at the end of the 1987–88 regular season. "I don't think we have to take a backseat to anyone."

Long before she made history, Wanda Oates made an impact. Oates, a longtime teacher at Ballou in Southeast Washington, sought to give high school girls some kind of athletic outlet years before Title IX changed the landscape of amateur sports in the United States. She started girls basketball in the Inter-High, often paying for uniforms and trophies out of her own pocket. As the Knights' coach at Ballou, which was located in one of the more troubled parts of the city, Oates won a slew of Inter-High regular-season and tournament titles and was a key force in getting the local newspapers to vote on All-Met basketball teams for girls as well as boys.

Oates also won league titles in boys soccer and softball and became the Inter-High's first female athletic director. She was held in such high esteem at the school that she landed the position as the football coach there in the mid-1980s before the school board stepped in and overturned the recommendation. She filed suit—one of many times she took the DC school system to court—claiming she was the victim of sexual discrimination.

Oates ultimately lost that battle but got her chance to make history a couple of years later when she was named coach of the boys basketball team in the summer of 1988. With that appointment, she became the first female coach of a boys' basketball team in the area and one of the few in the country.

"This was not a political move," said Robert Royster, the principal who convinced Oates to take the job. "I just felt she is the most competent—black or white, male or female—to do the job. She is talented and has always had the respect of the young people here. I don't envision her having any problems at all doing the job."

Oates, who was no shrinking violet, was equally confident. She was determined to strike a blow for gender equity and—having already fought so many battles by that point—didn't care what anybody else thought. In some circles, her feisty demeanor made her a hero; in others, it made her a pariah.

"I know there will be some underlying resentment by some people because I'm a woman," Oates said. "Those people are from the old-line school and are resistant to change. I have been successful coaching boys before. I'm only doing this for the students' welfare. These kids here are second-generation kids [at Ballou, where she'd been teaching for more than two decades], and their parents and older brothers and sisters know what I stand for."

Oates faced an uphill battle. Ballou had compiled a 26–84 record over the previous five years, but that didn't dampen her enthusiasm in the least.

"My teams will be as mentally and physically prepared as any team we play," she vowed. "I didn't anticipate any problems when I accepted the job because I know I can do the job. Many of the players are from single-parent homes and are used to the female figure being around. A lot of them look at me as if I was the mother figure, and I don't mind that at all."

Jeremy Watson, one of Oates's players, said, "She knows defenses and believes in attacking. Some guys on the other teams are saying we make layups in dresses and will play like girls, so we're anxious to show people we will be a good team."

They did just that. And Oates, to the surprise of many, proved prophetic. Her first Ballou team finished 15–11, going 11–9 in the ultra-competitive Inter-High, including a victory over eventual league champion Dunbar. The Knights had won 11 games or more only three times in the previous 17 years. Ballou turned in a respectable 13–13 record in Oates's second season as coach. Not much was expected in her third season because a half dozen of her players from the 1989–90 team had moved on, including Michael Robinson, who had flourished under Oates's tutelage to become the Inter-High's leading scorer with a 27.2 average.

With only four players back for the 1990–91 season, Oates took Ballou to heights it hadn't enjoyed in 20 years. Thanks to a 76–70 victory over Anacostia on February 21, Ballou won the Inter-High's East Division for the first time since 1971.

Against Anacostia, Oates's Ballou Knights pressed full-court, forced the action, and cashed in at the line, hitting 21 of 28 free throws. Her team had executed exactly as she wanted—so much so that she never even called a time out.

"A lot of people feel that women can't coach boys, but all we need is the opportunity," she said. "This is by far the greatest victory of my entire coaching career."

The Knights lost, 75–72, to Coolidge in the Inter-High playoffs, but they went down swinging. Ballou fell behind by 24 early and trailed by 16 at the half. But the Knights would've forced overtime if Marc Dozier's three-pointer at the buzzer hadn't been just off the mark.

Although no one knew it at the time, that was the high point for Oates as Ballou's boys' coach. The Knights kept slipping, and when they went 0–20 in 1993–94, her contract as coach was not renewed. She complained loud and long that her colleagues in the Inter-High had conspired against her, making charges that a number of schools were using overage players to gain an advantage. Nothing ever came of Oates's accusations, though, and her days of coaching boys basketball at her beloved Ballou were finished. But no matter how badly things might have ended, Oates still made history, and she made a difference. Only a few—very few—of her male colleagues could say the same.

Oates's arrival on the scene wasn't the only seismic shift in the local basketball scene during the 1988–89 season. In February came the news that Mackin and All Saints (which had merged with St. Anthony's) would cease to operate by order of the Washington archdiocese. The exodus of upper- and middle-class blacks from the city for the suburbs was ultimately what led to the decision. Dwindling enrollments at the diocesan high schools and rising costs led Cardinal James Hickey to conclude that closing both Mackin and All Saints was the best option.

Archbishop Carroll would continue to operate within the city boundaries and would go coed (it had been boys only) to accommodate those displaced. A couple of years later, similar concerns led St. John's, which had been an all-boys school since opening in 1851, to accept girls as well. The closures triggered all kinds of

Chapter Five

protests, charges, and countercharges, largely because the majority of those high school students affected by the decisions were black.

From a basketball standpoint, closing those schools represented a significant blow. For much of the previous 30 years, Mackin had marched a mere half step behind DeMatha atop the highly competitive Catholic League / Metro Conference. Under Paul Furlong, Harry Rest, and other coaches, the tiny Petworth school proved it could compete with anyone on a court, even though its own gym was too cramped to accommodate an actual game.

The Trojans were the only team other than DeMatha to win a league title between 1960 and 1977 when the Austin Carr–led squad did so in 1966–67. Mackin stayed good through the 1970s and early 1980s, though it was never able to unseat DeMatha again. And it kept churning out such topflight players as Donald "Duck" Williams, who would become a big star at Notre Dame; Jo Jo Hunter, the area's leading scorer with a 27-point average in 1976; and Johnny Dawkins, college basketball's Player of the Year at Duke in 1986.

The history at Brookland's St. Anthony's / All Saints was no less distinguished. Jack Sullivan had led an underdog Tonies team to the top of the local basketball heap with a victory in the Evening Star Tournament in 1953. A decade and a half later, John Thompson put together a 122–28 record there, including a 63–7 stretch from 1968–69 to 1971–72. During that time, St. Anthony's was never ranked lower than third in the final polls.

There were some good years in the 1970s and 1980s as well under Coaches Bob Grier and Dwight Datcher. The latter was the *Post*'s Coach of the Year in 1983.

St. Anthony's roster of stars was as impressive as Mackin's. Donald Washington went on to play at UNC and then in Europe for a decade. His high school teammate Merlin Wilson played for Thompson at Georgetown, where he—not Patrick Ewing, Dikembe Mutombo, or Alonzo Mourning—owns the highest rebounding average (11.4) in school history. Charles Smith, who played at All Saints, made the US Olympic team in 1988 and was the Big East Player of the Year for the Hoyas in 1989.

"We had some great teams back then, and there were some great people that came out of those programs," said Datcher, who played for Thompson at St. Anthony's before becoming the coach. "But if you start thinking about that stuff too long, you feel old. Still, we had some very talented guys come through that little tiny hole in the wall at 12th and Lawrence."

DeMatha senior Danny Ferry (35) waits for an assist under tight coverage at the basket. Spingarn completed its undefeated season with a 54–46 victory over DeMatha at Cole Field House. Sherman Douglas led Spingarn with 14 points and seven assists, but it was the Green Wave front line and a sagging zone defense that limited Ferry to 10 points (half his average) on 3-for-11 shooting.

DeMatha's Danny Ferry (35) tries for a layup against Dunbar's Darryl Prue (24). The schools would meet in the City Title Game in 1985 for the fifth time since the resumption of the private-public year-end series in 1973.

Danny Ferry in 1985.

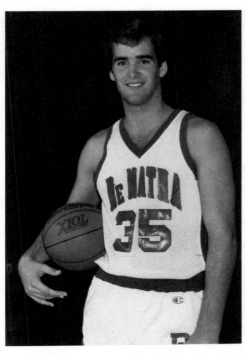

All-Met Sherman Douglas, 3rd row from bottom, 2nd from left, senior portrait in the 1985 Spingarn High School Yearbook.

(Pisces)
Crystal Davis
(Scorpio)

Earlean D. Davis
(Sagittarius)
Terressa Debose
(Libra)
Jerome Debrew
(Capricorn)
Briscoe Dickens
(Taurus)

Donovan Douglas
(Gemini)
Sherman Douglas
(Virgo)
Anthony Duckett
(Virgo)
Carolyn Duckett
(Libra)

Angela Ebron
Virgo)
Melissa Edwards
Wendy Edwards

Christopher Fisher
(Capricorn)
Tonya Fisher
(Aries)
Kevin Fortune
Al Foster
(Leo)

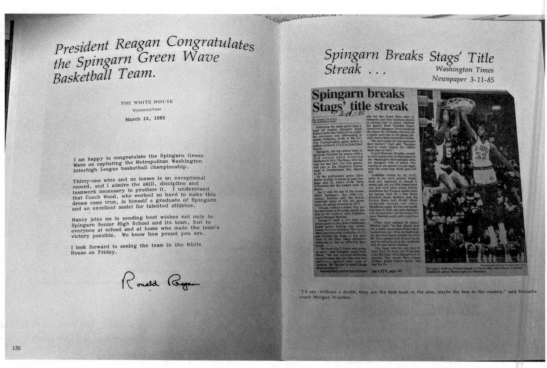

**Spingarn 1985 yearbook includes a letter of congratulations from President Reagan.**

**All-Met Sherman Douglas poses for a senior photo in the 1985 Spingarn High School Yearbook.**

# Boys' Basketball—The City Champs

Front, l-r, James Brooks, Clinton McCoy, Derrick Davis, Aaron Mahoney, Tauchios Owens. Back, Shawn Chisley, Carl Weldon, Fred Davy, Donald Hodge, Everett Robinson, Anthony Graham, Byron Hawkins and Tyrone Davis.

## Scores

| WE | | THEY | |
|---|---|---|---|
| 79 | Parkdale | 68 | |
| 82 | Walbrook (Balt.) | 65 | |
| 52 | Grant (Calif.) | 53 | |
| 71 | Wilson (Long Beach) | 40 | |
| 81 | Las Vegas High | 57 | |
| 57 | Santa Monica | 64 | |
| 58 | Rummel High | 59 | |
| 95 | Ballou | 46 | |
| 57 | Woodson | 45 | |
| 58 | Anacostia | 62 | |
| 64 | Cardozo | 67 | |
| 81 | Dunbar | 72 | |
| 86 | Wilson | 76 | |
| 78 | Eastern | 71 | |
| 77 | Roosevelt | 66 | |
| 64 | McKinley | 74 | |
| 85 | Spingarn | 78 | |
| 79 | Ballou | | |

| | | |
|---|---|---|
| 53 | Anacostia | 44 |
| 80 | Woodson | 52 |
| 65 | Wilson | 50 |
| 67 | Eastern | 65 |
| 66 | Dunbar | 67 |
| 65 | Wilson | 50 |
| 67 | Eastern | 65 |
| 61 | Roosevelt | 48 |
| 87 | McKinley | 56 |
| 83 | Spingarn | 68 |

**PLAYOFFS**

| | | |
|---|---|---|
| 77 | Eastern | 67 |
| 61 | Dunbar | 50 |

**CITY CHAMPIONSHIP**

| | | |
|---|---|---|
| 62 | Gonzaga | 61 |

**RECORD**

26  5

The 1985-86 Colts were not expected to do well this season after all-American David Butler was declared academically ineligible. The team had already lost Andre Jackson when he was murdered in October.

Coach Frank Williams then dedicated the season to Andre. The Colts compiled an 18-2 record in the Interhigh League and were it's regular season champs. Coolidge then won the Interhigh Tournament by beating Dunbar 61-50.

The Colts advanced to the City Championship game at the Cole Field House. They defeated the Metro High champs, the Gonzaga Eagles, 62-61 on a jump shot by MVP Derrick Davis with just five seconds left. This was Coolidge's first City Championship.

• 145

Calvin Coolidge High would beat Gonzaga for its first City Championship in 1986.

# A Tribute to Coach Frank R. Williams

**The Team** (Kneeling) Carl Hatcher, Leonard Lee, Derrick Harris, Clint McCoy, James Bright and Charles Hatcher. (Standing) Coach Leonard Farello, Gregory Hicks (manager), Derrick Price, Anthony Riley, Royal Richardson, Jason Ross, Donald Hodge, Chris Brummitt, Tyrone Chappell, Stanley Wright, John Hardy (manager), Coach Jarrel Robinson and Athletic Director, Arthur L. Riddle.

Coach Frank R. Williams died on May 24, 1987 and his team dedicated the 1988 season to his memory.

Under the new leadership of Coach Leonard Farello, his friend and co-worker, the team went on to post a regular-season record of 26-2. It lost no Interhigh games and played for the City Championship at Cole Field House, against Dematha, for the second time in three years.

Team members were driven to succeed for "Coach" and dedicated this season with its rewards, recognitions and accomplishments to him. They vowed to perform as he did as a player and as a coach and to emulate his character throughout life.

Coach Williams cared for his team. In the 15 seasons he was basketball coach, he pushed his charges to excel, not only on

the court but, in school and in life. The impact that he had upon people was evident during his funeral service. It was like a Coolidge alumni reunion, with former students paying their respects along with his present team, friends, family and associates.

Coach became ill during the 1987 season and tried to carry on as much as possible but, only coached part of the season. He knew that he was building a winner for 1988 and encouraged Coach Farello to keep the team on a weight program. He was right. Led by Donald Hodge, his 1988 Colts muscled their way to the top.

He realized two of his goals before his death, he won a city championship and he played in a new gym, the Colts Field House (a.k.a. The Frank R. Williams Memorial).

**Coach Leonard Farello poses next to a picture of the 1986 championship team visiting President Reagan at the White House.**

140

Dunbar 1988 yearbook tribute to Frank Williams. In 1987, the 16-year veteran coach died of brain cancer at 42. The Colts made it to the City Title game but lost to the DeMatha Stags.

# CITY AND INTER-HIGH CHAMPS

Get this straight —

Get him Roach

We go together

Dunbar's yearbook celebrates Coach Mike McLeese taking his team to the 1989 City Championship.

Dunbar High's Darryl Prue, a Georgetown University commit who ended up going to the University of West Virginia, was photographed for a press release when named Head Basketball Coach at T. C. Williams High School in Alexandria, VA. He was inducted into the WVU Hall of Fame in 2019.

# City Championship Game at Cole Field House

Colts
62

Eagles
61

The scoreboard tells it all.

Derrick Davis, the MVP, scored the winning basket.

Fifty-seven seconds left and down by three.

Carl Weldon makes two free throws to pull Coolidge closer.

Calvin Coolidge High would beat Gonzaga, 62–61, for its first City Championship in 1986.

Coach Williams runs the show.

Chasing down a loose ball.

Shooting against the odds.

## The Game

The Colts jumped out to an early 15-7 lead and held on to it until the final minutes of the third quarter. The Eagles led 49-46 after three. Coolidge slowed down its scoring pace every time, guard, Derrick Davis left the game.

The fourth quarter saw the lead change hands several times. Gonzaga's Mark Tillmon kept the pressure on Coolidge until, with the score 61-60 Eagles, he missed the first half of a one and one and Coolidge rebounded.

With five seconds remaining, Davis scored from 20 feet to give the Colts the lead and the game. The Eagles had one more shot but, Tillmon missed and Coolidge had its first City Championship.

|  | 1st | 2nd | 3rd | 4th | Final |
|---|---|---|---|---|---|
| Colts ... | 23 | 12 | 11 | 15 | 61 |
| Eagles ... | 15 | 14 | 20 | 11 | 60 |

150 .

The Coolidge yearbook would devote two pages to the Colts' win over the Gonzaga Eagles. Derrick Davis hit the last shot that clinched the victory for the Colts to win its first City championship.

# Basketball

Front row, l-r; James Brooks, Aaron Mahoney, Tyrone Davis, Clint McCoy and Byron Hawkins.
Back row; Ass't. Coach Jerell Robinson, Ass't. Coach Leonard Farello, Everret Robinson, Raymond Harris, Fred Davy, Donald Hodge, Anthony Graham, Carl Welden, Head Coach, Frank Williams.
Not pictured; Derrick Davis.

30 •

Coolidge High, city championship team in 1986.

Sylvia Weathers
Civil Service, Typing
Word Processing
"I'm going to get you."

Ramon White
History
"Hey."

Elizabeth Williams
Counselor
"Come back another time."

Frank Williams
Individual Sports 1
Health/Basketball Coach
"Hey, man."

• 13    9

Coach Frank Williams in the Coolidge 1986 yearbook. The Colts, under his fatherly guidance, set a school record with 25 victories.

Walt Williams made sure Crossland held off the Northwestern Wildcats, 79–71, for the Prince George's AA Boys Basketball Championship on February 25, 1987, at Crossland. Williams had a dunk and Bernard Hunt added a layup to give the hosts a safe 11-point lead with 18 seconds left. Jay Bias looks on.

# P.E. DEPARTMENT

AMES

Ms. Cox

Mr. Daves

Ms. Oates

Mr. Overton

Mr. Pearson

Ms. E. Sheppard

Wanda Oates of Ballou High (top right) would be the first woman to coach a boys basketball team, and in 1988 won the East championship of the Inter-High, which preceded DCIAA.

Len Bias school photo, 1980–81.

Len Bias represented all that was great about Prince George's county basketball during his high school and college playing years until his death on June 19, 1986.

Members of the 1987–88 All-Met First Team had some fun with their photo: (left to right) Henry Hall, Parkdale; Jerrod Mustaf, DeMatha; Walt Williams, Crossland; Anthony Higginbotham, Crossland; and (front) Michael Tate, Oxon Hill.

# CHAPTER SIX

# The Nineties

**WHEN THE 1990-91** DeMatha basketball team finished just the second perfect season in the storied history of the program, even the *Cumberland Times-News* (Maryland) took note. The Stags had topped off their unblemished season with a victory over the Roman Catholic High School Cahillites of Philadelphia in the Alhambra Catholic Invitational Tournament final in nearby Frostburg.

"Wootten, Stags finish unbeaten and unbelievable!" the *Times-News* proclaimed. The paper might also have added "and unexpected."

Nobody, not even the astute Morgan Wootten, saw this one coming. The DeMatha coach had noticed that the players who would compose the 1990–91 Stags had played extremely well together during the latter stages of the 1989–90 campaign, compiling a 26–8 record. It was an indication of DeMatha's standard of excellence that such a record constituted something of an off year. The Stags had failed to win the City Title, falling to Dunbar in the game for local bragging rights. They didn't win the Alhambra Tournament either, falling in the semifinals to Roman Catholic (which featured future pro football Hall of Famer Marvin Harrison).

Wootten often said that the team's goal every year was to win the league, the City Title Game, and the Alhambra Tournament title. Going undefeated was never a stated goal. Year in and year out, the competition in the Catholic League / Metro Conference / Washington Catholic Athletic Conference (WCAC) was too stiff to entertain such thoughts. Plus DeMatha always played a demanding nonleague schedule, which was designed to challenge and harden the Stags as they went along.

To presume the 1990–91 squad was capable of such a thing—DeMatha had gone undefeated just once before, in 1977–78—seemed folly. The team was not particularly tall, with six-foot-five junior Vaughn Jones serving as the de facto center. This squad did not feature a big name or any sit-up-and-take-notice superstar. In fact, the two players who earned All-Met mention at the end of the 30–0 campaign were Jones and point guard Duane Simpkins, both juniors.

"If ever you really wanted to point to an ideal team, that was one of them," Wootten said. "There was a lack of size, without an [Adrian] Dantley, without a [Danny] Ferry. But they did it. They played so well together, no one cared who got the credit. They were a great example of parking your ego at the door. They certainly showed that the strength of the wolf was in the pack. It was one of the most unselfish groups I think I've ever seen."

Because the Stags were unselfish, they ran great offense. Because they were so team oriented, they played strong team defense as well. But the real key to the team, in retrospect, was its knack for winning games. No matter the situation, the Stags always seemed to come up with the big play—or the lucky bounce—that turned the game their way.

"It was a team with great chemistry," noted Joe Wootten, the coach's son and one of four regulars on that team who later became a coach himself. "We were guys who really wanted to prove themselves."

And that's just what they did. The Stags were ranked No. 2 in the area in the preseason and established themselves as bona fide contenders with an early season 94–84 victory at No. 3 High Point. Jones pumped in a game-high 37 points, with 27 of them in the second half, as DeMatha handed the Eagles their first home loss in 29 games.

As impressive as that was, the team's penchant for late-game heroics was what turned the season into something special. In late January, DeMatha nipped St. John's, 69–65, in overtime, only because Simpkins tied the game at the end of regulation with a last-ditch three-pointer. A week later, a last-second jumper by Good Counsel's Kurt Small hung on the rim and refused to drop, enabling the Stags to escape with a 58–57 victory. "There was no way we should have won that game," Jones recalled.

Four days later, senior Ted Ellis was the hero in another nail-biter against St. John's. His late steal and four free throws gave DeMatha a 62–58 win over the Cadets.

The Stags won the league title, naturally, which brought them face-to-face with Dunbar for the City Title. The Crimson Tide (27–3) had won the last two titles, becoming the first Inter-High team to do so since Cardozo won the first two City Title Games back in the late 1950s. In fact, Coach Mike McLeese's team was the only squad other than DeMatha's and Cardozo's to win consecutive city titles.

Dunbar very nearly got its three-peat. But DeMatha, in a stunner, rallied from a 17-point deficit to pull yet another big game out of the fire, claiming a 72–71 victory. Jones hit the game winner, a short bank shot with 13 seconds left. Ellis led the way with 18 points, including a banked-in three-pointer that brought the Stags within one point with 44 seconds left. "We were so battled-tested that even being down 17, we didn't give up," Jones said.

The victory held special meaning for Jones, who'd missed a last-second shot the year before in the 1990 City Title Game loss to Dunbar. "I cried my eyes out because I was so hurt that we lost," he recalled. "I told the guys, 'I don't care who we play [for the city title], we're gonna beat them.' I was actually hoping it would be Dunbar."

But the job wasn't finished yet. Even though the Stags were league champs, city champs, 27–0, and ranked No. 1 in the final area poll, some unfinished business remained as far as Jones was concerned. The Alhambra Tournament loss to Roman Catholic the year before still stung, so the Stags set out to wipe out that unpleasant memory next.

They rose to the occasion once again, with Jones doing the bulk of the damage to close out the perfect season. He scored 28 points, grabbed 10 rebounds, and made six steals as the Stags (now 30–0) held off Harrison and Roman Catholic. The Stags survived a three-point attempt in the last 10 seconds to finish off the game, the tournament, and the perfect season.

The 1991–92 Catholic League season would be remarkable. DeMatha returned just three players from the undefeated 1990–91 squad, but two of them were senior standouts Jones and Simpkins. The Stags began the season ranked third in the *Post*'s poll. They were three spots ahead of rival St. John's team, now coached by Bob Wagner, who had replaced Joe Gallagher following the legend's retirement after 44 seasons.

The teams would meet an incredible five times in 1991–92. The Cadets won two of the first three games, including a 58–47 upset at American University's Bender Arena on January 12 that ended DeMatha's 42-game winning streak. Guard Eric Micoud powered St. John's with 23 points, just three fewer than Simpkins and Jones produced for DeMatha.

"We just got totally outplayed," Wootten lamented to the *Post*. "The score doesn't indicate how soundly we were beaten."

St. John's 66–56 victory in the March 4 Metro Conference playoff set up another meeting the next night to determine which squad would play Anacostia for the City Title Game. With that goal just three days away, the Stags came out on top. Micoud pumped in 26 points but just nine after halftime. In contrast, forward Jones scored nine of his 13 in the fourth quarter, and Simpkins's layup forced overtime at 49–49. The point guard, who led DeMatha with 14 points, then preserved the 52–51 squeaker by stripping Micoud of the ball in the final second of the extra period.

"Duane and Vaughn are used to playing in championships," Wootten told the *Post*. That was evident again when DeMatha outlasted DCIAA champion Anacostia (23–5) before an estimated crowd of 9,000 people at Maryland's Cole Field House. Simpkins, who was joining the Terrapins the next season, scored 20 points, but sophomore Chris Gray was critical during a 16–4 DeMatha run that raised its lead to 58–40 with just 4:58 left. The Stags wound up prevailing, 66–62.

And the Stags did it again on March 21, edging the Cadets, 51–49, at Frostburg State University to win the Alhambra title. Jones led the way with 19 points, and fellow All-Met Simpkins added 15, the same total that Micoud had scored to pace St. John's. "This is the greatest feeling of my life to go out a winner against a great team like St. John's that beat us twice," Jones said after the top-rated Stags finished 31–2.

While DeMatha rolled on, South Lakes emerged as Northern Virginia's top team in the late 1980s and early 1990s. Led by six-foot-eight All-Met forward Grant Hill, who would go on to excel at Duke and in the NBA en route to induction in the Naismith Memorial Basketball Hall of Fame, Coach Wendell Byrd's Seahawks won the Great Falls District title in 1989 and the Northern Region championship in 1990 before falling to Hampton in the state semifinals both seasons.

Hill scored 2,028 points in high school—110 behind school record-holder Joey Beard with whom he teamed for a year apiece at South Lakes and Duke—and set a Seahawks mark with 942 rebounds, 311 assists, 274 steals, and 160 blocked shots. As a senior, Hill was the *Post's* Player of the Year, but even as a sophomore, he scored 16 of his 36 points in the final 4:58 to rally the Seahawks from a 67–55 deficit against Washington-Lee to a 71–69 triumph in the Great Falls title game. "He was just head and shoulders above everybody, not just in Virginia, but in any tournament that he played in," Beard told the *Fairfax Connection* (Virginia).

At six foot ten, Beard was literally head and shoulders over almost everyone in high school. Still, South Lakes lost to the Chantilly Chargers in the Northern Region semifinal in 1990–91, which was Beard's sophomore year, and Theron Curry was the Seahawks' star. The Chargers then lost to Booker T. Washington in the state semifinals in 1991–92 despite the big man's 34 points and 10 rebounds. Beard averaged 22.5 points and 10 rebounds as a junior.

Then in 1992–93, Byrd's Seahawks became the first team to repeat as Northern Region champions since T. C. Williams did in 1982 and '83, advancing to the state finals after surviving, 46–43, Hayfield's slowdown style. Beard managed just eight points in that game. His high school career shockingly ended in his next game as Woodbridge stunned South Lakes, 50–49, in double overtime as the Vikings' box-and-one defense limited the All-Met center to a season-low four points.

Despite lacking a superstar for the first time since 1986, the Seahawks, led by six-foot-four swingman Troy Allen, won the Northern Region again in 1993–94. They fell once more in the state semifinals, 70–57, to the William Fleming Colonels of Roanoke. "We just didn't shoot well enough [32 percent] to beat a team of that caliber," Byrd said.

Shooting accuracy was rarely an issue for the area's top team during Beard's senior season. Dunbar, which had been outstanding during most of Coach Mike McLeese's five previous years, took its game to another level in 1992–93. The Crimson Tide began the season ranked second in the *Post's* poll and finished it on top with a 33–1 record, the only blemish being an early 80–67 loss to then No. 1 Anacostia. Dunbar avenged that defeat with an 82–73 triumph in the DC

Interscholastic Athletic Association (DCIAA) championship game. Despite 38 points by the Indians' Michael Powell, Dunbar's seniors Nathan Langley (24) and Earl Tyson (22) countered and combined for 46 points.

After previously being 0–47 against the Stags, Good Counsel beat powerhouse DeMatha for the second time in two months in the Metro Conference semifinals; however, they fell to the Lions in the final. So Dunbar moved on to meet Carroll for the City Title Game.

In front of an estimated 8,000 fans at Cole Field House, Carroll led Dunbar for all but a few seconds of the first 29 minutes of the first televised City Title Game. The Crimson Tide rallied to win, 68–66, despite 31 points and nine rebounds by the Lions' Marquise Newbie. Dunbar had finally forged a deadlock at 59–59 on a three-pointer by Claude Green, a shot that fellow senior Lorenzo Roach followed with one of his own to take the lead. Tyson (20 points), Langley (17), and Green (16) paced the attack as the Crimson Tide won its fourth City Title Game in seven years and its third under McLeese.

"When we were down [41–35] at halftime, I told my players that as bad as we were playing, we were still in it," McLeese said. "And we never let them completely get away. . . . We don't have the stars we had on some other [teams], but collectively this was our best team."

When the next season ended with Dunbar at 20–7 after a loss to McKinley in the DCIAA championship game, McLeese headed less than two miles uptown to coach at Howard University.

While McLeese moved to the next level at 38 years old, DeMatha's Morgan Wootten stayed put at 62. While on January 22, 1993, DeMatha became just the fifth high school in the nation to win 1,000 games, Wootten wasn't very happy with the Stags' 20–10 record in his 37th season in Hyattsville. But as the 1993–94 season dawned, DeMatha had added six-foot-ten center Greg Cristell from Florida and had zoomed from 11th to first in the rankings. "There's DeMatha, then there's everyone else," St. John's coach Bob Wagner told the *Post*.

On January 9, 1994, WCAC rival Gonzaga struck a blow for everyone else with a 53–48 upset of DeMatha to move atop the rankings at 14–0. The Purple Eagles limited the Stags to 19-of-61 shooting, and DeMatha missed 12 of 19 free throws.

Five nights later, McKinley knocked off defending city champion Dunbar, 82–76. Junior guard Victor Page poured in 42 points, with 27 of them in the first half, to end the Trainers' 10-game losing streak to the Crimson Tide.

Gonzaga's perfect season ended with a 70–69 loss to league foe Carroll on February 4 as guards Tony Parham and Kellii Taylor teamed for 47 points. The loss would start a season-ending 2–5 skid for Coach Dick Myers's Purple Eagles. That same night, McKinley beat Dunbar again, 69–61, behind 33 points from Page. The triumph raised the Trainers' record to 10–2 since he'd joined the team; he'd been ineligible for seven games following his transfer and extended time away from school to help care for his ailing mother.

Page, who led the area with 31 points per game, willed McKinley to the DCIAA title and a spot in the City Title Game against DeMatha. The Trainers were 18–3 with Page coming into Cole Field House, but they were no match for the Stags. Page scored 29 points, but senior forward Travis Lyons registered 25 points to go with 14 rebounds as DeMatha romped, 106–71. The Stags set City Title Game records for points and the margin of victory in Wootten's 13th appearance on the area's biggest stage.

"We do not have a [superstar] that could dominate. We just have a lot of people who can play and have great chemistry," Wootten said of his 26–3 team. "This is among the best teams . . . one through 14 that we have ever had."

Over in Prince George's County, that balance was also true for Crossland, which got a driving layup from Omari McKinsey with two seconds left in regulation to force overtime against county rival High Point. A free throw from Julian Peterson with three seconds left in the extra period allowed Crossland to squeak by, 63–62, for its first trip to the state semifinals in six years. But the 23–0 Cavaliers were throttled there by Southern of Baltimore, 71–53. The defeat enabled DeMatha to finish atop the *Post* poll yet again, one spot ahead of Crossland.

Prince George's best team of the late 1980s and early 1990s was probably High Point. Coach Ernie Welch's Eagles may have lacked star power for many years, but they made up for it with hard work and a relentless defense that simply wore other teams down. Welch had already been a success at Bladensburg, his alma mater, running up a 72–20 record and a pair of trips to the state tournament in four years (1977–81).

After a four-year hiatus from coaching, Welch got back into the game, taking over the High Point program for the 1985–86 season. He guided the Eagles to a 21–4 record—including a victory over DeMatha, the first by a county public school that anyone could recall—and to the county and region championships that first season.

Three years later, Welch and the Eagles rolled to their best season ever: a 24–1 record, the state Class 4A title, and a No. 13 national ranking in *USA Today*. That year was the beginning of a stunning 143–29 seven-year run (an .831 winning percentage) that included four straight Prince George's County Class 4A titles, five region championships, and a pair of state titles (1988–89 and 1991–92). When you consider the quality of play in the Prince George's Class 4A League at the time, that run of success looks even more impressive. From 1986 to 1993, county teams won the state 4A title six times: High Point won it twice (1989 and '92), with Crossland (1986), Northwestern (1987), Parkdale (1991), and the Largo Lions (1993) claiming one each.

"That was the best league in the state for a decade or so," Welch noted. "We were very proud of what we were doing. So were the kids."

In the five seasons during the stretch that High Point did not win the state title, the Eagles lost in the playoffs to the eventual state champ in 1990, 1991, and 1993. The loss to Annapolis in the 1990 state finals came in overtime, and the loss to Parkdale in the 1991 region playoffs was a three-point game that could have gone either way. In other words, with another turnover here or a missed free throw there in those two games, High Point could have walked off with four straight Class 4A basketball titles, something nobody in the state has done. That's how good the Eagles were at the time.

"Every game I played in high school, when I stepped on the court, I expected to win," said Kenny Avent, the athletic six-foot-four inside/outside star of High Point's 1992 championship team. "That's half the battle—being prepared, expecting to win. [Welch] got us to believe that on a nightly basis."

Welch's Eagles went into every game armed with a secret weapon—a defensive system Welch devised that was unlike anything their Prince George's County opponents had seen before. Welch had always been intrigued by the effectiveness of pressure defense, but he wanted something all his own. He'd learned his trade while serving as an assistant to Roy Henderson at Bladensburg beginning in the mid-1960s. Henderson (who took the Mustangs to the state finals in 1972 and won the title the next season) employed pressure defense to great effect, and Welch took note. He also sought out more experienced, more accomplished coaches at dozens of coaching clinics over the years and picked their brains about what might work and what wouldn't.

For years Welch had tried to devise his own system, something that was a hybrid of what he'd learned from the likes of Jack Ramsay, Vic Bubas, Morgan Wootten, and Dean Smith. Welch wanted something based on forcing the action rather than reacting to the offense, but he couldn't quite put his finger on it.

He was struck by an article he'd read in the mid-1980s in which Georgetown coach John Thompson talked about how his best defensive player would always start, no matter what. That got Welch to thinking. What might happen if you started your five best defensive players? What could you do then?

His mind raced at the possibilities. Designations such as point guard, wing guard, and small forward were meaningless now. Offensive positions didn't matter. Defense would be the priority, and if the Eagles played hard enough and fast enough, the offense would take care of itself.

To glamorize the unglamorous responsibilities each player would have—and to emphasize the new responsibilities—Welch came up with new names for all the positions. He delegated much of the responsibility for naming the positions to his young son, Scott, who was a fan of the Transformers action figures that were popular at the time. So instead of two guards, two forwards, and a center, High Point would have a forcer, an attacker, a thief, a raider, and—most ominously—a destroyer.

The forcer overplayed the dribbler into a double-team by the attacker.

Double-teams were designed to force lob passes, which then could be picked off by the thief. No matter what, the ball was to be kept out of the middle. There the raider and the destroyer were to provide the back line of defense and were always supposed to be ready to scramble toward a penetrator to block his path, draw a charge, or block a shot.

Welch wanted his players to force the action rather than react to it. As far as he was concerned, the faster the game the better. Consequently, he didn't worry so much about missed shots or turnovers, figuring that the quicker the pace the better off his team.

"People thought we were helter-skelter, but we weren't," recalled Wayne Bristol, a skinny, super-quick shooting guard who went on to become a valuable reserve at Maryland. "Ernie would say, 'If teams want to run with us, they won't be able to run with us in the fourth quarter.'"

The Eagles in those years simply wore teams down. Welch used his bench liberally; his substitutions resembled nothing so much as the line shifts employed in hockey. The frantic pace High Point strove for might have looked chaotic from the outside, but the Eagles knew what they were doing all the time.

Welch had an evenhanded substitution pattern. If you made a certain kind of mistake—for example, shot the ball off the dribble from the outside, failed to shoot once catching the ball in the post, failed to get back on defense, threw a bounce pass instead of chest pass—you came out of the game, and the next man checked in to take your place.

"When you messed up, you knew you were coming out," Bristol said. There were times when Bristol (an All-Met–caliber player) would go up for a jump shot—knowing it wasn't what Welch wanted—and look over to the scorers' table. "My sub was sitting there waiting for me," said Bristol.

That philosophy helped keep everyone fresh, helped keep the substitutes' minds in the game because they knew they would play, and helped mitigate the effects of an injury to a key player or foul trouble. That emphasis on defense also produced the post prolific offense in high-scoring Prince George's County during that time. In the four-year stretch (1988–92) that included a pair of state Class 4A titles, High Point averaged at least 86 points per game during the course of a season. Twice during that span, High Point averaged 92 points per game over a full season. Projected to a 40-minute college game, that would equate to a 115 points-per-game average. If a team could score at that rate over the course of a 48-minute NBA game, it would be an average of 138 points per game. Clearly, it would take a lot to outscore High Point.

Yet it actually happened in the 1990 Class 4A state final. High Point ran up against an equally athletic and up-tempo Annapolis squad in what had to have been one of the more remarkable state finals anytime, anywhere. In a game that left the officials and the fans almost breathless just trying to keep up with the action, Annapolis outgunned High Point, 106–102, in overtime for the title. Recalling the

Chapter Six

game years later, Bristol acknowledged that everyone involved knew early on that the game was going to reach the century mark—and probably for both teams.

That kind of scoring was nothing new for the Eagles. "It was a relentless style of play," Avent said. "A lot of people looked at how much we scored and thought we were just run-and-gun. But all the scoring was generated from our defensive pressure.

"We forced the tempo of the game, and we came at you in waves from opening tip to the final buzzer. The defense allowed us to put up the points we put up. There was lots of running in practice. No team in the area was in better shape."

Good conditioning was one thing Welch demanded. He had plenty of other rules as well that were spelled out in an extensive handbook he created, wrote, and passed out to his players before the season. The handbook covered everything from offensive and defensive sets to guidelines for behavior, and a discussion of proper dress. It included inspirational quotations from such disparate sources as Theodore Roosevelt and the musical *Man of La Mancha*.

The organizational skills came from Welch's years working with Henderson as a young assistant coach at Bladensburg. The philosophy and the rest of it were his own. Upon encountering the husky, demanding, sometimes blunt Welch, one might take him for one of those narrow-minded high school football coaches who was set in his ways and unwilling to compromise. Although Welch was clearly a product of growing up in Bladensburg in the 1940s and '50s, he somehow managed to keep an open mind about changing times and the most effective ways to reach his players.

He had a certain empathy for many of them, having grown up without a father himself. Back in his own high school days, Welch developed an ability to relate to many different kinds of kids—from the A students to the jocks to the hot-rodders of the 1950s whose primary after-school activity was working on their own cars in the driveway. In high school that trait had helped make him a class president—a position that many of his coaching colleagues would have been shocked to learn about.

Mostly, though, Welch gained his players' trust because they could see he wanted them to achieve both on and off the court. He believed in the importance of education—his grade point standards for his players were higher than the county's—and in helping the young men in his charge to achieve something in life. "I can't stand people who are all show and no go," he once said. "Give me doers." Even if Welch couldn't get all of his players college scholarships, he'd strive to get them to the point where they could at least get into college and compete academically in a classroom full of kids from more stable, well-to-do backgrounds.

"Ernie was a father figure to all of us," Bristol said. "He gave us the structure that we needed, the discipline that we needed. It wasn't all basketball with Ernie. To outsiders, he might have seemed like a mean guy, a strict guy. But he was very instrumental in my life."

While High Point was clearly the class of the county in the late 1980s and early 1990s, several other Class 4A schools in the county took turns grabbing the brass ring at Cole Field House. But basketball among the smaller schools in Prince George's County was also compelling and quite often of championship caliber.

Winning a state championship grew more difficult in the mid-1990s when the Baltimore City schools, which previously had their own governing body separate from the Maryland Public Secondary Schools Athletic Association, joined the rest of the state in high school athletic competition. Schools such as Dunbar and Lake Clifton were traditional powers and continued to shine upon joining the association. But Prince George's County teams still managed to win more than their share of state basketball titles during the 1990s.

Central, DuVal, and Forestville claimed seven state titles combined from 1990 to 1996. The Prince George's County 3A/2A/1A League included all three, plus traditional powers such as Fairmont Heights and Gwynn Park. Playing in such a competitive league during the regular season primed those teams for the region and state playoffs. There, the smaller Prince George's schools often came up against teams from western Maryland or the Eastern Shore—squads that were not used to Prince George's skill level and speed. A mismatch was often the result.

Central got it started with its run to win the Class 2A crown in 1990, escaping with a 79–77 victory over Hammond of Howard County in the final. The Falcons finished with a modest 17–10 record after claiming the crown and failing to make the *Washington Post*'s year-end top 20.

The *Post* couldn't—and didn't—ignore Coach Walter Fulton's Falcons after they claimed another Class 2A title in 1996. Central boasted the leading scorer in the Maryland suburban public schools that season in Kershaw Frager, who averaged better than 23 points per game. Thanks to the scoring of Frager and to Fulton's steadying hand, Central (24–3) ran off 17 straight victories to close the season, won the Class 2A title, and—stunningly—wound up the area's top-ranked team.

DuVal claimed the state 3A title the next year, led by the inside-outside tandem of Stacy Robinson and Carl Turner, and finished 20–5 overall. But what Coach Artie Walker seemed to specialize in during that period was the late-season run. After losing Robinson, his best player, during the 1991–92 regular season, DuVal stood at 12–13 at one point. But the Tigers pulled together and went all the way to the state semifinals.

Almost exactly the same thing happened during the Tigers' run to the 3A state final in 1993–94. That year, the Tigers were 9–10 at one point but found their stride in March, sweeping through the playoffs to another Class 3A title.

The most successful county team during the decade was its smallest. Somehow, tiny Forestville kept coming up with the big men who made the difference en route to the Knights' state titles in 1991, 1992, and 1995.

The six-foot-eight Kwamin Freeland was a huge presence inside for Gary Mc-Corkle's repeat Class 2A state champs in 1991 and 1992. Freeland once recorded 15 blocks in a game and was a two-time All-Met. In 1995 it was six-foot-five Joe Lofton who led the Knights to the title. Forestville had dropped down to 1A classification by that point, but Lofton came up big all season long. He averaged 27.5 points per game during the season as a whole, upping his game to average 29 points and 16 rebounds in a pair of wins at the state tournament.

Across the river in Dumfries, Virginia, superb basketball was being played at Potomac High. The Prince William County school had become a powerhouse under Coach Kendall Hayes. He had taken over at Potomac in 1985 on the heels of a winless Commonwealth District season. By 1988–89, the Panthers went 16–0 in district play.

Led by Notre Dame football signee B. J. Hawkins, the 1989–90 Panthers reeled off 20 straight victories. Their season ended at 24–5 with a 65–53 loss to Grant Hill and company of South Lakes in the state tournament.

Two years later, Potomac was the area's last unbeaten team at 18–0. However, the Panthers went just 3–3 the rest of the way, with their season ending in a 70–67 overtime loss to the Fauquier Falcons in the Commonwealth District semifinals.

By 1994–95, his 10th season, Hayes had a 146–71 career record and a truly loaded roster for the team's first campaign in the Cardinal District. With a starting frontcourt of senior forwards Tinail Harris and Mike Neal and junior center Rolan Roberts that averaged six foot five, Potomac was seventh in the *Post*'s preseason poll, a spot behind South Lakes. The Panthers were also the top team in Northern Virginia, being the winner of three straight Northern Region titles and gaining the spot in the state tournament that comes with that championship.

On December 10 Potomac showed that it was for real, blowing out traditionally strong Gar-Field, 65–45. Harris led the way with 17 points. A month and a day later, the second-ranked Panthers jumped on top of former Commonwealth rival Woodbridge (23–8) and cruised to a 56–46 victory as Harris scored 15 points, senior guard Erskin Fox added 12, and Roberts—wearing size 20 sneakers—contributed 10. The triumph gave Potomac its first sweep of Woodbridge since 1989–90, the last season that the Panthers had reached the state tournament.

"Right now, they are in a class by themselves," said Woodbridge coach Will Robinson. "I don't think anyone in the area can play with them when they play [their best]."

When St. John's upset DeMatha on February 3, Potomac (19–1) became the new No. 1, the first Northwest Region school to ascend to the top. However, Harris, who was averaging 20 points, felt that the Panthers still didn't get enough respect.

"The other night I was watching [television,] and they said that the ranking really doesn't stand for much, that it's just for fun," Harris told the *Post*. "Well, it stood for something when DeMatha and Dunbar were ranked first, [and] it better stand for something now. I just wish that there was a way that we could play some of those teams and decide it."

Potomac won the Cardinal District tournament with an 81–63 rout of Gar-Field, prompting Hayes to say, "We show no mercy on anybody. We take it to everybody." Then when the Panthers forced 25 turnovers in defeating Woodbridge, 62–50, in the Northern Region semifinals, Hayes said, "To see them play defense like that brings joy to my heart."

Hayes's joy kept growing as his defense forced 33 turnovers in a 66–43 romp over E. C. Glass of Lynchburg. Then Harris had 27 points and 14 rebounds in the 73–66 triumph over T. C. Williams that sent the Panthers to the state semifinals.

That magical ride was in danger when Potomac fell behind the Indian River Braves with Jason Capel (an eventual North Carolina recruit) by 10 points early, but Harris (18 points) and Roberts (15 points, five blocked shots) held steady. Roberts blocked a shot and followed with a bucket that gave Potomac its first lead with 3:29 remaining en route to the 63–58 nail-biter. "The kids have hearts like lions and they refused to give up," Hayes gushed.

There was little drama the next day. The Panthers established a 16-point advantage in the second quarter and cruised to a 62–53 victory over the Kecoughtan Warriors, who had edged second-ranked Robinson in the semifinals, for Potomac's first state championship and the first by a Northern Virginia school in 13 years. Harris led the way with 26 points.

"Everybody expected this, so I've felt like the [weight of the] world has been on my shoulders the last month," said Hayes. "It's a great feeling. Now I can wake up and not worry." His 28–1 team finished first in the *Post* poll in the wake of upstarts McNamara and Cardozo meeting in the City Title Game and after Springbrook blew a late lead in the Maryland Class 4A championship game.

Despite the graduations of Harris, Roberts, and Neal, Coach Hayes didn't have much to worry about the following season either. Potomac began the year ranked first and was 21–1 when it lost to William Fleming by a basket in the Northwest Region semifinals.

The Panthers were No. 6 in the 1996–97 preseason poll. They improved to 23–2 by rallying from an 11-point, fourth-quarter deficit to stun Woodbridge, 49–45, on February 28, ensuring a state tournament berth. Once there, Potomac avenged that defeat against William Fleming with a 67–57 victory, holding the Colonels to 29 percent shooting with a defense typical of a Hayes-coached squad. Senior Shajuan Williams, the Panthers' leading scorer, tallied 26 points.

Williams poured in another 24 points in a 74–58 triumph over the Yorktown Patriots in the next round. In the state semifinals, which matched the top two teams in the *Post*'s poll, Freshman Cliff Hawkins scored 19 points, and Demetrius

"Mookie" Felder, the only player left from the 1995 state champions, added 17 in the 68–54 conquest of Hayfield.

Hampton's Ronald Curry, who would go on to the NFL to catch 193 passes for the Oakland Raiders, scored 27 points in the state title game as Potomac fell, 67–52. Still, the Panthers (26–3) finished No. 1 in Virginia for the second time in three years.

With four starters back, Potomac was ranked fourth as the 1997–98 season began. By February 7 the Panthers—starting four guards—were 16–3. They got by No. 11 Woodbridge that night, 66–61, as Hawkins, who was averaging 18 points, scored 27. "He doesn't think anyone can stop him, and most of the time he's correct," Hayes said.

The same could have been said of the Panthers as a team. They beat Woodbridge again 15 days later, winning their fourth straight Cardinal District championship by a 68–58 count with Hawkins scoring 19 and Felder 16. However, Felder—who had faced misdemeanor charges of assault and battery the previous summer when accused of grabbing a 15-year-old student's buttocks—was given a third suspension of the season, this time for good after biting the Vikings' Nick Clay on the jaw and drawing blood. So there was definitely bad blood when the rivals met again two days later in the Northwest Region semifinals. Hawkins's pair of free throws with 2.9 seconds to go sealed the Panthers' 50–46 escape.

Sherman Rivers's 16 footer banked in at the buzzer for a 56–54 triumph over George Washington–Danville in the Northwest Region title game. Potomac had made just nine of 36 shots and fallen behind by 13 points at halftime before going on a 17–2 run fueled by a 2-1-2 zone press that turned the tables on the Eagles.

Next, Sabian Toussaint, who was averaging six points per game, scored 16 in the 60–58 squeaker over T. C. Williams that put the Panthers in the state semifinals for the third time in four years. Their foes? The Hampton Crabbers and Curry again. "I've been waiting for this all year," Hawkins said. "I want to guard him."

Hawkins got his wish in Norfolk, just 23 miles from Hampton's campus. He held Curry to 5-of-17 shooting while making 12 of his own 17 attempts and out-scoring everybody's All-American—31 to 13—as Potomac prevailed, 71–67. "I wanted to go out and do what I could do to earn his respect," Hawkins said. "I think I did."

No doubt about that, but the huge effort left the Panthers with little energy for the state championship game. They trailed by 14 at the half, shot 36 percent, and lost to GW-Danville, 71–50. Still, over the last four seasons, Potomac was 100–10 for a .909 winning percentage. By comparison, DeMatha, which was long the king of area hoops, was 118–20 (.855) during that span.

Meanwhile, the Stags lost one City Title game (1996), won another (1998), and split the WCAC championships, capturing two and falling once to McNamara and once to Gonzaga. Much more important, DeMatha almost lost its venerable and beloved coach.

On July 7, 1996, while working his summer camp at Mount St. Mary's University in Emmitsburg, Maryland, Morgan Wootten said he felt terrible as he was walking out of the cafeteria. Moments later the 65-year-old coach was on the ground. He was rushed to the hospital in desperate need of a liver transplant, which he received three days later. Twenty weeks later, Wootten was back on the sidelines as his 41st season at DeMatha began with a 77–72 triumph over St. John Neumann of Philadelphia.

Wootten had known since 1993 that he would need a liver transplant someday and admitted to being exhausted after the 1995–96 season, but he adamantly avoided paying attention to such warning signs. After 32 days in Johns Hopkins University Hospital, Wootten promised that he would listen to his body going forward, saying, "I told myself if I get tired, I'll sit down."

But giving up coaching wasn't going to happen once the doctors said that he could continue. DeMatha went 27–7 in Wootten's first post-transplant season, setting the stage for a 34–1 mark and a return to the top of the rankings in 1997–98. He finally retired on the eve of the 2002–03 season after another year ranked first and a staggering 1,274–192 (.869) record. When he retired, only one high school coach, Texan Robert Hughes, had won more games.

"I guess I would rather [retire] on the way up than on the way down," said the 71-year-old Wootten, whose teams were rarely down, having won five mythical national titles and finishing as the area's best in an incredible 22 of the final 42 of his 46 seasons.

Nine years before Wootten called it a day, the man who had hired him as a University of Maryland student to coach the Cadets' junior varsity football and basketball teams in 1953, St. John's Joe Gallagher, retired after 44 years. Gallagher was 870–292 as the basketball coach at his alma mater, winning 12 Catholic League crowns and the 1977 city title. He was also 171–32–10 in football, winning 11 league championships and eight city titles in 21 years. No wonder Wootten called Gallagher the best coach he ever faced.

"He was my mentor," Wootten said when Gallagher died at 93 in 2014. "He taught me so much. He impressed on me that a player would never forget [his] coach."

And Gallagher, who was famous for saying, "Never send a kid home from practice unhappy," will never be forgotten at St. John's, whose gym is named for the coach and his late wife, Doris.

Chapter Six

While Gallagher was closing out his career with the Cadets in 1991 at age 69, Chris Chaney was making history at the other end of the age spectrum at the tiny Canterbury School in Accokeek in southern Prince George's County. The former captain of the basketball team at Southern High in Anne Arundel County, Chaney played tennis at Maryland–Baltimore County, but basketball remained his love, and he was looking to coach the sport. Since public schools weren't an option without a college degree, Chaney turned to private schools at the suggestion of his high school coach.

Still too young to drink, the 20-year-old Chaney had thought he was being considered for an assistant coaching job at the Canterbury School, an Episcopal school in Accokeek, Maryland; however, he was hired as the head coach. He immediately led Canterbury to a blazing 12–2 start, a harbinger of what was to come in a career that is approaching its third decade. Sophomore guard Preston Tucker, a transfer from Eastern of the DCIAA, was leading the area at a stunning 38.8 points per game. Canterbury's other starting guard, freshman Terrell Holloway, was averaging 20.3 points. Pretty heady stuff for a team without its own gym in which to practice.

As the 1990s closed, Chaney was at his third school, leading the Newport Preparatory School Tigers in Kensington to top-five rankings in the *Post* in 1998 and 1999. And as the 2018 season began, the 48-year-old Chaney, now coaching the Scotland Campus Knights in Pennsylvania, had won 729 games. His record is greater than any high school coach yet to celebrate a 50th birthday and barely 600 from Robert Hughes's then national record of 1,333. Chaney never went back to finish his degree from the University of Maryland–Baltimore County and has turned down several college coaching opportunities, most notably to be an assistant at the University of Nebraska in 2007.

"It's been a great journey," said Chaney, who also coached big winners at Laurel Baptist, Princeton Day Academy, and New Hope Academy in Maryland; Laurinburg Institute and the Patterson School in North Carolina; and MMG Academy and DME Sports Academy in Florida. "I've been blessed to work with some great people along the way. If I continue the way I've been going, which is my plan, I think I'll beat the record."

Eighteen of Chaney's players have been drafted by NBA teams, including Louis Bullock, who starred for him at Canterbury and Laurel Baptist. More than 70 have played internationally, and more than 120 received college scholarships. Chaney, who ran a business called National Top Sports Institute from 2014 to 2016, has worked clinics in China, France, Italy, Nigeria, Belgium, Poland, and Iceland as well as a slew stateside.

In Chaney's second season at Laurel Baptist, his Eagles were the only ones to beat Stu Vetter's powerhouse of St. John's at Prospect Hall and future Duke captain Nate James. As Chaney recalled at an informal reunion of players,

When we were getting ready to play 'em, I asked the guys, "Do you want to play 'em or have a chance to beat 'em? Be careful what you ask for." When they said, "We want to beat 'em," I said, "OK." I pointed to four guys and said, "None of you are playing." I pointed to maybe four other guys and said, "None of you can shoot unless you have a wide-open layup." I told Louis that he could shoot whenever he wanted because I trusted his judgment. We ran the four corners. Louis had 40 points. That was a pretty big-time win. That kind of put us on the map.

That was also the case for Chaney, who left Laurel Baptist after three years for Newport, bringing star Dalonte Hill with him. Chaney also successfully recruited DerMarr Johnson, the eventual national Player of the Year, as well as future NBA players Rodney White and James White.

After five years at Newport, Chaney left the area for Laurinburg. In his fourth and final season, he coached the Tigers to a 40–0 record and the mythical national championship thanks to 15 Division I players. *Sports Illustrated* proclaimed it the best high school team ever.

"Our practices were like wars," Chaney said. "The guys asked, 'When do we get days off?' I said, 'Those are what we call games.'"

Despite that unparalleled success at Laurinburg, Chaney moved to the Patterson School for the 2005–6 season for its better facilities and a higher salary. Hassan Whiteside and Jordan Hill, both of whom wound up in the NBA, were among his Bulldog stars at Patterson.

After four years at Patterson, Chaney took a year off during which he visited college coaching buddies such as Tom Izzo, Brad Stevens, and Mike Brey. Then he spent a year each at Princeton Day in Beltsville, New Hope Academy in Landover, and the two Florida schools. After two years in business, Chaney was hired to start the program at Scotland Campus in 2016. It now includes 40 players from 12 countries and 12 states spread over two high school teams and two elite prep squads.

"When I started at Canterbury, I wouldn't have thought I would have gone to all these places and be tight with a lot of big-time college coaches and NBA people," said Chaney, who's in touch with many of his former players, including Bullock and Hill. "I put a lot of passion into my coaching. I'm really tough on the kids because I care so much about getting them ready to play in college. The great thing is that I think I've changed a lot of people's lives. That's what gets me going on an everyday basis."

While Wootten and Chaney (thus far) turned down the chance to coach on the next level, Gonzaga's Dick Myers had been there, done that. Myers, who retired in 2004 with a 714–262 record over 34 high school campaigns, was just 28 years old when he moved up from the high school ranks to coach Catholic University in 1971. The 1973–74 Cardinals boasted the two top scorers in school history, Bob Adrion and Glenn Kolonics, but couldn't manage a winning record.

After one more losing season, Myers was fired by Catholic in 1975. "It turned out to be one of the best things that happened to me," Myers told the *Post* after his retirement.

That's because Myers was quickly hired by Gonzaga. Inheriting a program that had won only three games the previous season, Myers debuted with a 16–11 record and stayed put until his retirement at 61. Always competing with national powerhouse DeMatha, Myers won league championships in 1997, 1999, and 2003 and the City Title Game in the latter season when he was named the area's Coach of the Year. Tom Sluby and Robert Churchwell, who starred for Myers at Gonzaga, went on to the NBA.

Seven years before Myers stepped down at Gonzaga, Red Jenkins, Northern Virginia's longest-tenured coach, retired after 35 years at W. T. Woodson. The 60-year-old Jenkins, who began his career coaching Gonzaga's freshmen for a year and then the Annandale junior varsity for three, won 538 games and 19 district championships at Woodson. Oddly, Jenkins always came up short of a regional title, most notably in 1979 when the Cavaliers led eventual state champion Mount Vernon by seven points and had the ball with just 1:30 remaining.

"Coaching in basketball is a cumulative thing," Jenkins told the *Fairfax Journal* on the eve of his 1997 retirement. "Maybe we've turned out some good people, which is what it's all about anyhow. So we don't win the region championship. I can live with that. It's not as important as the feeling I have for the players who played [for me]."

More than 80 of them went on to play in college. About his former coach, former Cavalier Tommy Amaker, who starred at Duke and now coaches at Harvard, told the *Journal*, "He was instrumental in the growth of basketball [in Northern Virginia]. He could call Coach [Bobby] Knight [of Indiana] or [Duke coach Mike Krzyzewski] and get those guys to speak at a clinic. That says a lot."

Herndon coach Gary Hall agreed: "[Red has] been a trailblazer and such an advocate for Northern Virginia basketball. He's opened doors for all of us."

Jenkins turned down offers to leave Woodson, most notably to be an assistant under Maryland coach Lefty Driesell. The smooth-talking Driesell had lured Jenkins's star, Pete Holbert, to College Park, but he couldn't persuade Jenkins to leave Fairfax.

Jenkins loved Fairfax so much that soon after leaving Woodson, he agreed to coach the Paul VI Panthers only three miles away. Jenkins went 70–53 in four seasons at Paul VI and resigned not long after what would be a career-ending loss to DeMatha in the WCAC semifinals.

"I had three goals when I came here," Jenkins told the *Post*. "First, I wanted to build respect for Paul VI basketball and become a contender. Second, I wanted to win 600 [career] games. And third, I wanted to beat DeMatha and play in the City Title Game. We didn't accomplish the last goal, but two out of three isn't too bad."

Neither was Jenkins's career.

🏀　　🏀　　🏀

Thomas Hargrove might not have been as high-profile a coach as Morgan Wootten, Joe Gallagher, Red Jenkins, or even DCIAA rival Mike McLeese of Dunbar, but the man was an institution at Anacostia in the 1980s and 1990s. In his 10th season at Anacostia, 1991–92, Hargrove guided second-team All-Met Mike Powell, University of Texas at Austin football recruit Lovell Pinkney, and the rest of the Indians to a 22–5 season and their first appearance in the City Title Game, where they fell to—who else?—DeMatha, 66–62.

"I think the guys got a little excited being here for the first time, on the big court [in Maryland's Cole Field House], and in front of the big crowd [of 9,000 fans]," Hargrove said. Anacostia's rally from an 18-point deficit came up only two baskets short.

Pinkney had graduated, but Powell and Keith Davis were back when the Indians were top ranked in the *Post*'s preseason poll of 1992–93. When Anacostia beat visiting Dunbar 80–67 on December 16, it marked the first No. 1 versus No. 2 matchup involving DCIAA squads in more than a decade.

The Indians had also edged the Crimson Tide, 66–64, in the 1992 DCIAA title game, so McLeese switched things up for the 1993 championship showdown, going to a rarely used zone defense. "I had to sell my guys on playing a zone and not getting too aggressive," McLeese said.

That change from man-to-man was critical in Dunbar's 82–73 upset on February 25. The Indians (29–4) lost despite Powell's 38 points and 10 steals.

"Last year was our time; this year is their time," said Hargrove, whose team shot just nine of 31 during the first half. "If we had just made a few outside shots, we could have brought them out of that zone. But we didn't . . . they were the better team."

Minus Powell and Davis, 1993–94 was a rebuilding year for Anacostia, which went 15–9. The Indians improved to 19–6 in 1994–95 and wound up ranked 16th. That set the stage for the following memorable 1995–96 season.

Anacostia was ranked ninth in the *Post*'s preseason poll but had fallen out of the top 20 by January 22. Edward Sheffey, who had led the DCIAA in scoring the previous season, had transferred to Oak Hill Academy in Virginia. Starting guard Ricardo Gibson missed the year after a heart ailment was diagnosed.

Their absences helped limit Anacostia to a 17–7 record and second place behind Eastern in the DCIAA East Division during the regular season. However, the Indians' 77–54 victory over the Ramblers on February 24 was a harbinger. Dwayne Payne, who was headed to Michigan State University to play quarterback, had 21 points in that game. The schools met five days later for the DCIAA championship, with Anacostia prevailing, 52–47. Andre Thomas scored 10 of his 18 points in the fourth quarter.

"We had a lot of adversity, [but] the kids hung in there and brought us to Cole Field House," Hargrove said.

Facing DeMatha in the City Title Game for the second time in five years, the Indians got 20 points from Thomas and 18 from Donte Smith while its 2-3 zone held the Stags to 29 percent shooting in the 61–48 shocker. "Anyone who saw the game, who knows basketball, knows DeMatha was not good enough to win," the gracious Wootten said.

He also declined to make a fuss over the presence of Payne, who should not have been allowed to play after being ejected from the DCIAA title game. DCIAA commissioner Allen Chin, formerly Anacostia's athletic director, said the ejection was never official because the referees didn't file a report with the league.

Hargrove kept it going in 1996–97 although the mostly new team needed some time to click. The Indians had seven losses by late January. But they would lose only one more game even after Coach Hargrove's absence due to a car crash on February 7.

With Hargrove's son, Kevin, taking temporary command, Anacostia defeated Cardozo, 67–56, to win the DCIAA again. Junior Lonnie Baxter, a big man transfer from Richard Montgomery, had 30 points, eight rebounds, and four blocks to overpower the Clerks.

This time, the Indians' City Title Game foe was Gonzaga, not DeMatha. And like Cardozo, the Eagles had no answer for the beefy Baxter, who scored 35 points and pulled down 12 boards in the 59–49 triumph.

"A lot of teams can have good seasons, but we want to be known as having a good program," said Kevin Hargrove, who went 7–0 while filling in for his father. "I think you can make a pretty good case that we are there."

No doubt about that. With Baxter off to a year of prep school before enrolling at Maryland, which he would help lead to the 2002 national championship, Donte Smith averaged an area-best 27 points for Anacostia in 1997–98. The Indians won the DCIAA East for the fifth time in seven years; then Jay Chapman's three-pointer at the buzzer beat Coolidge, 50–49, in the DCIAA championship game. Chapman, headed to play football at Syracuse, was a strong sidekick to fellow senior guard Smith, averaging 18.7 points.

"We're just going to try to keep [Smith and Chapman] to something within reason," DeMatha coach Morgan Wootten said before the City Title Game, the third between the schools in seven years. Smith scored 25 points against the Stags, but his teammates managed just 26 as DeMatha cruised, 74–51, behind 42 points combined from junior guards Joe Forte and Keith Bogans.

"I don't think we ever got into any kind of continuity," Hargrove lamented. "Some of our players were a little tentative. . . . Donte played his normal game, but as a team we just didn't step it up. [DeMatha] deserved to win. They were the better team today, but this defeat didn't tarnish our season."

Anacostia wound up ranked second with a 24–5 record. The Indians were 19–5 heading into the DCIAA playoffs in 1998–99, but their postseason ended after one game as they made just nine of 41 shots in a stunning 44–33 loss to Wilson.

🏀   🏀   🏀

Gaithersburg had long been a football power in Montgomery County. Its basketball program didn't rank with those of county rivals such as Blair, Springbrook, or Bethesda–Chevy Chase; however, the Trojans won the 4A Red Division title in 1997. They were headed for a repeat in 1998, having won 21 of 22 games—losing only to Wilson, 57–54—and ascending to seventh in the rankings.

But the superb season was in sudden jeopardy when Gaithersburg trailed the Magruder Colonels, 36–29, at halftime in its playoff opener. That's when Mike Ryan and Charles Johnson decided that their high school careers weren't going to end that way. The senior forwards, after teaming for just 13 in the first half, scored the Trojans' next 30 points as Gaithersburg rallied for the 69–63 victory.

Having produced a reprieve, the Trojans kept rolling all the way into the state semifinals against Annapolis. Johnson's 22 points and nine rebounds were critical in Gaithersburg's advancing to its first state championship game since 1958. The Trojans faced No. 7 Oxon Hill, which had edged the Mergenthaler Mustangs, 73–70, thanks to a closing 16–3 run. Sophomore center Mike Sweetney dominated with 19 points, 11 rebounds, and five blocks as the Clippers reached their first state final since 1957.

In the showdown between two schools that hadn't played for the state crown in four decades, Ryan played all but two minutes, and Johnson never left the floor. In what was believed to be the longest boys basketball title game in Maryland history, with five—count 'em, five—overtime periods, Gaithersburg won, 96–91. Remarkably, the championship was the first in Gaithersburg's 92 seasons.

"Every timeout and foul gave me a chance to catch my breath," said Johnson, who scored 30 points over those 52 minutes. "And every time they let us back in it, we got more energy to try to win it."

"We have a rule: if you're tired, you show me the fist," said Trojans coach Paul Foringer. "If [you do], I'll take you out to get a breather and some water. . . . Charles never showed me the fist, and he was still performing with tremendous intensity, so what could I do?"

Indeed, Johnson scored six points in the first quarter and six in the fifth and final four-minute overtime despite having picked up his fourth foul in the first overtime. The exits of Sweetney and Clipper senior forward Charlie Sharpe with five fouls apiece in the second and third overtimes, respectively, helped Johnson and the Trojans survive.

"Once [they] fouled out, I wasn't worried about Charles anymore, because there was nobody to draw a foul on him," Foringer explained. "But he was [also] smart and didn't get himself into any bad situations."

As the final full season of the 1990s began, it was no surprise that DeMatha was the area's top-ranked squad. In fact, the Stags—led by senior guards Keith Bogans, who had signed with Kentucky, and Joe Forte, a North Carolina signee—were also No. 1 in *USA Today*'s national poll. DeMatha looked strong early by beating top teams from St. Louis and Chicago on the road, but so did Gonzaga. The Eagles issued a warning to their WCAC rival by thumping Oxon Hill, 81–63, behind a combined 44 points from seniors Tom McCloskey and Tim Folan, who had known each other since they were toddlers. Sweetney, the Clippers' six-foot-eight standout, fouled out after scoring just 13 points.

Four days later at American University's Bender Arena, Gonzaga led DeMatha, 63–59, before Forte hit a jumper with 26 seconds to go and another 11 seconds later to force overtime. The Eagles' senior point guard Billy Glading sank the first of two free throws to put Gonzaga back on top, 66–65, with five seconds left in the extra session. When Forte's half-court shot hit the backboard and then the rim but didn't go through the net, he remained at 34 points, and the purple-clad fans stormed the court.

"These kids . . . you can't line them up like toy machines and expect them to perform the same way every time," Wootten said. "It doesn't happen."

What did happen next was Bogans received a 10-game suspension for fighting with Forte's younger brother, Jason, after a victory over Archbishop Molloy of New York on December 29. So the second-ranked Stags didn't have one of their two top players when they met new No. 1 Good Counsel at George Washington's Smith Center on January 8.

"We want to prove ourselves," the GW-bound Falcons standout Chris Monroe told the *Post*. "DeMatha is still getting more hype than we are. They've got a great name . . . and we want to be up there with them."

Make that on top of them. Monroe scored 32 points, and future Washington Wizard Roger Mason added 20 as Good Counsel improved to 15–1 with a 65–52 triumph. It was the Falcons' seventh in the last 15 meetings with the Stags after a 0–47 start to the series. Joe Forte was held to 12 points on 5-of-16 shooting.

A week later, Bogans and Jason Forte were back, their suspensions having been reduced to four games. The previous day Gonzaga lost senior starting forward Howard Blue for the season with a broken foot, a blow for the Eagles in the ultra-competitive WCAC in which they, the Falcons, and the Stags had all already been atop the rankings.

As the Catholic schools beat up on each other, 15th-ranked Dunbar moved into the top spot in the DCIAA West with an 82–73 victory at Cardozo on January 20. Point guard Brian Chase and forward Bernard Robinson, back from one-game suspensions, teamed for 30 points for third-year Crimson Tide coach Gary Lampkins.

In Maryland Sweetney overpowered Largo with 31 points and 17 rebounds in No. 7 Oxon Hill's 84–78 triumph on February 5, prompting Lions coach Lou Wilson to call him "the entire package." A week later, Sweetney poured in 43 points against High Point to raise his average to 22.5 points per game. The Georgetown commit was also averaging 13.7 rebounds.

And in Virginia, Herndon ascended to No. 2 in the rankings between Good Counsel and McNamara (yet another WCAC contender). When the Hornets got 20 points from senior guard Tim Gardiner in beating No. 15 South Lakes, 77–68, on February 11, they improved to 21–1 and a perfect 14–0 in the Concorde District. They advanced to the state championship game; however, two losses in their next three games, the latter by 67–54 to No. 18 Lee in the Northern Region quarterfinals, ended Herndon's super season at 23–3.

On February 26 DeMatha was No. 1, Good Counsel No. 2, Chaney's Newport Preparatory School No. 3, and Gonzaga No. 4. Just three days later, the Eagles were back on top. They had blown an 18-point lead in the WCAC championship game only to clamp down defensively on the Falcons in the last 3:30 and to win the first conference title of their 40 seasons, 48–43, before a sellout crowd of 5,000 fans at Bender Arena.

"We find ways . . . to make it exciting," Gonzaga coach Dick Myers told the *Post*. "Just when I think we are at our lowest point, [we] just bounced right back."

Dunbar had bounced to No. 5 in the rankings heading into the DCIAA championship game against Spingarn. Leading 27–24 at halftime at Coolidge, the Crimson Tide went on an 18–7 run to take control and cruised to the 63–51 victory as Chase and Robinson combined for 36 points, setting up a City Title Game meeting with Gonzaga.

Two days before that showdown, Sweetney and Oxon Hill aimed for a better fate in the state championship game than their five-overtime defeat against Gaithersburg in 1998. Unfortunately for the Clippers, the matchup with Lake Clifton would be just as agonizing. Oxon Hill had a small lead most of the way, but the score was tied in the final seconds when Lake Clifton's Teoine Carroll grabbed a rebound and put up a shot that glanced off the rim and dropped through the net for the 50–48 upset of the fourth-ranked Clippers.

"I don't have any words to describe how bad it feels," said Oxon Hill coach Billy Lanier, whose Clippers had won 22 in a row. "I feel terrible for my team. They did everything they were supposed to do." Except, for the second straight year, score the basket that ultimately mattered.

The City Title Game had moved to the MCI Center—the home court (now known as the Capital One Arena) of the Bullets and Wizards, and the Georgetown

Hoyas—but the big stage was old hat for Dunbar. The Crimson Tide was aiming for its sixth victory in 13 City Title Game appearances, both records being easily the most by a DCIAA school. In contrast, Gonzaga had lost two years earlier in its only shot at the big prize.

With a crowd of 7,000 fans watching, McCloskey scored off a feed from Pat Mitchell with 65 seconds remaining to give Gonzaga a 43–41 lead. It looked as if that might just be enough, but 34 seconds later, Robinson banked in a shot while being fouled. The free throw put Dunbar ahead and deflated the Eagles. "That was a heck of a move," Myers said. "That broke our backs."

After a timeout, Glading, whose shots had defeated DeMatha twice, took a three-pointer but missed badly. Robinson, fouled on the subsequent inbounds play, made one of two foul shots. As time ran down, McCloskey missed a three-pointer, and Mitchell's last-gasp attempt was blocked. The Crimson Tide had its third City Title of the decade, 45–43.

"I'm happy for [the players]," said Dunbar coach Lampkins, who followed his illustrious predecessors Joe Dean Davidson (one) and Mike McLeese (three) in winning a City Title. "Nobody can ever take that from them."

So with the first season of the new millennium approaching come autumn, a familiar program was on top of Washington area high school hoops with perennial kingpin DeMatha having *slipped* to fifth behind Gonzaga, Good Counsel, and Newport.

Senior shooting guard Claude Green in the 1993 Dunbar yearbook. Green would attend USC.

Claude Green
BASKETBALL PLAYER

VARSITY

Dunbar Crimson Tide Basketball Team
Claude Green, Leonard Durrett, Michael Gill, Frank Chambers, Roland Williams, Chris Yates, Alimamy Bangura, Nathan Langley, Earl Tyson, Donnell Brown, Reggie Taylor, Keith Thaxton, Lorenzo Roach, Anthony Brent, Jason Hinton

Dunbar, which had been outstanding during most of Coach Mike McLeese's five previous years, took its game to another level in 1992–93. The Crimson Tide began the season ranked second in the *Post*'s poll and finished it on top with a 33–1 record.

| MEN'S VARSITY BASKETBALL SCOREBOARD | | |
|---|---|---|
| | ANACOSTIA | OPPONENT |
| EDMONTON, CANADA INVITATIONAL | | |
| AN MYER, ALBERTA | 93 | 64 |
| JOHN TAYLOR, ALBERTA | 99 | 74 |
| WILSON, CALIFORNIA | 112 | 102 |
| RANCHO, NEVADA | 87 | 88 |
| | | |
| COOLIDGE | 70 | 63 |
| CALVERT, MARYLAND | 68 | 71 |
| LA PLATA, MARYLAND | 71 | 44 |
| | | |
| GWYNN PARK INVITATIONAL TOURNAMENT | | |
| PARKDALE, MARYLAND | 82 | 68 |
| GWYNN PARK, MARYLAND | 69 | 70 |
| | | |
| ROOSEVELT | 64 | 56 |
| WILSON | 84 | 69 |
| H.D. WOODSON | 85 | 80 |
| EASTERN | 76 | 59 |
| CARDOZO | 58 | 57 |
| BALLOU | 94 | 58 |
| PHELPS | 55 | 54 |
| SPINGARN | 73 | 60 |
| H.D. WOODSON | 60 | 56 |
| EASTERN | 82 | 68 |
| BALLOU | 72 | 50 |
| PHELPS | 44 | 40 |
| SPINGARN | 74 | 68 |
| | | |
| DCIAA PLAY-OFFS | | |
| WILSON | 56 | 55 |
| H.D. WOODSON | 46 | 47 |
| DUNBAR | 72 | 73 |

EAST DIVISION CHAMPIONS
3 OF THE LAST 4 YEARS

Andre Thomas passes to Javon Chaney as Ballou players look

Coach Thomas Hargrove

Edward Sheffey and Andre

The 1994 yearbook photo of Anacostia High School basketball Coach Thomas Hargrove. The Anacostia Indians improved to 19–6 in 1994–95 and wound up ranked 16th, setting the stage for the following memorable 1995–96 season.

Coach Joe Gallagher mentored Coach Morgan Wootten, and when they became rival coaches they remained close off the court.

All-Met Duane Simpkins points to the scoreboard celebrating the DeMatha City Championship title.

DeMatha's All-Met Duane Simpkins player photo. Simpkins would attend University of Maryland and coach at George Mason University.

Team photo after winning City Title game against Dematha

MVP Andre Thomas recieve trophy from Channel 7 Chris McKelvey City Title Game

Coach Hargrove and Asst. Head Coach Kevin Hargrove display City Championship trophy.

73

Coaches Thomas Hargrove and son Kevin of Anacostia High School. Anacostia beat DeMatha 52–47 for the DCIAA championship, with MVP Andre Thomas scoring 10 of his 18 points in the fourth quarter.

Dunbar Crimson Tide 1993 basketball team collage centers on a huddle with Coach Mike McLeese. Dunbar triumphed 82–73 in the DC Interscholastic Athletic Association (DCIAA) championship game.

"Two" for Roach!

Dunbar High's All-Met Lorenzo Roach (12) goes for two at the DCIA Championship against Archbishop Carroll in 1993. Roach would return to coach at Dunbar, replacing his own coach, Mike McLeese, in 2001.

# Dunbar 71
## DeMatha 69

Michael: Don't "Dis" Me Shultz!
Shultz: I'm sorry

Over my head?

Michael this is your last game at Dunbar

One Moment in Time

152  Closing

The 1993 Dunbar yearbook celebrates the city title win over DeMatha in 1993.

## Colts Lose to Stags in City Title Game 57-54

The outside game just was not there. "The ball just wouldn't go in. They clogged the middle against Hodge and we couldn't score from the outside," said Coach Farello to Donald Huff of The Washington Post.

The game was billed as a contest between two of the best centers in the country, Donald Hodge of Coolidge (27-3) and Jarrod Mustaf of DeMatha (27-3). Hodge was selected to the third team by Parade and Mustaf to the second team. Both played well with Hodge scoring 17 points and Mustaf 27 and both got 11 rebounds.

DeMatha led most of the way but, Coolidge got tough in the fourth quarter, holding the Stags scoreless for 5:28.

Derrick Harris' three pointer at the final buzzer was not enough to overcome poor shooting by the Colts during the rest of the game.

The Colts' 27-3 record earned them fourth place in The Washington Post ranking.

The Stags are on offense but, the Colts' defense has its eyes on the ball.

Donald Hod
of his 17 po

Derrick Price and Anthony Riley out hustle DeMatha for the rebound.

Derrick Price leaves the Stags behind as he dunks for two.

146

Coolidge High yearbook pages covered assistant coach Len Farello when he took over in 1987 after 16-year veteran Coach Frank Williams died of brain cancer at 42. The Colts made it to the City Title game but lost to the DeMatha Stags.

DeMatha's Coach Morgan Wootten and his son Joe, named for Wootten's mentor, Coach Joe Gallagher of St. John's.

# Afterword

**MY PARENTS INSTILLED** in me a love of watching sports, and when I was young I watched the same teams and the same games that my future husband was watching. I rooted for the Baltimore Bullets and for the Washington football team. I caught a fly ball in Memorial Stadium on East 33rd Street in Baltimore. I remember my father's excitement taking me to a Cavaliers game in the 1970s to see Austin Carr, who had graduated Mackin High in 1968. I attended all of my high school's basketball and football games, and covered the games for my county's paper. When it came time for college, I didn't miss a home football or basketball game. I liked to think I could hold my own in a sports conversation with anyone. But after a football game at the University of Maryland, John McNamara came up to me and told me with his honeyed voice and his sparkling blue eyes that our journalism teacher liked my writing, and he bought me a Michelob draft, and I was as concussed as any football player.

Even so, I'd be hard pressed to say I loved basketball or knew nearly as much about it as John did. After I started dating John exclusively, I attended games with him, and I even kept the books for charity and other games John played in. I enjoyed watching him not only keep up with but also pass, shoot, and score against local high school and college star players. But even sportswriters had trouble keeping up with John's knowledge. Both new fans and experts learned from him. We struggled to find peer reviewers for this book because John was the one who filled in blanks and broke ties when experts were stumped, especially about basketball. I never witnessed him get a baseball trivia question wrong either. He earned a vote in the Associated Press's basketball Top 25 Poll, even after layoffs and reorganizations at his paper moved him, inconsolable, from the sports desk.

John covered sports for the *Hagerstown Morning Herald* when we got married, and I finished grad school and started working in DC. Soon he was able to return to work in the metro area, and he took me to games with him on the weekends and some evenings when I could get away. He watched carefully and read everything he could, and his knowledge of high school basketball grew to encyclopedic depths.

I took on teaching at night since I knew he'd often be working late at a game. I certainly don't remember his version of the story in the beginning of this book, where I called the statesmen coaches "old-timers," but I did insist that John write down what he knew. This began a new chapter in our lives, when our evenings after work saw us retreat to our respective keyboards to write and work, separately but together. Even when he was home, he was researching and writing or setting up interviews with players and coaches for this book. Many nights and weekends he didn't come to the dinner table, but I brought a plate of food to his desk. We decided it was okay, temporarily; after all, when he finished his book, we'd be close to retirement, with years of leisure and quality time together stretching out ahead of us.

Those glorious leisure years never materialized. John was gunned down by a man who hated the news stories about his threats of violence and court appearances. The shooter had simmered for years until calls were sent out over the internet for "vigilante squads to start gunning journalists down on sight" since they were "enemies of the people." The shooter answered those calls.

John's welcoming voice was silenced. His eyes no longer sparkle. But his vast knowledge of basketball has been captured in his book. He was right to conclude that after all this time, he's "still in the game."

A. C.

# Acknowledgments

**THE ENTIRE WASHINGTON, DC,** area sports community rallied to help make this book a reality. John himself conducted over 150 interviews and spent hours with the expert and helpful staffs at Washington's Charles Sumner School Museum and Archives and at the Martin Luther King Jr. Memorial Library; the Black Heritage Museum of Arlington, Virginia; the Washington Catholic Athletic Conference; and the local public schools in Maryland, Virginia, and DC.

After his death, the support didn't waiver as Morgan Wootten, Gary Williams, and Johnny Holliday lent their considerable sports and media expertise to this endeavor. Writers Mike Ashley, Josh Barr, Doug Dull, Gerry Jackson, Tom Ponton, Bill Wagner, and especially Bob Gill and David Elfin contributed their time and expertise to this labor of love, even without knowing if this book would ever be published. To these remarkable, knowledgeable, and kind friends, I convey my enduring gratitude.

A. C.

# Appendix A

## Map

High school hoops in metro DC

1. American University
2. Anacostia High School
3. Archbishop Carroll High School
4. Armstrong Manual Training School*
5. Ballou High School
6. Bell (Vocational†) High School
7. Cardozo Senior High School (formerly Central High School*)
8. Chamberlain Vocational High School*
9. Coolidge High School
10. Devitt Preparatory School
11. Dunbar High School (formerly the Preparatory School for Colored Youth*)
12. Eastern High School
13. Gallaudet Preparatory School*
14. George Washington University
15. Georgetown University
16. Gonzaga High School
17. H.D. Woodson High School
18. Howard University
19. Mackin High School*
20. Maret High School
21. McKinley Technical High School
22. St. Anselm's Abbey School (formerly the Priory School*)
23. Sidwell Friends School
24. Spingarn High School
25. St. Albans School
26. St. Anthony Catholic School (formerly All Saints High School*)
27. St. John's College High School
28. The Catholic University of America
29. Theodore Roosevelt High School
30. Western High School*
31. Crossland High School, MD
32. DeMatha High School, MD
33. Landon High School, MD
34. Northwestern High School, MD
35. Springbrook High School, MD
36. University of Maryland at College Park, MD
37. Parker-Gray High School*, VA
38. Wakefield High School, VA
39. Washington-Lee High School, VA
40. Montgomery Blair High School

*no longer in existence
†currently named Bell Multicultural High School

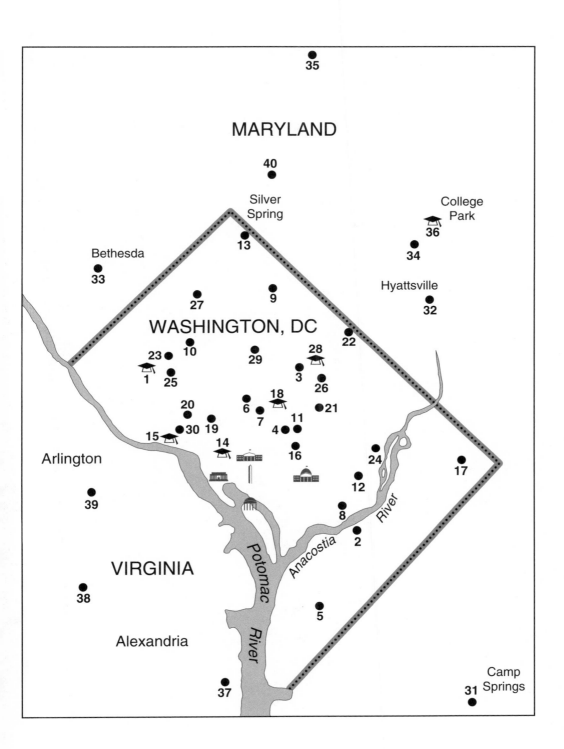

MARYLAND

35

40

Silver
Spring

College
Park
36

Bethesda
33

34

13

Hyattsville
32

27

9

WASHINGTON, DC

23
1   25
10

29

28

22

3
26

20
6

18
7

11
21

15
30  19

4

14

16

24

Arlington

39

12

17

8
2

VIRGINIA

38

5

Alexandria

Camp
Springs
31

37

Potomac
River

Anacostia
River

# Appendix B

## All-High, All-Catholic, All-Met, and All-Prep Compilation

### *STAR* ALL-HIGH, ALL-MET, AND ALL-CATHOLIC (1921–81)

#### 1921–22 All-High

H. Dey (Central), J. O'Dea (Eastern), L. McFadden (Central), Connor (Business), Shanks (Technical [Tech]), Birthright (Central), Dennis (Business), B. Supplee (Tech), A. Johnson (Central), Baird (Western)

#### 1922–23 All-High

D. Childress (Central), R. Garber (Western), H. Dey (Central), R. Dulin (Western), L. Cardwell (Eastern), P. Frisby (Western), J. O'Dea (Eastern), M. Miller (Central), T. Hook (Eastern), Connor (Business)

#### 1923–24 All-High

R. Bennie (Eastern), B. Kessler (Eastern), R. Dulin (Western), Smith (Eastern), Phillips (Western), R. Garber (Western), T. Hook (Eastern), T. Dean (Central), E. Furman (Business), H. Lamar (Western)

#### 1924–25 All-High

H. Lamar (Western), B. Scruggs (Eastern), B. Banta (Central), R. Dulin (Western), T. Dean (Central), H. Councilor (Tech), M. MacDonald (Central), R. Bennie (Eastern), B. Kessler (Eastern), A. Hecke (Eastern)

#### 1925–26 All-High

H. Councilor (Tech), M. MacDonald (Central), J. Radice (Eastern), A. Hecke (Eastern), E. Moser (Central), B. Werber (Tech), P. Walker (Western), B. Evans (Business), B. Wilson (Western), T. Cappelli (Eastern)

#### 1926–27 All-High

not available

#### 1927–28 All-High

*F* F. Burgess (Central), *F* L. Berger (Tech), *C* B. Burch (Central), *G* B. Wilson (Western), *G* N. Colley (Central)

Player positions, if known, are indicated with *F (forward)*, *C (center)*, and *G (guard)*.

## 1928–29 All-High

J. Goldblatt (Tech), P. Brown (Tech), B. Freeman (Western), T. Cappelli (Eastern), H. Thompson (Western), M. Hunt (Western), N. Newman (Business), J. Thompson (Western), C. Romig (Central), J. Lewis (Business)

## 1929–30 All-High

E. Russell (Tech), J. Thompson (Western), B. Freeman (Western), C. MacCartee (Tech), J. Robey (Eastern), W. Cross (Central), B. Lucas (Business), S. Chase (Business), G. Lassisse (Eastern), R. Lampson (Central)

## 1930–31 All-High

E. Russell (Tech), B. Lucas (Business), B. Noonan (Eastern), H. Broadbent (Central), D. Shirley (Eastern), T. Latona (Western), Buscher (Western), B. Duryee (Business), A. Willison (Tech), B. Burke (Central)

## 1931–32 All-High

B. Kane (Eastern), W. Wheeler (Tech), B. Lieb (Eastern), E. Russell (Tech), C. Shore (Business), T. Latona (Western), Reichhardt (Tech), B. Keyser (Central), Bayliss (Eastern), A. Waters (Eastern)

## 1932–33 All-High

B. Burke (Central), C. Shore (Central), J. Moulton (Central), K. Thomas (Tech), B. Nau (Central), T. Nolan (Eastern), A. Waters (Eastern), S. Olverson (Tech), J. Sherman (Roosevelt), J. Corcoran (Western)

## 1933–34 All-High

T. Nolan (Eastern), H. Bassin (Eastern), L. Dean (Eastern), B. Keyser (Central), F. Daly (Tech), J. Billings (Tech), J. Corcoran (Western), T. Davis (Eastern), C. Nau (Central), G. Edelin (Eastern)

## 1934–35 All-High

G. Edelin (Eastern), L. Dean (Eastern), J. Hanley (Western), P. Maloney (Western), F. Daly (Tech), J. Brennan (Western), B. Vermillion (Central), J. Billings (Tech), F. Scheible (Eastern), M. Mulitz (Tech)

## 1935–36 All-High

D. Fones (Central), C. Hollidge (Eastern), W. Thompson (Central), L. Dean (Eastern), B. Rea (Tech), G. Burns (Western), S. Kolius (Roosevelt), O. Shaner (Eastern), R. Scheible (Eastern), B. Vermillion (Central)

## 1936–37 All-High

G. Burns (Western), G. DeWitt (Western), J. Comer (Roosevelt), R. Lombardy (Eastern), W. Vermillion (Central), J. Vermillion (Tech), R. Fridrick (Roosevelt), C. Quantrille (Eastern), L. Lusby (Eastern), D. See (Tech)

## 1937–38 All-High

B. Custer (Western), L. Stanton (Western), C. Quantrille (Eastern), R. Lombardy (Eastern), L. Lusby (Eastern), H. Hancock (Eastern), R. Mantera (Eastern), J. Fanning (Central), G. West (Roosevelt), S. Schulman (Tech)

## 1938–39 All-High

L. Cooksey (Eastern), G. West (Roosevelt), C. Findley (Wilson), H. Hancock (Eastern),
E. Blank (Tech), H. Perlo (Roosevelt), M. Tannenbaum (Tech), E. Travis (Roosevelt),
J. Placos (Anacostia), F. Batiste (Eastern)

## 1939–40 All-High

B. Custer (Eastern), G. West (Roosevelt), E. Travis (Roosevelt), H. Perlo (Roosevelt),
M. MacDonald (Wilson), B. Fugler (Wilson), J. Karas (Western), C. Kligman (Central),
J. Placos (Anacostia), S. Schulman (Eastern)

## 1940–41 All-High

F. Ciango (Roosevelt), J. Walsh (Tech), D. Hillock (Wilson), M. Schulman (Eastern),
H. Perlo (Roosevelt), N. Craig (Eastern), W. Brewer (Tech), S. DiBlasi (Central), D. Cross
(Western), I. Schenker (Western)

## 1941–42 All-High

F. Vinson (Wilson), C. Howard (Roosevelt), D. Hillock (Wilson), T. Thomaides
(Central), J. Karas (Western), D. Cross (Western), E. LeukHardt (Anacostia), M. Lieb
(Eastern), H. Lawler (Central), F. Redinger (Roosevelt)

## 1942–43 All-High

not available

## 1943–44 All-High

S. Brown (Wilson), J. Kranking (Tech), G. Lafferty (Coolidge), M. Pappafotis (Eastern),
B. Lamon (Eastern), P. Panturis (Central), B. Kline (Anacostia), S. Dellinger (Eastern),
T. McLarney (Wilson), J. Moffatt (Tech)

## 1944–45 All-High

J. Moffatt (Tech), B. Graham (Eastern), A. D'Ambrosio (Eastern), B. Lamon (Eastern),
A. Davis (Tech), G. Baroutas (Central), A. Lann (Tech), W. Olson (Tech), G. Taylor
(Wilson), G. Abraham (Tech)

## 1945–46 All-High

G. Taylor (Wilson), B. Cannon (Coolidge), W. Olson (Tech), B. Selwyn (Central),
J. Castro (Western), D. Taylor (Coolidge), J. Houston (Roosevelt), S. Manos (Central),
A. Scribner (Wilson), C. Brotman (Tech)

## 1946–47 All-High

P. O'Neill (Wilson), D. Taylor (Coolidge), G. Schroeder (Anacostia), B. Kleinknecht
(Coolidge), A. Guifredda (Eastern), W. Gilroy (Eastern), A. Monaco (Wilson), B. Murray
(Tech), W. Brizendine (Western), P. Pacini (Tech)

## 1947–48 All-High

not available

## 1948–49 All-High

not available

<h2 style="text-align:center">1949–50 All-High</h2>

not available

<h2 style="text-align:center">1950–51 All-High</h2>

*First Team*
S. Kernan (McKinley Tech), B. Breen (McKinley Tech), B. Ryan (Anacostia), D. Scott (Wilson), L. Snouffer (Western)

*Second Team*
C. Hevener (Coolidge), J. Gradijan (Coolidge), H. Berger (Western), B. Smith (Roosevelt), S. Frank (Roosevelt)

<h2 style="text-align:center">1951–52 All-High</h2>

*First Team*
S. Kernan (McKinley Tech), B. Breen (McKinley Tech), L. Herzbrun (Wilson), J. Wexler (Western), F. Sullivan (McKinley Tech)

*Second Team*
B. Smith (Roosevelt), J. Caw (McKinley Tech), C. Pino (Coolidge), A. Baker (Coolidge), D. Torbett (Eastern)

<h2 style="text-align:center">1952–53 All-High</h2>

*First Team*
B. Wright (Roosevelt), P. Perlo (Roosevelt), J. Wexler (Western), L. Herzbrun (Wilson), A. Baker (Coolidge)

*Second Team*
H. Pollin (Roosevelt), F. Cohen (Western), G. D'Ambrosio (Eastern), J. Robertson (Wilson), D. DeAtley (Tech)

<h2 style="text-align:center">1952–53 All-Catholic</h2>

*First Team*
J. Sullivan (St. Anthony's), F. Harding (St. John's), R. Hawkins (St. John's), B. Rusevlyan (St. John's), D. Devlin (Gonzaga)

*Second Team*
D. Nalty (Georgetown Prep), B. Hessler (Carroll), T. Dunn (Gonzaga), F. Wittman (Carroll), P. Dell (Georgetown Prep)

<h2 style="text-align:center">1953–54 All-Met</h2>

*First Team*
Z. Zirkle (Anacostia), L. Luce (Wilson), E. Baylor (Spingarn), D. Yates (George Washington [GWHS]), B. Rusevlyan (St. John's)

<h2 style="text-align:center">1954–55 All-Met</h2>

*First Team*
L. Luce (Wilson), D. Brown (Montgomery Blair), C. Jenkins (Armstrong), D. Preziotti (Roosevelt), R. Bennett (Gonzaga)

## 1955–56 All-Met

*First Team*
L. Luce (Wilson), T. McCloskey (Gonzaga), W. Smith (Fairmont Heights), W. Jones (Dunbar), M. Agee (GWHS)

## 1956–57 All-Met

*First Team*
B. Sheehan (St. John's), J. Howell (Carroll), M. Beasley (Montgomery Blair), W. Densmore (GWHS), E. Warley (Dunbar)

*Second Team*
W. Smith (Fairmont Heights), J. Shipman (Bethesda–Chevy Chase [B-CC]), E. Cage (DeMatha), T. Matan (Gonzaga), W. Griffin (Parker-Gray)

## 1957–58 All-Met

*First Team*
E. Cage (DeMatha), T. Brown (Montgomery Blair), B. Chavis (Eastern), G. Leftwich (Carroll), R. Scott (Cardozo)

*Second Team*
G. Schweickhardt (Wakefield), B. Daniels (Montgomery Blair), T. Hoover (Carroll), F. Neal (Western), W. Eddins (Washington-Lee [W-L])

## 1958–59 All-Met

*First Team*
F. Hetzel (Landon), T. Hoover (Carroll), J. Thompson (Carroll), G. Leftwich (Carroll), E. Doran (Hammond)

*Second Team*
E. Malloy (Carroll), E. Littles (McKinley Tech), B. Spotts (DeMatha), C. MacCartee (B-CC), E. Lucas (Cardozo)

## 1959–60 All-Met

*First Team*
J. Buckley (Bladensburg), F. Hetzel (Landon), J. Thompson (Carroll), G. Leftwich (Carroll), M. Lentz (Mount Vernon)

*Second Team*
F. Dubofsky (St. John's), W. Skinner (Carroll), O. Johnson (Spingarn), K. Stewart (Northwood), W. Lee (Fairmont Heights)

*Third Team*
D. Endres (DeMatha), B. Levi (Spingarn), T. Barrett (Bladensburg), B. Terwilliger (Wakefield), D. Young (Eastern)

## 1960–61 All-Met

*First Team*
M. Lentz (Mount Vernon), O. Johnson (Spingarn), F. Hetzel (Landon), T. Barrett (Bladensburg), J. Austin (DeMatha)

*Second Team*
B. Windsor (Montgomery Blair), R. Wilkins (Spingarn), G. Manger (Landon), D. Roth (St. John's), R. Duques (Wakefield)

*Third Team*
R. Savoy (Mackin), J. Petty (Cardozo), G. Spadetti (Wakefield), M. O'Connell (Surrattsville), K. Doane (Richard Montgomery)

## 1961–62 All-Met

*First Team*
J. Austin (DeMatha), J. Jones (DeMatha), B. Lewis (St. John's), D. Bing (Spingarn), J. Chambers (Eastern)

*Second Team*
D. Yates (Walt Johnson), E. Hummer (W-L), S. Jackson (Montgomery Blair), G. Logan (Spingarn), P. Cranford (Sasscer)

*Third Team*
R. Greene (Eastern), B. Berger (Landon), B. Wills (Lee), B. Butler (Mackin), J. Pratt (Priory)

## 1962–63 All-Met

*First Team*
B. Lewis (St. John's), E. Hummer (W-L), R. Greene (Eastern), J. McBride (DeMatha), E. Taylor (McKinley Tech)

*Second Team*
B. Butler (Mackin), B. Agnew (B-CC), J. Howard (St. Stephen's), J. Kemper (GWHS), B. Cunningham (Eastern)

*Third Team*
B. Owens (Douglass), J. Johnson (Fairmont Heights), B. Dodson (Hammond), R. Farmer (Northwood), T. Gorham (Cardozo)

## 1963–64 All-Met

*First Team*
B. Cunningham (Eastern), J. McBride (Dunbar), B. Butler (Mackin), B. Keller (St. John's), B. Williams (DeMatha)

*Second Team*
S. Swift (GWHS), J. Johnson (Fairmont Heights), J. Kennedy (DeMatha), P. Scott (Cardozo), B. Owens (Douglass)

*Third Team*
B. McCarthy (DeMatha), R. Williams (Eastern), R. Ruhling (Montgomery Blair), D. Rhoades (Surrattsville), R. Farmer (Northwood)

## 1964–65 All-Met

*First Team*
B. Williams (DeMatha), B. Whitmore (DeMatha), A. White (Western), T. Little (Mackin), S. Swift (GWHS)

*Second Team*
J. Hummer (W-L), G. Oliverio (W. T. Woodson), B. Gaskins (Cardozo), R. Coleman (Mackin), E. Thorne (McKinley Tech)

*Third Team*
W. Hetzel (Landon), W. Allen (Richard Montgomery), M. Epps (Phelps), H. Crittendon (Wakefield), M. Wiles (DeMatha)

## 1965–66 All-Met

*First Team*
E. Austin (DeMatha), J. Hummer (W-L), A. Carr (Mackin), W. Hetzel (Landon), L. Grillo (Carroll)

*Second Team*
L. West (Eastern), J. Hampton (Fairmont Heights), S. Catlett (DeMatha), W. Allen (Richard Montgomery), B. Gaskins (Cardozo)

*Third Team*
P. Toomay (Edison), G. Smythe (St. Stephen's), H. Fox (Northwestern), B. Freeman (Whitman), B. Petrini (DeMatha)

## 1966–67 All-Met

*First Team*
W. Allen (Richard Montgomery), A. Carr (Mackin), S. Catlett (DeMatha), C. Jones (St. John's), L. McCoy (Western)

*Second Team*
B. Gordon (Richard Montgomery), H. Fox (Northwestern), B. Lowe (Edison), E. Epps (Cardozo), G. Browne (Whitman)

*Third Team*
R. Clarke (Spingarn), M. Christian (Northwestern), G. Williams (Mackin), W. Lockett (DeMatha), R. Barnett (GWHS)

## 1967–68 All-Met

*First Team*
A. Nash (DeMatha), H. Fox (Northwestern), J. O'Brien (J.E.B. Stuart), G. Browne (Whitman), M. Gantt (Douglass)

*Second Team*
J. Brown (DeMatha), R. Ford (Mackin), D. Bullock (Cardozo), E. Oliver (Fairmont Heights), E. Lewis (McKinley Tech)

*Third Team*
P. Coder (Peary), J. McCloskey (St. John's), V. LeBuffe (Gonzaga), R. Hogue (McKinley Tech), R. Lambert (GWHS)

## 1968–69 All-Met

*First Team*
M. Bossard (McKinley Tech), J. O'Brien (J.E.B. Stuart), F. Lewis (Western), J. Brown (DeMatha), H. Mathews (Mackin)

*Second Team*
D. Freitag (St. John's), H. Black (Wakefield), R. Milam (McKinley Tech), J. Pecorak (W. T. Woodson), L. Harris (Cardozo)

*Third Team*
E. Peterson (Springbrook), R. Hogue (McKinley Tech), R. Hatcher (Madison), S. Hegens (Spingarn), S. Robinson (Douglass)

## 1969–70 All-Met

*First Team*
R. Hite (DeMatha), W. Daniels (Eastern), D. Washington (St. Anthony's), J. McDaniel (Fairmont Heights), E. Peterson (Springbrook)

*Second Team*
S. Graham (B-CC), S. Nuce (Peary), I. Copeland (DuVal), T. Pecorak (W. T. Woodson), M. Lundy (Roosevelt)

*Third Team*
D. Elliott (Bladensburg), M. Michaels (DuVal), G. Price (Coolidge), S. Washington (Spingarn), P. DeHaven (Edison)

## 1970–71 All-Met

*First Team*
C. Campbell (Ballou), D. Washington (St. Anthony's), J. Briscoe (Parkdale), A. Dantley (DeMatha), J. McDaniel (Fairmont Heights)

*Second Team*
T. Cox (St. John's), M. Simons (McLean), S. Graham (B-CC), W. Thomas (Roosevelt), G. Carrington (Bell)

*Third Team*
A. McCain (Churchill), J. Monroe (McKinley Tech), R. Pulley (Bladensburg), K. Kee (Phelps), H. Estes (GWHS)

## 1971–72 All-Met

*First Team*
A. Dantley (DeMatha), G. Carrington (Bell), B. Buckley (Bladensburg), J. Harrison (McKinley Tech), H. Estes (T. C. Williams)

*Second Team*
A. Daniels (Carroll), B. Braman (Springbrook), D. Stolldorf (Annandale), K. Kee (Phelps), M. Wilson (St. Anthony's)

*Third Team*
M. Giles (Central), S. White (Richard Montgomery), R. Campbell (Ballou), J. Clements (St. John's), S. Klitenic (Northwood)

## 1972–73 All-Met

*First Team*
A. Dantley (DeMatha), L. Wright (Western), L. Herron (Mackin), B. Braman (Springbrook), D. Koesters (West Springfield)

*Second Team*

S. Klitenic (Northwood), A. Daniels (Carroll), B. Buckley (Bladensburg), B. Langloh (DeMatha), L. Joiner (Eastern)

*Third Team*

C. Holmes (DeMatha), J. Fuhrmann (Jefferson), L. Stover (Suitland), J. Gorham (McKinley Tech), R. Lee (Einstein)

### 1973–74 All-Met

*First Team*

D. Williams (Mackin), D. Koesters (West Springfield), K. Carr (DeMatha), T. Jones (Eastern), C. Davis (Peary)

*Second Team*

C. Jackson (Williams), L. Joiner (Eastern), K. Herron (Mackin), C. Vanlandingham (Potomac), C. Esherick (Springbrook)

*Third Team*

P. Dosh (St. John's), M. Oliver (Eastern), P. Greene (Parkdale), S. Mitchell (Woodward), R. Ledbetter (Crossland)

### 1974–75 All-Met

*First Team*

J. Thweat (Dunbar), C. Whitney (DeMatha), A. Dutch (Carroll), J. Tillman (Eastern), B. Magid (Montgomery Blair)

*Second Team*

M. Mills (T. C. Williams), S. Castellan (St. Anselm's), C. Shelton (Dunbar), B. Frazier (H. D. Woodson), S. Robinson (Dunbar)

*Third Team*

A. Hunter (Mackin), H. Krusen (Northwood), B. Dankos (Good Counsel), G. Jones (Madison), S. Proctor (Gwynn Park)

### 1975–76 All-Met

*First Team*

B. Bryant (Carroll), C. Whitney (DeMatha), C. Shelton (Dunbar), J. Duren (Dunbar), J. Hunter (Mackin)

*Second Team*

B. Roman (Lee), J. Ratiff (Eastern), T. Jackson (Paint Branch), J. Gregory (Coolidge), H. Gray (Bowie)

*Third Team*

H. Krusen (Northwood), B. Dankos (Good Counsel), C. Banks (Gwynn Park), C. Scott (Robinson), S. Lincoln (Eastern)

### 1976–77 All-Met

*First Team*

J. Ratiff (Eastern), T. Jackson (Paint Branch), J. Ellis (St. John's), K. Matthews (Dunbar), C. Harris (T. C. Williams)

*Second Team*

G. Jordan (McKinley Tech), M. Clark (Gwynn Park), G. Hopkins (DuVal), M. Pitchford (St. John's), J. Brawner (Spingarn)

*Third Team*

C. Rosenberg (Woodward), C. Gregory (Coolidge), D. Mulquin (Georgetown Prep), R. Semeta (West Springfield), J. Atchison (Lee)

## 1977–78 All-Met

*First Team*

B. Barnes (St. John's), C. Branch (DeMatha), J. Holston (Dunbar), E. Swails (McKinley Tech), G. Dennis (Robinson)

*Second Team*

D. McCoy (Spingarn), S. Speaks (Bladensburg), M. Nickens (Mackin), D. Morley (DeMatha), E. Smith (Churchill)

*Third Team*

B. Fields (Osbourn Park), V. Fenwick (Suitland), M. Mulquin (Georgetown Prep), P. DeVito (DeMatha), P. Ward (Coolidge)

## 1978–79 All-Met

*First Team*

S. Lowe (DeMatha), D. Whittenburg (DeMatha), T. Bailey (Bladensburg), M. Tissaw (Robinson), P. Holbert (W. T. Woodson)

*Second Team*

D. Bonner (Dunbar), K. Darmody (O'Connell), K. Payne (Mackin), K. Black (Mackin), T. Sluby (Gonzaga)

*Third Team*

M. Daniels (Cardozo), E. Harris (Einstein), G. Holmes (Fairmont Heights), K. Wilder (Groveton), J. Brown (Mount Vernon)

## 1979–80 All-Met

*First Team*

T. Sluby (Gonzaga), T. Kearney (Marshall), E. Jones (Spingarn), A. Jones (Dunbar), A. Branch (DeMatha)

*Second Team*

A. Russell (T. C. Williams), P. Holbert (W. T. Woodson), O. Wilson (Gar-Field), M. Jones (High Point), B. Ellerbee (Bowie), B. Baylor (Montgomery Blair), A. McKinney (Walter Johnson), C. Rucker (Mackin), J. Jones (Spingarn), J. Pannell (McKinley Tech)

## 1980–81 All-Met

*First Team*

A. Jones (Dunbar), S. Charles (Dunbar), A. Branch (DeMatha), W. Martin (McKinley Tech), J. Dawkins (Mackin)

*Second Team*

G. Ford (Groveton), K. Racine (St. John's), J. Howard (Carroll), N. Gibson (Laurel),
J. Hamilton (Spingarn), L. Davis (T. Roosevelt), B. Howard (Rockville), C. Yates (Flint
Hill), L. Bias (Northwestern), G. Mitchell (Seneca Valley)

## *TIMES-HERALD* ALL-HIGH AND ALL-CATHOLIC (1927–53)

### 1927–28 All-High

F. Burgess (Central), T. Cappelli (Eastern), J. Forney (Tech), J. Goldblatt (Tech),
N. Colley (Central), L. Berger (Tech), B. Jones (Business), B. Burch (Central), B. Wilson
(Western), C. Essex (Eastern)

### 1928–29 All-High

T. Cappelli (Eastern), J. Goldblatt (Tech), B. Freeman (Western), J. Lewis (Business),
H. Thompson (Western), J. Thompson (Western), C. Romig (Central), P. Brown (Tech),
M. Hunt (Western), J. Ryan (Eastern)

### 1929–30 All-High

J. Thompson (Western), W. Cross (Central), B. Freeman (Western), C. MacCartee (Tech),
R. Lampson (Central), E. Russell (Tech), S. Chase (Business), J. Robey (Eastern),
G. Lassisse (Eastern)

### 1930–31 All-High

B. Lieb (Eastern), B. Lucas (Business), B. Duryee (Business), D. Shirley (Eastern),
F. Cumberland (Central), B. Kane (Eastern), T. Latona (Western), R. Yowell (Western),
A. Willison (Tech), G. Nemorofsky (Business)

### 1931–32 All-High

T. Latona (Western), B. Kane (Eastern), B. Lieb (Eastern), E. Russell (Tech), C. Shore
(Business), B. Burke (Central), W. Wheeler (Tech), B. Keyser (Central), K. Thomas
(Tech), B. Nau (Central)

### 1932–33 All-High

C. Shore (Central), T. Nolan (Eastern), J. Moulton (Central), B. Nau (Central),
K. Thomas (Tech), A. Waters (Eastern), B. Burke (Central), T. Davis (Eastern), B. Harris
(Roosevelt), F. Daly (Tech)

### 1933–34 All-High

T. Nolan (Eastern), H. Bassin (Eastern), T. Davis (Eastern), F. Daly (Tech), L. Dean (Eastern), J. Billings (Tech), Cavanaugh (Roosevelt), B. Keyser (Central), G. Edelin (Eastern),
M. Mulitz (Tech)

### 1934–35 All-High

P. Maloney (Western), J. Hanley (Western), F. Daly (Tech), G. Edelin (Eastern), L. Dean
(Eastern), B. Dodderidge (Western), J. Brennan (Western), W. Thompson (Central),
F. Scheible (Eastern), M. Mulitz (Tech)

## 1935–36 All-High

D. Fones (Central), S. Kolius (Roosevelt), C. Hollidge (Eastern), W. Rea (Tech), L. Dean (Eastern), G. Burns (Western), S. Lomax (Western), O. Shaner (Eastern), B. Vermillion (Central), H. Scheible (Eastern)

## 1936–37 All-High

G. Burns (Western), G. DeWitt (Western), J. Comer (Roosevelt), R. Lombardy (Eastern), B. Vermillion (Central), C. Colton (Eastern), J. Vermillion (Tech), R. Fridrick (Roosevelt), H. Schulze (Western), C. Clark (Central)

## 1937–38 All-High

L. Lusby (Eastern), J. Fanning (Central), C. Quantrille (Eastern), R. Lombardy (Eastern), L. Stanton (Western), B. Custer (Western), G. West (Roosevelt), J. Smith (Roosevelt), M. Tannenbaum (Tech), B. Holloran (Western)

## 1938–39 All-High

H. Hancock (Eastern), H. Perlo (Roosevelt), C. Findley (Wilson), L. Cooksey (Eastern), E. Blank (Tech), G. West (Roosevelt), B. Holloran (Western), S. Schulman (Tech), J. Horn (Western), H. Martin (Central)

## 1939–40 All-High

G. West (Roosevelt), B. Custer (Eastern), E. Travis (Roosevelt), H. Perlo (Roosevelt), M. Schulman (Eastern), C. Kligman (Central), J. Walsh (Tech), I. Schenker (Western), M. MacDonald (Wilson), J. Hilleary (Western)

## 1940–41 All-High

F. Ciango (Roosevelt), J. Walsh (Tech), D. Hillock (Wilson), S. Schulman (Eastern), H. Perlo (Roosevelt), J. Karas (Western), C. Howard (Roosevelt), S. DiBlasi (Central), J. Hilleary (Western), R. Poston (Eastern)

## 1941–42 All-High

F. Vinson (Wilson), C. Howard (Roosevelt), D. Hillock (Wilson), D. Cross (Western), J. Karas (Western), T. Thomaides (Central), S. Moore (Western), E. LeukHardt (Anacostia), B. Penn (Coolidge), L. Capone (Eastern)

## 1942–43 All-High

K. Harder (Tech), C. Howard (Roosevelt), B. Deck (Eastern), C. Thompson (Tech), F. Seaton (Eastern), O. Kennedy (Roosevelt), B. Citrenbaum (Roosevelt), B. Brewer (Tech), H. Pizza (Tech), B. Jawish (Wilson)

## 1943–44 All-High

Robert Lamon (Eastern), J. Kranking (Tech), G. Lafferty (Coolidge), S. Brown (Wilson), M. Pappafotis (Eastern), W. Kline (Anacostia), P. Panturis (Central), S. Dellinger (Eastern), T. McLarney (Wilson), F. Wacker (Western)

## 1944–45 All-High
Robert Lamon (Eastern), T. McLarney (Wilson), S. Manos (Central), A. Lann (Tech), J. Moffatt (Tech), J. Castro (Western), G. Taylor (Wilson), E. Charnock (Eastern), B. Graham (Eastern), G. Baroutas (Central)

## 1945–46 All-High
B. Cannon (Coolidge), S. Manos (Central), W. Olson (Tech), G. Taylor (Wilson), D. Taylor (Coolidge), B. Timmons (Tech), J. Houston (Roosevelt), A. Scribner (Wilson), L. Selwyn (Central), J. Castro (Western)

## 1946–47 All-High
P. O'Neill (Wilson), B. Kleinknecht (Coolidge), G. Schroeder (Anacostia), D. Taylor (Coolidge), A. Guiffreda (Eastern), A. Monaco (Wilson), P. Pacini (Tech), H. Sponsler (Central), W. Brizendine (Western), B. Murray (Tech)

## 1947–48 All-High
J. Pantos (Central), H. Sponsler (Central), W. Warner (Anacostia), J. Whitcomb (Wilson), W. Brizendine (Western), B. Johnson (Central), B. Hibbs (Roosevelt), B. Wickers (Tech), J. Brown (Eastern), B. Paugh (Roosevelt)

## 1948–49 All-High
not available

## 1949–50 All-High
not available

## 1950–51 All-High
S. Kernan (Tech), B. Breen (Tech), D. Torbett (Eastern), L. Snouffer (Western), B. Ryan (Anacostia), B. Smith (Roosevelt), D. Scott (Wilson), J. Gradijan (Coolidge), G. Marshall (Tech), J. Ferrari (Chamberlain)

## 1950–51 All-Catholic
B. Gaskins (St. John's), B. Reese (St. John's), F. Fuqua (DeMatha), G. LeCompte (Gonzaga), B. Hall (St. Anthony's), A. Torre (St. Anthony's), T. Cassidy (St. Anthony's), J. Byrne (Gonzaga), J. Klopher (St. Paul's), B. Sweeney (St. John's)

## 1951–52 All-High
S. Kernan (Tech), B. Breen (Tech), J. Wexler (Western), B. Smith (Roosevelt), L. Herzbrun (Wilson), A. Baker (Coolidge), B. Wright (Roosevelt), D. Torbett (Eastern), J. Caw (Tech), B. Hilleary (Anacostia)

## 1952–53 All-High
L. Herzbrun (Wilson), J. Wexler (Western), A. Baker (Coolidge), B. Wright (Roosevelt), H. Pollin (Roosevelt), G. D'Ambrosio (Eastern), P. Perlo (Roosevelt), T. DiChiacchio (Tech), J. Pelligrino (Wilson), J. Linthicum (Eastern)

# DAILY NEWS ALL-HIGH, ALL-MET, AND ALL-PREP (1946–70)

## 1946–47 All-High

F P. O'Neill (Wilson), F B. Kleinkenecht (Coolidge), C G. Schroeder (Anacostia), G P. Pacini (Tech), G D. Taylor (Coolidge), F A. Giuffreda (Eastern), F A. Monaco (Wilson), C B. Wickers (Tech), G N. Simon (Roosevelt), G B. Murray (Tech)

## 1946–47 All-Prep

F J. G. (St. John's), F J. Lattimer (St. John's), C J. O'Keefe (Gonzaga), G B. Pusey (Gonzaga), G P. Currin (St. John's), F G. Bogley (W-L), F B. Spicer (Landon), C J. Chalfont (Gonzaga), G D. Essex (W-L), G B. Martins (Devitt)

## 1947–48 All-High

F J. Whitcomb (Wilson), F W. Brizendine (Western), C W. Warner (Anacostia), G J. Pantos (Central), G B. Hibbs (Roosevelt), F B. Wickers (Tech), F H. Sponsler (Central), C J. Brown (Eastern), G B. Johnson (Central), G D. Janigan (Wilson)

## 1947–48 All-Prep

F J. G. (St. John's), F J. Spicer (Gonzaga), C T. Fannon (St. John's), G B. Martins (St. John's), G C. Conlin (Gonzaga), F R. Kingsbury (St. Albans), F A. Weaver (St. John's), C M. Nolan (Gonzaga), G V. Durkin (St. John's), G J. Larkins (Gonzaga)

## 1948–49 All-High

F L. Speros (Wilson), F T. Sgro (Tech), C F. Gleason (Central), G J. Pantos (Central), G B. Poston (Western), F D. Eslin (Coolidge), F J. Stringer (Central), C J. Young (Wilson), G K. Luxenberg (Coolidge), G B. Zamsky (Roosevelt)

## 1948–49 All-Prep

F R. Kingsbury (St. Albans), F B. MacDonald (St. John's), C M. Nolan (Gonzaga), G J. Larkins (Gonzaga), G D. Kokes (St. John's), F J. Duchense (Priory), F L. Pennini (St. Anthony's), C J. O'Donnell (Georgetown Prep), G L. Crowley (Georgetown Prep), G B. McLindon (Georgetown Prep)

## 1949–50 All-High

F T. Sgro (Tech), F D. Scott (Wilson), C B. Ryan (Anacostia), G F. Dyer (Eastern), G T. Gregory (Central), F R. Brooks (Anacostia), F J. Kolley (Chamberlain), C H. Weintraub (Western), G L. Snouffer (Western), G J. O'Donnell (Eastern)

## 1949–50 All-Prep

F M. Nolan (Gonzaga), F B. MacDonald (St. John's), C R. Kingsbury (St. Albans), G F. Fuqua (DeMatha), G B. McLindon (St. John's), F B. Alvord (St. Albans), F J. LaCompte (Gonzaga), C L. Pennini (St. Anthony's), G J. Hayden (Priory), G C. Gamble (Episcopal)

## 1950–51 All-High

S. Kernan (Tech), B. Breen (Tech), G. Marshall (Tech), B. Ryan (Anacostia), L. Snouffer (Western), H. Berger (Western), J. Kolley (Chamberlain), D. Scott (Wilson), A. Baker (Coolidge), J. Gradijan (Coolidge)

### 1950–51 All-Prep

B. Gaskins (St. John's), F. Fuqua (DeMatha), G. LeCompte (Gonzaga), B. Hall (St. Anthony's), B. Reese (St. John's), J. Eckholm (Priory), B. McCauley (Devitt), J. Byrne (Gonzaga), B. Sweeney (St. John's), L. Roe (Devitt)

### 1951–52 All-High

S. Kernan (Tech), B. Breen (Tech), B. Marshall (Tech), J. Wexler (Western), L. Herzbrun (Wilson), A. Baker (Coolidge), J. Caw (Tech), F. Sullivan (Tech), Harrison (Coolidge), B. Smith (Roosevelt)

### 1951–52 All-Prep

T. Cassidy (St. Anthony's), B. Hall (St. Anthony's), B. Reese (St. John's), J. Eckholm (Priory), J. Murphy (DeMatha), R. Sweeny (St. John's), J. Sullivan (St. Anthony's), J. Manning (St. Paul's), C. Mochwart (Sidwell Friends), F. Digirolomo (Gonzaga)

### 1952–53 All-High

L. Herzbrun (Wilson), J. Wexler (Western), B. Wright (Roosevelt), A. Baker (Coolidge), P. Perlo (Roosevelt), H. Poin (Roosevelt), G. D'Ambrosio (Eastern), F. Cohen (Western), J. Robertson (Wilson), S. Bobb (Coolidge)

### 1952–53 All-Prep

J. Sullivan (St. Anthony's), R. Hawkins (St. John's), B. Rusevlyan (St. John's), F. Harding (St. John's), T. Dunn (Gonzaga), B. Russell (DeMatha), D. Devlin (Gonzaga), G. Shugars (St. Anthony's), D. Nalty (Georgetown Prep), J. Miller (Kendall)

### 1953–54 All-High

L. Luce (Wilson), Z. Zirkle (Anacostia), D. Butler (Anacostia), H. Jepson (Tech), T. DiChiacchio (Tech), F. Cohen (Western), R. Windsor (Bell), K. Erickson (Roosevelt), D. Weingarten (Coolidge), J. Laventhol (Wilson)

### 1953–54 All-Prep

R. Bennett (Gonzaga), B. Cassidy (St. Anthony's), H. Dant (St. Anthony's), B. Rusevlyan (St. John's), H. Phelan (Landon), B. Hessler (Carroll), J. Frazier (St. John's), R. Smith (Gonzaga), F. Thornett (Gonzaga), M. Boyd (Episcopal)

### 1954–55 All-Met

L. Luce (Wilson), R. Bennett (Gonzaga), D. Preziotti (Roosevelt), D. Yates (GWHS), D. Brown (Blair), C. Jenkins (Armstrong), D. Dell (Landon), B. Hessler (Carroll), J. Frazier (St. John's), J. Wooldridge (W-L)

### 1955–56 All-Met

L. Luce (Wilson), T. McCloskey (Gonzaga), W. Smith (Fairmont Heights), W. Jones (Dunbar), B. Tallant (Chamberlain), S. Anslie (Episcopal), D. Dell (Landon), M. Agee (GWHS), T. Farrington (B-CC), R. Fox (Herndon)

## 1956–57 All-Met

M. Beasley (Montgomery Blair), W. Densmore (GWHS), E. Warley (Dunbar), W. Smith (Fairmont Heights), B. Sheehan (St. John's), J. Shipman (B-CC), W. Griffin (Parker-Gray), E. Cage (DeMatha), J. Howell (Carroll), T. Matan (Gonzaga)

## 1957–58 All-Met

E. Cage (DeMatha), T. Hoover (Carroll), R. Scott (Cardozo), T. Brown (Blair), B. Chavis (Eastern), F. Neal (Western), B. Daniels (Blair), T. Hodges (G. Mason), G. Leftwich (Carroll), G. Schwieckhardt (Wakefield)

## 1958–59 All-Met

G. Leftwich (Carroll), T. Hoover (Carroll), J. Thompson (Carroll), F. Hetzel (Landon), E. Malloy (Carroll), E. Lucas (Cardozo), J. Jones (Eastern), C. MacCartee (B-CC), R. Smith (Fairmont Heights), B. Spotts (DeMatha)

## 1959–60 All-Met

J. Buckley (Bladensburg), G. Leftwich (Carroll), M. Lentz (Mount Vernon), O. Johnson (Spingarn), J. Thompson (Carroll), F. Hetzel (Landon), T. Barrett (Bladensburg), D. Endres (DeMatha), K. Stewart (Northwood), W. Skinner (Carroll)

## 1960–61 All-Met

F. Hetzel (Landon), M. Lentz (Mount Vernon), J. Austin (DeMatha), O. Johnson (Spingarn), T. Barrett (Bladensburg), B. Windsor (Blair), G. Manger (Landon), R. Wilkins (Spingarn), G. Spadetti (Wakefield), R. Duques (Wakefield)

## 1961–62 All-Met

J. Austin (DeMatha), J. Jones (DeMatha), D. Bing (Spingarn), B. Lewis (St. John's), J. Chambers (Eastern), E. Hummer (W-L), D. Yates (Walter Johnson), G. Ward (DeMatha), B. Butler (Mackin), S. Jackson (Montgomery Blair), G. Logan (Spingarn)

## 1962–63 All-Met

R. Greene (Eastern), E. Hummer (W-L), B. Lewis (St. John's), J. McBride (DeMatha), E. Taylor (McKinley Tech), B. Agnew (B-CC), B. Butler (Mackin), J. Caruso (High Point), R. Cunningham (Eastern), H. Owens (Douglass)

## 1963–64 All-Met

B. Butler (Mackin), R. Cunningham (Eastern), B. Keller (St. John's), J. McBride (Dunbar), B. Williams (DeMatha), J. Johnson (Fairmont Heights), J. Lewis (Groveton), H. Owens (Douglass), P. Scott (Cardozo), C. Williams (Eastern)

## 1964–65 All-Met

R. Coleman (Mackin), T. Little (Mackin), S. Swift (GWHS), B. Whitmore (DeMatha), B. Williams (DeMatha), W. Jones (Cardozo), J. Hummer (W-L), J. Morgan (McKinley Tech), A. White (Western), M. Wiles (DeMatha)

### 1965–66 All-Met

E. Austin (DeMatha), A. Carr (Mackin), B. Gaskins (Cardozo), W. Hetzel (Landon),
J. Hummer (W-L), S. Catlett (DeMatha), H. Fox (Northwestern), L. Grillo (Carroll),
P. Toomay (Edison), L. West (Eastern)

### 1966–67 All-Met

W. Allen (Richard Montgomery), A. Carr (Mackin), S. Catlett (DeMatha), H. Fox
(Northwestern), E. Epps (Cardozo), M. Christian (Northwestern), B. Gordon (Richard
Montgomery), C. Jones (St. John's), W. Lockett (DeMatha), L. McCoy (Western)

### 1967–68 All-Met

H. Fox (Northwestern), A. Nash (DeMatha), J. Brown (DeMatha), G. Browne (Whitman), J. O'Brien (J.E.B. Stuart), M. Gantt (Douglass), E. Lewis (McKinley Tech),
D. Bullock (Cardozo), R. Ford (Mackin), M. Jackson (Cardozo)

### 1968–69 All-Met

J. Brown (DeMatha), M. Bossard (McKinley Tech), R. Milam (McKinley Tech),
A. Covington (Mackin), I. Copeland (DuVal), J. O'Brien (J.E.B. Stuart), F. Lewis (Western), H. Mathews (Mackin), R. Hogue (McKinley Tech), H. Black (Wakefield)

### 1969–70 All-Met

D. Washington (St. Anthony's), R. Hite (DeMatha), W. Daniels (Eastern), D. Elliott
(Bladensburg), I. Copeland (DuVal), J. McDaniel (Fairmont Heights), E. Peterson
(Springbrook), S. Washington (Spingarn), S. Graham (B-CC), E. Shaw (Eastern)

## POST ALL-HIGH AND ALL-MET (1919–2002)

### 1919–20 All-High

J. Lemon (Central), Hutchinson (Tech), Loehler (Tech), Conrad (Western), D. Newby
(Central), Hillman (Central), Gosnell (Tech), Grove (Western), Parker (Tech), Held
(Business)

### 1920–21 All-High

not available

### 1921–22 All-High

H. Dey (Central), Birthright (Central), McFadden (Central), Baird (Western), Shanks
(Tech), Connor (Business), Aubinoe (Tech), J. O'Dea (Eastern), House (Tech), Buckley
(Central)

### 1922–23 All-High

D. Childress (Central), T. Hook (Eastern), P. Frisby (Western), McNulty (Western),
B. Kessler (Eastern), J. O'Dea (Eastern), R. Dulin (Western), H. Dey (Central), Hannegan
(Western), Merle Miller (Central)

### 1923–24 All-High

R. Garber (Western), T. Hook (Eastern), Smith (Eastern), B. Kessler (Eastern), R. Dulin
(Western), Phillips (Western), R. Bennie (Eastern), Adams (Tech), T. Dean (Central),
Furman (Business)

## 1924–25 All-High

H. Lamar (Western), W. Hale (Central), B. Werber (Tech), R. Bennie (Eastern), R. Dulin (Western), M. MacDonald (Central), Scruggs (Eastern), T. Hook (Eastern), Dean (Central), G. Kessler (Eastern)

## 1925–26 All-High

H. Councilor (Tech), M. MacDonald (Central), B. Banta (Central), E. Moser (Central), J. Radice (Eastern), B. Werber (Tech), G. Madigan (Eastern), C. May (Business), P. Walker (Western), Evans (Business)

## 1926–27 All-High

F. Burgess (Central), P. Nee (Central), S. Tash (Central), W. Swift (Central), B. Wilson (Western), B. Jones (Business), L. Berger (Tech), A. Buscher (Western), C. Hogarth (Eastern), Crouch (Central)

## 1927–28 All-High

F. Burgess (Central), T. Cappelli (Eastern), B. Burch (Central), B. Wilson (Western), N. Colley (Central), L. Berger (Tech), J. Forney (Tech), B. Jones (Business), J. Goldblatt (Tech)

## 1928–29 All-High

J. Thompson (Western), T. Cappelli (Eastern), B. Freeman (Western), J. Goldblatt (Tech), P. Brown (Tech), C. MacCartee (Tech), B. Lucas (Business), C. Romig (Central), M. Hunt (Western), J. Lewis (Business)

## 1929–30 All-High

F J. Thompson (Western), F E. Russell (Tech), C B. Freeman (Western), G C. MacCartee (Tech), G G. Lassisse (Tech), F W. Cross (Central), F B. Lucas (Business), C S. Chase (Business), G R. Lampson (Central), G J. Robey (Eastern)

## 1930–31 All-High

F B. Lucas (Business), F E. Russell (Tech), C B. Noonan (Eastern), G D. Shirley (Eastern), G H. Broadbent (Central), F A. Latona (Western), F B. Lieb (Eastern), C B. Duryee (Business), G E. DeLisio (Central), G A. Willison (Tech)

## 1931–32 All-High

F B. Kane (Eastern), F A. Latona (Western), C B. Lieb (Eastern), G E. Russell (Tech), G C. Shore (Business), F W. Wheeler (Tech), F B. Courtney (Eastern), C B. Keyser (Central), G A. Waters (Eastern), G B. Nau (Central)

## 1932–33 All-High

F T. Nolan (Eastern), F B. Burke (Central), C J. Moulton (Central), G K. Thomas (Tech), G B. Nau (Central), F C. Shore (Central), F A. Waters (Eastern), C T. Davis (Eastern), G B. Harris (Roosevelt), G L. Dean (Eastern)

## 1933–34 All-High

F T. Nolan (Eastern), F H. Bassin (Eastern), C C. Keyser (Central), G L. Dean (Eastern), G F. Daly (Tech), F J. Billings (Tech), F J. Cocoran (Western), C T. Davis (Eastern), G G. Edelin (Eastern), G C. Nau (Central)

## 1934–35 All-High

*F* F. Daly (Tech), *F* G. Edelin (Eastern), *C* J. Billings (Tech), *G* P. Maloney (Western), *G* L. Dean (Eastern), *F* C. Nau (Central), *F* B. Brennan (Western), *C* J. Hanley (Western), *G* F. Scheible (Eastern), *G* M. Mulitz (Tech)

## 1935–36 All-High

*F* C. Hollidge (Eastern), *F* D. Fones (Central), *C* S. Kolius (Roosevelt), *G* L. Dean (Eastern), *G* B. Rea (Tech), *G* F. Bailey (Roosevelt), *F* G. Burns (Western), *G* F. Scheible (Eastern)

## 1936–37 All-High

*F* R. Lombardy (Eastern), *F* G. Burns (Western), *C* J. Comer (Roosevelt), *G* G. DeWitt (Western), *G* B. Vermillion (Central), *F* J. Vermillion (Tech), *F* J. Williamson (Tech), *C* C. Quantrille (Eastern), *G* R. Fridrich (Roosevelt), *G* F. Bailey (Roosevelt)

## 1937–38 All-High

*F* A. Panago (Central), *F* B. Custer (Western), *C* C. Quantrille (Eastern), *G* R. Lombardy (Eastern), *G* L. Lusby (Eastern), *F* J. Fanning (Central), *F* H. Hancock (Eastern), *C* L. Stanton (Western), *G* G. West (Roosevelt), *G* C. Findley (Wilson)

## 1938–39 All-High

*F* E. Blank (Tech), *F* G. West (Roosevelt), *C* S. Schulman (Tech), *G* H. Hancock (Eastern), *G* F. Batiste (Eastern), *F* J. Horn (Western), *F* L. Cooksey (Eastern), *C* B. Fugler (Wilson), *G* H. Perlo (Roosevelt), *G* M. Tannenbaum (Tech)

## 1939–40 All-High

*F* J. Shumate (B-CC), *F* G. West (Roosevelt), *C* B. Custer (Eastern), *G* B. Mulvihill (Gonzaga), *G* H. Perlo (Roosevelt), *F* Newmyer (Friends), *F* R. Barrett (Georgetown Prep), *C* E. Travis (Roosevelt), *G* M. Schulman (Eastern), *G* M. McDonald (Wilson)

## 1940–41 All-Met

*F* H. Perlo (Roosevelt), *F* F. Ciango (Roosevelt), *C* P. Baker (Landon), *G* M. Schulman (Eastern), *G* B. Mulvihill (Gonzaga), *F* J. Walsh (Tech), *F* B. Barrett (Georgetown Prep), *C* D. Hillock (Wilson), *G* T. Robertson (Roosevelt), *G* R. McNab (W-L)

## 1941–42 All-Met

*F* F. Vinson (Wilson), *F* E. Elliott (St. Albans), *C* D. Hillock (Wilson), *G* J. Karas (Western), *G* C. Howard (Roosevelt), *F* Dudley (St. John's), *F* Kidwell (Hyattsville), *C* Showell (Georgetown Prep), *G* Cross (Western), *G* Hamill (Episcopal)

## 1942–43 All-Met

*F* C. Howard (Roosevelt), *F* C. Bailey (GWHS), *C* K. Harder (Tech), *G* F. Seaton (Eastern), *G* C. Thompson (Tech), *F* Pizza (Tech), *F* Elliott (St. Albans), *C* Hensley (GWHS), *G* Brewer (Tech), *G* Phillips (W-L)

## 1943–44 All-High

not available

## 1944–45 All-High

*F* B. Lamon (Eastern), *F* J. Moffatt (Tech), *C* S. Manos (Central), *G* A. Lann (Tech), *G* T. McLarney (Wilson), *F* G. Taylor (Wilson), *F* J. Castro (Western), *C* B. Lake (Coolidge), *G* E. Charnock (Eastern), *G* G. Baroutas (Central)

## 1945–46 All-High

*F* B. Cannon (Coolidge), *F* G. Taylor (Wilson), *C* W. Olson (McKinley Tech), *G* D. Taylor (Coolidge), *G* S. Manos (Central), *F* B. Timmons (Tech), *F* J. Castro (Western), *C* A. Scribner (Wilson), *G* J. Houston (Roosevelt), *G* B. Selwyn (Central)

## 1946–47 All-Met

*F* G. Schroeder (Anacostia), *G* P. O'Neil (Wilson), *C* M. Boaz (GWHS), *F* J. G. (St. John's), *G* D. Taylor (Coolidge), *F* D. Harlow (Woodward), *G* J. Castro (Woodward), *C* J. O'Keefe (Gonzaga), *G* B. Brown (GWHS), *F* B. Chalfont (W-L)

## 1947–48 All-Met

*F* J. G. (St. John's), *F* B. Rorer (GWHS), *C* R. Kingsbury (St. Albans), *G* W. Brizendine (Western), *G* J. Pantos (Central), *F* J. Whitcomb (Wilson), *F* T. Fannon (St. John's), *C* W. Warner (Anacostia), *G* J. Dohner (GWHS), *G* D. Latimer (B-CC)

## 1948–49 All-Met

*F* J. Pantos (Central), *F* B. Poston (Western), *C* R. Kingsbury (St. Albans), *G* T. Larkins (Gonzaga), *G* J. Gahagan (GWHS), *F* F. Geneau (B-CC), *F* B. Smith (GWHS), *C* T. Daukas (GWHS), *G* W. Lytle (Hyattsville), *G* D. Kokes (St. John's)

## 1949–50 All-Met

not available

## 1950–51 All-Met

*First Team*
*F* S. Kernan (McKinley Tech), *F* G. LeCompte (Gonzaga), *C* B. Kessler (GWHS), *G* B. Reese (St. John's), *G* L. Snouffer (Western)

*Second Team*
*F* B. Breen (McKinley Tech), *F* B. Tompkins (Montgomery Blair), *C* F. Fuqua (DeMatha), *G* B. Ryan (Anacostia), *G* J. Eckholm (Priory)

## 1951–52 All-Met

*First Team*
*F* S. Kernan (McKinley Tech), *F* B. Reese (St. John's), *C* R. Kessler (GWHS), *G* J. Eckholm (Priory), *G* B. Breen (McKinley Tech)

*Second Team*
*F* T. Cassidy (St. Anthony's), *F* L. McMenamin (GWHS), *C* J. Wexler (Western), *G* L. Herzbrun (Wilson), *G* B. Edmondson (Mount Vernon)

*Third Team*
*F* C. Hardy (GWHS), *F* J. Caw (McKinley), *C* F. Sullivan (McKinley Tech), *G* J. Hill (W-L), *G* D. Green (Bladensburg)

## 1952–53 All-Met

*First Team*
F R. Hawkins (St. John's), F B. Edmondson (Mount Vernon), C J. Sullivan (St. Anthony's), G L. Herzbrun (Wilson), G P. Perlo (Roosevelt)

*Second Team*
F B. Morton (GWHS), F F. Smith (Spingarn), C J. Wexler (Western), G B. Wright (Roosevelt), G F. Harding (St. John's)

*Third Team*
F C. Mochwart (Sidwell Friends), F W. Rice (Armstrong), C L. McMenamin (GWHS), G E. Phoenix (Dunbar), G J. Schilling (W-L)

## 1953–54 All-Met

*First Team*
F D. Yates (GWHS), F L. Luce (Wilson), C E. Baylor (Spingarn), G B. Rusevlyan (St. John's), G B. Edmondson (Mount Vernon)

*Second Team*
F R. Crown (Suitland), F B. Cassidy (St. Anthony's), C D. Watson (W-L), G Z. Zirkle (Anacostia), G H. Phelan (Landon)

*Third Team*
F W. Williams (Dunbar), F R. Bennett (Gonzaga), C H. Jepson (McKinley Tech), G A. Sonner (B-CC), G M. Boyd (Episcopal)

## 1954–55 All-Met

*First Team*
F D. Yates (GWHS), F D. Brown (Montgomery Blair), C C. Jenkins (Armstrong), G R. Bennett (Gonzaga), G D. Preziotti (Roosevelt)

*Second Team*
F D. Dell (Landon), F B. Warley (Phelps), C J. Woolridge (W-L), G L. Luce (Wilson), G B. Hessler (John Carroll)

*Third Team*
F B. Bolen (McKinley Tech), F J. Weingarten (Coolidge), C K. Eriksson (Roosevelt), G O. Hooks (Armstrong), G D. Rhine (Anacostia)

## 1955–56 All-Met

*First Team*
F T. McCloskey (Gonzaga), F W. Jones (Dunbar), C W. Smith (Fairmont Heights), G L. Luce (Wilson), G M. Agee (GWHS)

*Second Team*
F J. Mandes (St. John's), F D. Dell (Landon), C S. Ainslie (Episcopal), G B. Sawyer (Fairfax), G C. Johnson (Northwestern)

*Third Team*
F B. Brown (W-L), F E. Cage (DeMatha), C B. Tallant (Chamberlain), G S. Shriver (Suitland), G J. Collins (St. John's)

## 1956–57 All-Met

*First Team*
F M. Beasley (Montgomery Blair), F W. Densmore (GWHS), C W. Griffin (Parker-Gray),
G W. Smith (Fairmont Heights), G B. Sheehan (St. John's)

*Second Team*
F J. Shipman (B-CC), F F. Neal (Western), C E. Cage (DeMatha), G M. DelNegro
(GWHS), G H. Brown (Cardozo)

*Third Team*
F T. Coleman (Gonzaga), F G. Patterson (Gallaudet Prep), C H. Gray (Phelps),
G B. Hewitt (Annandale), G J. Howell (John Carroll)

## 1957–58 All-Met

*First Team*
T. Hoover (John Carroll), T. Brown (Montgomery Blair), D. Lockman (Wakefield),
E. Cage (DeMatha), R. Scott (Cardozo)

*Second Team*
F. Neal (Western), B. Daniels (Montgomery Blair), G. Leftwich (John Carroll),
K. Sanders (W-L), G. Meeks (Fort Hill)

*Third Team*
B. Chavis (Eastern), G. Catlett (Hedgesville), D. Slattery (Gonzaga), D. Smith (Walkers-
ville), R. Price (St. Stephen's)

## 1958–59 All-Met

*First Team*
E. Lucas (Cardozo), M. Molloy (John Carroll), F. Hetzel (Landon), T. Hoover (John
Carroll), G. Leftwich (John Carroll)

*Second Team*
J. Thompson (John Carroll), J. Jones (Eastern), T. Geith (Annandale), C. MacCartee
(B-CC), R. Smith (Fairmont Heights)

*Third Team*
O. Johnson (Spingarn), F. Harrison (Cardozo), E. Littles (McKinley Tech), B. Spotts
(DeMatha), E. Doran (Hammond)

## 1959–60 All-Met

*First Team*
J. Buckley (Bladensburg), J. Thompson (John Carroll), F. Hetzel (Landon), O. Johnson
(Spingarn), M. Lentz (Mount Vernon), G. Leftwich (John Carroll)

*Second Team*
D. Endres (DeMatha), H. Burchette (Coolidge), F. Dubofsky (St. John's), K. Stewart
(Northwood), S. Chisholm (GWHS)

*Third Team*
W. Lee (Fairmont Heights), D. Young (Eastern), W. Skinner (John Carroll), A. Wheeler
(Dunbar), T. Barrett (Bladensburg)

## 1960–61 All-Met

*First Team*
J. Austin (DeMatha), F. Hetzel (Landon), O. Johnson (Spingarn), M. Lentz (Mount Vernon), R. Duques (Wakefield)

*Second Team*
T. Barrett (Bladensburg), B. Windsor (Montgomery Blair), G. Manger (Landon), G. Spadetti (Wakefield), D. Roth (St. John's)

*Third Team*
J. Jones (DeMatha), K. Doane (Richard Montgomery), W. Burroughs (W-L), V. Jackson (Cardozo), D. Bing (Spingarn)

## 1961–62 All-Met

*First Team*
E. Hummer (W-L), J. Jones (DeMatha), D. Bing (Spingarn), J. Austin (DeMatha), S. Jackson (M. Blair)

*Second Team*
J. Chambers (Eastern), B. Lewis (St. John's), B. Wills (Lee), D. Yates (Walter Johnson), B. Butler (Mackin)

*Third Team*
P. Cranford (Sasscer), J. Pratt (Priory), R. Greene (Eastern), D. McCollum (St. Stephen's), J. O'Neal (Western)

## 1962–63 All-Met

*First Team*
E. Hummer (W-L), B. Lewis (St. John's), J. Howard (St. Stephen's), B. Butler (Mackin), J. McBride (DeMatha), B. Agnew (B-CC), B. Dodson (Hammond), J. Johnson (Fairmont Heights), E. Taylor (McKinley Tech), R. Greene (Eastern)

## 1963–64 All-Met

*First Team*
W. Campbell (J.E.B. Stuart), J. Johnson (Fairmont Heights), B. Williams (DeMatha), J. Lewis (Groveton), B. Cunningham (Eastern), R. Ruhling (Montgomery Blair), J. Kennedy (DeMatha), P. Scott (Cardozo), B. Butler (Mackin), J. McBride (Dunbar)

*Second Team*
H. Brantley (Bell), B. Keller (St. John's), B. McCarthy (DeMatha), B. Owens (Douglass), R. Renaudin (Georgetown Prep)

*Third Team*
R. Farmer (Northwood), J. Hummer (W-L), T. Little (Mackin), M. O'Brien (St. Anthony's), S. Swift (GWHS)

## 1964–65 All-Met

*First Team*
J. Hummer (W-L), B. Williams (DeMatha), W. Allen (Richard Montgomery), B. Whitmore (DeMatha), R. Coleman (Mackin), G. Oliverio (W. T. Woodson), M. Wiles (DeMatha), T. Little (Mackin), A. White (Western), S. Swift (GWHS)

*Second Team*
S. Catlett (DeMatha), B. Gaskins (Cardozo), E. Thorne (McKinley Tech), A. Carr (Mackin), R. Farrell (Montgomery Blair)

*Third Team*
J. Morgan (McKinley Tech), W. Hetzel (Landon), J. Radin (Groveton), P. G. (Gonzaga), J. Pyles (Oxon Hill)

## 1965–66 All-Met

*First Team*
S. Catlett (DeMatha), J. Hummer (W-L), W. Hetzel (Landon), L. West (Eastern), W. Allen (Richard Montgomery), A. Carr (Mackin), B. Gaskins (Cardozo), H. Fox (Northwestern), E. Austin (DeMatha), L. Grillo (John Carroll)

*Second Team*
P. Toomay (Edison), J. Pyles (Oxon Hill), R. Truehart (McKinley Tech), B. Freeman (Whitman), B. Petrini (DeMatha)

*Third Team*
C. Fox (Herndon), T. Chilcutt (Fort Hunt), B. Vines (Eastern), S. Gaines (Bell), J. Hampton (Fairmont Heights)

## 1966–67 All-Met

*First Team*
A. Carr (Mackin), W. Allen (Richard Montgomery), S. Catlett (DeMatha), H. Fox (Northwestern), L. McCoy (Western), C. Jones (St. John's), R. Clarke (Spingarn), E. Epps (Cardozo), G. Browne (Whitman), D. Oliverio (W. T. Woodson)

*Second Team*
W. Lockett (DeMatha), D. Tilley (Whitman), B. Gordon (Richard Montgomery), S. Savoy (Mackin), W. Holland (Eastern)

*Third Team*
A. Nash (DeMatha), B. Lowe (Edison), M. Christian (Northwestern), N. Moon (Chamberlain), R. Barnett (GWHS)

## 1967–68 All-Met

*First Team*
A. Nash (DeMatha), H. Fox (Northwestern), D. Bullock (Cardozo), J. O'Brien (J.E.B. Stuart), J. Brown (DeMatha), E. Lewis (McKinley Tech), G. Browne (Whitman), M. Gantt (Douglass), P. Coder (Peary), R. Ford (Mackin)

*Second Team*
E. Oliver (Fairmont Heights), J. Thomas (Sherwood), R. Hogue (McKinley Tech), M. Jackson (Cardozo), J. McCloskey (St. John's)

*Third Team*
R. Lambert (GWHS), D. Dunmore (Ballou), D. Harps (Coolidge), L. Harris (Cardozo), V. LeBuffe (Gonzaga)

## 1968–69 All-Met

*First Team*

J. Brown (DeMatha), M. Bossard (McKinley Tech), F. Lewis (Western), S. Hegens (Spingarn), J. O'Brien (J.E.B. Stuart), H. Mathews (Mackin), J. Garvin (Phelps), L. Harris (Cardozo), R. Milam (McKinley Tech), D. Freitag (St. John's)

*Second Team*

R. Hogue (McKinley Tech), A. Jez (Carroll), W. Simmons (Gwynn Park), I. Copeland (DuVal), G. Gibbs (Mackin)

*Third Team*

E. Peterson (Springbrook), P. Wagner (St. Anthony's), E. Quash (GWHS), T. Bassett (McKinley Tech), S. Garrett (DeMatha)

## 1969–70 All-Met

*First Team*

D. Washington (St. Anthony's), R. Hite (DeMatha), W. Daniels (Eastern), J. McDaniel (Fairmont Heights), G. Price (Coolidge), E. Peterson (Springbrook), D. Elliott (Bladensburg), S. Washington (Spingarn), C. Redding (John Carroll), T. Pecorak (W. T. Woodson)

*Second Team*

S. Graham (B-CC), A. Baker (St. Anthony's), I. Copeland (DuVal), E. Shaw (Eastern), J. Simms (Good Counsel)

*Third Team*

S. Nuce (Peary), D. Willis (DeMatha), M. Lundy (Roosevelt), T. Lewis (GWHS), M. Permenter (Sidwell Friends)

## 1970–71 All-Met

*First Team*

D. Washington (St. Anthony's), J. Briscoe (Parkdale), A. Dantley (DeMatha), C. Campbell (Ballou), G. Carrington (Bell), S. Graham (B-CC), J. McDaniel (Fairmont Heights), T. Cox (St. John's), M. Simons (McLean), W. Thomas (Roosevelt)

*Second Team*

A. McCain (Churchill), C. Crosswhite (Whitman), R. Pulley (Bladensburg), K. Kee (Phelps), M. Permenter (Sidwell Friends)

*Third Team*

D. Thomas (W. T. Woodson), J. Monroe (McKinley Tech), W. Parker (Ballou), B. Newton (Mackin), B. Jones (St. John's)

## 1971–72 All-Met

*First Team*

G. Carrington (Bell), K. Kee (Phelps), J. Harrison (McKinley Tech), J. Monroe (McKinley Tech), M. Wilson (St. Anthony's), J. Smith (St. Anthony's), A. Dantley (DeMatha), R. Campbell (Ballou), B. Buckley (Bladensburg), H. Estes (T. C. Williams)

*Second Team*

B. Langloh (DeMatha), B. Braman (Springbrook), J. Clements (St. John's), M. Giles (Central), G. Brooks (St. Anthony's)

*Third Team*
D. Stolldorf (Annandale), M. Hartley (St. John's), L. Herron (Mackin), W. Askew (Cardozo), A. Daniels (Carroll)

## 1972–73 All-Met

*First Team*
A. Dantley (DeMatha), L. Wright (Western), B. Buckley (Bladensburg), D. Koesters (West Springfield), A. Daniels (John Carroll), B. Langloh (DeMatha), L. Joiner (Eastern), J. Smith (Western), L. Herron (Mackin), B. Braman (Springbrook)

*Second Team*
C. Holmes (DeMatha), D. Williams (Mackin), J. Gorham (McKinley Tech), M. Hartley (St. John's), S. Klitenic (Northwood)

*Third Team*
J. Furhmann (Jefferson), D. Wiley (Cardozo), R. Ledbetter (Largo), D. Cook (Springbrook), S. McDaniel (Carroll)

## 1973–74 All-Met

*First Team*
D. Williams (Mackin), K. Carr (DeMatha), L. Joiner (Eastern), K. Herron (Mackin), D. Koesters (West Springfield), P. Dosh (St. John's), T. Jones (Eastern), C. Vanlandingham (Potomac), C. Jackson (T. C. Williams), C. Davis (Peary)

*Second Team*
A. Dutch (Carroll), M. Oliver (Eastern), R. Ledbetter (Crossland), C. Esherick (Springbrook), H. Nickens (Spingarn)

*Third Team*
V. Allen (DeMatha), S. Young (Gaithersburg), B. Wetesnik (West Springfield), P. Greene (Parkdale), B. Frazier (H. D. Woodson)

## 1974–75 All-Met

*First Team*
S. Robinson (Dunbar), A. Dutch (John Carroll), B. Magid (Montgomery Blair), S. Castellan (St. Anselm's), C. Whitney (DeMatha), J. Tillman (Eastern), J. Thweatt (Dunbar), G. Jones (James Madison), L. Reid (Bladensburg), B. Frazier (H. D. Woodson)

*Second Team*
S. Proctor (Gwynn Park), C. Shelton (Dunbar), M. Morton (Eastern), K. Sinnett (St. John's), J. Hunter (Mackin)

*Third Team*
B. Green (St. Albans), A. Williams (McKinley Tech), M. Murray (Hayfield), D. Casey (Rockville), M. Mills (T. C. Williams)

## 1975–76 All-Met

*First Team*
C. Scott (Robinson), H. Gray (Bowie), J. Hunter (Mackin), J. Ratiff (Eastern), C. Whitney (DeMatha), J. Duren (Dunbar), B. Bryant (Carroll), C. Shelton (Dunbar), T. Jackson (Paint Branch), J. Gregory (Coolidge)

*Second Team*

B. Roman (Lee), S. Lincoln (Eastern), A. Hammaker (Mount Vernon), M. Pitchford
(St. John's), H. Krusen (Northwood)

*Third Team*

M. Owens (Einstein), L. Moreno (Spingarn), C. Lyles (Parkdale), C. Brewer (Robinson),
B. Lewis (Central)

### 1976–77 All-Met

*First Team*

J. Atchison (Lee), C. Harris (T. C. Williams), K. Matthews (Dunbar), J. Ratiff (Eastern),
G. Hopkins (DuVal), T. Jackson (Paint Branch), M. Pitchford (St. John's), G. Jordan
(McKinley Tech), M. Clark (Gwynn Park), C. Gregory (Coolidge)

*Second Team*

J. Ellis (St. John's), R. Wright (Eastern), E. Dozier (Carroll), A. Corbin (H. D. Woodson),
V. Fenwick (Suitland)

*Third Team*

B. Neal (Oxon Hill), D. Mulquin (Georgetown Prep), R. Semeta (West Springfield),
C. Rosenberg (Woodward), J. Brawner (Spingarn)

### 1977–78 All-Met

*First Team*

S. Speaks (Bladensburg), V. Fenwick (Suitland), G. Dennis (Robinson), C. Branch
(DeMatha), D. McCoy (Spingarn), B. Barnes (St. John's), E. Swails (McKinley Tech),
J. Holston (Dunbar), E. Smith (Churchill), M. Nickens (Mackin)

*Second Team*

G. Butler (Sherwood), R. Crooks (Mackin), W. Wilson (Montgomery Blair), B. Johnson
(Spingarn), D. Morley (DeMatha)

*Third Team*

P. Ward (Coolidge), S. Wolz (Springbrook), T. Tibbs (Dunbar), B. Fields (Osbourn Park),
P. DeVito (DeMatha)

### 1978–79 All-Met

*First Team*

K. Black (Mackin), D. Whittenburg (DeMatha), S. Lowe (DeMatha), K. Payne (Mackin),
P. Holbert (W. T. Woodson), M. Tissaw (Robinson), T. Bailey (Bladensburg), M. Daniels
(Cardozo), K. Darmody (O'Connell), D. Bonner (Dunbar)

*Second Team*

T. Sluby (Gonzaga), J. Brown (Mount Vernon), G. Holmes (Fairmont Heights), L. Geddie
(Spingarn), K. Wilder (Groveton)

*Third Team*

J. Pannell (McKinley Tech), E. Harris (Einstein), D. Seals (High Point), B. Donohue
(St. John's), M. Mulquin (Georgetown Prep)

## 1979–80 All-Met

*First Team*
B. Baylor (Montgomery Blair), A. Branch (DeMatha), L. McGainey (Potomac),
P. Holbert (W. T. Woodson), A. Jones (Dunbar), E. Jones (Spingarn), T. Kearney
(Marshall), J. Pannell (McKinley Tech), A. Russell (T. C. Williams), T. Sluby (Gonzaga)

*Second Team*
A. McKinney (Walter Johnson), M. Jones (High Point), C. Cottom (Spingarn), O. Wilson
(Gar-Field), C. Rucker (Mackin)

*Third Team*
C. Yates (Flint Hill), J. Jones (Spingarn), M. Wright (Cardozo), R. Matthews (Rockville),
S. Perry (Gar-Field)

## 1980–81 All-Met

*First Team*
A. Branch (DeMatha), S. Charles (Dunbar), L. Davis (T. Roosevelt), J. Dawkins
(Mackin), B. Ellerbee (Bowie), J. Hamilton (Spingarn), A. Jones (Dunbar), K. Lomax
(St. Anthony's), W. Martin (McKinley Tech), C. Yates (Flint Hill)

*Second Team*
G. Ford (Groveton), B. Howard (Rockville), L. Bias (Northwestern), N. Gibson (Laurel),
D. Webster (Coolidge)

*Third Team*
K. Harvey (Fairmont Heights), Von Robinson (Bell), K. Racine (St. John's), G. Mitchell
(Seneca Valley), B. Ferry (DeMatha)

## 1981–82 All-Met

*First Team*
J. Dawkins (Mackin), D. Webster (Coolidge), L. Davis (T. Roosevelt), G. Potts (St. John's),
J. Baxter (Carroll), L. Bias (Northwestern), T. Amaker (W. T. Woodson), M. Jackson
(South Lakes), E. Davis (T. Roosevelt), D. Turner (Seneca Valley)

*Second Team*
A. McCloud (H. D. Woodson), D. Tucker (Mount Vernon), W. Hughes (Good Counsel),
M. Graham (Spingarn), D. Pressley (Mackin)

*Third Team*
T. Graves (McNamara), S. Walters (Northwood), V. Butler (High Point), T. Allen
(Hayfield), B. King (Park View)

## 1982–83 All-Met

*First Team*
B. Campbell (Dunbar), K. Saunders (McKinley Tech), L. DeBellotte (Cardozo),
T. Amaker (W. T. Woodson), C. Green (Spingarn), K. Scarborough (Eastern), R. Rice
(St. John's), G. Jackson (Flint Hill), B. Bolton (DeMatha), W. Lancaster (St. Anthony's)

*Second Team*
D. Tucker (Mount Vernon), T. Shaw (T. C. Williams), F. Ross (Potomac), B. King (Park
View), T. Coffey (Maret)

*Third Team*
B. Day (H. D. Woodson), M. Jones (Paint Branch), C. Valentine (DeMatha), D. Lewis (Carroll), E. Brent (Mount Vernon)

## 1983–84 All-Met

*First Team*
T. Coffey (Maret), D. Ferry (DeMatha), B. King (Park View), D. Lewis (Carroll), B. Milstead (Potomac), D. Prue (Dunbar), T. Shaw (T. C. Williams), D. Simms (Flint Hill), J. Thompson (Gonzaga), C. Valentine (DeMatha)

*Second Team*
F. Smith (Mount Vernon), W. Lancaster (Coolidge), J. Burney (Wilson), D. Jones (Suitland), K. Sanders (McKinley Tech)

*Third Team*
S. Douglas (Spingarn), T. Jones (Dunbar), C. Thomas (Seneca Valley), P. Gamble (St. Anthony's), J. Smith (Friendly)

## 1984–85 All-Met

*First Team*
D. Butler (Coolidge), C. Cheeks (Wilson), S. Douglas (Spingarn), D. Ferry (DeMatha), P. Gamble (All Saints), G. Hill (Flint Hill), E. Moore (Cardozo), R. Peters (Suitland), D. Prue (Dunbar), M. Tillmon (Gonzaga)

*Second Team*
T. Brent (Forestville), D. Gregg (Northwestern), S. Hood (DeMatha), M. Tate (St. John's), B. Winston (All Saints)

*Third Team*
T. Anderson (Coolidge), A. Duckett (Spingarn), L. Harris (Suitland), M. Mundy (Springbrook), D. Scott (Flint Hill)

## 1985–86 All-Met

*First Team*
D. Davis (Coolidge), T. Gibson (Dunbar), S. Hood (DeMatha), M. Jackson (Anacostia), M. Karver (B-CC), D. Scott (Flint Hill), G. Sitney (High Point), M. Tillmon (Gonzaga), A. Tucker (McKinley Tech), D. Williams (Eastern)

*Second Team*
S. Jefferson (Flint Hill), B. Pollard (Bishop Ireton), J. Turner (E. Roosevelt), C. Venable (Northwestern), M. White (Crossland)

*Third Team*
J. Barnes (Maret), K. Berry (Woodbridge), Q. Burton (Hammond), P. Carter (Gonzaga), D. Lewis (Dunbar)

## 1986–87 All-Met

*First Team*
T. Gibson (Dunbar), J. Gwynn (DeMatha), E. Harris (St. John's), D. Scott (Flint Hill), G. Sitney (High Point), A. Tucker (McKinley Tech), B. Tucker (Potomac [Md.]), C. Venable (Northwestern), C. Weldon (Coolidge), B. Young (Mt. Hebron)

*Second Team*

A. Beagle (Dunbar), C. Lewis (Carroll), D. Williams (Eastern), C. Alford (Crossland), J. Hymes (Springbrook)

*Third Team*

H. Davis (Lake Braddock), M. Miles (Hayfield), J. Bias (Northwestern), J. Mustaf (DeMatha), A. Bain (Flint Hill)

## 1987–88 All-Met

*First Team*

A. Bain (Flint Hill), J. Bias (Northwestern), H. Davis (Lake Braddock), W. Davis (Cardozo), H. Hall (Parkdale), D. Hodge (Coolidge), J. Mustaf (DeMatha), C. Palmer (W-L), M. Tate (Oxon Hill), W. Williams (Crossland)

*Second Team*

A. Higginbotham (Crossland), G. Hill (South Lakes), S. Clifton (Springbrook), J. Morton (Gonzaga), R. Leonard (Spingarn)

*Third Team*

S. Simpkins (Maret), H. Scruggs (Bishop Ireton), Q. Harris (McNamara), J. Scott (South Lakes), C. Hawkins (Gwynn Park)

## 1988–89 All-Met

*First Team*

A. Bain (Flint Hill), G. Hill (South Lakes), G. Lynch (Flint Hill), L. Moten (Carroll), D. Simpkins (Friendly), R. Slater (Laurel), C. Smith (Coolidge), M. Smith (Dunbar), M. Tate (Oxon Hill), M. Williams (Potomac)

*Second Team*

D. Armstrong (Yorktown), J. Bryson (Largo), B. Hill (W. T. Woodson), A. Lee (High Point), K. McLinton (Springbrook)

*Third Team*

T. Bergan (DeMatha), A. J. Hoff (Einstein), R. Peyton (Chantilly), L. Thompson (Dunbar), J. Williams (Fairmont Heights)

## 1989–90 All-Met

*First Team*

C. Ast (High Point), K. Blakeney (DeMatha), R. Childress (Flint Hill), R. Churchwell (Gonzaga), K. Gregory (Cardozo), C. Harrison (Carroll), G. Hill (South Lakes), L. Moten (Carroll), D. Simpkins (Friendly), M. Smith (Dunbar)

*Second Team*

K. Hunter (Wakefield), M. McGlone (Bladensburg), L. Morgan (Gonzaga), D. Murray (Dunbar), M. Robinson (Ballou)

*Third Team*

R. Garner (Potomac [Md.]), F. Martin (Anacostia), J. Morgan (Cardozo), D. Ross (McNamara), C. Simpson (St. Stephen's)

## 1990–91 All-Met

*First Team*

W. Bristol (High Point), I. Church (Parkdale), V. Jones (DeMatha), J. Marshall (Dunbar), N. Nelson-Richards (Good Counsel), J. Rhodes (Dunbar), S. Short (Harker Prep D. Vanterpool (Montgomery Blair), J. Warren (West Springfield), A. Willis (West Potomac)

*Second Team*

K. Freeland (Forestville), R. Garner (Potomac), O. Johnson (Largo), L. Kalombo (Herndon), C. Turner (DuVal)

*Third Team*

D. Edwards (Annapolis), T. Ellis (DeMatha), R. Inge (Paint Branch), B. Lammersen (Madison), J. Stuckey (Coolidge)

## 1991–92 All-Met

*First Team*

D. Franklin (Chantilly), J. Beard (South Lakes), K. Freeland (Forestville), E. Hipp (Harker Prep), R. Inge (Paint Branch), V. Jones (DeMatha), D. Simpkins (DeMatha), G. Williams (W. T. Woodson), S. Winfree (Dunbar), S. Zwikker (Harker Prep)

*Second Team*

J. Lansdown (Broad Run), E. Micoud (St. John's), T. Moore (Newport Prep [Newport]), M. Norris (Cardozo), M. Powell (Anacostia)

*Third Team*

K. Avent (High Point), G. Jones (Cardozo), M. Miles (Largo), R. Misenko (Potomac [Va.]), A. Thompson (Parkdale)

## 1992–93 All-Met

*First Team*

N. Langley (Dunbar), K. Avent (High Point), J. Beard (South Lakes), C. Green (Dunbar), A. McQueen (St. Albans), M. Newbie (Carroll), W. Peters (Potomac [Md.]), M. Powell (Anacostia), T. Treadwell (Good Counsel), G. Williams (W. T. Woodson)

*Second Team*

O. Clark (Forestville), K. Davis (Anacostia), G. Jones (Cardozo), R. Miller (Largo), C. Robinson (Watkins Mill)

*Third Team*

D. Barrett (Meade), M. Doyle (Pallotti), K. Shakur (Montgomery Blair), K. Taylor (Carroll), E. Tyson (Dunbar)

## 1993–94 All-Met

*First Team*

V. Page (McKinley Tech), M. Brown (Potomac [Md.]), L. Bullock (Canterbury), C. Howard (Southern), T. Lyons (DeMatha), K. McFarland (Gonzaga), D. Owens (Bowie), R. Shelton (Louisa County), K. Taylor (Carroll), C. Turner (Lee)

*Second Team*

J. Childress (Canterbury), R. Felton (Hayfield), W. Peters (Potomac [Md.]), T. Ridges (Springbrook), J. Stinson (High Point)

*Third Team*
T. Allen (South Lakes), R. Dodson (Herndon), B. Dunlap (Woodbridge), M. Horton
(T. C. Williams), E. Poole (High Point)

## 1994–95 All-Met

*First Team*
L. Bullock (Laurel Baptist), B. Beal (West Potomac), M. Gill (Dunbar), T. Harris
(Potomac [Va.]), T. Hill (DeMatha), D. Jackson (T. C. Williams), J. Lofton (Forestville),
J. Outtz (Good Counsel), T. Ridges (Springbrook), A. Wills (Kennedy)

*Second Team*
O. Jones (St. Stephen's), M. Horton (T. C. Williams), D. Presley (DeMatha), J. Smith
(Broadneck), M. Smith (Wakefield)

*Third Team*
W. Callahan (Robinson), J. Childress (National Christian), C. King (Gar-Field),
F. McQueen (Dunbar), C. Rooths (St. John's)

## 1995–96 All-Met

*First Team*
R. Roberts (Potomac [Va.]), J. Adams (Northern), A. Brown (Gonzaga), D. Clark
(Bullis), A. Demory (Woodbridge), K. Frager (Central [Md.]), J. Lofton (Forestville),
X. Singletary (Dunbar), A. Stanley (W-L), A. Thomas (Anacostia)

*Second Team*
N. Burton (McKinley Tech), I. Conwell (Oakland Mills), D. Dove (Gwynn Park),
D. Kelly (Carroll), H. Wrotten (Annandale)

*Third Team*
C. Burns (North Stafford), G. Diggs (Annapolis), J. Drewry (Montgomery Blair),
K. Flood (Central [Md.]), E. Holmes (Hayfield)

## 1996–97 All-Met

*First Team*
A. Brown (Gonzaga), R. Boumtje Boumtje (Carroll), M. Felder (Potomac [Va.]),
C. Felton (Hayfield), D. Hill (Newport), T. Nixon (Oxon Hill), S. Pearson (Cardozo),
W. Smith (Spingarn), S. Tyndell (Sherwood), J. Williams (Broadneck)

*Second Team*
L. Baxter (Anacostia), M. McCoy (Lackey), D. Smith (Anacostia), K. Staton (Wakefield),
M. Zak (South Lakes)

*Third Team*
K. Bogans (DeMatha), M. Crawford (James Wood), C. Johnson (Gaithersburg), S. Miles
(Hayfield), T. Rowles (Parkdale)

## 1997–98 All-Met

*First Team*
D. Smith (Anacostia), K. Bogans (DeMatha), P. Doctor (Gwynn Park), J. Forte
(DeMatha), D. Franklin (Chantilly), C. Johnson (Gaithersburg), D. Johnson (Newport),
C. Hawkins (Potomac [Va.]), D. Morris (Pallotti), T. Washington (Carroll)

*Second Team*
R. Anderson (Wakefield), J. Chapman (Anacostia), N. Clay (Woodbridge), B. Jenkins (Montgomery Blair), D. Payne (Coolidge)

*Third Team*
T. Clegg (Suitland), M. Countiss (Leonardtown), C. Felton (Hayfield), J. Gipson (Spotsylvania), R. Mason (Good Counsel)

### 1998–99 All-Met

*First Team*
J. Forte (DeMatha), K. Bogans (DeMatha), B. Chase (Dunbar), T. Dobbins (Maret), J. Gilchrist (Notre Dame), R. Mason (Good Counsel), P. Mitchell (Gonzaga), C. Monroe (Good Counsel), M. Sweetney (Oxon Hill), R. White (Newport)

*Second Team*
T. Haynesworth (Dunbar), A. Lappegard (Largo), D. Pope (Surrattsville), B. Robinson (Dunbar), V. Samnick (Newport)

*Third Team*
P. Johnson (DuVal), R. Ross (Lake Braddock), J. Sanders (Hayfield), D. Saunders (Spingarn), M. Young (McNamara)

### 1999–2000 All-Met

*First Team*
M. Sweetney (Oxon Hill), S. Brooks (Central), M. Diakite (Montrose Christian), S. Ford (Gwynn Park), D. Hawkins (Carroll), D. Holland (Eleanor Roosevelt), M. Johnson (Annapolis), M. Moss (Wheaton), D. Saunders (Spingarn), M. Young (McNamara)

*Second Team*
K. Brown (Oakton), B. Edelin (DeMatha), C. Hicks (Spingarn), M. Lewis (Montrose Christian), J. Wise (Paint Branch)

*Third Team*
K. Bell (Riverdale Baptist), H. Blue (Gonzaga), T. Hawkins (Annapolis), J. Palumbo (St. John's), J. White (Newport)

### 2000–2001 All-Met

*First Team*
D. West (Eleanor Roosevelt), E. Basden (Eleanor Roosevelt), L. Butler (Oxon Hill), J. Hargett (National Christian), J. Ingram (T. C. Williams), C. McCray (Fairmont Heights), M. Neal (Annapolis), L. Watkins (Montrose Christian), S. Wiggins (Spingarn), J. Wise (Paint Branch)

*Second Team*
T. Bethel (Montrose Christian), J. Collins (DeMatha), P. Goss (Oxon Hill), K. Jolley (Fairmont Heights), A. Miller (H. D. Woodson)

*Third Team*
B. Harrod (Friendly), R. Little (Paul VI Catholic), D. Morrow (Ballou), M. Orfini (Gonzaga), J. Thomas (Thomas Johnson)

## 2001–2002 All-Met

*First Team*

J. Thomas (Thomas Johnson), C. Cage (Bladensburg), W. Dunston (Bullis), T. Galloway (Notre Dame), T. Garrison (DeMatha), L. Hinnant (Gwynn Park), T. Kelley (Dunbar), C. McCray (Fairmont Heights), A. Smith (O'Connell), K. Steenberge (River Hill)

*Second Team*

A. Mayhand (H. D. Woodson), L. Owens (Annapolis), P. Paelay (Magruder), J. Steward (Hayfield), W. Williams (DeMatha)

*Third Team*

M. Estep (Chopticon), R. Hughes (Mount Vernon), L. Kleiza (Montrose Christian), M. Malik (Spingarn), C. Williams (Oxon Hill)

# Photo Credits

*A good faith effort has been made to identify and credit the owner of each image. Any errors will be corrected in subsequent printings.*

**Chapter 1**

*EB Henderson Team Photo:* courtesy of the Henderson family (Addison Scurlock collection) and the Black Fives Foundation (13)

*Howard University Basketball Team:* courtesy of the Henderson family (Addison Scurlock collection) (13)

*EB Henderson Retirement Portrait:* courtesy of the Henderson family (Addison Scurlock collection) (13)

*Roosevelt High School Yearbook:* courtesy of the Charles Sumner Museum and Archives (14)

*Red Auerbach:* courtesy of the Digital Collections Research Center at George Washington University Libraries (14)

*Auerbach Military Headshot:* courtesy of the National Archives (14)

*Earl Lloyd Graduation:* courtesy of the Charles Sumner Museum and Archives (15)

*Earl Lloyd vs. Fort Wayne Pistons:* courtesy of the Associated Press (15)

*Earl Lloyd:* courtesy of the Stevenson Collection / NBAE / Getty Images (16)

*Jack George:* courtesy of LaSalle University (16)

**Chapter 2**

*Kernan as "Best Athlete":* courtesy of the Charles Sumner Museum and Archives (58)

*Woodrow Wilson Team '51–'52:* courtesy of the Charles Sumner Museum and Archives (58)

*Elgin Baylor's Yearbook Entry:* courtesy of the Charles Sumner Museum and Archives (59)

*Dave Brown in the Spingarn Yearbook:* courtesy of the Charles Sumner Museum and Archives (60)

*Brown Team Photo:* courtesy of the Charles Sumner Museum and Archives (60)

*Llewellyn Luce Headshot:* courtesy of the Charles Sumner Museum and Archives (61)

*Spingarn Yearbook '57–'58:* courtesy of the Charles Sumner Museum and Archives (61)

*Dwyer Team Photo '58–'59:* courtesy of the Archbishop Carroll High School Archives (62)

*Dwyer Team Photo '59–'60:* courtesy of the Archbishop Carroll High School Archives (62)

*Dywer with Tom Hoover:* courtesy of the Archbishop Carroll High School Archives (63)

*Bob Dwyer in 2001:* courtesy of the Archbishop Carroll High School Archives (63)

*Carrasco Plaque:* courtesy of Professor Davíd L. Carrasco family collection (63)

*Carrasco in Mexico '68:* courtesy of Professor Davíd L. Carrasco family collection (63)

*Cardozo Coaches '57:* courtesy of the Charles Sumner Museum and Archives (64)

*Spingarn Yearbook '59–'60:* courtesy of the Charles Sumner Museum and Archives (64)

**Chapter 3**

*Spingarn Trophy Presentation:* courtesy of the Charles Sumner Museum and Archives (108)
*Inter-High Champions Team Photo:* courtesy of the Charles Sumner Museum and Archives (109)
*Dave Bing vs. Eastern High:* courtesy of the Charles Sumner Museum and Archives (109)
*Spingarn Yearbook '60:* courtesy of the Charles Sumner Museum and Archives (110)
*Spingarn Yearbook Season Summary:* courtesy of the Charles Sumner Museum and Archives (111)
*Spingarn Yearbook Spingarn-Eastern Game:* courtesy of the Charles Sumner Museum and Archives (112)
*Roundtree Trophy Presentation:* courtesy of the Charles Sumner Museum and Archives (113)
*Spingarn's "S" Club:* courtesy of the Charles Sumner Museum and Archives (113)
*Student Council '61-'62:* courtesy of the Charles Sumner Museum and Archives (114)
*Spingarn HI-Y Club:* courtesy of the Charles Sumner Museum and Archives (114)
*Roundtree in Spain:* courtesy of the Charles Sumner Museum and Archives (115)
*Spingarn Yearbook Class of '62:* courtesy of the Charles Sumner Museum and Archives (115)
*Wootten and Team Huddle:* courtesy of the Charles Sumner Museum and Archives (116)
*Montgomery Blair Class of '63:* courtesy of the Charles Sumner Museum and Archives (116)
*DeMatha Starters Photo:* courtesy of the DeMatha High School Archives (116)
*James Brown Jump Shot:* courtesy of the DeMatha High School Archives (117)
*Harold Fox Layup:* courtesy of the MLK Library (117)
*James Brown:* courtesy of the DeMatha High School Archives (118)
*James Brown Game Photo:* courtesy of the Charles Sumner Museum and Archives (118)
*James Brown vs. McKinley:* courtesy of the DeMatha High School Archives (119)
*Michael Bossard vs. Ballou:* courtesy of the MLK Library (119)
*McKinley Yearbook '69:* courtesy of the Charles Sumner Museum and Archives (120)
*Skeeter Swift Game Photo:* courtesy of Skeeter Swift (personal collection) (121)
*Swift, Wheatley, and Hummer:* courtesy of Skeeter Swift (personal collection) (121)
*Skeeter Swift:* courtesy of Skeeter Swift (personal collection) (122)
*Swift Jump Shot:* courtesy of Skeeter Swift (personal collection) (122)
*Adrian Dantley:* courtesy of the Charles Sumner Museum and Archives (122)

**Chapter 4**

*Georgetown vs. St. Anthonys:* courtesy of the MLK Library (168)
*Fairmont Heights Victory:* courtesy of the MLK Library (168)
*DeMatha's Adrian Dantley (vs. St. Johns):* courtesy of the Charles Sumner Museum and Archives (169)
*DeMatha's Adrian Dantley (vs. Spingarn):* courtesy of the MLK Library (169)
*Coach Williamson:* courtesy of the Charles Sumner Museum and Archives (169)
*Gene Doane at Blair:* courtesy of the Montgomery County Sentinel (170)
*Dunbar's John Duren:* courtesy of the MLK Library (170)
*Dunbar Defeats DeMatha:* courtesy of the Charles Sumner Museum and Archives (171)
*Blair Brian Magid:* courtesy of the MLK Library (171)
*T. C. Williams Team Huddle:* courtesy of the MLK Library (172)
*Coach Joe Davidson:* courtesy of the Charles Sumner Museum and Archives (173)
*Gwynn Park's Sonny Proctor:* courtesy of the MLK Library (174)
*Mackin's Jo Jo Hunter:* courtesy of the MLK Library (174)
*DeMatha vs. Dunbar at Cole:* courtesy of the Charles Sumner Museum and Archives (175)
*Dereck Whittenburg:* courtesy of the Charles Sumner Museum and Archives (175)
*Brian Magid:* courtesy of Brian Magid (175)

## Chapter 5

*Danny Ferry '84:* courtesy of the DeMatha High School Archives (214)
*Danny Ferry Layup '85:* courtesy of the DeMatha High School Archives (214)
*Danny Ferry '85:* courtesy of the DeMatha High School Archives (215)
*Sherman Douglas Yearbook Senior Photo:* courtesy of the Charles Sumner Museum and
    Archives (215)
*Spingarn '85 Yearbook:* courtesy of the Charles Sumner Museum and Archives (216)
*Sherman Douglas Yearbook Pose:* courtesy of the Charles Sumner Museum and Archives (216)
*Coolidge Team Photo:* courtesy of the Charles Sumner Museum and Archives (217)
*Dunbar's Tribute to Coach Williams:* courtesy of the Charles Sumner Museum and Archives (218)
*Dunbar's Yearbook Celebrates Coach McLeese:* courtesy of the Charles Sumner Museum and
    Archives (219)
*Dunbar's Darryl Prue:* courtesy of T .C. Williams High School Archives (219)
*City Championship at Cole Field House:* courtesy of the Charles Sumner Museum and
    Archives (220)
*Calvin Coolidge City Champs:* courtesy of the Charles Sumner Museum and Archives (221)
*Coolidge Team '86:* courtesy of the Charles Sumner Museum and Archives (222)
*Frank Williams:* courtesy of the Charles Sumner Museum and Archives (222)
*Walt Williams Slam Dunk:* courtesy of Walt Williams (personal collection) (223)
*PE Department:* courtesy of the Charles Sumner Museum and Archives (224)
*Len Bias '80–81:* courtesy of the Bias family (personal collection) (225)
*Len Bias Dunk:* courtesy of the *Baltimore Sun* (225)
*Walt Williams All-Met Five:* courtesy of Walt Williams (personal collection) (226)

## Chapter 6

*Claude Green Yearbook Pose:* courtesy of the Charles Sumner Museum and Archives (250)
*Dunbar Crimson Tide:* courtesy of the Charles Sumner Museum and Archives (250)
*Anacostia's Coach Hargrove:* courtesy of the Charles Sumner Museum and Archives (251)
*Coaches Gallagher and Wootten:* courtesy of Morgan Wootten (personal collection) (252)
*Duane Simpkins Celebrates:* courtesy of the DeMatha High School Archives (253)
*Duane Simpkins player photo:* courtesy of the DeMatha High School Archives (253)
*Coach Hargrove and son Kevin:* courtesy of the Charles Sumner Museum and Archives (254)
*Basketball City Championship:* courtesy of the Charles Sumner Museum and Archives (255)
*"Two for Roach":* courtesy of the Charles Sumner Museum and Archives (256)
*Dunbar vs. DeMatha:* courtesy of the Charles Sumner Museum and Archives (257)
*Colts vs. Stags:* courtesy of the Charles Sumner Museum and Archives (258)
*Coach Wootten:* courtesy of Morgan Wootten (personal collection) (259)

# Index

Page numbers in italics signify photos.